Of The SEVEN

Of The Seven

The Eighth Empire

Duane Andry

authorHOUSE®

AuthorHouse™
1663 Liberty Drive
Bloomington, IN 47403
www.authorhouse.com
Phone: 1-800-839-8640

Published by AuthorHouse 03/01/2012

ISBN: 978-1-4685-5822-7 (sc)
ISBN: 978-1-4685-5824-1 (hc)
ISBN: 978-1-4685-5823-4 (e)

Library of Congress Control Number: 2012903978

Unless otherwise indicated, Bible quotations are taken from the King James Version of the Bible.

www.lifelearningseries.com

CONTENTS

PREFACE

There came a man, Jesus. He was conceived by the overshadowing of the Holy Ghost; and born of a virgin named Mary, who, along with Joseph her husband, is of the seed of David the king.

This same man Jesus was sanctified by God, with the filling of the Holy Ghost, which remained upon him. At this time he was announced to those with him, and thus to the world, as being the beloved Son of God. And at that time, we were directed, by the voice of God, to "hear ye him". This is the one who is the Son of man, and who is also, the Son of God.

After the anointing of the Holy Ghost, This same man Jesus continued his ministry on the earth, with mighty signs and wonders. Because of these signs, he engendered the displeasure of the religious/political powers of his day. They, thinking to rid the world of this, *nuisance*, crucified and killed this body, on the cross. And by doing so, they brought into effect God's will for the salvation of mankind and for the return of His children to His straight way of righteousness. Jesus Christ, the Lamb of God, is the last sacrifice sanctioned by God to carry away the sins of the world through his blood. "It is finished."

This same man Jesus is spoken of throughout the pages of the Bible, the Holy Word of God. And this Bible was transcribed by holy men, as they were moved by the Spirit of God. It is in the light of this Bible that I present this message; for the remission of sin and the salvation of mankind.

Introduction

Matthew 16:27-28

For the Son of man shall come in the glory of his Father with his angels; and then he shall reward every man according to his works.

Verily I say unto you, There be some standing here, which shall not taste of death, till they see the Son of man coming in his kingdom.

Daniel 8:1-17

In the third year of the reign of king Belshazzar a vision appeared unto me, even unto me Daniel, after that which appeared unto me at the first. And I saw in a vision; and it came to pass, when I saw, that I was at Shushan in the palace, which is in the province of Elam; and I saw in a vision, and I was by the river of Ulai. Then I lifted up mine eyes, and saw, and, behold, there stood before the river a ram which had two horns: and the two horns were high; but one was higher than the other, and the higher came up last. I saw the ram pushing westward, and northward, and southward; so that no beasts might stand before him, neither was there any that could deliver out of his hand; but he did according to his will, and became great.

And as I was considering, behold, an he goat came from the west on the face of the whole earth, and touched not the ground: and the goat had a notable horn between his eyes. And he came to the ram that had two horns, which I had seen standing before the river, and ran unto him in the fury of his power. And I saw him come close unto the ram, and he was moved with choler against him, and smote the ram, and brake his two horns: and there was no power in the ram to stand before him, but he cast him down to the ground, and stamped upon him: and there was none that could deliver the ram out of his hand.

Therefore the he goat waxed very great: and when he was strong, the great horn was broken; and for it came up four notable ones toward the four winds of heaven. And out of one of them came forth a little horn, which waxed exceeding great, toward the south, and toward the east, and toward the pleasant land. And it waxed great, even to the host of heaven; and it cast down some of the host and of the stars to the ground, and stamped upon them. Yea, he magnified himself even to the prince of the host, and by him the daily sacrifice was taken away, and the place of his sanctuary was cast down. And an host was given him against the daily sacrifice by reason of transgression, and it cast down the truth to the ground; and it practiced, and prospered.

Then I heard one saint speaking, and another saint said unto that certain saint which spake, How long shall be the vision concerning the daily sacrifice, and the transgression of desolation, to give both the sanctuary and the host to be trodden under foot? And he said unto me, Unto two thousand and three hundred days; then shall the sanctuary be cleansed.

And it came to pass, when I, even I Daniel, had seen the vision, and sought for the meaning, then, behold, there stood before me as the appearance of a man. And I heard a man's voice between the banks of Ulai, which called, and said, Gabriel, make this man to understand the vision.

So he came near where I stood: and when he came, I was afraid, and fell upon my face: but he said unto me, Understand, O son of man: for at the time of the end shall be the vision.

Revelation 17:7-11

And the angel said unto me, Wherefore didst thou marvel? I will tell thee the mystery of the woman, and of the beast that carrieth her, which hath the seven heads and ten horns. The beast that thou sawest was, and is not; and shall ascend out of the bottomless pit, and go into perdition: and they that dwell on the earth shall wonder, whose names were not written in the book of life from the foundation of the world, when they behold the beast that was, and is not, and yet is.

And here is the mind which hath wisdom. The seven heads are seven mountains, on which the woman sitteth. And there are seven kings: five are fallen, and one is, and the other is not yet come; and when he cometh, he must continue a short space. And the beast that was, and is not, even he is the eighth, and is of the seven, and goeth into perdition.

Eschatology

1. The branch of theology that is concerned with the end of the world or of humankind.
2. A belief or a doctrine concerning the ultimate or final things, such as death, the destiny of humanity, the Second Coming, or the Last Judgment.

This is what every religious person seems to be very much focused on these days. Maybe it's because the world has become so unbearable for such a large mass of humans that we find ourselves searching for an escape. But not just any escape: The escape: the Ultimate escape. This is by no means a new phenomenon, but it seems to be taking on a life of its own. There is, in the Bible, a rather low key question from the disciples to Jesus.

> *And Jesus went out, and departed from the temple: and his disciples came to him for to shew him the buildings of the temple. And Jesus said unto them, See ye not all these things? verily I say unto you, There shall not be left here one stone upon another, that shall not be thrown down.*

> *And as he sat upon the mount of Olives, the disciples came unto him privately, saying, Tell us, when shall these things be? and what shall be the sign of thy coming, and of the end of the world?*
>
> (Matthew 24:1-3)

Jesus gave them the answer.

> *And Jesus answered and said unto them, Take heed that no man deceive you. For many shall come in my name, saying, I am Christ; and shall deceive many. And ye shall hear of wars and rumours of wars: see that ye be not troubled: for all these things must come to pass, but the end is not yet.*
>
> *For nation shall rise against nation, and kingdom against kingdom: and there shall be famines, and pestilences, and earthquakes, in divers places. All these are the beginning of sorrows.*
>
> *Then shall they deliver you up to be afflicted, and shall kill you: and ye shall be hated of all nations for my name's sake. And then shall many be offended, and shall betray one another, and shall hate one another. And many false prophets shall rise, and shall deceive many. And because iniquity shall abound, the love of many shall wax cold.*
>
> *But he that shall endure unto the end, the same shall be saved.*
>
> (Matthew 24:4)

The answer requires clarification for our modern mind.

Is the question from the disciple one question or two? Is he asking about the date of the destruction that Jesus said was coming to the structures, ***and*** about the signs of the time of the end? Or is this just a compound question with only one necessary answer; that is to say, is it that both the destruction and the time of the end will happen at the same time? And, might this, *end*, be the same one that is referred to in the prophecy of Daniel, where it says . . .

> *And I heard a man's voice between the banks of Ulai, which called, and said, Gabriel, make this man to understand the vision.*

> *So he came near where I stood: and when he came, I was afraid, and fell upon my face: but he said unto me, Understand, O son of man: for at the time of the end shall be the vision.*
>
> *Now as he was speaking with me, I was in a deep sleep on my face toward the ground: but he touched me, and set me upright.*
>
> *And he said, Behold, I will make thee know what shall be in the last end of the indignation: for at the time appointed the end shall be.*
>
> (Daniel 8:16-19)

If the prophecy of Jesus and the prophecy of Daniel both refer to the same period of time, it has a definite connection to the time of Jesus of Nazareth, the Christ. But, does the combined intersection of the prophecies of Jesus and Daniel extend beyond the time of Jesus. If so, we have questions that arise about the application of the answer to now. How does the answer that Jesus gave fit in with modern times? How far in the future should these prophecies of Jesus be taken? How broad an application do they have? For instance; are they for Israel, only, or are they for the entire world? Moreover, besides these words of Jesus, and the associated prophecy of Daniel, there are other portions of Scripture that refer to the time that was to come, as viewed from that day in Jesus' life.

There is a whole book of the Bible that presents prophecy about various terminating issues in time: *the Revelation of Jesus Christ, which God gave unto him, to show unto his servants things which must shortly come to pass; and he sent and signified it by his angel unto his servant John.* This book is commonly referred to as, The Revelation, and we use that shortened form, as well, in this work. The Revelation starts by delivering words *for reproof, for correction, for instruction in righteousness* to the seven churches. This type of delivery is in accordance with the purpose of all Scripture.

> *All scripture is given by inspiration of God, and is profitable for doctrine, for reproof, for correction, for instruction in righteousness: That the man of God may be perfect, thoroughly furnished unto all good works.*
>
> (2 Timothy 3:16-17)

The seven churches of The Revelation refer directly to ones that existed at the time of the scribe of the Revelation, John the Revelator.

Moreover, these seven churches are patterns that one can find in churches of today. So, does the message also apply to the churches of today? To this, I believe every religious scholar would say a resounding, yes. Therefore, the admonition that was sent to the seven churches is not a part of our mission, in presenting this work of exploration of Scripture to you and to the world.

So what is our mission?

Our mission is to discover—by the leading and sharing of the indwelling Holy Ghost—those parts of the book of Revelation that are still open, so to speak. There has been much conjecture about the revelations of both Jesus and Daniel, along with those of several other prophets. There have been some attempts to directly apply their messages to our times, and to some future time. But is this according to the will of God? Did God intend for the prophecies in these various places in the Bible to be lumped together? Or, were they sent forth to describe specific events that are close, in time, to the delivery of the prophecy? For Daniel's prophecy, Scripture specifically answers that question that belongs to the prophecy of Daniel, in reference to the time-reference for the revelation.

> *And I heard, but I understood not: then said I, O my Lord, what shall be the end of these things?*
>
> *And he said, Go thy way, Daniel: for the words are closed up and sealed till the time of the end. Many shall be purified, and made white, and tried; but the wicked shall do wickedly: and none of the wicked shall understand; but the wise shall understand. And from the time that the daily sacrifice shall be taken away, and the abomination that maketh desolate set up, there shall be a thousand two hundred and ninety days. Blessed is he that waiteth, and cometh to the thousand three hundred and five and thirty days.*
>
> *But go thou thy way till the end be: for thou shalt rest, and stand in thy lot at the end of the days.*
>
> (Daniel 12:8-13)

Why are such questions important?

Such questions are important because many people are performing their service to God based on the answer to these and many other similar questions. There are potentially billions of people who look forward to the events of, what is called, the time of the end. They are being persuaded to consider these coming events as being an escape from the current presumed misery of our existence. Even those who are prosperous are searching for this escape.

There are many people that are reserving their best service to God until some time to be determined in the future. They feel that one day they will *really* be able to serve God, in the still-to-come Kingdom of God on earth. They withhold from their fellow man the compassion that should be shown by those who truly honor God.

Furthermore, there are some portions of humanity that place the burden of the total development of mankind at the feet of Jesus, and walk away. "When he returns, he will make all things right," they say. They seem to be walking away from their required service to God; which is, to work to make it all right, right now.

There is an increasing sense of frustration with the things of this world. The ending message of Revelation is shouted from many mouths.

> *He which testifieth these things saith, Surely I come quickly. Amen.*
>
> *Even so, come, Lord Jesus.*
>
> (Revelation 22:20)

However, many are doing so without clear understanding of the full mission of God, in Jesus Christ. There are many people who have forgotten that we must take up our cross daily, and follow him. Or, maybe they have just conveniently discarded this message.

> *And he said to them all, If any man will come after me, let him deny himself, and take up his cross daily, and follow me.*
>
> (Luke 9:23)

Many have forgotten, or displaced, the fact that we will have tribulation as a regular part of life.

> *These things I have spoken unto you, that in me ye might have peace. In the world ye shall have tribulation: but be of good cheer; I have overcome the world.*
>
> (John 16:33)

We want it all to be made right; and we want this to be done ***now***. We have not stopped to count the cost. Let us just look at an example from Revelation. When that end time comes, anguish will still be present for those who are outside. Anguish will not be totally eliminated, nor will it be, necessarily, understood to be anguish. The ones in certain states of spiritual anguish may think of the anguish as being a productive part of their lives. They may consider themselves as being as normal in their carnality, as the followers of God's way think themselves to be normal in their spirituality.

> *Blessed are they that do his commandments, that they may have right to the tree of life, and may enter in through the gates into the city. For without are dogs, and sorcerers, and whoremongers, and murderers, and idolaters, and whosoever loveth and maketh a lie.*
>
> (Revelation 22:14-15)

Without further insight, and considering the writings of Revelation as being the description of an eternal state of existence, there will be some places that are without hope—and this would be forever. Considering the weight of the words in Revelation, there are some parties in our reality who are condemned (I am not even sure this is an adequate word for it)—angels, for sure; humans, *maybe*. These are they who inhabit the lake that burns with fire and brimstone.

> *And I saw the beast, and the kings of the earth, and their armies, gathered together to make war against him that sat on the horse, and against his army.*
>
> *And the beast was taken, and with him the false prophet that wrought miracles before him, with which he deceived them that had received the mark of the beast, and them that worshipped his image. These both were cast alive into a lake of fire burning with brimstone.*
>
> (Revelation 19:19-20)

> *And when the thousand years are expired, Satan shall be loosed out of his prison, And shall go out to deceive the nations which are in the four quarters of the earth, Gog and Magog, to gather them together to battle: the number of whom is as the sand of the sea.*

> *And they went up on the breadth of the earth, and compassed the camp of the saints about, and the beloved city: and fire came down from God out of heaven, and devoured them.*
>
> *And the devil that deceived them was cast into the lake of fire and brimstone, where the beast and the false prophet are, and shall be tormented day and night for ever and ever.*
>
> (Revelation 20:7-10)

> *And death and hell were cast into the lake of fire. This is the second death.*
>
> *And whosoever was not found written in the book of life was cast into the lake of fire.*
>
> (Revelation 20:14-15)

> *But the fearful, and unbelieving, and the abominable, and murderers, and whoremongers, and sorcerers, and idolaters, and all liars, shall have their part in the lake which burneth with fire and brimstone: which is the second death.*
>
> (Revelation 21:8)

As humans we might feel comfortable with the image of Satan, death and hell going into this place. For Satan it might not be much different from the state he was in before that. For death and hell, they are not listed in the Bible as having feelings. They seem to be placed in the Lake only because there is no more use for them anywhere else. But, what about the others?

If *the beast* and *the false prophet* are humans, and if there are any humans not mentioned in the book, this is a most horrendous thing to think about. Imagine being in a fire that never goes out. No matter how much wisdom you acquire while you are there, and even when you want to bow your knee, you will not benefit by it, according to a common interpretation of the Scripture in Revelation.

Personally, I have tried to imagine a human so horrendous that I would wish that they could never be transformed: and I have failed to do so. In my mind is a circuit that prays to God that every human is transformed, and conformed into the image of His Son. To be frank, humans are just too stupid to not mess up. For someone as powerful as God, it seems like fighting with an infant—no; like fighting with an embryo. Forgive me, Dad, if I am getting too emotional; but, You have made this a most serious matter for me.

As often as it crosses my mind, I petition God in this matter; asking that He make His will universal, and not just optional. Here, I am referring to the word, *willing*, which is referenced in this Scripture.

> *The Lord is not slack concerning his promise, as some men count slackness; but is longsuffering to us-ward, not willing that any should perish, but that all should come to repentance.*
>
> (1 John 3:9)

I hope you, who are reading this, or who hear about it, do the same thing too. Every person I have ever met who told me that they did not believe in the message of God in Jesus Christ, I saw as a work in progress. My mind says, "You do not believe now, maybe; but, you will. My Father will pull you to Him, and you will believe." I am naive about these things. This is my reason for being assigned this mission. I guess God got a little tired of me just sitting in my comfortable chair, asking Him to make it happen. He finally said to me, "Well, if you want to make it known, then do so." So, with the help of the Holy Ghost, I will; in the name of Jesus, and according to his request.

> *These things have I spoken unto you, being yet present with you. But the Comforter, which is the Holy Ghost, whom the Father will send in my name, he shall teach you all things, and bring all things to your remembrance, whatsoever I have said unto you.*
>
> (John 14:25-26)

So this is a search in the Scripture to discover what is still outstanding in the historical march toward the complete, visible judgment of God over all people in the earth: dead and alive, past and present, saved and unsaved.

The Bible mentions seven dynasties that will arise leading up to the final events of the Bible. This is where I will search for the answer. What is that seventh dynasty? Has it come and gone? Is it here now? Or, is it yet to come? And once I find this dynasty, and if it is either here, or, yet to come, then what is the message that I want God to give to its king?

Even, perhaps when the king of the seventh dynasty arises, the surrounding activity may only be a test of God's children's devotion to Him, and of their belief in Him. The test may not be an irrevocable condemnation of the collection of people. In reference to this sort of activity of God, I am thinking of the nation of Nineveh. It too was, like the world in which we now live is, thought to be doomed. Indeed, the writing had already been given, and the prophecy was in the mouth of the prophet. But in God's wisdom, this was just a prod, to move Nineveh to Him.

> *And Jonah began to enter into the city a day's journey, and he cried, and said, Yet forty days, and Nineveh shall be overthrown.*
>
> *So the people of Nineveh believed God, and proclaimed a fast, and put on sackcloth, from the greatest of them even to the least of them. For word came unto the king of Nineveh, and he arose from his throne, and he laid his robe from him, and covered him with sackcloth, and sat in ashes. And he caused it to be proclaimed and published through Nineveh by the decree of the king and his nobles, saying, Let neither man nor beast, herd nor flock, taste any thing: let them not feed, nor drink water: But let man and beast be covered with sackcloth, and cry mightily unto God: yea, let them turn every one from his evil way, and from the violence that is in their hands. Who can tell if God will turn and repent, and turn away from his fierce anger, that we perish not?*
>
> *And God saw their works, that they turned from their evil way; and God repented of the evil, that he had said that he would do unto them; and he did it not.*
>
> (Jonah 3:4-10)

We have to not conceal from you the fact that such repentance may not be pleasant for the people of that kingdom, including some of the LORD'S election. Among the people for which this can be unpleasant, they will insist on the fulfillment of unyielding fiery judgment. It is my prayer that God speaks to them, as He did to Jonah. Moreover, as with

Jonah, it is my prayer that the LORD'S word of forgiveness is the last word on the matter.

> *So Jonah went out of the city, and sat on the east side of the city, and there made him a booth, and sat under it in the shadow, till he might see what would become of the city.*
>
> *And the LORD God prepared a gourd, and made it to come up over Jonah, that it might be a shadow over his head, to deliver him from his grief.*
>
> *So Jonah was exceeding glad of the gourd. But God prepared a worm when the morning rose the next day, and it smote the gourd that it withered. And it came to pass, when the sun did arise, that God prepared a vehement east wind; and the sun beat upon the head of Jonah, that he fainted, and wished in himself to die, and said, It is better for me to die than to live.*
>
> *And God said to Jonah, Doest thou well to be angry for the gourd?*
>
> *And he said, I do well to be angry, even unto death.*
>
> *Then said the LORD, Thou hast had pity on the gourd, for the which thou hast not laboured, neither madest it grow; which came up in a night, and perished in a night: And should not I spare Nineveh, that great city, wherein are more than sixscore thousand persons that cannot discern between their right hand and their left hand; and also much cattle?*
>
> (Jonah 4:5-11)

Maybe the seventh king is also a prod to move the entire world to God. As Jonah told Nineveh to repent, and they did; in like fashion, I pray to God to bring up a prophet who will guide the nations to repentance. And so, the mission has been given to me to try. Please pray with me, those of you who love the Lord, as I try to find the king, and the answer that will cause a worldwide conversion, and thus stay the hand of God; if

He is still ready to strike. It is a tall order, indeed. But, so was Nineveh; and God did it there.

> *Then came the word of the LORD unto Jeremiah, saying, Behold, I am the LORD, the God of all flesh: is there any thing too hard for me?*
>
> (Jeremiah 32:26-27)

We are about to proceed deeper into the identification of the seventh empire, as we draw this chapter to a close. Also, even though it may be a shady place, we will partake of anything that can provide spiritual nourishment. First, however, please indulge me as I pray.

> *Father, please move in me. I am Your vessel; no matter how damaged I may be, no matter how insufficient I am. I know that You have sufficiency that is more than enough for the entire human race. Please share some of that with me, through the Holy Ghost that you have sent to dwell in me. As this book is being developed, please keep the Comforter at full power. I know this is asking a lot, but I don't know what else to ask.*
>
> *You have allowed me to think about searching for another Nineveh. If you show me that this eschatological Nineveh has already come and gone, I will deliver that message, to those who read this book. However, if the eschatological Nineveh still exists, or is yet to come; please prepare the message that will cause the conversion of the entirety. Such a thing is of such a small amount of effort for You: You have unlimited power. This is also well within the scope of the power that you gave to Your Son, Jesus Christ. He declared to us, and we know this to be true, that he received all power in heaven and earth.*
>
> *It is You and Your Son's joint mission, as You also called me to do, to convert the world. One nation, albeit a most powerful nation, with a most powerful calamity poised to fall on all mankind from it, is well within the power grid that you reserved for this activity.*

Please activate that power grid to effect a shocking change, now, or in the present-future; if fulfillment does not already abide in the past. Again, if the eschatological Nineveh is already past, You have already spared us the destruction that we thought would befall us. For this, I am forever grateful. In that event, teach us how to move in You in the light of our current situation.

In this, I need Your help. In this, I want Your help. It is for this reason that, from before the foundation of the world, Your Son prepared the sacrifice. And this sacrifice is for all mankind. Activate Your redemptive power, for the benefit of all mankind, as You convert the eschatological nation. For, once this happens, then all men will see the power of God; as they saw it with your selected people in Egypt. This time, however, it is the power to shake mind and hearts; and, governments.

Yes, LORD, I do know that it is the government that must take the lead. It was the king of Nineveh that proclaimed the fast. This is also required in the eschatological Nineveh. Move the heart of the government, as you moved the heart of that king.

There is so much more that I want to say, but I really do not know what it is. Please Holy Ghost; speak for me to my Father. Please Lord Jesus, accept this request, and conform it to your way. For it is in your name that I ask it, and for your sake. Amen.

Father, take control
Of this here I do;
Fill it with words
That glorify You.

Take from my mind
Any wayward thought;
Move me to do
Just what I ought.

To my Father and His Son,
I send this prayer.
"Fill me with the Holy Ghost,
So that I may dare

To speak the word,
In a way most bold;
To share Your wisdom,
So that all will behold

The Design that You have
Sealed in this world,
Filled with the power
To help it unfurl.

Take away any thought
That says I must know
Where you will lead,
Or where we will go.

Give, to me,
The child's heart.
Make **my** *wisdom*
Swiftly depart;

Replacing it with Yours,
So ancient and true,
Which will take hold,
My spirit to subdue.

It is not for me alone
That I send this prayer,
But that in this work,
All may see You there.

Your glory and majesty
Let every mouth proclaim.
This, my fervent prayer,
Is sent in Jesus' name."

The Word from the Bible

Daniel 2:31-36

Thou, O king, sawest, and behold a great image. This great image, whose brightness was excellent, stood before thee; and the form thereof was terrible. This image's head was of fine gold, his breast and his arms of silver, his belly and his thighs of brass, His legs of iron, his feet part of iron and part of clay.

Thou sawest till that a stone was cut out without hands, which smote the image upon his feet that were of iron and clay, and brake them to pieces. Then was the iron, the clay, the brass, the silver, and the gold, broken to pieces together, and became like the chaff of the summer threshingfloors; and the wind carried them away, that no place was found for them: and the stone that smote the image became a great mountain, and filled the whole earth.

This is the dream; and we will tell the interpretation thereof before the king.

Numbers 12:5-8

And the LORD came down in the pillar of the cloud, and stood in the door of the tabernacle, and called Aaron and Miriam: and they both came forth.

And he said, Hear now my words: If there be a prophet among you, I the LORD will make myself known unto him in a vision, and will speak unto him in a dream. My servant Moses is not so, who is faithful in all mine house. With him will I speak mouth to mouth, even apparently, and not in dark speeches; and the similitude of the LORD shall he behold: wherefore then were ye not afraid to speak against my servant Moses?

Deuteronomy 18:15-19

The LORD thy God will raise up unto thee a Prophet from the midst of thee, of thy brethren, like unto me; unto him ye shall hearken; According to all that thou desiredst of the LORD thy God in Horeb in the day of the assembly, saying, Let me not hear again the voice of the LORD my God, neither let me see this great fire any more, that I die not.

And the LORD said unto me, They have well spoken that which they have spoken. I will raise them up a Prophet from among their brethren, like unto thee, and will put my words in his mouth; and he shall speak unto them all that I shall command him. And it shall come to pass, that whosoever will not hearken unto my words which he shall speak in my name, I will require it of him.

Genesis 14:18-20

And Melchizedek king of Salem brought forth bread and wine: and he was the priest of the most high God. And he blessed him, and said, Blessed be Abram of the most high God, possessor of heaven and earth: And blessed be the most high God, which hath delivered thine enemies into thy hand.

And he gave him tithes of all.

Psalm 110:1-7

A Psalm of David.

The LORD said unto my Lord, Sit thou at my right hand, until I make thine enemies thy footstool. The LORD shall send the rod of thy strength out of Zion: rule thou in the midst of thine enemies. Thy people shall be willing in the day of thy power, in the beauties of holiness from the womb of the morning: thou hast the dew of thy youth. The LORD hath sworn, and will not repent, Thou art a priest for ever after the order of Melchizedek.

The Lord at thy right hand shall strike through kings in the day of his wrath. He shall judge among the heathen, he shall fill the places with the dead bodies; he shall wound the heads over many countries. He shall drink of the brook in the way: therefore shall he lift up the head.

Chapter One

Daniel Complete

The Book of Daniel is often used as a part of the formula leading up to the time of the end of the kingdom of man. This, however, is not the purpose of the book of Daniel. This book is a revelation to Daniel, in prophecy, of the events that were to occur in the time leading up to the coming of the Messiah, and of the return of the Messiah in the period closely following his coming.

> *Know therefore and understand, that from the going forth of the commandment to restore and to build Jerusalem unto the Messiah the Prince shall be seven weeks, and threescore and two weeks: the street shall be built again, and the wall, even in troublous times.*
>
> *And after threescore and two weeks shall Messiah be cut off, but not for himself: and the people of the prince that shall come shall destroy the city and the sanctuary; and the end thereof shall be with a flood, and unto the end of the war desolations are determined. And he shall confirm the covenant with many for one week: and in the midst of the week he shall cause the sacrifice and the oblation to cease, and for the overspreading of abominations he shall make it desolate, even until the consummation, and that determined shall be poured upon the desolate.*
>
> (Daniel 9:25-27)

The Babylonian king, Nebuchadnezzar, had a dream. This dream started Daniel on a quest. This quest would take him to an understanding of the prophecy of the earthly kingdoms that would precede the coming of the eternal Kingdom of God, in the Messiah. Let us go through the interpretation of king Nebuchadnezzar's dream, piece by piece.

> *Thou, O king, art a king of kings: for the God of heaven hath given thee a kingdom, power, and strength, and glory. And wheresoever the children of men dwell, the beasts of the field and the fowls of the heaven hath he given into thine hand, and hath made thee ruler over them all. Thou art this head of gold.*
>
> (Daniel 2:37-38)

This Scripture introduces us to the place in God's design for the kingdom of man that is held by the kingdom of Babylon, when it was ruled by a select and specific king of Babylon. This is obviously already fulfilled. The Babylonian empire continued until Belshazzar, who was the last king of Babylon.

> *Belshazzar the king made a great feast to a thousand of his lords, and drank wine before the thousand. Belshazzar, whiles he tasted the wine, commanded to bring the golden and silver vessels which his father Nebuchadnezzar had taken out of the temple which was in Jerusalem; that the king, and his princes, his wives, and his concubines, might drink therein.*
>
> *Then they brought the golden vessels that were taken out of the temple of the house of God which was at Jerusalem; and the king, and his princes, his wives, and his concubines, drank in them. They drank wine, and praised the gods of gold, and of silver, of brass, of iron, of wood, and of stone.*
>
> *In the same hour came forth fingers of a man's hand, and wrote over against the candlestick upon the plaster of the wall of the king's palace: and the king saw the part of the hand that wrote.*
>
> (Daniel 5:1-5)

Then, Belshazzar's kingdom was taken from him because of his arrogance toward God.

> *This is the interpretation of the thing: MENE; God hath numbered thy kingdom, and finished it.*

(Daniel 5:26)

It was prophesied by Daniel that a kingdom would arise to displace the rule of Babylon.

> ***And after thee shall arise another kingdom inferior to thee . . .***
>
> (Daniel 2:39)

In fulfillment of that prophecy, the dominant kingdom of the world, in that day, was then given to king Darius. This was the start of the second dominant empire of that day. It arose as foretold in Daniel's prophecy, which he had received from God.

> *TEKEL; Thou art weighed in the balances, and art found wanting.*
>
> *PERES; Thy kingdom is divided, and given to the Medes and Persians.*
>
> *Then commanded Belshazzar, and they clothed Daniel with scarlet, and put a chain of gold about his neck, and made a proclamation concerning him, that he should be the third ruler in the kingdom. In that night was Belshazzar the king of the Chaldeans slain.*
>
> *And Darius the Median took the kingdom, being about threescore and two years old.*
>
> (Daniel 5:27-31)
>
> *And I saw in a vision; and it came to pass, when I saw, that I was at Shushan in the palace, which is in the province of Elam; and I saw in a vision, and I was by the river of Ulai. Then I lifted up mine eyes, and saw, and, behold, there stood before the river a ram which had two horns: and the two horns were high; but one was higher than the other, and the higher came up last. I saw the ram pushing westward, and northward, and southward; so that no beasts might stand before him, neither was there any that*

> *could deliver out of his hand; but he did according to his will, and became great.*
>
> (Daniel 8:2-4)

> *The ram which thou sawest having two horns are the kings of Media and Persia.*
>
> (Daniel 8:20)

But this kingdom would not continue as the center of the political sphere of the earth. There is another, a third kingdom, which is foretold. The third kingdom is that of Greece.

> ***. . . and another third kingdom of brass, which shall bear rule over all the earth.***
>
> (Daniel 2:39)

> *And as I was considering, behold, an he goat came from the west on the face of the whole earth, and touched not the ground: and the goat had a notable horn between his eyes. And he came to the ram that had two horns, which I had seen standing before the river, and ran unto him in the fury of his power. And I saw him come close unto the ram, and he was moved with choler against him, and smote the ram, and brake his two horns: and there was no power in the ram to stand before him, but he cast him down to the ground, and stamped upon him: and there was none that could deliver the ram out of his hand.*
>
> (Daniel 8:5-7)

> *And the rough goat is the king of Grecia: and the great horn that is between his eyes is the first king.*
>
> (Daniel 8:21)

The third kingdom, Greece, would later be supplanted by the Roman Empire.

> *Now that being broken, whereas four stood up for it, four kingdoms shall stand up out of the nation, but not in his power.*
>
> (Daniel 8:22)

The fourth kingdom is activated, thusly.

> ***And the fourth kingdom shall be strong as iron**: forasmuch as iron breaketh in pieces and subdueth all things: and as iron that breaketh all these, shall it break in pieces and bruise. And whereas thou sawest the feet and toes, part of potters' clay, and part of iron, the kingdom shall be divided; but there shall be in it of the strength of the iron, forasmuch as thou sawest the iron mixed with miry clay. And as the toes of the feet were part of iron, and part of clay, so the kingdom shall be partly strong, and partly broken. And whereas thou sawest iron mixed with miry clay, they shall mingle themselves with the seed of men: but they shall not cleave one to another, even as iron is not mixed with clay.*
>
> (Daniel 2:40-43)

> *Therefore the he goat waxed very great: and when he was strong, the great horn was broken; and for it came up four notable ones toward the four winds of heaven. And out of one of them came forth a little horn, which waxed exceeding great, toward the south, and toward the east, and toward the pleasant land. And it waxed great, even to the host of heaven; and it cast down some of the host and of the stars to the ground, and stamped upon them.*
>
> (Daniel 8:8-10)

> *And in the latter time of their kingdom, when the transgressors are come to the full, a king of fierce countenance, and understanding dark sentences, shall stand up. And his power shall be mighty, but not by his own power: and he shall destroy wonderfully, and shall prosper, and practice, and shall destroy the mighty and the holy people. And through his policy also he shall cause craft to prosper in his hand; and he shall magnify himself in his heart, and by peace shall destroy many: he shall also stand up against the Prince of princes; but he shall be broken without hand.*
>
> (Daniel 8:23-25)

For the sake of reference, let us say that the crucifixion of Jesus Christ occurred approximately 30 AD. This is the time when there was a kingdom that chose to *stand up against the Prince of princes.*

The kingdom of Daniel 2:40-43 is the Roman Empire. This empire was made up of Rome and Greece. From the historical record, we know that one part of it consisted of the gladiators (*partly strong*) and the other part more scholastic (*partly broken*). The Greeks and the Romans did not always get along. There was a kind of a feud between whether the scholastic side of man or the warrior side of man should be dominant. Even though it might seem obvious that the warriors would be able to destroy the scholar, this did not happen. Instead, this empire gave us some of the far reaching principles of governance; which includes that of involving more of the people in governance. This is the pattern that was taken up by what we now call democracy. In that day, though, representation of the people was mostly done by the privileged people, but sometimes a senator or other politician would arise from the ranks of the common man. The following is the lingering legacy of the Roman Empire.

> *Yea, he magnified himself even to the prince of the host, and by him the daily sacrifice was taken away, and the place of his sanctuary was cast down. And an host was given him against the daily sacrifice by reason of transgression, and it cast down the truth to the ground; and it practiced, and prospered.*
>
> *Then I heard one saint speaking, and another saint said unto that certain saint which spake, How long shall be the vision concerning the daily sacrifice, and the transgression of desolation, to give both the sanctuary and the host to be trodden under foot? And he said unto me, Unto two thousand and three hundred days; then shall the sanctuary be cleansed.*
>
> (Daniel 8:11-14)

Again, for the sake of reference, we note that about six weeks (42 years) after the crucifixion of Christ, which would take us to about 72 AD, the events started that resulted in the warfare that would eventually destroy ancient Jerusalem. This happened over a period of about *two thousand and three hundred days*. At the end of the war that destroyed ancient Jerusalem, there is the mass destruction at Massada. These two went on for about one week of years.

Thus he said, The fourth beast shall be the fourth kingdom upon earth, which shall be diverse from all kingdoms, and shall devour the whole earth, and shall tread it down, and break it in pieces. And the ten horns out of this kingdom are ten kings that shall arise: and another shall rise after them; and he shall be diverse from the first, and he shall subdue three kings.

And he shall speak great words against the most High, and shall wear out the saints of the most High, and think to change times and laws: and they shall be given into his hand until a time and times and the dividing of time.

(Daniel 7:23-25)

Another significant event of this time, which we introduce for reference sake, is the decline and destruction of the Roman Empire. This did not start until around 410 AD (almost three centuries and a fraction of a century after 72 AD), or, *until a time and times and the dividing of time.* It could be said that this is when the power of the Roman Empire was taken away, and there was a quenching of the Empire's ability to either *speak great words against the most High* or *wear out the saints of the most High.* The actual fall of the Empire has been set at 476 AD. (We will look at this in greater detail later.)

The Roman Empire is the Empire that was in control of the crucifixion of Jesus of Nazareth (*he shall also stand up against the Prince of princes*), which is, now, history. Another matter of history is the fact that this is the kingdom that performed some of the most heinous torture of Christians; in an attempt to *wear out the saints of the most High.* The Roman Empire was responsible for such things as throwing Christians to the lions, and using them for gladiator training. However, as we know, they were not allowed to continue; now, this too is history.

But the judgment shall sit, and they shall take away his dominion, to consume and to destroy it unto the end.

(Daniel 7:26)

The kingdom in Rome was replaced by rulers who did look to God for their direction. They also turned to Jesus Christ, sometimes even for the governance of their peoples. And, of course, we know that the kingdom, or at least part of it, spawned another power, under the control of some of the professed people of God. We call this, the office of the Pope in the Vatican in Rome, of the Catholic Church. Some may attempt to apply the Scripture in Daniel 7:27 to this power; but, they do not fit with one another.

> *And the kingdom and dominion, and the greatness of the kingdom under the whole heaven, shall be given to the people of the saints of the most High, whose kingdom is an everlasting kingdom, and all dominions shall serve and obey him.*
>
> (Daniel 7:27)

There is a different place of origin of the power that is of the Roman Pope than that which energizes the kingdom of Daniel 7:27. We will return to this later.

It is not right to consider the passage in Daniel 7:27 as being applicable to an earthly kingdom. There is a logical break that must be understood. The break after the first part of the statement: *And the kingdom and dominion, and the greatness of the kingdom under the whole heaven, shall be given to the people of the saints of the most High.* This could include an earthly kingdom, or center of power, which was taken away from those who persecuted the Christians, and given to rulers who promoted Christian principles. And these rulers even made Christianity the national religion, in some cases. This, however, had its problems: Christianity cannot be a mandated service to God.

After the transition from persecution of Christianity, in the kingdoms of the world, in the time of the New Testament's revelation, as the environment of that day changes to reverence for the way of Christ, there is a transition; from the natural, to the spiritual. In this case, the, natural, includes matters of the mind and of human logic. The, logical to spiritual, transition is found in the next thought in this area of Scripture. It is in the words that tell us of the kingdom of the *most High, whose kingdom is an everlasting kingdom, and all dominions shall serve and obey him.* To understand this, note that the passage ends with the word *him* not them. Thus, it is referring to only one; and not to the saints of the Most High. This one is the Most High, who is our Father God; so, too, is the Divine One that is given service in the kingdom that is the reference of the following passage from Daniel.

> *And in the days of these kings shall the God of heaven set up a kingdom, which shall never be destroyed: and the kingdom shall not be left to other people, but it shall break in pieces and consume all these kingdoms, and it shall stand for ever. Forasmuch as thou sawest that the stone was cut out of the mountain without hands, and that it brake in pieces the iron, the brass, the clay, the silver, and the gold; the great God hath made known to the king what shall come to pass hereafter: and the dream is certain, and the interpretation thereof sure.*
>
> (Daniel 2:44-45)

This is the start of the everlasting kingdom of Christ; which is the kingdom that God set up. However, it is not framed by an earthly kingdom. The rise of Christianity in Rome is just a fulfillment of the prophecy that gives a measure of power in the earth to the saints. The kingdom of Christ is far more pervasive than that. In Jesus Christ's message to mankind, he tells of the establishment of his kingdom with man, but *not of this world.*

> *Then Pilate entered into the judgment hall again, and called Jesus, and said unto him, Art thou the King of the Jews?*
>
> *Jesus answered him, Sayest thou this thing of thyself, or did others tell it thee of me?*
>
> *Pilate answered, Am I a Jew? Thine own nation and the chief priests have delivered thee unto me: what hast thou done?*
>
> *Jesus answered, My kingdom is not of this world: if my kingdom were of this world, then would my servants fight, that I should not be delivered to the Jews: but now is my kingdom not from hence.*
>
> (John 18:33-36)

The fulfillment of this prophecy of Daniel was on its way to completion when Jesus Christ rose from the dead, and received all power in Heaven and earth. This is when the Kingdom of God in Christ, with man, emerged on the earth as an everlasting kingdom. Jesus received two things: the promise of God that he would deliver all to him, and the ability to manage all that the Father would give him.

David tells us about the promise:

> *A Psalm of David.*
> *The LORD said unto my Lord, Sit thou at my right hand, until I make thine enemies thy footstool.*
> (Psalm 110:1)

Jesus tells us about the empowerment:

> *Then the eleven disciples went away into Galilee, into a mountain where Jesus had appointed them. And when they saw him, they worshipped him: but some doubted.*
>
> *And Jesus came and spake unto them, saying, All power is given unto me in heaven and in earth.*
> (Matthew 28:16-18)

A disciple of Christ announces its impending arrival of both, as scheduled for his day:

> *But he, being full of the Holy Ghost, looked up stedfastly into heaven, and saw the glory of God, and Jesus standing on the right hand of God, And said, Behold, I see the heavens opened, and the Son of man standing on the right hand of God.*
> (Acts 7:55-56)

Jesus Christ is the one who, at that time, took control of all aspects of the kingdom of man. There was only a matter of demonstrating to mankind that God was indeed certifying Christ's reign among the heathen. This he did in Jerusalem, and with the Roman Empire. It was then quite clear that God had taken back the direction of mankind, and given it to His Son. But, as we will see later, there is still one more matter that God will take care of. But don't you love a mystery? No? Well, this matter will become clear, later.

"Wait a minute," you say. "This can't be the end of the story, look at the world around us. This is not the world that Christ would have if he was here on earth, ruling."

It is absolutely correct to say that the story is not finished with the establishment of the rule of Jesus Christ, over all. Please remember what the LORD said he would do for the chosen one. It is somewhat selfishly idealistic to rush both mankind and the kingdom of man through the intermediate phases of their return to the fullness of God's grace. Furthermore, it is stingy of those who would stop the development that Christ will achieve by exercise of his strength to rule, under the loving direction of the Father. Please, let progress be progressive.

> *I will declare the decree: the LORD hath said unto me, Thou art my Son; this day have I begotten thee. Ask of me, and I shall give thee the heathen for thine inheritance, and the uttermost parts of the earth for thy possession.*
>
> (Psalm 2:7-8)

Then, think back to the following portion of the history of the LORD'S inheritance, which we call the nation of Israel.

> *In that day shall there be a highway out of Egypt to Assyria, and the Assyrian shall come into Egypt, and the Egyptian into Assyria, and the Egyptians shall serve with the Assyrians. In that day shall Israel be the third with Egypt and with Assyria, even a blessing in the midst of the land: Whom the LORD of hosts shall bless, saying, Blessed be Egypt my people, and Assyria the work of my hands, and Israel mine inheritance.*
>
> (Isaiah 19:23-25)

With the nation of Israel, the LORD established an everlasting covenant. But, did they do everything just the way they were supposed to? Though God has the ability to command anyone to do anything that He wants them to do; was this the way he treated His inheritance?

No, the LORD allowed His inheritance to grow. He gave—and still gives—them challenges to move them along. He works with them to bring them to perfection. Though as a matter of power, God could do so; the Father does not just command them to be obedient. What God has promised that he will do is, to change their hearts to ones that want to serve Him.

> *But this shall be the covenant that I will make with the house of Israel; After those days, saith the LORD, I will put my law in their inward parts, and write it in their hearts; and will be their God, and they shall be my people. And they shall teach no more every man his neighbour, and every man his brother, saying, Know the LORD: for they shall all know me, from the least of them unto the greatest of them, saith the LORD: for I will forgive their iniquity, and I will remember their sin no more.*
>
> (Jeremiah 31:33-34)

> *And it shall come to pass afterward, that I will pour out my spirit upon all flesh; and your sons and your daughters shall prophesy, your old men shall dream dreams, your young men shall see visions: And also upon the servants and upon the handmaids in those days will I pour out my spirit.*
>
> (Joel 2:28-29)

Do you think that the Lord Jesus Christ might have learned a few things from the Father? Do you think that he was paying attention when the lessons were being given out to the nation of Israel? Do you think that Jesus might also be a Leader to his inheritance, such as the Father is to His? Do you think that maybe Jesus uses his Father's method of moving his inheritance to serving God? I think so, and I think that it is called *rewards* and *judgment*.

> *And I saw a great white throne, and him that sat on it, from whose face the earth and the heaven fled away; and there was found no place for them. And I saw the dead, small and great, stand before God; and the books were opened: and another book was opened, which is the book of life: and the dead were judged out of those things which were written in the books, according to their works. And the sea gave up the dead which were in it; and death and hell delivered up the dead which were in them: and they were judged every man according to their works.*
>
> (Revelation 20:11-13)

Yes, this world is under the control of the Son. Yes, he does know just how bad his inheritance is behaving. And yes, just like the Father, Whom Jesus loves dearly (and so do I), he is willing to persevere with us in longsuffering love. This is love: first, for the Father; and then, because of that, for us—all of us. Mankind is a work in progress. Mankind is being moved to perfection under the tutelage of the Greatest Teachers of all time; God the Father and Jesus Christ, the Son of God.

But does this mean that we will be allowed to continue as we are forever?

If you have the stomach for it, ask one of your brothers in the nation of Israel. Ask him how God has moved this nation to honor Him. Or if you don't have a strong stomach, or are just isolated from the nation of Israel, look in the Bible. In the Old Testament it sometimes gets very graphic about what was allowed to happen, and what was done to the nation of Israel to bring it into conformance with the image of one that is God's son, which Israel is.

> *And the LORD said unto Moses, When thou goest to return into Egypt, see that thou do all those wonders before Pharaoh, which I have put in thine hand: but I will harden his heart, that he shall not let the people go. And thou shalt say unto Pharaoh, Thus saith the LORD, Israel is my son, even my firstborn: And I say unto thee, Let my son go, that he may serve me: and if thou refuse to let him go, behold, I will slay thy son, even thy firstborn.*
>
> (Exodus 4:21-23)

In consideration of the rigors of being a son of God, think about what God must be allowing His Son to do to bring each of us into conformance with the image of His Son. For, as the Father pressed His firstborn son, Israel; so, too, the Son of God presses each one of us that is elected to be, or is already, now, a smaller-in-size child of God. This pertains to every individual human, as well as every human organization that has living cells that are human beings. Be proud to declare your relationship with the Father, and with the Father through the Son.

> *And we know that all things work together for good to them that love God, to them who are the called according to his purpose. For whom he did foreknow, he also did predestinate to be conformed to*

> *the image of his Son, that he might be the firstborn among many brethren. Moreover whom he did predestinate, them he also called: and whom he called, them he also justified: and whom he justified, them he also glorified. What shall we then say to these things? If God be for us, who can be against us?*
>
> (Romans 8:28-31)

The nations of the world might want to start listening to the lesson of the nation of Israel. Please, do not waste all that good teaching, which has been procured for us by this most noble nation. Yes, I know; it is said that experience is the best teacher. But those who made this statement did not have to experience the very heavy handed Teaching of the most High God. God the Father's Hand is not like human hands; it is much larger, and **much** heavier. Please, learn from example, rather than from experience. This is the gift of the nation of Israel, by the will of God, to the world. This is the gift that Daniel pronounced, and that Jesus perpetuated.

> *And at that time shall Michael stand up, the great prince which standeth for the children of thy people: and there shall be a time of trouble, such as never was since there was a nation even to that same time: and at that time thy people shall be delivered, every one that shall be found written in the book. And many of them that sleep in the dust of the earth shall awake, some to everlasting life, and some to shame and everlasting contempt. And they that be wise shall shine as the brightness of the firmament; and they that turn many to righteousness as the stars for ever and ever.*
>
> *But thou, O Daniel, shut up the words, and seal the book, even to the time of the end: many shall run to and fro, and knowledge shall be increased.*
>
> *Then I Daniel looked, and, behold, there stood other two, the one on this side of the bank of the river, and the other on that side of the bank of the river. And one said to the man clothed in linen, which was upon the waters of the river, How long shall it be to the end of these wonders?*
>
> *And I heard the man clothed in linen, which was upon the waters of the river, when he held up his right hand and his left hand unto*

heaven, and sware by him that liveth for ever that it shall be for a time, times, and an half; and when he shall have accomplished to scatter the power of the holy people, all these things shall be finished.

And I heard, but I understood not: then said I, O my Lord, what shall be the end of these things?

And he said, Go thy way, Daniel: for the words are closed up and sealed till the time of the end. Many shall be purified, and made white, and tried; but the wicked shall do wickedly: and none of the wicked shall understand; but the wise shall understand. And from the time that the daily sacrifice shall be taken away, and the abomination that maketh desolate set up, there shall be a thousand two hundred and ninety days. Blessed is he that waiteth, and cometh to the thousand three hundred and five and thirty days.

But go thou thy way till the end be: for thou shalt rest, and stand in thy lot at the end of the days.

(Daniel 12:1-13)

The resurrection of Jesus Christ started the training session for his inheritance, which is, us. Therefore, we will have much more to reveal about the lessons that he has already given. Again, please learn from these examples; and do not try to, as they say, reinvent the wheel. The lives that are in the Old Testament were set in our history for our edification, toward perfection.

Moreover, brethren, I would not that ye should be ignorant, how that all our fathers were under the cloud, and all passed through the sea; And were all baptized unto Moses in the cloud and in the sea; And did all eat the same spiritual meat; And did all drink the same spiritual drink: for they drank of that spiritual Rock that followed them: and that Rock was Christ.

But with many of them God was not well pleased: for they were overthrown in the wilderness.

Now these things were our examples, to the intent we should not lust after evil things, as they also lusted.

Neither be ye idolaters, as were some of them; as it is written, The people sat down to eat and drink, and rose up to play.

Neither let us commit fornication, as some of them committed, and fell in one day three and twenty thousand.

Neither let us tempt Christ, as some of them also tempted, and were destroyed of serpents.

Neither murmur ye, as some of them also murmured, and were destroyed of the destroyer.

Now all these things happened unto them for ensamples: and they are written for our admonition, upon whom the ends of the world are come.

Wherefore let him that thinketh he standeth take heed lest he fall. There hath no temptation taken you but such as is common to man: but God is faithful, who will not suffer you to be tempted above that ye are able; but will with the temptation also make a way to escape, that ye may be able to bear it.

(1 Corinthians 10:1-13)

Great messages were sent
For Daniel to proclaim;
To reveal the LORD,
And spread His fame

To nations allowed,
By God, to rule
Over Israel, His son,
His precious jewel.

The wayward son
Was sent away
To be prepared
For the blessed day

Of deliverance of
The kingdom of man,
According to God's
Design, as of a plan:

In reality, active before
This earth was made;
Before a single brick
Of anything was laid.

It is God's Work,
Which causes us, all,
To rebound from
Adam's first fall.

It manifests God's will,
In establishing a being
That is prepared for
This amazing thing:

Communion with God,
As if face to face,
As the blessed destiny
Of the human race.

Daniel announced
The first phase, to be:
The Anointed of God,
Sent by His decree

To teach every one
How the hearts of men
Might enter the kingdom
That will never end.

CHAPTER 1A

Complete Understanding

Rightly Dividing Scripture

In presenting Scripture it is imperative that we have a complete understanding of what is being said, and why. This even governs what you read here. A person may have a thing fully memorized, and yet not be able to use the knowledge. Memorization is not sufficient for consistent application. This means that either we have to study the word ourselves or we have to receive insight from somewhere else, to know how to turn our knowledge into action. This is why God allowed the Bible to be written, thereby putting it in a form that man can read, absorb, categorize for life's circumstances, and then apply to these circumstances.

However, caution must be exercised in our handling of Scripture. When we say, a form that man can read, this does not mean that it can be transformed into any form that man decides to change the Bible; for instance, to fit a certain linguistic skill set, lifestyle, or even age group.

The words in the Bible have precise meaning. We cannot attempt to take shortcuts to understanding, by reframing the message of the Bible in words that are only close to the meaning.

> *Knowing this first, that no prophecy of the scripture is of any private interpretation. For the prophecy came not in old time by the will of man: but holy men of God spake as they were moved by the Holy Ghost.*
>
> (2 Peter 1:20-21)

We are not told to revise the Bible for understanding, but, instead, to study it for edification. It is not to man that we are responsible in this endeavor; but to God.

> *Of these things put them in remembrance, charging them before the Lord that they strive not about words to no profit, but to the subverting of the hearers. Study to show thyself approved unto God, a workman that needeth not to be ashamed, rightly dividing the word of truth. But shun profane and vain babblings: for they will increase unto more ungodliness.*
>
> (2 Timothy 2:14-16)

The study of the Bible must be done in cooperation with the Holy Ghost. For mankind; no matter how it is enunciated, translated, or explicated, it will stay as a mystery, until it is studied under the direction of the Spirit of truth. There are no mysteries to God, and there are no mysteries to those who are of God. Understanding is given by God through His direct revelations in the Law and the prophets, along with Jesus and the apostles, as presented in the Bible.

In the Old Testament, the mystery was still present in the kingdom of man. However, in the time of the overspreading of the Old Covenant with a new one, and to begin to disperse the cloud from the mystery; God sent his angel to a family of Israel. Near the turn of the calendar, the angel appeared to the man and woman to tell them of a son to be born. This son is now known by the title John the Baptist. The child, John, is the living news, as by the gift he received, even from his birth, of the way we achieve understanding of God.

> *But the angel said unto him, Fear not, Zacharias: for thy prayer is heard; and thy wife Elisabeth shall bear thee a son, and thou shalt call his name John. And thou shalt have joy and gladness; and many shall rejoice at his birth. For he shall be great in the sight of the Lord, and shall drink neither wine nor strong drink; and he shall be filled with the Holy Ghost, even from his mother's womb. And many of the children of Israel shall he turn to the Lord their God.*
>
> (Luke 1:13-16)

Now, don't get panicky. You have not missed the boat. If you are a new-comer, a late-comer, or a soon-to-comer to the Holy Ghost, you are never too late. You see, Jesus told us of another chance we get to be born, and thus to receive the Holy Ghost from the new womb of the Spirit. In fact, Jesus let us know that this is not an optional thing; it is mandatory.

> *There was a man of the Pharisees, named Nicodemus, a ruler of the Jews: The same came to Jesus by night, and said unto him, Rabbi, we know that thou art a teacher come from God: for no man can do these miracles that thou doest, except God be with him.*
>
> *Jesus answered and said unto him, Verily, verily, I say unto thee, Except a man be born again, he cannot see the kingdom of God.*
>
> *Nicodemus saith unto him, How can a man be born when he is old? can he enter the second time into his mother's womb, and be born?*
>
> *Jesus answered, Verily, verily, I say unto thee, Except a man be born of water and of the Spirit, he cannot enter into the kingdom of God. That which is born of the flesh is flesh; and that which is born of the Spirit is spirit.*
>
> (John 3:1-6)

Wherever you are in life; understanding is given by submission to the influence of the Holy Ghost. This understanding flows through the Bible, and through the message of Christ, in the Gospel. Then, it spreads from there, taking its place in all aspects of life. The Gospel is not just religion; it is life. For, the Gospel is the power of the Word of God.

> *In the beginning was the Word, and the Word was with God, and the Word was God. The same was in the beginning with God. All things were made by him; and without him was not any thing made that was made. In him was life; and the life was the light of men. And the light shineth in darkness; and the darkness comprehended it not.*
>
> (John 1:1-5)

To provide some assistance with what to expect from the Holy Ghost, let us consider three ways of dividing of the word of truth. The ways are these: prophecy, interpretation, and, proclamation. Let us look at each one in a little more detail and to a greater depth.

Prophecy is that mysterious stuff, which has a language of its own. This is the language of much of the Old Testament; especially, in those books attributed to the prophets; such as, Isaiah, Joel, Amos and Malachi. As a raw piece of communication, there is not much that can be done with unrefined prophecy as it is given. That is to say that prophecy must be accepted as it is given, as we wait for the interpretation. Here is the declared intention of God in delivering prophecy.

> *And the LORD came down in the pillar of the cloud, and stood in the door of the tabernacle, and called Aaron and Miriam: and they both came forth. And he said, Hear now my words: If there be a prophet among you, I the LORD will make myself known unto him in a vision, and will speak unto him in a dream.*
>
> (Numbers 12:5-6)

But, God is good—naturally! God provides the second division of the word of truth: interpretation. This we see in much of Daniel. When Daniel became concerned about his lack of understanding, an angel of God came to Daniel, to clarify the prophecy. We saw this in the prophecies of the events leading up to the Messiah.

> *I Daniel was grieved in my spirit in the midst of my body, and the visions of my head troubled me. I came near unto one of them that stood by, and asked him the truth of all this. So he told me, and made me know the interpretation of the things.*
>
> (Daniel 7:15-16)

Once we know the interpretation, then this division of Scripture moves us to the third division: proclamation. Proclamation is almost exclusively the form in the New Testament of the Bible—remember; the word, almost. In the New Testament, the old form of mysterious prophecy is almost gone—again, remember the word, almost.

> *And he said unto them, Ye are they which justify yourselves before men; but God knoweth your hearts: for that which is highly esteemed among men is abomination in the sight of God. The law and the prophets were until John: since that time the kingdom of God is preached, and every man presseth into it. And it is easier for heaven and earth to pass, than one tittle of the law to fail.*
>
> (Luke 16:15-17)

In the New Testament, by way of acts of declaration, the mystery that is the major content of the Old Testament has been revealed.

> *Now to him that is of power to stablish you according to my gospel, and the preaching of Jesus Christ, according to the revelation of the mystery, which was kept secret since the world began, But now is made manifest, and by the scriptures of the prophets, according to the commandment of the everlasting God, made known to all nations for the obedience of faith: To God only wise, be glory through Jesus Christ for ever. Amen.*
>
> (Romans 16:25)

> *But we speak the wisdom of God in a mystery, even the hidden wisdom, which God ordained before the world unto our glory: Which none of the princes of this world knew: for had they known it, they would not have crucified the Lord of glory. But as it is written, Eye hath not seen, nor ear heard, neither have entered into the heart of man, the things which God hath prepared for them that love him.*
>
> *But God hath revealed them unto us by his Spirit: for the Spirit searcheth all things, yea, the deep things of God. For what man knoweth the things of a man, save the spirit of man which is*

> *in him? even so the things of God knoweth no man, but the Spirit of God.*
>
> *Now we have received, not the spirit of the world, but the spirit which is of God; that we might know the things that are freely given to us of God. Which things also we speak, not in the words which man's wisdom teacheth, but which the Holy Ghost teacheth; comparing spiritual things with spiritual.*
>
> (1 Corinthians 2:7-13)

The revelation of the mystery, in the time of Jesus of Nazareth, is perfectly consistent with the message given by Moses. Moses told of the Prophet that would come, and that would stand as a precursor to understanding.

> *The LORD thy God will raise up unto thee a Prophet from the midst of thee, of thy brethren, like unto me; unto him ye shall hearken; According to all that thou desiredst of the LORD thy God in Horeb in the day of the assembly, saying, Let me not hear again the voice of the LORD my God, neither let me see this great fire any more, that I die not.*
>
> *And the LORD said unto me, They have well spoken that which they have spoken. I will raise them up a Prophet from among their brethren, like unto thee, and will put my words in his mouth; and he shall speak unto them all that I shall command him. And it shall come to pass, that whosoever will not hearken unto my words which he shall speak in my name, I will require it of him.*
>
> (Deuteronomy 18:15-19)

Being *like unto* Moses means that God speaks to the Prophet directly: no dark sayings. It also means that the Prophet is worthy of the same high respect that the LORD required of Israel for Moses.

> *My servant Moses is not so, who is faithful in all mine house. With him will I speak mouth to mouth, even apparently, and not in dark speeches; and the similitude of the LORD shall he behold: wherefore then were ye not afraid to speak against my servant Moses?*
>
> (Numbers 12:7-8)

So, in the New Testament era, we see the flourishing of the proclamation in the Old Testament. This does not mean that there were no proclamations in the Old Testament. There were indeed proclamations. However, the New Testament is, substantially, all proclamation. Let us take a deeper look at the nature of the proclamation, as it is presented by the servant of God.

The proclamation can be divided into three categories. These are commandments, examples and guidelines. Now, be very careful in the weight that you give to the guidelines of Scripture. Generally speaking, and in their more common application, guidelines are things that can be modified as fits the mind of the recipient. This is not the way that they are presented in the messages of the Bible. In the way of the Bible, a guideline may only be modified if there is a very good reason to do so. Here is an example of a time when a guideline emerged from the combination of two commandments.

> *And Nadab and Abihu, the sons of Aaron, took either of them his censer, and put fire therein, and put incense thereon, and offered strange fire before the LORD, which he commanded them not. And there went out fire from the LORD, and devoured them, and they died before the LORD.*
>
> *Then Moses said unto Aaron, This is it that the LORD spake, saying, I will be sanctified in them that come nigh me, and before all the people I will be glorified.*
>
> *And Aaron held his peace.*

> *And Moses diligently sought the goat of the sin offering, and, behold, it was burnt: and he was angry with Eleazar and Ithamar, the sons of Aaron which were left alive, saying, Wherefore have ye not eaten the sin offering in the holy place, seeing it is most holy, and God hath given it you to bear the iniquity of the congregation, to make atonement for them before the LORD? Behold, the blood of it was not brought in within the holy place: ye should indeed have eaten it in the holy place, as I commanded.*
>
> *And Aaron said unto Moses, Behold, this day have they offered their sin offering and their burnt offering before the LORD; and such things have befallen me: and if I had eaten the sin offering to day, should it have been accepted in the sight of the LORD?*

And when Moses heard that, he was content.
(Leviticus 10:1-3; 16-20)

Guidelines in Scripture must be followed, or unpleasant consequences may result. This gives all three the requirement for reasoned obedience; for, all of these proclamations, which are of the Bible, are Scripture, and they can be found in the categories given by the apostle Paul, in the following.

All scripture is given by inspiration of God, and is profitable for doctrine, for reproof, for correction, for instruction in righteousness: That the man of God may be perfect, thoroughly furnished unto all good works.
(2 Timothy 3:16-17)

Let us look at the commandments, examples and guidelines in their increasing levels of intensity, from the less intense to the most. This is the reverse of their order above. It also goes from a lesser population of humans to a greater one.

Instruction in righteousness (Guidelines)

This is primarily for the group of believers who have set their minds, and their hearts, on things above. I say this because, to be corrected unto righteousness, you must have already decided that it is productive to be righteous. This includes those who are under conviction, by the Holy Ghost, to move in the direction of righteousness. Of such was the man reading Esaias the prophet (Isaiah).

And he arose and went: and, behold, a man of Ethiopia, an eunuch of great authority under Candace queen of the Ethiopians, who had the charge of all her treasure, and had come to Jerusalem for to worship, Was returning, and sitting in his chariot read Esaias the prophet.

Then the Spirit said unto Philip, Go near, and join thyself to this chariot. And Philip ran thither to him, and heard him read the prophet Esaias, and said, Understandest thou what thou readest?

And he said, How can I, except some man should guide me? And he desired Philip that he would come up and sit with him.

(Acts 8:27-31)

For the committed servant of God, Scripture contain many guidelines for enhancing life. Not all guidelines can be followed by all. However, if they can be followed, there are added benefits that one may receive. Here are two examples.

And I say unto you, Whosoever shall put away his wife, except it be for fornication, and shall marry another, committeth adultery: and whoso marrieth her which is put away doth commit adultery.

His disciples say unto him, If the case of the man be so with his wife, it is not good to marry.

But he said unto them, All men cannot receive this saying, save they to whom it is given.

(Matthew 19:9-11)

Follow after charity, and desire spiritual gifts, but rather that ye may prophesy. For he that speaketh in an unknown tongue speaketh not unto men, but unto God: for no man understandeth him; howbeit in the spirit he speaketh mysteries. But he that prophesieth speaketh unto men to edification, and exhortation, and comfort. He that speaketh in an unknown tongue edifieth himself; but he that prophesieth edifieth the church. I would that ye all spake with tongues, but rather that ye prophesied: for greater is he that prophesieth than he that speaketh with tongues, except he interpret, that the church may receive edifying.

(1 Corinthians 14:1-5)

Correction; Reproof
(Examples)

This is a broader category. It covers all those who have accepted membership in the family of God; this does not mean, just Christians. The broader collection includes the nation of Israel, the extended nation of Islam, and any other religious group that is of the people of God.

> *God that made the world and all things therein, seeing that he is Lord of heaven and earth, dwelleth not in temples made with hands; Neither is worshipped with men's hands, as though he needed any thing, seeing he giveth to all life, and breath, and all things; And hath made of one blood all nations of men for to dwell on all the face of the earth, and hath determined the times before appointed, and the bounds of their habitation; That they should seek the Lord, if haply they might feel after him, and find him, though he be not far from every one of us: For in him we live, and move, and have our being; as certain also of your own poets have said, For we are also his offspring. Forasmuch then as we are the offspring of God, we ought not to think that the Godhead is like unto gold, or silver, or stone, graven by art and man's device.*
>
> (Acts 17:24-29)

We are they that are eligible for the chastisement of God, when we misbehave. Yes, it is an honor to be chastised by the LORD; for, through this, we know that we are they *whom the LORD loveth.*

> *My son, despise not the chastening of the LORD; neither be weary of his correction: For whom the LORD loveth he correcteth; even as a father the son in whom he delighteth.*
>
> (Proverbs 3:11-12)

> *And ye have forgotten the exhortation which speaketh unto you as unto children, My son, despise not thou the chastening of the Lord, nor faint when thou art rebuked of him: For whom the Lord loveth he chasteneth, and scourgeth every son whom he receiveth.*
>
> (Hebrews 12:5-6)

God is not limited to physical harm to get our attention. The LORD can provide psychological pressure to move us to excellence; and this is often done by examples from the Bible. The whole Bible proclaims the commandment of Jesus Christ, as he gave it to his followers.

> *Ye are the salt of the earth: but if the salt have lost his savour, wherewith shall it be salted? it is thenceforth good for nothing, but to be cast out, and to be trodden under foot of men.*
>
> *Ye are the light of the world. A city that is set on an hill cannot be hid. Neither do men light a candle, and put it under a bushel, but on a candlestick; and it giveth light unto all that are in the house.*
>
> *Let your light so shine before men, that they may see your good works, and glorify your Father which is in heaven.*
>
> (Matthew 5:13-16)

An example from the Bible always serves as the best reproof. With this reproof sealed in our mind, we can no longer say that it cannot be done. We see clearly, through example, where it has been done. Our choices of actions, and obedience, are then clear:

- Do it because we can
- Petition God to make us ready, and to move us to do it
- Walk away, because we just don't love the LORD that much—right now

Our mission, as servants of God, is to behave in either the first or second fashion, and never in the third. For, the words of Jesus in Matthew 5:13-16 tell us that we have both an obligation, and the power, to become the examples for the present Age. This is the type of behavior that the apostle Paul exhorted even the young men to express in the word. Among these young men is Timothy.

> *These things command and teach.*
>
> *Let no man despise thy youth; but be thou an example of the believers, in word, in conversation, in charity, in spirit, in faith, in purity.*

Till I come, give attendance to reading, to exhortation, to doctrine. Neglect not the gift that is in thee, which was given thee by prophecy, with the laying on of the hands of the presbytery. Meditate upon these things; give thyself wholly to them; that thy profiting may appear to all.

Take heed unto thyself, and unto the doctrine; continue in them: for in doing this thou shalt both save thyself, and them that hear thee.

(1 Timothy 4:11-16)

Doctrine (Commandments)

This is the all-inclusive category. It includes all mankind, regardless of standing with God. These are the commandments that all men must follow. The price of variance is this: a tainted, and sometimes, worthless life. For this reason, I will never accept any doctrine that cannot be found clearly in the written words in the Bible.

Among the doctrine of God for the modern Age are the non-blood commandments of the Law of Moses. However, as of the dawn of the Modern Age, in the New Age of the Gospel of God's Kingdom with man, the doctrinal elements in the Law relating to the efficacy of the blood sacrifice of animals are fulfilled in Christ.

Brethren, my heart's desire and prayer to God for Israel is, that they might be saved. For I bear them record that they have a zeal of God, but not according to knowledge. For they being ignorant of God's righteousness, and going about to establish their own righteousness, have not submitted themselves unto the righteousness of God. For Christ is the end of the law for righteousness to every one that believeth.

(Romans 10:1-4)

Especially binding are the proclamations of the apostles. This is so because their proclamations were repetitions of the word given to them by Jesus. By carrying the message of the Gospel to the world, the apostles were following Jesus' doctrine and commandments.

> *Afterward he appeared unto the eleven as they sat at meat, and upbraided them with their unbelief and hardness of heart, because they believed not them which had seen him after he was risen. And he said unto them, Go ye into all the world, and preach the gospel to every creature.*
>
> *He that believeth and is baptized shall be saved; but he that believeth not shall be damned. And these signs shall follow them that believe; In my name shall they cast out devils; they shall speak with new tongues; They shall take up serpents; and if they drink any deadly thing, it shall not hurt them; they shall lay hands on the sick, and they shall recover.*
>
> (Mark 16:14-18)

No other proclamations, by any other man, will ever be binding. No other servant of God, from then to now, has been given the power necessary to deliver a new message of God. Jesus' message is the only set of proclamations to which we ever need to turn for life.

> *From that time many of his disciples went back, and walked no more with him.*
>
> *Then said Jesus unto the twelve, Will ye also go away?*
>
> *Then Simon Peter answered him, Lord, to whom shall we go? thou hast the words of eternal life. And we believe and are sure that thou art that Christ, the Son of the living God.*
>
> (John 6:66-69)

The choice here is very simple. You either choose to follow the Scripture in the Bible, or you choose not to follow them. The choice to adhere to the Gospel of the Kingdom is a choice to follow God. The choice not to follow the gospel of Jesus Christ, in the doctrine given by him, as written in the Bible, is a choice not to follow God.

Now therefore fear the LORD, and serve him in sincerity and in truth: and put away the gods which your fathers served on the other side of the flood, and in Egypt; and serve ye the LORD. And if it seem evil unto you to serve the LORD, choose you this day whom ye will serve; whether the gods which your fathers served that were on the other side of the flood, or the gods of the Amorites, in whose land ye dwell: but as for me and my house, we will serve the LORD.

(Joshua 24:14-15)

Rightly dividing the word of truth: do it, or not; this is your choice. Where you go in life—and in God—is determined by the path you choose.

And Elijah came unto all the people, and said, How long halt ye between two opinions? if the LORD be God, follow him: but if Baal, then follow him. And the people answered him not a word.

(1 Kings 18:21)

THE WORD FROM THE BIBLE

Revelation 1:1-3

The Revelation of Jesus Christ, which God gave unto him, to show unto his servants things which must shortly come to pass; and he sent and signified it by his angel unto his servant John: Who bare record of the word of God, and of the testimony of Jesus Christ, and of all things that he saw. Blessed is he that readeth, and they that hear the words of this prophecy, and keep those things which are written therein: for the time is at hand.

2 Kings 24:10-17

At that time the servants of Nebuchadnezzar king of Babylon came up against Jerusalem, and the city was besieged. And Nebuchadnezzar king of Babylon came against the city, and his servants did besiege it.

And Jehoiachin the king of Judah went out to the king of Babylon, he, and his mother, and his servants, and his princes, and his officers: and the king of Babylon took him in the eighth year of his reign.

And he carried out thence all the treasures of the house of the LORD, and the treasures of the king's house, and cut in pieces all the vessels of gold which Solomon king of Israel had made in the temple of the LORD, as the LORD had said. And he carried away all Jerusalem, and all the princes, and all the mighty men of valour, even ten thousand captives, and all the craftsmen and smiths: none remained, save the poorest sort of the people of the land.

And he carried away Jehoiachin to Babylon, and the king's mother, and the king's wives, and his officers, and the mighty of the land, those carried he into captivity from Jerusalem to Babylon. And all the men of might, even seven thousand, and craftsmen and smiths a thousand, all that were strong and apt for war, even them the king of Babylon brought captive to Babylon.

And the king of Babylon made Mattaniah his father's brother king in his stead, and changed his name to Zedekiah.

Chapter Two

Revelation

The Recap

PREAMBLE ON THE PROPHET JESUS

Please study for a moment the following statement by Jesus. This statement has been the inspiration for quite a bit of speculation, and no small number of books, songs and sermons.

> *Then shall two be in the field; the one shall be taken, and the other left. Two women shall be grinding at the mill; the one shall be taken, and the other left.*
>
> (Matthew 24:40-41)

This statement recalls the actions of Nebuchadnezzar as written in 2 Kings. Rather than go into a lengthy theological discussion, I will let the Holy Ghost reveal to you the significance, or lack thereof, of the passage in 2 Kings as set beside the statement of Jesus. Jesus made this declarative statement in order to forewarn about the time of the destruction of the temple in Jerusalem, and the ravaging thereof that would be done by the conquering forces, around 70 AD. This would be done in the same fashion as Nebuchadnezzar did, in his day.

> *And he carried away all Jerusalem, and all the princes, and all the mighty men of valour, even ten thousand captives, and all the craftsmen and smiths: none remained, save the poorest sort of the people of the land.*
>
> (2 Kings 24:14)

Let us go on a journey, slowly. To begin, we have to find the road, before we can travel along it. Fortunately for us, the road has already been paved by the events of the Bible. The road was created by God, in the times of the Old Testament, and paved by the prophets in that Testament. The prophets did an excellent job of paving the road. So, let us now turn once again to them, in order for us to pave our road forward from where they left off.

> *And he said unto them, Ye are they which justify yourselves before men; but God knoweth your hearts: for that which is highly esteemed among men is abomination in the sight of God. The law and the prophets were until John: since that time the kingdom of God is preached, and every man presseth into it. And it is easier for heaven and earth to pass, than one tittle of the law to fail.*
>
> (Luke 16:15-17)

As Jesus said, John came preaching the Kingdom of Heaven, and many pressed into it. We are a part of that eager crowd of seekers. Therefore, since we are among the crowd, we need to store the message of the contribution of John to our road forward. This needs to be put in its place, as a continuation of the prophets.

> *In those days came John the Baptist, preaching in the wilderness of Judaea, And saying, Repent ye: for the kingdom of heaven is at hand. For this is he that was spoken of by the prophet Esaias, saying, The voice of one crying in the wilderness, Prepare ye the way of the Lord, make his paths straight. And the same John had his raiment of camel's hair, and a leathern girdle about his loins; and his meat was locusts and wild honey.*
>
> *Then went out to him Jerusalem, and all Judaea, and all the region round about Jordan, And were baptized of him in Jordan, confessing their sins.*
>
> *But when he saw many of the Pharisees and Sadducees come to his baptism, he said unto them, O generation of vipers, who hath warned you to flee from the wrath to come? Bring forth therefore fruits meet for repentance: And think not to say within yourselves,*

We have Abraham to our father: for I say unto you, that God is able of these stones to raise up children unto Abraham.

(Matthew 3:1-9)

John is not the end of our search. John is not the road that we are seeking. John told us these things, himself.

I indeed baptize you with water unto repentance: but he that cometh after me is mightier than I, whose shoes I am not worthy to bear: he shall baptize you with the Holy Ghost, and with fire: Whose fan is in his hand, and he will throughly purge his floor, and gather his wheat into the garner; but he will burn up the chaff with unquenchable fire.

(Matthew 3:11-12)

Even thought he is not the one that constructed the road; still, John did tell us where we can find the road to righteousness in God.

And John bare record, saying, I saw the Spirit descending from heaven like a dove, and it abode upon him. And I knew him not: but he that sent me to baptize with water, the same said unto me, Upon whom thou shalt see the Spirit descending, and remaining on him, the same is he which baptizeth with the Holy Ghost. And I saw, and bare record that this is the Son of God.

Again the next day after John stood, and two of his disciples; And looking upon Jesus as he walked, he saith, Behold the Lamb of God!

(John 1:32-36)

By a revelation that was sent through Moses, we received the word that the Prophet is the one that knows the road to righteousness in God.

The LORD thy God will raise up unto thee a Prophet from the midst of thee, of thy brethren, like unto me; unto him ye shall hearken; According to all that thou desiredst of the LORD thy God in Horeb in the day of the assembly, saying, Let me not hear again the voice of the LORD my God, neither let me see this great fire any more, that I die not.

> *And the LORD said unto me, They have well spoken that which they have spoken. I will raise them up a Prophet from among their brethren, like unto thee, and will put my words in his mouth; and he shall speak unto them all that I shall command him. And it shall come to pass, that whosoever will not hearken unto my words which he shall speak in my name, I will require it of him.*
>
> (Deuteronomy 18:15-19)

By the confirmation that is provided by observation of the works of his day, we see actions that point us to the Prophet. Moreover, as observers of these actions; the people of his day felt that Jesus was the Prophet spoken of by Moses, as well as by many of the other Old Testament prophets.

> *And Jesus said, Make the men sit down. Now there was much grass in the place. So the men sat down, in number about five thousand. And Jesus took the loaves; and when he had given thanks, he distributed to the disciples, and the disciples to them that were set down; and likewise of the fishes as much as they would. When they were filled, he said unto his disciples, Gather up the fragments that remain, that nothing be lost.*
>
> *Therefore they gathered them together, and filled twelve baskets with the fragments of the five barley loaves, which remained over and above unto them that had eaten.*
>
> *Then those men, when they had seen the miracle that Jesus did, said, This is of a truth that prophet that should come into the world.*
>
> *When Jesus therefore perceived that they would come and take him by force, to make him a king, he departed again into a mountain himself alone.*
>
> (John 6:10-15)

Many of us know Jesus as that Prophet; and as much, much more. However, I will stop at this *common denominator* among religions. I will even tone it down, just a bit, for now. To tone it down a bit, let us just say that if he is the Prophet, then he must be a prophet. In a fashion similar to the environment of the LORD God as it appeared to the congregation of Israel.

> *And all the people saw the thunderings, and the lightnings, and the noise of the trumpet, and the mountain smoking: and when the people saw it, they removed, and stood afar off. And they said unto Moses, Speak thou with us, and we will hear: but let not God speak with us, lest we die.*
>
> *And Moses said unto the people, Fear not: for God is come to prove you, and that his fear may be before your faces, that ye sin not.*
>
> *And the people stood afar off, and Moses drew near unto the thick darkness where God was.*
>
> (Exodus 20:18-21)

Let us construct a logical *thick darkness*, to allow our eyes to receive the portion of Jesus that we all can bear. For, the fullness of Jesus is indeed bright. The brightness of Jesus is expressed in the fact that the Prophet is only one, and he speaks with the full authority of God. Meanwhile the part that we can bear more easily is that, as a prophet, Jesus is one of many, and his words are perceived as being less threatening. So, let us first review Jesus' work as part of the collective set of prophets. One of his works of prophecy amazed a woman of his day—and for very good reason.

> *There cometh a woman of Samaria to draw water: Jesus saith unto her, Give me to drink. (For his disciples were gone away unto the city to buy meat.)*
>
> *Then saith the woman of Samaria unto him, How is it that thou, being a Jew, askest drink of me, which am a woman of Samaria? for the Jews have no dealings with the Samaritans.*
>
> *Jesus answered and said unto her, If thou knewest the gift of God, and who it is that saith to thee, Give me to drink; thou wouldest have asked of him, and he would have given thee living water.*
>
> *The woman saith unto him, Sir, thou hast nothing to draw with, and the well is deep: from whence then hast thou that living water? Art thou greater than our father Jacob, which gave us the well, and drank thereof himself, and his children, and his cattle?*

> *Jesus answered and said unto her, Whosoever drinketh of this water shall thirst again: But whosoever drinketh of the water that I shall give him shall never thirst; but the water that I shall give him shall be in him a well of water springing up into everlasting life.*
>
> *The woman saith unto him, Sir, give me this water, that I thirst not, neither come hither to draw.*
>
> *Jesus saith unto her, Go, call thy husband, and come hither.*
>
> *The woman answered and said, I have no husband.*
>
> *Jesus said unto her, Thou hast well said, I have no husband: For thou hast had five husbands; and he whom thou now hast is not thy husband: in that saidst thou truly.*
>
> *The woman saith unto him, Sir, I perceive that thou art a prophet.*
>
> (John 4:7-19)

However, this prophetic insight was about past events. In our modern times, we would say that he could have had an advance crew to prime his mind. They could have done the research, and brought him the information. The woman knew better, in her mind; however, let us maintain a healthy skepticism.

So, what marks a prophet as a prophet of God?

This was answered by the LORD, in the time of Moses

> *And if thou say in thine heart, How shall we know the word which the LORD hath not spoken? When a prophet speaketh in the name of the LORD, if the thing follow not, nor come to pass, that is the thing which the LORD hath not spoken, but the prophet hath spoken it presumptuously: thou shalt not be afraid of him.*
>
> (Deuteronomy 18:21-22)

Be careful here, though. Also, in the time of Moses, we were told that, sometimes a prophet will appear to be so only to test the masses. In certain instances, we have to look to the context of the prophecy. For, when the content is defective, then the prophet is not a true, devoted servant of God.

> *If there arise among you a prophet, or a dreamer of dreams, and giveth thee a sign or a wonder, And the sign or the wonder come to*

pass, whereof he spake unto thee, saying, Let us go after other gods, which thou hast not known, and let us serve them; Thou shalt not hearken unto the words of that prophet, or that dreamer of dreams: for the LORD your God proveth you, to know whether ye love the LORD your God with all your heart and with all your soul. Ye shall walk after the LORD your God, and fear him, and keep his commandments, and obey his voice, and ye shall serve him, and cleave unto him.

(Deuteronomy 13:1-4)

No problem here: Jesus is exempt from this brisk caution. For, Jesus did not tell anyone to *go after other gods*; he was always consistent and persistent in telling everyone to follow God the Father. Even the religious leaders of his day confirmed this aspect of Jesus' prophetic behavior and of his election by God.

And one of the scribes came, and having heard them reasoning together, and perceiving that he had answered them well, asked him, Which is the first commandment of all?

And Jesus answered him, The first of all the commandments is, Hear, O Israel; The Lord our God is one Lord: And thou shalt love the Lord thy God with all thy heart, and with all thy soul, and with all thy mind, and with all thy strength: this is the first commandment. And the second is like, namely this, Thou shalt love thy neighbour as thyself. There is none other commandment greater than these.

And the scribe said unto him, Well, Master, thou hast said the truth: for there is one God; and there is none other but he: And to love him with all the heart, and with all the understanding, and with all the soul, and with all the strength, and to love his neighbour as himself, is more than all whole burnt offerings and sacrifices.

And when Jesus saw that he answered discreetly, he said unto him, Thou art not far from the kingdom of God.

And no man after that durst ask him any question.

(Mark 12:28-34)

So, let us acknowledge that we have in Jesus a prophet of God. Thus, we have a prophet to look to for the continuation of the road that passes from the Old Testament to the New Testament, through the New Covenant. In Jesus, we have someone to whom we can listen; and, too, we have someone who will show us, and tell us, of the foundation that is laid by God. We will discuss this latter point a little more, in a moment.

For now, let us return to John the Baptist's ministry. John the Baptist was the herald of the Kingdom of God, with all mankind: he is *the voice of one crying in the wilderness*. So that we will not become confused, let us keep John's ministry separate from that of the Prophet's; in that John confirmed for us that he is not the Prophet.

> *And this is the record of John, when the Jews sent priests and Levites from Jerusalem to ask him, Who art thou? And he confessed, and denied not; but confessed, I am not the Christ. And they asked him, What then? Art thou Elias? And he saith, I am not. Art thou that prophet? And he answered, No.*
>
> (John 1:19-21)

Therefore, let us say, for the sake of discussion, that Jesus of Nazareth is the Prophet. Even so, why should we listen to him? Forgive me for the fervor of the answer, but here it is: Because Dad said so! Okay, please forgive me again; sometimes when I refer to God, I speak as a child. Rather than speaking in that fashion, let me say, because God the Father said so. And let me add that God the Father said so in the hearing of a tiny cloud of witnesses.

> *And after six days Jesus taketh Peter, James, and John his brother, and bringeth them up into an high mountain apart, And was transfigured before them: and his face did shine as the sun, and his raiment was white as the light. And, behold, there appeared unto them Moses and Elias talking with him.*
>
> *Then answered Peter, and said unto Jesus, Lord, it is good for us to be here: if thou wilt, let us make here three tabernacles; one for thee, and one for Moses, and one for Elias.*

While he yet spake, behold, a bright cloud overshadowed them: and behold a voice out of the cloud, which said, This is my beloved Son, in whom I am well pleased; hear ye him.

And when the disciples heard it, they fell on their face, and were sore afraid.

And Jesus came and touched them, and said, Arise, and be not afraid.

And when they had lifted up their eyes, they saw no man, save Jesus only.

(Matthew 17:1-8)

So, I have decided to listen to him. Before we go further, though; what is the foundation that has been laid by God? Well, again, let us move slowly to the answer. The road paved by the prophets of the Old Testament, led somewhere.

For, behold, the day cometh, that shall burn as an oven; and all the proud, yea, and all that do wickedly, shall be stubble: and the day that cometh shall burn them up, saith the LORD of hosts, that it shall leave them neither root nor branch. But unto you that fear my name shall the Sun of righteousness arise with healing in his wings; and ye shall go forth, and grow up as calves of the stall. And ye shall tread down the wicked; for they shall be ashes under the soles of your feet in the day that I shall do this, saith the LORD of hosts. Remember ye the law of Moses my servant, which I commanded unto him in Horeb for all Israel, with the statutes and judgments.

Behold, I will send you Elijah the prophet before the coming of the great and dreadful day of the LORD: And he shall turn the heart of the fathers to the children, and the heart of the children to their fathers, lest I come and smite the earth with a curse.

(Malachi 4:1-6)

The road paved by the prophets of the Old Testament, led to the Messiah; who is also called, the Son of God.

I can of mine own self do nothing: as I hear, I judge: and my judgment is just; because I seek not mine own will, but the will of the Father which hath sent me. If I bear witness of myself, my witness is not true. There is another that beareth witness of me; and I know that the witness which he witnesseth of me is true.

Ye sent unto John, and he bare witness unto the truth. But I receive not testimony from man: but these things I say, that ye might be saved. He was a burning and a shining light: and ye were willing for a season to rejoice in his light. But I have greater witness than that of John: for the works which the Father hath given me to finish, the same works that I do, bear witness of me, that the Father hath sent me. And the Father himself, which hath sent me, hath borne witness of me.

Ye have neither heard his voice at any time, nor seen his shape. And ye have not his word abiding in you: for whom he hath sent, him ye believe not.

Search the scriptures; for in them ye think ye have eternal life: and they are they which testify of me.

(John 5:30-39)

Jesus: The name Jesus is an anglicized form of the Latin Iesus, which itself is derived from the Greek name Iesous. Iesous was the Greek transliteration of the Aramaic name Yeshua, which itself was the later Aramaic form of the Hebrew name Yehoshua. Yeshua means "salvation". Others translate it as "He will save," "the LORD saves," "salvation of YHWH," or "the LORD is salvation."

However, a person cannot be the end of the road. Jesus is a person. There must be more. And, there is more.

The discovery of the purpose of Jesus is critical to moving beyond the person, to the mission. This discovery does not just include the training that the disciples received. The need for training is a part of every soul, continually. All mankind has the need for information about that road which has been built by the will of God, passing through the current

Age in the Son of God. Jesus delivered a question that needed an answer from the disciples, and still needs the same answer from every Christian, today.

> *When Jesus came into the coasts of Caesarea Philippi, he asked his disciples, saying, Whom do men say that I the Son of man am?*
>
> *And they said, Some say that thou art John the Baptist: some, Elias; and others, Jeremias, or one of the prophets.*
>
> *He saith unto them, But whom say ye that I am?*
>
> (Matthew 16:13-15)

Christ: Christ is the English representation of the Greek word Χριστός (Christos). The Christian religion takes its name from Christ, as a title given to Jesus of Nazareth, always capitalized as a singularly descriptive title meaning literally The Anointed One. The term "Christ" pertains to the role to be performed by the "chosen one of God" (another possible translation of "Christ").

The Old Testament prophets were pointing the way to the Christ; not just to the Prophet. Furthermore, from the tone of Peter's answer, we may surmise that Jesus is more than just the message, but that he represents the road.

> *And Simon Peter answered and said, Thou art the Christ, the Son of the living God.*
>
> *And Jesus answered and said unto him, Blessed art thou, Simon Barjona: for flesh and blood hath not revealed it unto thee, but my Father which is in heaven.*
>
> (Matthew 16:16-17)

By Peter's confession, Jesus is the Messiah, the Christ; who is, too, the Son of the Living God. Then, rather than separating our study of Jesus' ministry, in consideration of the message as set apart from the road; maybe it would be more accurate to say that the message of Jesus is the road; for, Dad did say, *hear ye him*. And even more accurate is to say that . . . well, let us just let Jesus tell us.

And I say also unto thee, That thou art Peter, and upon this rock I will build my church; and the gates of hell shall not prevail against it.

(Matthew 16:18)

The road, and the destination, is the church of God in Christ. And it is built on the rock. This rock is the foundation that is laid by God in the church. This rock is the truth that Jesus is the Christ, the Son of the Living God. Paul delivers the word of God on this matter.

For we are labourers together with God: ye are God's husbandry, ye are God's building. According to the grace of God which is given unto me, as a wise masterbuilder, I have laid the foundation, and another buildeth thereon. But let every man take heed how he buildeth thereupon. For other foundation can no man lay than that is laid, which is Jesus Christ.

(1 Corinthians 3:9-11)

Now, do not take what follows in the wrong spirit—Jesus does not stand alone as a foundational representative of God's truth. There is at least one other significant foundational description that exists, which is this: the foundation to the holy city.

And there came unto me one of the seven angels which had the seven vials full of the seven last plagues, and talked with me, saying, Come hither, I will show thee the bride, the Lamb's wife. And he carried me away in the spirit to a great and high mountain, and showed me that great city, the holy Jerusalem, descending out of heaven from God, Having the glory of God: and her light was like unto a stone most precious, even like a jasper stone, clear as crystal; And had a wall great and high, and had twelve gates, and at the gates twelve angels, and names written thereon, which are the names of the twelve tribes of the children of Israel: On the east three gates; on the north three gates; on the south three gates; and on the west three gates.

And the wall of the city had twelve foundations, and in them the names of the twelve apostles of the Lamb.

(Revelation 21:9-14)

These are the foundations that supported the building of the new home of the family of God, in Christ; but still, there is only one foundation to the church of Christ. The foundation is Jesus Christ. Furthermore, it is the church of Christ which is the road paved by the prophet Jesus Christ. This is the way that leads to the Kingdom of God. And the final sealant for the path to the kingdom was laid down as the blood of Jesus Christ, who is the Lamb of God. This is what we preach in the church.

This is *the way* that we share with the world. No parts missing; no new coatings needed. The road is paved and sealed: if anyone, or anything, tries to lay down a new coat, it will wash off. And nothing can penetrate the covering of the blood of Jesus. The impenetrable and irreplaceable power of the blood is in the fact that it represents life for life. As the Scripture says, *life for life* is one of the payments for transgressions. We continually transgress against God; therefore, by right, He could demand our life for the lives that we have destroyed by our actions; whether the life is physical or metaphysical. However, in this case, it is Jesus' life for our life; or, more correctly, Jesus' life for a tremendously large number of lives—one life at a time. In Christ, and in his church, our road is sure to the Kingdom of God. Only one caution though.

> *Enter ye in at the strait gate: for wide is the gate, and broad is the way, that leadeth to destruction, and many there be which go in thereat: Because strait is the gate, and narrow is the way, which leadeth unto life, and few there be that find it.*
>
> (Matthew 7:13-14)

Jesus, the way: Jesus, the prophet: in our search for the thing that is of the seven, let us start with Jesus, and his words to Israel, and to the world. Jesus is the beginning of the journey to knowledge of the Kingdom of God, and to the understanding of its way. Maybe, Jesus, as the representative of God, is also the end. Hopefully, you believe that he is, for this is what is revealed by the apostle of Jesus Christ.

> *Brethren, my heart's desire and prayer to God for Israel is, that they might be saved. For I bear them record that they have a zeal of God, but not according to knowledge. For they being ignorant of God's righteousness, and going about to establish their own righteousness, have not submitted themselves unto the righteousness*

of God. For Christ is the end of the law for righteousness to every one that believeth.

(Romans 10:1-4)

Please continue reading. There is more to the man, Jesus of Nazareth; which we will reveal to you. Wherefore let us start, on the next page, to increase our understanding of Jesus Christ, the Son of God.

The Revelation of Jesus Christ, which God gave unto him, to show unto his servants things which must shortly come to pass

The exploration of the character of Jesus, the Messiah, leads us naturally into the last book of the Bible, The Revelation of Saint John the divine, as it is titled. The beginning verse describes some of the content of the book. However, it should not be used to imply that it contains all of the content of the book. For instance in the first verse we read the phrase: *to show unto his servants things which must shortly come to pass.* This might give the impression that this is only about the author's future, if viewed in isolation. However, in the body of the book we see many references to things that have already occurred. This is the place where I need to give a slight lesson, for those who need it, in literary communication. This also applies to any other communication where the communicator intends to give a complete picture of the nature of an event or person.

As the author indicated, the content of this book is provided by God. It is given by God to Jesus Christ, to show some things to his servants. The author of the book is Jesus, who is the angel of God. Jesus delivers the words to one of his servants, John. By the writing and distribution of this book, John will give this information to others of Jesus' servants—serving as the angel, or representative, of Jesus. The purpose of showing these things to his servants is the same as the purpose of showing anything to any servant; which is, to equip them for service. Thus, there is a need for information beyond just the amount that is needed to perform the particular action.

For a servant to truly serve his master, he must have some knowledge of why it must be done. Please, do not get servant and slave confused. A slave needs no information, except for the task to be performed. Also, a slave is not trusted with complex matters: only simple ones. A servant is different. A servant is trusted with the understanding of the lord of his service. In this way, the servant can give the best service possible.

One of the things that must always be done in order to give a complete understanding of the matter is what may be called "setting the stage". To just say what is happening, without some insight on what led up to it, give a very incomplete picture. It is difficult, if not impossible to understand anything fully—or in this case, *things which must shortly come to pass*—without knowing what went into its development. This is true also of the Book of Revelation. The first hint that we are reading fulfilled events occurs with the pronouncement of another one of the angels of Heaven.

> *And the angel which I saw stand upon the sea and upon the earth lifted up his hand to heaven, And sware by him that liveth for ever and ever, who created heaven, and the things that therein are, and the earth, and the things that therein are, and the sea, and the things which are therein, that there should be time no longer: But in the days of the voice of the seventh angel, when he shall begin to sound, the mystery of God should be finished, as he hath declared to his servants the prophets.*
>
> (Revelation 10:5-7)

This is a fulfillment of the unfolding of the proclamation of Jesus Christ to his twelve disciples . . .

> *And when he was alone, they that were about him with the twelve asked of him the parable. And he said unto them, Unto you it is given to know the mystery of the kingdom of God: but unto them that are without, all these things are done in parables: That seeing they may see, and not perceive; and hearing they may hear, and not understand; lest at any time they should be converted, and their sins should be forgiven them.*
>
> (Mark 4:10-12)

. . . Which is supported by a revelation from God to Paul, the apostle to the Romans . . .

> *Now to him that is of power to stablish you according to my gospel, and the preaching of Jesus Christ, according to the revelation of the mystery, which was kept secret since the world began, But now is made manifest, and by the scriptures of the prophets, according to the commandment of the everlasting God, made known to all nations for the obedience of faith: To God only wise, be glory through Jesus Christ for ever. Amen.*
>
> (Romans 16:25-27)

. . . That is the same apostle Paul that further affirmed to the Ephesians, as he told them that the mystery which has been revealed is itself, Jesus Christ.

> *For this cause I Paul, the prisoner of Jesus Christ for you Gentiles, If ye have heard of the dispensation of the grace of God which is given me to you-ward: How that by revelation he made known unto me the mystery; (as I wrote afore in few words, Whereby, when ye read, ye may understand my knowledge in the mystery of Christ) Which in other ages was not made known unto the sons of men, as it is now revealed unto his holy apostles and prophets by the Spirit; That the Gentiles should be fellowheirs, and of the same body, and partakers of his promise in Christ by the gospel: Whereof I was made a minister, according to the gift of the grace of God given unto me by the effectual working of his power.*
>
> *Unto me, who am less than the least of all saints, is this grace given, that I should preach among the Gentiles the unsearchable riches of Christ; And to make all men see what is the fellowship of the mystery, which from the beginning of the world hath been hid in God, who created all things by Jesus Christ: To the intent that now unto the principalities and powers in heavenly places might be known by the church the manifold wisdom of God, According to the eternal purpose which he purposed in Christ Jesus our Lord: In whom we have boldness and access with confidence by the faith of him.*
> (Ephesians 3:1-12)

First, the doctrine has to be established; then, things can proceed from there. In the same way as Paul said, we will not go over the doctrine of Jesus Christ, again.

> *Therefore leaving the principles of the doctrine of Christ, let us go on unto perfection; not laying again the foundation of repentance from dead works, and of faith toward God, Of the doctrine of baptisms, and of laying on of hands, and of resurrection of the dead, and of eternal judgment. And this will we do, if God permit.*
> (Hebrews 6:1-3)

However, you can find the recap of this doctrine in the book of Revelation, starting at the beginning of chapter 1 and proceeding to the last verse of chapter fourteen: this is the destruction of Jerusalem that was foretold by Jesus.

> *And the angel thrust in his sickle into the earth, and gathered the vine of the earth, and cast it into the great winepress of the wrath of God. And the winepress was trodden without the city, and blood came out of the winepress, even unto the horse bridles, by the space of a thousand and six hundred furlongs.*
>
> (Revelation 14:19-20)

This portion of The Revelation describes the events that had occurred prior to the time of The Revelation of Saint John the divine. Following these events, there are *things which must shortly come to pass.* However, before these things, we will look at those things that were going on during the times of the writing of the book by John, the Revelator. For now, however, this is where we will pause in our journey through Revelation. We will resume from this point as we proceed further. We will start with the following.

> *And I saw another sign in heaven, great and marvellous, seven angels having the seven last plagues; for in them is filled up the wrath of God. And I saw as it were a sea of glass mingled with fire: and them that had gotten the victory over the beast, and over his image, and over his mark, and over the number of his name, stand on the sea of glass, having the harps of God. And they sing the song of Moses the servant of God, and the song of the Lamb, saying, Great and marvellous are thy works, Lord God Almighty; just and true are thy ways, thou King of saints. Who shall not fear thee, O Lord, and glorify thy name? for thou only art holy: for all nations shall come and worship before thee; for thy judgments are made manifest.*
>
> (Revelation 15:1-4)

A book of prophecy,
The final one,
Reveals a marvelous
Work to be done.

A mystery that was
So long concealed,
Now in its pages,
To all, revealed.

The LORD of host
Reveals the plan
Established before
There was even one man.

This life map was issued
With just one goal:
Bring man to God,
Each and every soul.

The message of Adam
Is the very early part;
Revealing man's need
For a servant's heart.

Then, to show all mankind
What it surely must do,
The pot of worship
Was allowed to stew.

It started to simmer
When a son was born;
As, from Egypt's grip
It was forcefully torn:

The nation of Israel,
Carrying the Law of God,
Moved toward perfection
By His mighty rod.

Then, the pot really boiled
When the nation gave birth
To he who has brought
God's peace, to all the earth:

Jesus of Nazareth,
At the time of the end,
To receive the kingdom
That God shall defend.

CHAPTER 2A

Without Augmentation

Rightly Dividing Scripture

The Bible is not a history book, and must not be viewed as such. The Bible does have some historical content, which can be validated by the records kept by man. The uniqueness of the Bible, though, is in that it has both more, and less, than is contained in the records of mankind. This is the strength of the Bible's design.

The Bible has less detail about such things as, the complete history of the kings, international relations, the making of great men from their childhood, and the activities of the first ladies of power. These things are, quite frankly, not relevant to the story.

The Bible contains the information that God has provided to us, in order for us to understand what the most ambitious project of all time is. I admit that I am somewhat biased about this in saying that the most ambitious project of all is raising a family in the light of the LORD. Godly family development is the underlying theme of the entire Bible; on a cosmological level. The Bible begins as the story of a single parent family. The single parent is God; and a Most Powerful Parent, indeed, is He.

> *For since the beginning of the world men have not heard, nor perceived by the ear, neither hath the eye seen, O God, beside thee, what he hath prepared for him that waiteth for him. Thou meetest him that rejoiceth and worketh righteousness, those that remember thee in thy ways: behold, thou art wroth; for we have sinned: in those is continuance, and we shall be saved.*
>
> *But we are all as an unclean thing, and all our righteousnesses are as filthy rags; and we all do fade as a leaf; and our iniquities,*

> *like the wind, have taken us away. And there is none that calleth upon thy name, that stirreth up himself to take hold of thee: for thou hast hid thy face from us, and hast consumed us, because of our iniquities.*
>
> *But now, O LORD, thou art our father; we are the clay, and thou our potter; and we all are the work of thy hand.*
>
> (Isaiah 64:4-8)

Yes, the Parent is God the Father; and, there is no God beside Him.

> *Thus saith the LORD the King of Israel, and his redeemer the LORD of hosts; I am the first, and I am the last; and beside me there is no God.*
>
> (Isaiah 44:6)

> *Unto thee it was showed, that thou mightest know that the LORD he is God; there is none else beside him. Out of heaven he made thee to hear his voice, that he might instruct thee: and upon earth he showed thee his great fire; and thou heardest his words out of the midst of the fire. And because he loved thy fathers, therefore he chose their seed after them, and brought thee out in his sight with his mighty power out of Egypt; To drive out nations from before thee greater and mightier than thou art, to bring thee in, to give thee their land for an inheritance, as it is this day.*
>
> *Know therefore this day, and consider it in thine heart, that the LORD he is God in heaven above, and upon the earth beneath: there is none else.*
>
> (Deuteronomy 4:35-39)

In His family, the Parent, God the Father, has absolute control. This is required to prevent power struggles and to eliminate confusion among the children.

> *No man can serve two masters: for either he will hate the one, and love the other; or else he will hold to the one, and despise the other. Ye cannot serve God and mammon.*
>
> (Matthew 6:24)

God the Father has no need for a mate, since He has the power to create children by the power of His Word. The first human child of God, on earth, is called Adam. A few of his descendants, in reverse order, are listed below.

> *Which was the son of Cainan, which was the son of Arphaxad, which was the son of Sem, which was the son of Noe, which was the son of Lamech, Which was the son of Mathusala, which was the son of Enoch, which was the son of Jared, which was the son of Maleleel, which was the son of Cainan, Which was the son of Enos, which was the son of Seth, which was the son of Adam, which was the son of God.*
>
> (Luke 3:36-38)

In a certain sense, Eve is God's daughter by creation. In another sense, Eve is God's granddaughter, because she was born from Adam. (Things happened a little differently at the start of humanity).

> *And the LORD God caused a deep sleep to fall upon Adam, and he slept: and he took one of his ribs, and closed up the flesh instead thereof; And the rib, which the LORD God had taken from man, made he a woman, and brought her unto the man.*
>
> *And Adam said, This is now bone of my bones, and flesh of my flesh: she shall be called Woman, because she was taken out of Man.*
>
> (Genesis 2:21-23)
>
> *Therefore shall a man leave his father and his mother, and shall cleave unto his wife: and they shall be one flesh.*
>
> (Genesis 2:24)

And all the children of Adam and Eve are God's sons and daughters, by acquisition. This is the family structuring that Jacob introduced to us by his statement to Joseph, about Joseph's first two sons.

> *And Jacob said unto Joseph, God Almighty appeared unto me at Luz in the land of Canaan, and blessed me, And said unto me, Behold, I will make thee fruitful, and multiply thee, and I will*

> *make of thee a multitude of people; and will give this land to thy seed after thee for an everlasting possession. And now thy two sons, Ephraim and Manasseh, which were born unto thee in the land of Egypt before I came unto thee into Egypt, are mine; as Reuben and Simeon, they shall be mine.*
>
> (Genesis 48:3-5)

So, we can understand that in the pattern that He inspired Jacob to introduce, the LORD God retains full and absolute Parental control over all. He is our Father—not our grandfather, or really-great-grandfather. God is the Father, according to the rules of acquisition—which He revealed in Jacob.

Since God is our Perfect Father, what He says is Law. Therefore, those whom He sends carry His authority, when they are behaving according to His assignment given to them, and according to His Law. It is the Law of God that is perfect, not the person, organization or the nation that is sent with the Law. There is none good but God.

> *And, behold, one came and said unto him, Good Master, what good thing shall I do, that I may have eternal life?*
>
> *And he said unto him, Why callest thou me good? there is none good but one, that is, God: but if thou wilt enter into life, keep the commandments.*
>
> (Matthew 19:16-17)

For this, and many other reasons, what God says, and what He sends, must be accepted without augmentation, or diminution. The Bible contains both the Law and the reason for the Law, as set forth by God. The Bible contains all that we need to know in order to understand the workings of the family of God, and our place in it. The sum total of Scripture is sufficient unto itself as this guide for mankind. Our Father, through his servant Moses, told us how to behave in respect to His word.

> *Now therefore hearken, O Israel, unto the statutes and unto the judgments, which I teach you, for to do them, that ye may live, and go in and possess the land which the LORD God of your fathers giveth you. Ye shall not add unto the word which I command*

> *you, neither shall ye diminish ought from it, that ye may keep the commandments of the LORD your God which I command you.*
> (Deuteronomy 4:1-2)

The family that God is raising is a perfect family. This does not mean that each piece is perfect—yet—but only that the raising of the family and the final state of the family is perfection. Since the people who make up the process are not perfect, they cannot be relied upon to add to the Family building plan, which is the Bible. This includes the restriction from what has been attempted by mankind through what is known as tradition. There is no need for us to complete Scripture as based on tradition. In fact, there is a real danger in doing that.

If we add to the Scripture through tradition, or by any other means, the Father is prepared to obviously, and forcefully, disavow such additions.

> *For I testify unto every man that heareth the words of the prophecy of this book, If any man shall add unto these things, God shall add unto him the plagues that are written in this book: And if any man shall take away from the words of the book of this prophecy, God shall take away his part out of the book of life, and out of the holy city, and from the things which are written in this book.*
> (Revelation 22:18-19)

Furthermore, since it is a complete plan, there is no need for a "fill in the blanks" type project. There is no need for us to complete Scripture based on the historical record. That which is excluded from the Bible is excluded for a reason; which is God's reason. When we indulge in historical augmentation, or even proof, of Scripture as recorded in the Bible, we introduce thoughts and concepts that are unnecessary. In fact, the concepts we add from the historical records are often introducing sin that we need not ponder.

> *For ye were sometimes darkness, but now are ye light in the Lord: walk as children of light: (For the fruit of the Spirit is in all goodness and righteousness and truth;) Proving what is acceptable unto the Lord.*

And have no fellowship with the unfruitful works of darkness, but rather reprove them. For it is a shame even to speak of those things which are done of them in secret.

(Ephesians 5:8-12)

We must not add anything to the Bible. Especially, it is not up to us to add to Scripture such things as seem expedient to us. This is not to say that we are not allowed the permissive will of God. However, understand this: the permissive will of the Father is not the absolute will of the Father. When we execute God's permissive will, our lives are, in a large part of it, controlled by our power. When we submit to the absolute will of the Father, we operate in His power. This is the example of Jesus Christ, the Son of God. Jesus lived in, and submitted himself to, the absolute will of God the Father. For this reason, he is able to proclaim the indwelling of the full power of God.

Then the eleven disciples went away into Galilee, into a mountain where Jesus had appointed them. And when they saw him, they worshipped him: but some doubted.

And Jesus came and spake unto them, saying, All power is given unto me in heaven and in earth.

(Matthew 28:16-18)

The leaders of Jesus' day chose the permissive will of God. They decided to run the show under their own power. They were absolutely determined to serve God according to their own logic, and to lead under their own power. To do this, they placed a carnal cover over the evidence of the Father that was directing them to His absolute will. One of the examples of this is seen in their treatment of the resurrection of Jesus Christ.

Now when they were going, behold, some of the watch came into the city, and shewed unto the chief priests all the things that were done.

And when they were assembled with the elders, and had taken counsel, they gave large money unto the soldiers, Saying, Say ye,

> *His disciples came by night, and stole him away while we slept. And if this come to the governor's ears, we will persuade him, and secure you.*
>
> *So they took the money, and did as they were taught: and this saying is commonly reported among the Jews until this day.*
>
> (Matthew 28:11-15)

The results are obvious. God the Father will allow certain actions, according to His permissive will; however, when this will is invoked, we also receive the, sometimes unmerciful, consequences of the actions.

> *But let every man prove his own work, and then shall he have rejoicing in himself alone, and not in another. For every man shall bear his own burden. Let him that is taught in the word communicate unto him that teacheth in all good things. Be not deceived; God is not mocked: for whatsoever a man soweth, that shall he also reap. For he that soweth to his flesh shall of the flesh reap corruption; but he that soweth to the Spirit shall of the Spirit reap life everlasting.*
>
> (Galatians 6:4-8)

Jesus, the Son of God, received God's approval; moreover, this was proclaimed by apostles that were inspired, and more, by the Spirit of truth, the Holy Ghost. Furthermore, the inspiration of the Spirit is directed at us, to inspire us to replication of the spirit of the Son of God.

> *Let this mind be in you, which was also in Christ Jesus: Who, being in the form of God, thought it not robbery to be equal with God: But made himself of no reputation, and took upon him the form of a servant, and was made in the likeness of men: And being found in fashion as a man, he humbled himself, and became obedient unto death, even the death of the cross.*
>
> *Wherefore God also hath highly exalted him, and given him a name which is above every name: That at the name of Jesus every knee should bow, of things in heaven, and things in earth, and*

things under the earth; And that every tongue should confess that Jesus Christ is Lord, to the glory of God the Father.

(Philippians 2:5-11)

On the other hand; because they basked in the perceived liberty of controlling their lives, in God's permissive will; the spiritual leaders of Jesus' day received God's condemnation as the recompense, with harsh consequences pending.

Strive to enter in at the strait gate: for many, I say unto you, will seek to enter in, and shall not be able. When once the master of the house is risen up, and hath shut to the door, and ye begin to stand without, and to knock at the door, saying, Lord, Lord, open unto us; and he shall answer and say unto you, I know you not whence ye are: Then shall ye begin to say, We have eaten and drunk in thy presence, and thou hast taught in our streets. But he shall say, I tell you, I know you not whence ye are; depart from me, all ye workers of iniquity.

There shall be weeping and gnashing of teeth, when ye shall see Abraham, and Isaac, and Jacob, and all the prophets, in the kingdom of God, and you yourselves thrust out. And they shall come from the east, and from the west, and from the north, and from the south, and shall sit down in the kingdom of God.

And, behold, there are last which shall be first, and there are first which shall be last.

(Luke 13:24-30)

The contrast is both glaringly obvious and personally penetrating, between submitting to God's absolute will and basking in a perception of self-control in the LORD'S permissive will.

Blessed are they that do his commandments, that they may have right to the tree of life, and may enter in through the gates into the city. For without are dogs, and sorcerers, and whoremongers, and murderers, and idolaters, and whosoever loveth and maketh a lie.

(Revelation 22:14-15)

So, we know now that the Bible is the Father's plan for raising the family of mankind. The Father is raising the family from the infancy of Adam, to the stability of eternal existence in identity with the Son of God, which is Jesus Christ.

> *And we know that all things work together for good to them that love God, to them who are the called according to his purpose. For whom he did foreknow, he also did predestinate to be conformed to the image of his Son, that he might be the firstborn among many brethren.*
>
> (Romans 8:28-29)

So, what do we do?

We follow the Word! We serve God! We announce the good news of the Father's mission, and of our place in it.

> *And I, brethren, when I came to you, came not with excellency of speech or of wisdom, declaring unto you the testimony of God. For I determined not to know any thing among you, save Jesus Christ, and him crucified.*
>
> (1 Corinthians 2:1-2)

We must allow each man to be moved to the Father by the Father. Let the Father's hand do the drawing, and not our own. This is the way to Perfection, which was prepared by His Son, Jesus Christ.

> *Now is the judgment of this world: now shall the prince of this world be cast out. And I, if I be lifted up from the earth, will draw all men unto me.*
>
> (John 12:31-32)

We must accept our position of service, and let the Father grow the Family.

> *For while one saith, I am of Paul; and another, I am of Apollos; are ye not carnal? Who then is Paul, and who is Apollos, but ministers by whom ye believed, even as the Lord gave to every man? I have planted, Apollos watered; but God gave the increase. So then*

> *neither is he that planteth any thing, neither he that watereth; but God that giveth the increase.*
>
> (1 Corinthians 3:4-7)

Furthermore, we must be willing to wait until we are assigned a task by the Father.

> *Come, behold the works of the LORD, what desolations he hath made in the earth. He maketh wars to cease unto the end of the earth; he breaketh the bow, and cutteth the spear in sunder; he burneth the chariot in the fire. Be still, and know that I am God: I will be exalted among the heathen, I will be exalted in the earth. The LORD of hosts is with us; the God of Jacob is our refuge. Selah.*
>
> (Psalm 46:8-11)

And, we must be ready when the Father assigns a task. We must be ready, first in the heart, and then in the head; as much as is possible, with the grace that God has given us.

> *But and if ye suffer for righteousness' sake, happy are ye: and be not afraid of their terror, neither be troubled; But sanctify the Lord God in your hearts: and be ready always to give an answer to every man that asketh you a reason of the hope that is in you with meekness and fear: Having a good conscience; that, whereas they speak evil of you, as of evildoers, they may be ashamed that falsely accuse your good conversation in Christ. For it is better, if the will of God be so, that ye suffer for well doing, than for evil doing.*
>
> (1 Peter 3:14-17)

How do we get ready?

> *Of these things put them in remembrance, charging them before the Lord that they strive not about words to no profit, but to the subverting of the hearers. Study to show thyself approved unto God, a workman that needeth not to be ashamed, rightly dividing the*

> *word of truth. But shun profane and vain babblings: for they will increase unto more ungodliness.*
>
> (2 Timothy 2:14-16)

It is not for us to provoke or instigate the question of placement in the Family. We need only be ready to work as the Father tells us to—without modification. And, there is lots of work to do.

> *And Jesus went about all the cities and villages, teaching in their synagogues, and preaching the gospel of the kingdom, and healing every sickness and every disease among the people. But when he saw the multitudes, he was moved with compassion on them, because they fainted, and were scattered abroad, as sheep having no shepherd. Then saith he unto his disciples, The harvest truly is plenteous, but the labourers are few; Pray ye therefore the Lord of the harvest, that he will send forth labourers into his harvest.*
>
> (Matthew 9:35-38)

THE WORD FROM THE BIBLE

1 Samuel 15:22-23

And Samuel said, Hath the LORD as great delight in burnt offerings and sacrifices, as in obeying the voice of the LORD? Behold, to obey is better than sacrifice, and to hearken than the fat of rams. For rebellion is as the sin of witchcraft, and stubbornness is as iniquity and idolatry.

Because thou hast rejected the word of the LORD, he hath also rejected thee from being king.

Matthew 12:1-8

At that time Jesus went on the sabbath day through the corn; and his disciples were an hungred, and began to pluck the ears of corn and to eat. But when the Pharisees saw it, they said unto him, Behold, thy disciples do that which is not lawful to do upon the sabbath day.

But he said unto them, Have ye not read what David did, when he was an hungred, and they that were with him; How he entered into the house of God, and did eat the shewbread, which was not lawful for him to eat, neither for them which were with him, but only for the priests? Or have ye not read in the law, how that on the sabbath days the priests in the temple profane the sabbath, and are blameless?

But I say unto you, That in this place is one greater than the temple. But if ye had known what this meaneth, I will have mercy, and not sacrifice, ye would not have condemned the guiltless. For the Son of man is Lord even of the sabbath day.

Matthew 23:34-39

Wherefore, behold, I send unto you prophets, and wise men, and scribes: and some of them ye shall kill and crucify; and some of them shall ye scourge in your synagogues, and persecute them from city to city: That upon you may come all the righteous blood shed upon the earth, from the blood of righteous Abel unto the blood of Zacharias son of Barachias, whom ye slew between the temple and the altar. Verily I say unto you, All these things shall come upon this generation.

O Jerusalem, Jerusalem, thou that killest the prophets, and stonest them which are sent unto thee, how often would I have gathered thy children together, even as a hen gathereth her chickens under her wings, and ye would not! Behold, your house is left unto you desolate. For I say unto you, Ye shall not see me henceforth, till ye shall say, Blessed is he that cometh in the name of the Lord.

CHAPTER THREE

Why Remove, Totally, Jerusalem

When left unchecked, cancer is like mold on bread; it will spread to infect the whole body of whatever it is a part. This is the situation that had happened with Jerusalem and the temple, in the time of Christ. A cancer had spread throughout the religious worship among the people of God. This cancer had taken over the entire community, and it had to be wiped out. Even so, ONLY God can determine the time and method of disposition of this community, as well as of any other portion of this nation.

In the day of Jesus Christ, he came with this message: that God had proclaimed that the cancer in Jerusalem had become terminal. There were no more treatments scheduled to control the cancer. The cancer had to be removed, and this would happen decisively. In that day, the time of the end of the spiritual center of God at the Jerusalem, for that day, had come. Jesus made the announcement.

> *And Jesus went out, and departed from the temple: and his disciples came to him for to shew him the buildings of the temple. And Jesus said unto them, See ye not all these things? verily I say unto you, There shall not be left here one stone upon another, that shall not be thrown down.*
>
> *And as he sat upon the mount of Olives, the disciples came unto him privately, saying, Tell us, when shall these things be? and what shall be the sign of thy coming, and of the end of the world?*
>
> *And Jesus answered and said unto them, Take heed that no man deceive you. For many shall come in my name, saying, I am Christ;*

> *and shall deceive many. And ye shall hear of wars and rumours of wars: see that ye be not troubled: for all these things must come to pass, but the end is not yet. For nation shall rise against nation, and kingdom against kingdom: and there shall be famines, and pestilences, and earthquakes, in divers places. All these are the beginning of sorrows.*
>
> *Then shall they deliver you up to be afflicted, and shall kill you: and ye shall be hated of all nations for my name's sake. And then shall many be offended, and shall betray one another, and shall hate one another. And many false prophets shall rise, and shall deceive many. And because iniquity shall abound, the love of many shall wax cold. But he that shall endure unto the end, the same shall be saved.*
>
> *And this gospel of the kingdom shall be preached in all the world for a witness unto all nations; and then shall the end come.*
>
> *When ye therefore shall see the abomination of desolation, spoken of by Daniel the prophet, stand in the holy place, (whoso readeth, let him understand:) Then let them which be in Judaea flee into the mountains: Let him which is on the housetop not come down to take any thing out of his house: Neither let him which is in the field return back to take his clothes. And woe unto them that are with child, and to them that give suck in those days!*
>
> *But pray ye that your flight be not in the winter, neither on the sabbath day: For then shall be great tribulation, such as was not since the beginning of the world to this time, no, nor ever shall be. And except those days should be shortened, there should no flesh be saved: but for the elect's sake those days shall be shortened.*
>
> (Matthew 24:1-22)

But how did things go so bad in Jerusalem? What was so special about Jerusalem that it required the direct selection, by God, for purging? To answer these, and many other questions, let us look at the former time of the glory of Jerusalem.

In the early days of Israel, God established Jerusalem as the place on which He placed his name. The LORD recruited king Solomon to do the preparation.

Then Solomon assembled the elders of Israel, and all the heads of the tribes, the chief of the fathers of the children of Israel, unto king Solomon in Jerusalem, that they might bring up the ark of the covenant of the LORD out of the city of David, which is Zion. And all the men of Israel assembled themselves unto king Solomon at the feast in the month Ethanim, which is the seventh month. And all the elders of Israel came, and the priests took up the ark.

(1 Kings 8:1-3)

. . . So that the priests could add the finishing human touches . . .

And they brought up the ark of the LORD, and the tabernacle of the congregation, and all the holy vessels that were in the tabernacle, even those did the priests and the Levites bring up. And king Solomon, and all the congregation of Israel, that were assembled unto him, were with him before the ark, sacrificing sheep and oxen, that could not be told nor numbered for multitude.

And the priests brought in the ark of the covenant of the LORD unto his place, into the oracle of the house, to the most holy place, even under the wings of the cherubims. For the cherubims spread forth their two wings over the place of the ark, and the cherubims covered the ark and the staves thereof above. And they drew out the staves, that the ends of the staves were seen out in the holy place before the oracle, and they were not seen without: and there they are unto this day. There was nothing in the ark save the two tables of stone, which Moses put there at Horeb, when the LORD made a covenant with the children of Israel, when they came out of the land of Egypt.

(1 Kings 8:4-9)

. . . So that the LORD could make His presence known therein . . .

And it came to pass, when the priests were come out of the holy place, that the cloud filled the house of the LORD, So that the priests could not stand to minister because of the cloud: for the glory of the LORD had filled the house of the LORD.

Then spake Solomon, The LORD said that he would dwell in the thick darkness. I have surely built thee an house to dwell in, a settled place for thee to abide in for ever.

(1 Kings 8:10-13)

. . . With Solomon serving as the face of public certification.

And it came to pass, when Solomon had finished the building of the house of the LORD, and the king's house, and all Solomon's desire which he was pleased to do, That the LORD appeared to Solomon the second time, as he had appeared unto him at Gibeon.

And the LORD said unto him,

I have heard thy prayer and thy supplication, that thou hast made before me: I have hallowed this house, which thou hast built, to put my name there for ever; and mine eyes and mine heart shall be there perpetually.

(1 Kings 9:1-3)

The Israelites were told to reverence this place. They had certain continual ceremonies that they were to follow relative to Jerusalem. Even before the place was selected, Israel was told what they must do once it had been selected by God as the place on which the LORD placed His name.

But when ye go over Jordan, and dwell in the land which the LORD your God giveth you to inherit, and when he giveth you rest from all your enemies round about, so that ye dwell in safety; Then there shall be a place which the LORD your God shall choose to cause his name to dwell there; thither shall ye bring all that I command you; your burnt offerings, and your sacrifices, your tithes, and the heave offering of your hand, and all your choice vows which ye vow unto the LORD: And ye shall rejoice before the LORD your God, ye, and your sons, and your daughters, and your menservants, and your maidservants, and the Levite that is within your gates; forasmuch as he hath no part nor inheritance with you.

(Deuteronomy 12:10-12)

This was the main place for the performance of sacrifices and offerings, which is a most necessary part of the observance of the law of Moses. Thus, the requirements of the LORD could be fulfilled in Jerusalem, *the place which the LORD shall choose in one of thy tribes.*

> *Take heed to thyself that thou offer not thy burnt offerings in every place that thou seest: But in the place which the LORD shall choose in one of thy tribes, there thou shalt offer thy burnt offerings, and there thou shalt do all that I command thee.*
>
> (Deuteronomy 12:13-14)

> *When the LORD thy God shall enlarge thy border, as he hath promised thee, and thou shalt say, I will eat flesh, because thy soul longeth to eat flesh; thou mayest eat flesh, whatsoever thy soul lusteth after. If the place which the LORD thy God hath chosen to put his name there be too far from thee, then thou shalt kill of thy herd and of thy flock, which the LORD hath given thee, as I have commanded thee, and thou shalt eat in thy gates whatsoever thy soul lusteth after. Even as the roebuck and the hart is eaten, so thou shalt eat them: the unclean and the clean shall eat of them alike.*
>
> *Only be sure that thou eat not the blood: for the blood is the life; and thou mayest not eat the life with the flesh. Thou shalt not eat it; thou shalt pour it upon the earth as water. Thou shalt not eat it; that it may go well with thee, and with thy children after thee, when thou shalt do that which is right in the sight of the LORD.*
>
> *Only thy holy things which thou hast, and thy vows, thou shalt take, and go unto the place which the LORD shall choose. And thou shalt offer thy burnt offerings, the flesh and the blood, upon the altar of the LORD thy God: and the blood of thy sacrifices shall be poured out upon the altar of the LORD thy God, and thou shalt eat the flesh.*
>
> (Deuteronomy 12:20-27)

The first king of the nation of Israel, Saul, gives us a preview of the cancer that would form in the observances of the services of God. Even though he had been told to wait for Samuel, the one who was designated by God to perform the sacrifices; still, Saul decided to do it himself. He became impatient and fearful, and he thought that, for that reason, he did not have time to honor God's requirement. However, it is ironic that even though he did not have time to honor God's requirement, he still expected that God should honor his sacrifice. As they say, "what's wrong with this picture?"

> *And he tarried seven days, according to the set time that Samuel had appointed: but Samuel came not to Gilgal; and the people were scattered from him. And Saul said, Bring hither a burnt offering to me, and peace offerings. And he offered the burnt offering. And it came to pass, that as soon as he had made an end of offering the burnt offering, behold, Samuel came; and Saul went out to meet him, that he might salute him.*
>
> *And Samuel said, What hast thou done?*
>
> *And Saul said, Because I saw that the people were scattered from me, and that thou camest not within the days appointed, and that the Philistines gathered themselves together at Michmash; Therefore said I, The Philistines will come down now upon me to Gilgal, and I have not made supplication unto the LORD: I forced myself therefore, and offered a burnt offering.*
>
> *And Samuel said to Saul, Thou hast done foolishly: thou hast not kept the commandment of the LORD thy God, which he commanded thee: for now would the LORD have established thy kingdom upon Israel for ever. But now thy kingdom shall not continue: the LORD hath sought him a man after his own heart, and the LORD hath commanded him to be captain over his people, because thou hast not kept that which the LORD commanded thee.*
>
> (1 Samuel 13:8-14)

As the nation continued; over the course of time, the leaders, both spiritual and secular, introduced serious illness into the worship of God. This illness is the start of the cancer that would spread throughout the city on which God had placed his name.

> *Hear this, I pray you, ye heads of the house of Jacob, and princes of the house of Israel, that abhor judgment, and pervert all equity. They build up Zion with blood, and Jerusalem with iniquity. The heads thereof judge for reward, and the priests thereof teach for hire, and the prophets thereof divine for money: yet will they lean upon the LORD, and say, Is not the LORD among us? none evil can come upon us. Therefore shall Zion for your sake be plowed as a field, and Jerusalem shall become heaps, and the mountain of the house as the high places of the forest.*
>
> (Micah 3:9-12)

Cancer is a funny type of disease. In some ways it really might not be called a disease: this is because cancer has a way of mimicking the body's cellular structure. It presents the same face as other cells of the body. However, cancer has the ability to multiply at a much faster rate than the other cells of the body. So, there is a two-pronged attack. First, as you have read, it looks like the bodies cells; this keeps it from being destroyed by the immune systems of the body. Such was the state of things in Jerusalem, wherein there were many cells of religiosity that looked like the other, more devout, cells of Israel.

For these, look somewhat like though caustic, cells, there was much Scripture from which the religious leaders could draw to keep the people under their control. However, in many cases, these leaders had not been sent by God. Among these pretenders were those ones that elevated Jerusalem and its administration even above God. Jesus of Nazareth opened our eyes to this group's behavior.

> *Then came to Jesus scribes and Pharisees, which were of Jerusalem, saying, Why do thy disciples transgress the tradition of the elders? for they wash not their hands when they eat bread.*
>
> *But he answered and said unto them, Why do ye also transgress the commandment of God by your tradition? For God commanded, saying, Honour thy father and mother: and, He that curseth father or mother, let him die the death. But ye say, Whosoever shall say to his father or his mother, It is a gift, by whatsoever thou mightest be profited by me; And honour not his father or his mother, he shall be*

> *free. Thus have ye made the commandment of God of none effect by your tradition.*
>
> *Ye hypocrites, well did Esaias prophesy of you, saying, This people draweth nigh unto me with their mouth, and honoureth me with their lips; but their heart is far from me. But in vain they do worship me, teaching for doctrines the commandments of men.*
>
> (Matthew 15:1-9)

Yes, there is Scripture that calls for the reverence of the holy city, Jerusalem, and the temple. This Scripture was adhered to by Daniel, who is one of the most devout of the patriarchs. The example of Daniel's life could have been used as an example to persuade the people to continue to perform according to the old teachings.

> *Then these presidents and princes assembled together to the king, and said thus unto him, King Darius, live for ever. All the presidents of the kingdom, the governors, and the princes, the counsellors, and the captains, have consulted together to establish a royal statute, and to make a firm decree, that whosoever shall ask a petition of any God or man for thirty days, save of thee, O king, he shall be cast into the den of lions. Now, O king, establish the decree, and sign the writing, that it be not changed, according to the law of the Medes and Persians, which altereth not. Wherefore king Darius signed the writing and the decree.*
>
> *Now when Daniel knew that the writing was signed, he went into his house; and his windows being open in his chamber toward Jerusalem, he kneeled upon his knees three times a day, and prayed, and gave thanks before his God, as he did aforetime.*
>
> (Daniel 6:6-10)

But, instead of holding fast in word of God, Israel did not fulfill its contract with God, as it was given to them and recorded in Scripture. Thus, at a certain time, of God's designation, the uniqueness of the worship in the nation was disavowed by the LORD: this also applied to Jerusalem, based on what it had become. Just as the LORD had placed His name on this place in the nation of Israel, He also took His name from it, at the same intensity of God's power. The LORD announced this, through the record of events in the history of Israel.

> *And the king commanded all the people, saying, Keep the passover unto the LORD your God, as it is written in the book of this covenant. Surely there was not holden such a passover from the days of the judges that judged Israel, nor in all the days of the kings of Israel, nor of the kings of Judah; But in the eighteenth year of king Josiah, wherein this passover was holden to the LORD in Jerusalem.*
>
> *Moreover the workers with familiar spirits, and the wizards, and the images, and the idols, and all the abominations that were spied in the land of Judah and in Jerusalem, did Josiah put away, that he might perform the words of the law which were written in the book that Hilkiah the priest found in the house of the LORD. And like unto him was there no king before him, that turned to the LORD with all his heart, and with all his soul, and with all his might, according to all the law of Moses; neither after him arose there any like him.*
>
> *Notwithstanding the LORD turned not from the fierceness of his great wrath, wherewith his anger was kindled against Judah, because of all the provocations that Manasseh had provoked him withal. And the LORD said, I will remove Judah also out of my sight, as I have removed Israel, and will cast off this city Jerusalem which I have chosen, and the house of which I said, My name shall be there.*
>
> (2 Kings 23:21-27)

Furthermore, because of Israel's failure to perform the contractual requirements in righteousness, God also invalidated their offerings as being sufficient for recompense for sins.

> *I hate, I despise your feast days, and I will not smell in your solemn assemblies. Though ye offer me burnt offerings and your meat offerings, I will not accept them: neither will I regard the peace offerings of your fat beasts. Take thou away from me the noise of thy*

songs; for I will not hear the melody of thy viols. But let judgment run down as waters, and righteousness as a mighty stream. Have ye offered unto me sacrifices and offerings in the wilderness forty years, O house of Israel?

(Amos 5:21-25)

There must have been a deep root of arrogance in the children of Israel, in that they did not respond to the pronouncement, and repent because of it. There are examples in Scripture that highlight the great benefit of repentance. For instance, the people of Nineveh were under sentence from God in a similar fashion. However, they heeded God, and repented of their evil ways. They returned to the fulfillment of the contract in righteousness that God required of them.

And the word of the LORD came unto Jonah the second time, saying, Arise, go unto Nineveh, that great city, and preach unto it the preaching that I bid thee.

So Jonah arose, and went unto Nineveh, according to the word of the LORD. Now Nineveh was an exceeding great city of three days' journey. And Jonah began to enter into the city a day's journey, and he cried, and said, Yet forty days, and Nineveh shall be overthrown.

So the people of Nineveh believed God, and proclaimed a fast, and put on sackcloth, from the greatest of them even to the least of them. For word came unto the king of Nineveh, and he arose from his throne, and he laid his robe from him, and covered him with sackcloth, and sat in ashes.

And he caused it to be proclaimed and published through Nineveh by the decree of the king and his nobles, saying, Let neither man nor beast, herd nor flock, taste any thing: let them not feed, nor drink water: But let man and beast be covered with sackcloth, and cry mightily unto God: yea, let them turn every one from his evil way, and from the violence that is in their hands. Who can tell if God will turn and repent, and turn away from his fierce anger, that we perish not?

And God saw their works, that they turned from their evil way; and God repented of the evil, that he had said that he would do unto them; and he did it not.

(Jonah 3:1-10)

So, why didn't the people of the nation of Israel, in the time of Jesus of Nazareth, do as the people of Nineveh did? Why didn't Israel return to God after hearing the words from the prophets, repenting in a fashion such as the king of Nineveh had his people do?

The nation of Israel did not return to the LORD, in repentance, because the problem was much more systemic than that of Nineveh. It was not just the error of the moment, but a habit in life. It became their lifestyle. This habit was not just practiced by the common man, but from the top as well. Israel did not have leaders that were willing to return to God. What they had were the scribes and Pharisees, who wanted to keep their hold on the people. They wanted this control for various reasons; none of which had anything to do with God. So, to retain this control, they invoked the other attribute of a cancer. The scribes and Pharisees started rapid reproduction process in their laws; spawning them in forms that were aberrations of the Law of God as presented in the law of Moses.

Woe unto you, ye blind guides, which say, Whosoever shall swear by the temple, it is nothing; but whosoever shall swear by the gold of the temple, he is a debtor! Ye fools and blind: for whether is greater, the gold, or the temple that sanctifieth the gold?

And, Whosoever shall swear by the altar, it is nothing; but whosoever sweareth by the gift that is upon it, he is guilty. Ye fools and blind: for whether is greater, the gift, or the altar that sanctifieth the gift?

Whoso therefore shall swear by the altar, sweareth by it, and by all things thereon. And whoso shall swear by the temple, sweareth by it, and by him that dwelleth therein. And he that shall swear by heaven, sweareth by the throne of God, and by him that sitteth thereon.

Woe unto you, scribes and Pharisees, hypocrites! for ye pay tithe of mint and anise and cummin, and have omitted the weightier matters of the law, judgment, mercy, and faith: these ought ye to

> *have done, and not to leave the other undone. Ye blind guides, which strain at a gnat, and swallow a camel.*
> (Matthew 23:16-24)

Yes, this is the second thing that cancer does in the body. It starts a rapid replication of cells that are misfits. These cells are not necessarily carbon copies of the original cell that formed them. They can take on different natures. They are not true replicas, and they are not totally different. For this reason, it is difficult for anyone, other than a highly trained surgeon, to tell which cells to remove, and which to leave alone. When you think about this attribute of cancer, think also about the wheat and the tares. The tare is another representation of the cancer that infests mankind. It cannot be removed except by a skilled husbandman. And this husbandman for the tares in mankind, as is the surgeon for Jerusalem in the time of Jesus Christ, comes from God.

> *Another parable put he forth unto them, saying, The kingdom of heaven is likened unto a man which sowed good seed in his field: But while men slept, his enemy came and sowed tares among the wheat, and went his way. But when the blade was sprung up, and brought forth fruit, then appeared the tares also. So the servants of the householder came and said unto him, Sir, didst not thou sow good seed in thy field? from whence then hath it tares?*
>
> *He said unto them, An enemy hath done this.*
>
> *The servants said unto him, Wilt thou then that we go and gather them up?*
>
> *But he said, Nay; lest while ye gather up the tares, ye root up also the wheat with them. Let both grow together until the harvest: and in the time of harvest I will say to the reapers, Gather ye together first the tares, and bind them in bundles to burn them: but gather the wheat into my barn.*
> (Matthew 13:24-30)

In the day of Jesus Christ, God commanded that it was time to remove the cancer.

But, why not just do with the cancer what is sometimes done with certain malignancies in mankind? Why not just wall it off? Why not just isolate it, and let it still live in isolation? Why not just take the power from Jerusalem, and yet still leave the temple standing?

To answer those questions, I will ask you one. How does one isolate God?

This is the statement that was being made by the scribes, Pharisees and the other rulers of the nation of Israel, in that day. They were not saying that they were working with an engine of mankind. They were saying that they were working with the engine of God: but they were not!

> *It is also written in your law, that the testimony of two men is true. I am one that bear witness of myself, and the Father that sent me beareth witness of me.*
>
> *Then said they unto him, Where is thy Father?*
>
> *Jesus answered, Ye neither know me, nor my Father: if ye had known me, ye should have known my Father also.*
>
> (John 8:17-19)

The religious leaders were proclaiming that their actions were authorized by God. If this is allowed to stand among mankind, there is no man who would challenge it; for, no man can stand against the representative of God. And with the large volume of additions to the Law of Moses, there really was not anyone who could fully understand what the, then, modern religion said, and what it did not say. At least, that was the perceived shield of the religious leader, as evidenced by their actions.

However, the scribes, Pharisees and the other rulers of the nation of Israel in that day had forgotten about one thing: God can determine who is speaking for Him, and who is not. And God had already said what had to happen to the person who spoke in His behalf, but who was not sent by Him. (This can also be applied to organizations, communities, nations, and the entire earth.)

> *If there arise among you a prophet, or a dreamer of dreams, and giveth thee a sign or a wonder, And the sign or the wonder come to pass, whereof he spake unto thee, saying, Let us go after other gods, which thou hast not known, and let us serve them; Thou shalt not hearken unto the words of that prophet, or that dreamer of dreams:*

> *for the LORD your God proveth you, to know whether ye love the LORD your God with all your heart and with all your soul.*
>
> *Ye shall walk after the LORD your God, and fear him, and keep his commandments, and obey his voice, and ye shall serve him, and cleave unto him.*
>
> *And that prophet, or that dreamer of dreams, shall be put to death; because he hath spoken to turn you away from the LORD your God, which brought you out of the land of Egypt, and redeemed you out of the house of bondage, to thrust thee out of the way which the LORD thy God commanded thee to walk in. So shalt thou put the evil away from the midst of thee.*
>
> (Deuteronomy 13:1-4)

So, the action sealed the sentence. By portraying themselves as God's representative, without having the authorization of God, the entire religious order; the entire city of Jerusalem had become the prophet that was worthy of death. (And again, only God can determine the time, and the method, of delivering judgment against any portion of His people.) This is why Jerusalem had to be removed, totally. Let God be true, though every man be a liar.

> *Think not that I am come to destroy the law, or the prophets: I am not come to destroy, but to fulfil. For verily I say unto you, Till heaven and earth pass, one jot or one tittle shall in no wise pass from the law, till all be fulfilled.*
>
> (Matthew 5:17-18)

Let me complete this thought by giving you an introduction to the replacement that God prepared from before the foundation of the world.

"Why," you ask, "was a replacement prepared before a failure was evident?"

I really do not believe that you need to ask such a question, since I would like to think that you are aware of God's strong "habit" of advance preparation (omniscience as projected through foreknowledge) but since the question is here, I will explain. God does not see history unfolding:

God sees time as complete. All that is, and all that will be, and all that was, are for ever in the view of God. Therefore, even before it becomes evident to mankind that it is needed, God knows what is needed. God is a very proactive manufacturer. For God's purposes, just-in-time is already too late. He absolutely knows His product, in all its cycles; and, this product is mankind.

> *Remember the former things of old: for I am God, and there is none else; I am God, and there is none like me, Declaring the end from the beginning, and from ancient times the things that are not yet done, saying, My counsel shall stand, and I will do all my pleasure:*
>
> (Isaiah 46:9-10)

The ***way***—which God prepared to replace the worship accorded to the temple in Jerusalem—is not just another earthly temple; it *is one greater than the temple* (Matthew 12:6). This better way is the eternal sacrifice of the Lamb of God, and his proclamation of the highlighted law of love, as declared in a new commandment. This is the message of the Gospel in Jesus Christ. There will be much more about this throughout the remainder of this book, so we will just introduce you to it, for now.

> *For the law having a shadow of good things to come, and not the very image of the things, can never with those sacrifices which they offered year by year continually make the comers thereunto perfect. For then would they not have ceased to be offered? because that the worshippers once purged should have had no more conscience of sins. But in those sacrifices there is a remembrance again made of sins every year. For it is not possible that the blood of bulls and of goats should take away sins.*
>
> *Wherefore when he cometh into the world, he saith, Sacrifice and offering thou wouldest not, but a body hast thou prepared me: In burnt offerings and sacrifices for sin thou hast had no pleasure. Then said I, Lo, I come (in the volume of the book it is written of me,) to do thy will, O God.*

Above when he said, Sacrifice and offering and burnt offerings and offering for sin thou wouldest not, neither hadst pleasure therein; which are offered by the law; Then said he, Lo, I come to do thy will, O God. He taketh away the first, that he may establish the second. By the which will we are sanctified through the offering of the body of Jesus Christ once for all.

(Hebrews 10:1-10)

But when the Pharisees had heard that he had put the Sadducees to silence, they were gathered together. Then one of them, which was a lawyer, asked him a question, tempting him, and saying, Master, which is the great commandment in the law?

Jesus said unto him, Thou shalt love the Lord thy God with all thy heart, and with all thy soul, and with all thy mind. This is the first and great commandment. And the second is like unto it, Thou shalt love thy neighbour as thyself. On these two commandments hang all the law and the prophets.

(Matthew 22:34-40)

A new commandment I give unto you, That ye love one another; as I have loved you, that ye also love one another. By this shall all men know that ye are my disciples, if ye have love one to another.

(John 13:34-35)

If ye love me, keep my commandments. And I will pray the Father, and he shall give you another Comforter, that he may abide with you for ever; Even the Spirit of truth; whom the world cannot receive, because it seeth him not, neither knoweth him: but ye know him; for he dwelleth with you, and shall be in you. I will not leave you comfortless: I will come to you.

Yet a little while, and the world seeth me no more; but ye see me: because I live, ye shall live also. At that day ye shall know that I am in my Father, and ye in me, and I in you. He that hath my commandments, and keepeth them, he it is that loveth me: and he that loveth me shall be loved of my Father, and I will love him, and will manifest myself to him.

(John 14:15-21)

Was it really so bad
That they moved apace
To defy God
Before His face?

This is the same thing
They had done, before,
To the One that
All men should adore;

Like a child with a balloon,
Trying to make it break,
Or a spoiled brat,
Wanting to take and take.

But aren't all parents
Made to give and give?
Isn't this the way
We all should live:

To indulge the child
To the end of time;
Even when there is
No reason or rhyme?

Or, must we remember,
As God did do;
To the world, around us,
We owe something, too?

Our child's behavior
Does not stand alone;
To civilization and life,
All must atone.

Righteousness demands
That the price we pay
Is, to listen to God
In all He doth say.

If not, God's grace
Will accomplish its release
To another place where
It will continually increase.

This is what God did,
As He took from His son,
That special access
Now shared by everyone.

CHAPTER 3A

Proper Application

Rightly Dividing Scripture

Matthew 23:23-24

> Woe unto you, scribes and Pharisees, hypocrites! for ye pay tithe of mint and anise and cummin, and have omitted the weightier matters of the law, judgment, mercy, and faith: these ought ye to have done, and not to leave the other undone. Ye blind guides, which strain at a gnat, and swallow a camel.

Bless our hearts, we religious folk. We want so much for the Bible to cover every aspect of our lives everywhere we look in the text. But this is not what the Bible is. Let us not take the Scripture as a means of describing everything in life in every passage. It is not a complete guide to the human soul. It will not stand alone as the only thing you need to have in order to live a full life in God. Be cautious with this one, however. It is a complete set of directions for understanding righteousness in God. There is no other text needed for that purpose. There is no need for further enhancement by tradition or history.

> *All scripture is given by inspiration of God, and is profitable for doctrine, for reproof, for correction, for instruction in righteousness: That the man of God may be perfect, thoroughly furnished unto all good works.*
>
> (2 Timothy 3:16-17)

But, gasp, understanding righteousness in God is not all that the human condition is about. This is not the only thing that is required by God of man. The Bible points the way to a world outside of itself in a very interesting passage.

> *Yea, a man may say, Thou hast faith, and I have works: show me thy faith without thy works, and I will show thee my faith by my works. Thou believest that there is one God; thou doest well: the devils also believe, and tremble. But wilt thou know, O vain man, that faith without works is dead?*
>
> (James 2:18-20)

This brings up what is sometimes viewed to be a conflict in the Bible between the writings of the apostle Paul and the writings of the apostle James. Paul seems to be pointing to the Bible as the finished work of righteousness in God. James, on the other hand, seems to point to a world outside of the Bible that completes the Bible in fulfilling righteousness. Some think that both men cannot be right. Well, unfortunately, both men are right. Let us look closely at each one, taking the apostle Paul first.

> *Now we know that what things soever the law saith, it saith to them who are under the law: that every mouth may be stopped, and all the world may become guilty before God. Therefore by the deeds of the law there shall no flesh be justified in his sight: for by the law is the knowledge of sin.*
>
> *But now the righteousness of God without the law is manifested, being witnessed by the law and the prophets; Even the righteousness of God which is by faith of Jesus Christ unto all and upon all them that believe: for there is no difference: For all have sinned, and come short of the glory of God; Being justified freely by his grace through the redemption that is in Christ Jesus: Whom God hath set forth to be a propitiation through faith in his blood, to declare his righteousness for the remission of sins that are past, through the forbearance of God; To declare, I say, at this time his righteousness: that he might be just, and the justifier of him which believeth in Jesus.*

> *Where is boasting then? It is excluded. By what law? of works? Nay: but by the law of faith. Therefore we conclude that a man is justified by faith without the deeds of the law.*
> (Romans 3:19-28)

In reading the apostle Paul's writing, we are introduced to one of the seeming dilemmas of Scripture, and it is this: the focus of Scripture can be precisely narrow or extremely broad. When we read this writing by the apostle Paul, we must view it from a narrow perspective. Paul is not talking about works, generally, here; he is talking about works of the law. Though, we must ask you to store in your mind that the things that are done for Christ are not of the same nature as the vaporous redemptive ability that is in works of the law. For, whereas the things of the law have only temporary power, the things that are done for Christ's sake and in his name will last, and they do fulfill righteousness.

> *According to the grace of God which is given unto me, as a wise masterbuilder, I have laid the foundation, and another buildeth thereon. But let every man take heed how he buildeth thereupon. For other foundation can no man lay than that is laid, which is Jesus Christ.*
>
> *Now if any man build upon this foundation gold, silver, precious stones, wood, hay, stubble; Every man's work shall be made manifest: for the day shall declare it, because it shall be revealed by fire; and the fire shall try every man's work of what sort it is. If any man's work abide which he hath built thereupon, he shall receive a reward. If any man's work shall be burned, he shall suffer loss: but he himself shall be saved; yet so as by fire.*
> (1 Corinthians 3:10-15)

Let us go back a little further, in the history of the Bible. We need to establish the need for something greater than the works of the law, as being the necessary ingredient for righteousness. Let us go back to the example of Abraham (Abram). Before the law of Moses was, Abraham is. Therefore, it is logical for us to say that the apostle Paul is not talking about the works that Abraham (Abram) did. Abraham's works could not have been *works of the law*, by intent, because the Law had not been revealed at that time. Though, the life of Abraham did fulfill the Law, and we know that Abraham's actions were deemed, by the LORD, to be righteous.

> *After these things the word of the LORD came unto Abram in a vision, saying, Fear not, Abram: I am thy shield, and thy exceeding great reward.*
>
> *And Abram said, Lord GOD, what wilt thou give me, seeing I go childless, and the steward of my house is this Eliezer of Damascus? And Abram said, Behold, to me thou hast given no seed: and, lo, one born in my house is mine heir.*
>
> *And, behold, the word of the LORD came unto him, saying, This shall not be thine heir; but he that shall come forth out of thine own bowels shall be thine heir.*
>
> *And he brought him forth abroad, and said, Look now toward heaven, and tell the stars, if thou be able to number them: and he said unto him, So shall thy seed be.*
>
> *And he believed in the LORD; and he counted it to him for righteousness.*
>
> (Genesis 15:1-6)

The apostle Paul is saying, specifically, that by following the entire law, exactly as it is written, you still will not obtain righteousness just by doing so. This is not what the law was designed to do. The law of Moses was designed to govern the conduct of the nation of Israel. This conduct of the nation of Israel was to show forth the God of the universe, in His interaction with mankind. They were to be the living examples to the world of the grace of God. The law of Moses did not give them righteousness; it only gave them order. And it was this order, and the subsequent power of God, shining in, and projected from, that order, which moved empires to revere God. Two examples among these empires are Babylon under king Nebuchadnezzar, and the empire of king Darius the Median.

> *Then Nebuchadnezzar spake, and said, Blessed be the God of Shadrach, Meshach, and Abednego, who hath sent his angel, and delivered his servants that trusted in him, and have changed the*

king's word, and yielded their bodies, that they might not serve nor worship any god, except their own God. Therefore I make a decree, That every people, nation, and language, which speak any thing amiss against the God of Shadrach, Meshach, and Abednego, shall be cut in pieces, and their houses shall be made a dunghill: because there is no other God that can deliver after this sort.

(Daniel 3:28-29)

Then was the king exceeding glad for him, and commanded that they should take Daniel up out of the den.

So Daniel was taken up out of the den, and no manner of hurt was found upon him, because he believed in his God.

And the king commanded, and they brought those men which had accused Daniel, and they cast them into the den of lions, them, their children, and their wives; and the lions had the mastery of them, and brake all their bones in pieces or ever they came at the bottom of the den.

Then king Darius wrote unto all people, nations, and languages, that dwell in all the earth; Peace be multiplied unto you. I make a decree, That in every dominion of my kingdom men tremble and fear before the God of Daniel: for he is the living God, and stedfast for ever, and his kingdom that which shall not be destroyed, and his dominion shall be even unto the end. He delivereth and rescueth, and he worketh signs and wonders in heaven and in earth, who hath delivered Daniel from the power of the lions.

(Daniel 6:23-27)

These kings were not heirs to the promise of God that had been given to Israel. They were, however, able to see the road to righteousness. Whether they achieved it or not is a matter for God to reveal when we each see Him—and then, too, we will know the fate of all who we have read about in the Bible.

But the righteousness which is of faith speaketh on this wise, Say not in thine heart, Who shall ascend into heaven? (that is, to bring Christ down from above:) Or, Who shall descend into the deep?

> *(that is, to bring up Christ again from the dead.) But what saith it? The word is nigh thee, even in thy mouth, and in thy heart: that is, the word of faith, which we preach; That if thou shalt confess with thy mouth the Lord Jesus, and shalt believe in thine heart that God hath raised him from the dead, thou shalt be saved. For with the heart man believeth unto righteousness; and with the mouth confession is made unto salvation. For the scripture saith, Whosoever believeth on him shall not be ashamed.*
>
> (Romans 10:6-11)

But even though we cannot say whether these two kings now rest in the LORD'S salvation; it is true to say that these two empires had, in them, a child of Israel, and that the child of Israel was following the law of Moses. However, it was not the law of Moses that gave Daniel, Shadrach, Meshach and Abednego their unique position in the will and mind of God. Rather, it was their devotion to God, beyond the law of Moses, which moved Daniel, Shadrach, Meshach and Abednego to the place of this distinction. They were justified in the sight of God by the works of righteousness that He accepted from the indwelling nature of righteousness that He gave to them. It was not even they who gave themselves the capacity to perform works of righteousness; but rather, it is God THAT sustained them.

> *Put them in mind to be subject to principalities and powers, to obey magistrates, to be ready to every good work, To speak evil of no man, to be no brawlers, but gentle, showing all meekness unto all men. For we ourselves also were sometimes foolish, disobedient, deceived, serving divers lusts and pleasures, living in malice and envy, hateful, and hating one another. But after that the kindness and love of God our Saviour toward man appeared, Not by works of righteousness which we have done, but according to his mercy he saved us, by the washing of regeneration, and renewing of the Holy Ghost; Which he shed on us abundantly through Jesus Christ our Saviour; That being justified by his grace, we should be made heirs according to the hope of eternal life.*
>
> (Titus 3:1-7)

When we look at the event that happened after the selection of the first king of Israel, king Saul, we see further evidence that even our righteous behavior is a gift from God.

> *And it was so, that when he had turned his back to go from Samuel, God gave him another heart: and all those signs came to pass that day. And when they came thither to the hill, behold, a company of prophets met him; and the spirit of God came upon him, and he prophesied among them.*
>
> (1 Samuel 10:9-10)

When Saul was selected, God empowered him to fulfill the requirements of the office for which He had selected him. This is taught to us by the apostle Paul, through these words written in the Bible.

> *And we know that all things work together for good to them that love God, to them who are the called according to his purpose. For whom he did foreknow, he also did predestinate to be conformed to the image of his Son, that he might be the firstborn among many brethren. Moreover whom he did predestinate, them he also called: and whom he called, them he also justified: and whom he justified, them he also glorified.*
>
> *What shall we then say to these things? If God be for us, who can be against us?*
>
> (Romans 8:28-31)

Thus, with this understanding, we can move to one of the broad concepts of Scripture. This is the concept that was presented by the apostle James.

When the apostle James spoke of works, he was identifying that which every religious person must do for God. At the beginning of the revelation of our assignment to perform work for the LORD, we see how God empowered king Saul to perform those works of righteousness that would be required of a king. Moving rapidly ahead in time, from the time of king Saul, to now, we have an even clearer statement of our transformation to a qualified state. Support for the message of the above mentioned information is in this promise of the Son of God, Jesus Christ . . .

> *If ye love me, keep my commandments. And I will pray the Father, and he shall give you another Comforter, that he may abide with you for ever; Even the Spirit of truth; whom the world cannot receive, because it seeth him not, neither knoweth him: but ye know him; for he dwelleth with you, and shall be in you.*
>
> (John 14:15-17)

In addition to announcing God's preparation of our soul and spirit for service to the Father, Jesus provided further insight of the nature of service to God. Jesus stated that once we are truly immersed in the Spirit of truth, we will have no option but to move in a certain way. This applies only to those who accept the direction of the Spirit of truth, the Holy Ghost, which is in them.

> *And we have known and believed the love that God hath to us. God is love; and he that dwelleth in love dwelleth in God, and God in him. Herein is our love made perfect, that we may have boldness in the day of judgment: because as he is, so are we in this world. There is no fear in love; but perfect love casteth out fear: because fear hath torment. He that feareth is not made perfect in love.*
>
> *We love him, because he first loved us. If a man say, I love God, and hateth his brother, he is a liar: for he that loveth not his brother whom he hath seen, how can he love God whom he hath not seen? And this commandment have we from him, That he who loveth God love his brother also.*
>
> (1 John 4:16-21)

Our major task in accomplishing the will of God is to stay out of the way.

> *Quench not the Spirit.*
>
> (1 Thessalonians 5:19)

Thus, we must not take scriptural passages and try to apply them either too broadly or too narrowly.

I could give maybe a thousand or more examples of the pitfalls that await those who strain to follow the teaching of the apostles, rather than yielding to the ease of understanding that we get by the leading of the Holy Ghost, as it helps us rightly divide the word of truth. However, if I did, no one would even be able to lift this book, let alone read it. It is sufficient for you to know that all these matters and many others are handled by the Holy Ghost. However, I will give some general categories.

Double Meanings

Do not look too closely at the Bible for double meanings. There are very few double meanings in the Bible—I am inclined to say, none—that have not been revealed. You see, the time of the prophets, which we call the Old Testament, was a time of mystery (mystery is not double meaning). This is the time of the unfolding of the coming of the Messiah. There were many obscure passages that were written that were pointing at specific events of the nation of Israel; but that were foreshadowing events that would occur in the life of the Messiah. From among those events, I will share one that seems, to me, to be obscure.

New Testament:

> *When Herod the king had heard these things, he was troubled, and all Jerusalem with him. And when he had gathered all the chief priests and scribes of the people together, he demanded of them where Christ should be born.*
>
> *And they said unto him, In Bethlehem of Judaea: for thus it is written by the prophet, And thou Bethlehem, in the land of Juda, art not the least among the princes of Juda: for out of thee shall come a Governor, that shall rule my people Israel.*
>
> *Then Herod, when he had privily called the wise men, enquired of them diligently what time the star appeared. And he sent them to Bethlehem, and said, Go and search diligently for the young child;*

> *and when ye have found him, bring me word again, that I may come and worship him also.*
>
> *When they had heard the king, they departed; and, lo, the star, which they saw in the east, went before them, till it came and stood over where the young child was. When they saw the star, they rejoiced with exceeding great joy. And when they were come into the house, they saw the young child with Mary his mother, and fell down, and worshipped him: and when they had opened their treasures, they presented unto him gifts; gold, and frankincense and myrrh.*
>
> *And being warned of God in a dream that they should not return to Herod, they departed into their own country another way.*
>
> *And when they were departed, behold, the angel of the Lord appeareth to Joseph in a dream, saying, Arise, and take the young child and his mother, and flee into Egypt, and be thou there until I bring thee word: for Herod will seek the young child to destroy him.*
>
> *When he arose, he took the young child and his mother by night, and departed into Egypt: And was there until the death of Herod: that it might be fulfilled which was spoken of the Lord by the prophet, saying, Out of Egypt have I called my son.*
>
> (Matthew 2:3-15)

Old Testament:

> *When Israel was a child, then I loved him, and called my son out of Egypt.*
>
> (Hosea 11:1)

The first, New Testament, Scripture tells of Jesus, and the reason he ended up in Egypt. The second, Old Testament, Scripture seems to be testimony about the nation of Israel, and how God delivered them from Pharaoh in Egypt. When reading only the second one, there is no way of knowing that it relates to the first; or, is there?

The one piece of information that is needed is that the son of God, the nation of Israel, was being patterned in its life and travel to foreshadow the life of the Son of God, the Messiah, who is Jesus Christ. To those who have read this, previously, I send this question: Haven't you ever asked yourself why God chose Egypt to have Joseph be sold to? There were many other nations who were, maybe not quite as powerful, but that existed at that time. For instance, why didn't the *Ishmeelites* just enslave Joseph, themselves (or even, the *Midianites merchantmen*; though, it is understandable that they sell things, of which Joseph was one)? They had original possession of this apparently discarded soul.

> *And it came to pass, when Joseph was come unto his brethren, that they stript Joseph out of his coat, his coat of many colours that was on him; And they took him, and cast him into a pit: and the pit was empty, there was no water in it. And they sat down to eat bread: and they lifted up their eyes and looked, and, behold, a company of Ishmeelites came from Gilead with their camels bearing spicery and balm and myrrh, going to carry it down to Egypt. And Judah said unto his brethren, What profit is it if we slay our brother, and conceal his blood? Come, and let us sell him to the Ishmeelites, and let not our hand be upon him; for he is our brother and our flesh.*
>
> *And his brethren were content.*
>
> *Then there passed by Midianites merchantmen; and they drew and lifted up Joseph out of the pit, and sold Joseph to the Ishmeelites for twenty pieces of silver: and they brought Joseph into Egypt.*
>
> (Genesis 37:23-28)

And even when Joseph was sold to Egypt, why did things have to turn out bad for his extended family, as they did after they had gone so profitably?

> *Now these are the names of the children of Israel, which came into Egypt; every man and his household came with Jacob. Reuben, Simeon, Levi, and Judah, Issachar, Zebulun, and Benjamin, Dan, and Naphtali, Gad, and Asher. And all the souls that came out of the loins of Jacob were seventy souls: for Joseph was in Egypt already.*
>
> *And Joseph died, and all his brethren, and all that generation. And the children of Israel were fruitful, and increased abundantly, and multiplied, and waxed exceeding mighty; and the land was filled with them.*

Now there arose up a new king over Egypt, which knew not Joseph. And he said unto his people, Behold, the people of the children of Israel are more and mightier than we: Come on, let us deal wisely with them; lest they multiply, and it come to pass, that, when there falleth out any war, they join also unto our enemies, and fight against us, and so get them up out of the land.

Therefore they did set over them taskmasters to afflict them with their burdens. And they built for Pharaoh treasure cities, Pithom and Raamses. But the more they afflicted them, the more they multiplied and grew. And they were grieved because of the children of Israel. And the Egyptians made the children of Israel to serve with rigour: And they made their lives bitter with hard bondage, in morter, and in brick, and in all manner of service in the field: all their service, wherein they made them serve, was with rigour.

(Exodus 1:1-14)

Why wasn't Joseph remembered for what he did for the nation of Egypt? He was, at one point, considered the second ruler of the kingdom.

Now therefore let Pharaoh look out a man discreet and wise, and set him over the land of Egypt. Let Pharaoh do this, and let him appoint officers over the land, and take up the fifth part of the land of Egypt in the seven plenteous years. And let them gather all the food of those good years that come, and lay up corn under the hand of Pharaoh, and let them keep food in the cities. And that food shall be for store to the land against the seven years of famine, which shall be in the land of Egypt; that the land perish not through the famine.

And the thing was good in the eyes of Pharaoh, and in the eyes of all his servants. And Pharaoh said unto his servants, Can we find such a one as this is, a man in whom the Spirit of God is?

And Pharaoh said unto Joseph, Forasmuch as God hath shewed thee all this, there is none so discreet and wise as thou art: Thou shalt be over my house, and according unto thy word shall all my people be ruled: only in the throne will I be greater than

> *thou. And Pharaoh said unto Joseph, See, I have set thee over all the land of Egypt.*
>
> *And Pharaoh took off his ring from his hand, and put it upon Joseph's hand, and arrayed him in vestures of fine linen, and put a gold chain about his neck; And he made him to ride in the second chariot which he had; and they cried before him, Bow the knee: and he made him ruler over all the land of Egypt.*
>
> (Genesis 41:33-43)

But once we get to the time of the Messiah, the questions, above, and many other things, are cleared up.

Please note that at the time of the writing of Hosea 11:1 there was no double meaning that could have been applied to it, though it is a part of the mystery of the Old Testament. It is only in the light of the greater information in the New Testament about the Messiah that we see the hidden meaning. This is the sort of afterthought that highlights the mystery of Scripture, and is not an indication of a double meaning. Again, we say, there are no double meanings in Scripture, only unrevealed facts, as seen from the perspective of the time of their occurrence. When the Messiah arrived, many of the unrevealed facts—indeed, all of the both unrevealed and undiscovered facts—of the way of righteousness were revealed. This is the mystery that is no more.

> *Howbeit we speak wisdom among them that are perfect: yet not the wisdom of this world, nor of the princes of this world, that come to nought: But we speak the wisdom of God in a mystery, even the hidden wisdom, which God ordained before the world unto our glory: Which none of the princes of this world knew: for had they known it, they would not have crucified the Lord of glory. But as it is written, Eye hath not seen, nor ear heard, neither have entered into the heart of man, the things which God hath prepared for them that love him. But God hath revealed them unto us by his Spirit: for the Spirit searcheth all things, yea, the deep things of God.*
>
> *For what man knoweth the things of a man, save the spirit of man which is in him? even so the things of God knoweth no man, but*

> *the Spirit of God. Now we have received, not the spirit of the world, but the spirit which is of God; that we might know the things that are freely given to us of God. Which things also we speak, not in the words which man's wisdom teacheth, but which the Holy Ghost teacheth; comparing spiritual things with spiritual.*
>
> *But the natural man receiveth not the things of the Spirit of God: for they are foolishness unto him: neither can he know them, because they are spiritually discerned. But he that is spiritual judgeth all things, yet he himself is judged of no man. For who hath known the mind of the Lord, that he may instruct him? But we have the mind of Christ.*
>
> (1 Corinthians 2:6-16)

Thus, we have an example of the first among the broad categories of applications of Scripture: revelation of mysteries' meanings, without duplicity. Such, too, is the way that the church must behave.

> *How is it then, brethren? when ye come together, every one of you hath a psalm, hath a doctrine, hath a tongue, hath a revelation, hath an interpretation. Let all things be done unto edifying.*
>
> *If any man speak in an unknown tongue, let it be by two, or at the most by three, and that by course; and let one interpret. But if there be no interpreter, let him keep silence in the church; and let him speak to himself, and to God.*
>
> *Let the prophets speak two or three, and let the other judge. If any thing be revealed to another that sitteth by, let the first hold his peace. For ye may all prophesy one by one, that all may learn, and all may be comforted. And the spirits of the prophets are subject to the prophets.*
>
> *For God is not the author of confusion, but of peace, as in all churches of the saints.*
>
> (1 Corinthians 14:26-33)

Focus on the Audience

The second category tells us that we must understand that, in the Bible, the audience is clearly stated in Scripture; whether Jew or Gentile. Sometimes this can become a bit of a stumbling block when reading the Old Testament. We sometimes want to take words that were directed specifically at the nation of Israel, and apply them generally to all peoples. This includes the category of manifestations of mysteries that were contained in the Old Testament.

Where there is a general application that we are to take from the specific statement to the nation of Israel, it has been included in the teaching of Jesus and the apostles, in the New Testament. Where it is not so included, we must not take it upon ourselves to do so.

Consider this Old Testament directive that was eliminated in the New Testament: *Eye for eye, tooth for tooth.*

> *If men strive, and hurt a woman with child, so that her fruit depart from her, and yet no mischief follow: he shall be surely punished, according as the woman's husband will lay upon him; and he shall pay as the judges determine.*
>
> *And if any mischief follow, then thou shalt give life for life, Eye for eye, tooth for tooth, hand for hand, foot for foot, Burning for burning, wound for wound, stripe for stripe.*
>
> (Exodus 21:22-25)

> *Ye have heard that it hath been said, An eye for an eye, and a tooth for a tooth: But I say unto you, That ye resist not evil: but whosoever shall smite thee on thy right cheek, turn to him the other also. And if any man will sue thee at the law, and take away thy coat, let him have thy cloak also. And whosoever shall compel thee to go a mile, go with him twain. Give to him that asketh thee, and from him that would borrow of thee turn not thou away.*
>
> (Matthew 5:38-42)

Consider this passage of the law of Moses as it was enhanced by the full weight of God's intention, with His permissive will removed.

When a man hath taken a wife, and married her, and it come to pass that she find no favour in his eyes, because he hath found some uncleanness in her: then let him write her a bill of divorcement, and give it in her hand, and send her out of his house.

(Deuteronomy 24:1)

The Pharisees also came unto him, tempting him, and saying unto him, Is it lawful for a man to put away his wife for every cause?

And he answered and said unto them, Have ye not read, that he which made them at the beginning made them male and female, And said, For this cause shall a man leave father and mother, and shall cleave to his wife: and they twain shall be one flesh? Wherefore they are no more twain, but one flesh. What therefore God hath joined together, let not man put asunder.

They say unto him, Why did Moses then command to give a writing of divorcement, and to put her away?

He saith unto them, Moses because of the hardness of your hearts suffered you to put away your wives: but from the beginning it was not so. And I say unto you, Whosoever shall put away his wife, except it be for fornication, and shall marry another, committeth adultery: and whoso marrieth her which is put away doth commit adultery.

(Matthew 19:3-9)

Advancing in Righteousness

Then, there is the vast summation that wipes out a significant portion of the pressure of the law of Moses. No, I should not say, wipes out: the Bible actually says that it completes it. This means that; where once it was necessary to have this type of interaction with God, the great pressure that accompanied this interaction has been rendered unnecessary by intervention of a greater action toward God that replaces it.

> *Brethren, my heart's desire and prayer to God for Israel is, that they might be saved. For I bear them record that they have a zeal of God, but not according to knowledge. For they being ignorant of God's righteousness, and going about to establish their own righteousness, have not submitted themselves unto the righteousness of God. For Christ is the end of the law for righteousness to every one that believeth.*
>
> (Romans 10:1-4)

These are only three of the categories of cautions that we must apply to the application of Scripture, particularly the application of Old Testament Scripture. We must not just read the words, perform the actions, and expect God to be pleased. This was stated, specifically, by God, in reference to that most sacred action of, sacrifice to the LORD. Even before the final stroke of the Old Testament was delivered, the LORD removed the effectiveness of this action, and replaced it with a greater one. Samuel announced it.

> *And Samuel said, Hath the LORD as great delight in burnt offerings and sacrifices, as in obeying the voice of the LORD? Behold, to obey is better than sacrifice, and to hearken than the fat of rams.*
>
> (1 Samuel 15:22)

Amos reaffirmed it:

Shall not the day of the LORD be darkness, and not light? even very dark, and no brightness in it? I hate, I despise your feast days, and I will not smell in your solemn assemblies. Though ye offer me burnt offerings and your meat offerings, I will not accept them: neither will I regard the peace offerings of your fat beasts. Take thou away from me the noise of thy songs; for I will not hear the melody of thy viols. But let judgment run down as waters, and righteousness as a mighty stream. Have ye offered unto me sacrifices and offerings in the wilderness forty years, O house of Israel?

(Amos 5:20-25)

A scribe, of the New Age, witnessed to a superior service to the LORD than sacrifices and offerings, as he responded to words of Jesus Christ.

And the scribe said unto him, Well, Master, thou hast said the truth: for there is one God; and there is none other but he: And to love him with all the heart, and with all the understanding, and with all the soul, and with all the strength, and to love his neighbour as himself, is more than all whole burnt offerings and sacrifices.

And when Jesus saw that he answered discreetly, he said unto him, Thou art not far from the kingdom of God.

And no man after that durst ask him any question.

(Mark 12:32-34)

This portion of the law of Moses, the first place position of sacrifices and offerings—as perceived and stressed by religious leaders—had been made secondary to the weightier matters of the Law, which Jesus states in Matthew 23:23-24, written at the start of this chapter. These matters are the ones to which we are pointed by the Bible. To point us in the direction of righteousness is the proper application of the message of the Bible.

So, are we to dismiss the Old Testament?

Absolutely not!!!

Knowing this first, that no prophecy of the scripture is of any private interpretation. For the prophecy came not in old time by

> *the will of man: but holy men of God spake as they were moved by the Holy Ghost.*
>
> (1 Peter 1:20-21)

We are, however, to dismiss any application that ***we*** may add, thinking that it is appropriate. We need, instead, to yield to those applications that are brought forth to us by the Spirit of truth, the Holy Ghost. This is the final answer to the application of Scripture. It must be applied under the direction, and at the leading, of the Holy Ghost. Any other application of Scripture, even *for doctrine, for reproof, for correction, for instruction in righteousness*, will be ineffective without the absolute leading of the Holy Ghost. This is the purpose for which Christ requested of God the Father that the Spirit of truth be sent to us. Let us therefore not quench the Spirit; instead, we must let it do for us that for which it has come to reside with us. Let us, as they say, "Let go, and let God".

> *These things have I spoken unto you, being yet present with you. But the Comforter, which is the Holy Ghost, whom the Father will send in my name, he shall teach you all things, and bring all things to your remembrance, whatsoever I have said unto you. Peace I leave with you, my peace I give unto you: not as the world giveth, give I unto you. Let not your heart be troubled, neither let it be afraid.*
>
> (John 14:25-27)

THE WORD FROM THE BIBLE

Psalm 82:1-8

A Psalm of Asaph.

God standeth in the congregation of the mighty; he judgeth among the gods. How long will ye judge unjustly, and accept the persons of the wicked? Selah.

Defend the poor and fatherless: do justice to the afflicted and needy. Deliver the poor and needy: rid them out of the hand of the wicked. They know not, neither will they understand; they walk on in darkness: all the foundations of the earth are out of course. I have said, Ye are gods; and all of you are children of the most High. But ye shall die like men, and fall like one of the princes.

Arise, O God, judge the earth: for thou shalt inherit all nations.

1 Samuel 8:1-9

And it came to pass, when Samuel was old, that he made his sons judges over Israel. Now the name of his firstborn was Joel; and the name of his second, Abiah: they were judges in Beersheba. And his sons walked not in his ways, but turned aside after lucre, and took bribes, and perverted judgment.

Then all the elders of Israel gathered themselves together, and came to Samuel unto Ramah, And said unto him, Behold, thou art old, and thy sons walk not in thy ways: now make us a king to judge us like all the nations.

But the thing displeased Samuel, when they said, Give us a king to judge us. And Samuel prayed unto the LORD.

And the LORD said unto Samuel, Hearken unto the voice of the people in all that they say unto thee: for they have not rejected thee, but they have rejected me, that I should not reign over them. According to all the works which they have done since the day that I brought them up out of Egypt even unto this day, wherewith they have forsaken me, and served other gods, so do they also unto thee. Now therefore hearken unto their voice: howbeit yet protest solemnly unto them, and show them the manner of the king that shall reign over them.

Hosea 8:1-7

Set the trumpet to thy mouth. He shall come as an eagle against the house of the LORD, because they have transgressed my covenant, and trespassed against my law. Israel shall cry unto me, My God, we know thee. Israel hath cast off the thing that is good: the enemy shall pursue him. They have set up kings, but not by me: they have made princes, and I knew it not: of their silver and their gold have they made them idols, that they may be cut off.

Thy calf, O Samaria, hath cast thee off; mine anger is kindled against them: how long will it be ere they attain to innocency? For from Israel was it also: the workman made it; therefore it is not God: but the calf of Samaria shall be broken in pieces. For they have sown the wind, and they shall reap the whirlwind: it hath no stalk: the bud shall yield no meal: if so be it yield, the strangers shall swallow it up.

Chapter Four

Bring you before the Court

At the time of this writing, there is a lot of murmuring about the hindrances that Christians are facing in the United States of America from governmental intervention. This is primarily focused on the courts. Please, please forgive me—or not—for being cold, heartless, and downright mean. I have just three words for this state of affairs.

So . . . !
And . . . ?
Well . . .

Think about the plight of the early Christians. It is not necessarily true that each one of us will experience this level of separation, but we really should not complain over little inconveniences, in the light of what the pioneering Christians—then known as, the disciples of Christ—were told to prepare themselves.

> *And as he sat upon the mount of Olives, the disciples came unto him privately, saying, Tell us, when shall these things be? and what shall be the sign of thy coming, and of the end of the world?*
>
> *And Jesus answered and said unto them, Take heed that no man deceive you. For many shall come in my name, saying, I am Christ; and shall deceive many. And ye shall hear of wars and rumours of wars: see that ye be not troubled: for all these things must come to pass, but the end is not yet. For nation shall rise against nation, and kingdom against kingdom: and there shall be famines, and*

> *pestilences, and earthquakes, in divers places. All these are the beginning of sorrows.*
>
> *Then shall they deliver you up to be afflicted, and shall kill you: and ye shall be hated of all nations for my name's sake. And then shall many be offended, and shall betray one another, and shall hate one another. And many false prophets shall rise, and shall deceive many. And because iniquity shall abound, the love of many shall wax cold. But he that shall endure unto the end, the same shall be saved.*
>
> (Matthew 24:3-13)

In other words, you can either believe that Jesus possessed a true prophetic gift from God the Father, or not. If not, and if you believe that Christians should be misery-exempt special, then you have a reason to pout or to petition God to fix His oversight. Also, even when you believe that Jesus did have an Old Testament style prophetic gift, you can, too, try to believe that somewhere in his words is a hidden exception. You can especially try to believe that there must be a special exception for a nation that portrays itself as being *under* God. However, no such exemption is obvious in these words of Jesus. I am just totally thankful that he only said, *some of you*, and not, *all of you*. So maybe it is time for us to accept the compensatory gift that Jesus delivered then, and still delivers now, to those who believe.

> *These things have I spoken unto you, being yet present with you. But the Comforter, which is the Holy Ghost, whom the Father will send in my name, he shall teach you all things, and bring all things to your remembrance, whatsoever I have said unto you.*
>
> *Peace I leave with you, my peace I give unto you: not as the world giveth, give I unto you. Let not your heart be troubled, neither let it be afraid.*
>
> (John 14:25-27)

And, maybe it is time for us to lean on the promise of the word of God.

> *And we know that all things work together for good to them that love God, to them who are the called according to his purpose. For whom he did foreknow, he also did predestinate to be conformed to*

the image of his Son, that he might be the firstborn among many brethren. Moreover whom he did predestinate, them he also called: and whom he called, them he also justified: and whom he justified, them he also glorified.

What shall we then say to these things? If God be for us, who can be against us?

(Romans 8:28-31)

But, please, do not take this the wrong way. In countries, such as the United States of America, where I am, we do have the right to resist. This is provided by the government, in the current contracts with us; such things as, the Constitution and the Declaration of Independence. But when we invoke these contractual rights, let us be clear about what we are leaning on. With the exercise of these contractual rights, we are depending on the government; we are depending on Caesar. And this freedom of dependence is in accordance with Scripture.

Then went the Pharisees, and took counsel how they might entangle him in his talk. And they sent out unto him their disciples with the Herodians, saying, Master, we know that thou art true, and teachest the way of God in truth, neither carest thou for any man: for thou regardest not the person of men. Tell us therefore, What thinkest thou? Is it lawful to give tribute unto Caesar, or not?

But Jesus perceived their wickedness, and said, Why tempt ye me, ye hypocrites? Shew me the tribute money.

And they brought unto him a penny.

And he saith unto them, Whose is this image and superscription?

They say unto him, Caesar's.

Then saith he unto them, Render therefore unto Caesar the things which are Caesar's; and unto God the things that are God's.

When they had heard these words, they marvelled, and left him, and went their way.

(Matthew 22:15-22)

In a certain encounter in the life of the apostle Paul, we have a righteous example of the exercise of government-citizen contractual rights. In this encounter, the apostle Paul exercised his rights, in order to promote the mission of God, and to introduce the good news of the Gospel to those who were controlled by the government. Paul did not do so just to protect his rights, or because he felt constrained to gain permission from Caesar to preach. The reason for the exercise of his rights begins when a governmental official sat down in, what may be called, a town hall meeting.

> *And when he was come, the Jews which came down from Jerusalem stood round about, and laid many and grievous complaints against Paul, which they could not prove. While he answered for himself,*
>
> *Neither against the law of the Jews, neither against the temple, nor yet against Caesar, have I offended any thing at all.*
>
> *But Festus, willing to do the Jews a pleasure, answered Paul, and said, Wilt thou go up to Jerusalem, and there be judged of these things before me?*
>
> *Then said Paul, I stand at Caesar's judgment seat, where I ought to be judged: to the Jews have I done no wrong, as thou very well knowest. For if I be an offender, or have committed any thing worthy of death, I refuse not to die: but if there be none of these things whereof these accuse me, no man may deliver me unto them. I appeal unto Caesar.*
>
> *Then Festus, when he had conferred with the council, answered, Hast thou appealed unto Caesar? unto Caesar shalt thou go.*
>
> (Acts 25:7-12)

However, even Paul chose his battles well, in that he did, as they say, "know when to hold them, and know when to fold them; know when to walk away, and know when to run". The following is a time when Paul walked away briskly, with a little help from his friends.

> *Now when they had passed through Amphipolis and Apollonia, they came to Thessalonica, where was a synagogue of the Jews: And Paul, as his manner was, went in unto them, and three sabbath days reasoned with them out of the scriptures, Opening*

and alleging, that Christ must needs have suffered, and risen again from the dead; and that this Jesus, whom I preach unto you, is Christ. And some of them believed, and consorted with Paul and Silas; and of the devout Greeks a great multitude, and of the chief women not a few.

But the Jews which believed not, moved with envy, took unto them certain lewd fellows of the baser sort, and gathered a company, and set all the city on an uproar, and assaulted the house of Jason, and sought to bring them out to the people. And when they found them not, they drew Jason and certain brethren unto the rulers of the city, crying, These that have turned the world upside down are come hither also; Whom Jason hath received: and these all do contrary to the decrees of Caesar, saying that there is another king, one Jesus. And they troubled the people and the rulers of the city, when they heard these things. And when they had taken security of Jason, and of the other, they let them go.

And the brethren immediately sent away Paul and Silas by night unto Berea: who coming thither went into the synagogue of the Jews.

(Acts 17:1-10)

In the current age, many of us have not been so wise in our battles. I will give you an example. In my time, there is a renewed furor about the display of the Ten Commandments. The furors that I have seen are driven by the efforts of Christians. Being a Christian myself, this seems odd to me. As a follower of Christ, I believe in the message he gave to us at the transformation of our reality, in the relevant part of it that is written below.

And I heard a great voice out of heaven saying, Behold, the tabernacle of God is with men, and he will dwell with them, and they shall be his people, and God himself shall be with them, and be their God. And God shall wipe away all tears from their eyes; and there shall be no more death, neither sorrow, nor crying, neither shall there be any more pain: for the former things are passed away.

> *And he that sat upon the throne said, Behold, I make all things new. And he said unto me, Write: for these words are true and faithful.*
>
> *And he said unto me, It is done. I am Alpha and Omega, the beginning and the end. I will give unto him that is athirst of the fountain of the water of life freely. He that overcometh shall inherit all things; and I will be his God, and he shall be my son.*
>
> (Revelation 21:3-7)

God said, *Behold, I make all things new.* One of the new things is a summation of the Ten Commandments, and pretty much all of the rest of the Law.

> *But when the Pharisees had heard that he had put the Sadducees to silence, they were gathered together. Then one of them, which was a lawyer, asked him a question, tempting him, and saying, Master, which is the great commandment in the law?*
>
> *Jesus said unto him, Thou shalt love the Lord thy God with all thy heart, and with all thy soul, and with all thy mind. This is the first and great commandment. And the second is like unto it, Thou shalt love thy neighbour as thyself. On these two commandments hang all the law and the prophets.*
>
> (Matthew 22:34-40)

The renewed concentration on the Ten Commandments strikes me as the same kind of legalism that led the children of Israel into trouble. It is once again resurrecting the works type philosophy/theology of existence. It is my understanding of the mission that Jesus Christ, the Son of God, which he set before us through the words of the New Testament, is to simplify our worship.

> *Come unto me, all ye that labour and are heavy laden, and I will give you rest. Take my yoke upon you, and learn of me; for I am meek and lowly in heart: and ye shall find rest unto your souls. For my yoke is easy, and my burden is light.*
>
> (Matthew 11:28-30)

Jesus did not seem to be interested in maintaining the status quo. Wherefore he set out to establish, among his followers, the new cutting-edge state of being: that blessed state of being known as love. If we are going down that legalistic path, we might also petition for the display of the Lord's Prayer. I am repeating here, for you, the Lord's Prayer, recalled by two witnesses, Matthew and Luke.

> *After this manner therefore pray ye: Our Father which art in heaven, Hallowed be thy name. Thy kingdom come, Thy will be done in earth, as it is in heaven. Give us this day our daily bread. And forgive us our debts, as we forgive our debtors. And lead us not into temptation, but deliver us from evil: For thine is the kingdom, and the power, and the glory, for ever. Amen.*
>
> (Matthew 6:9-13)

> *And it came to pass, that, as he was praying in a certain place, when he ceased, one of his disciples said unto him, Lord, teach us to pray, as John also taught his disciples.*
>
> *And he said unto them, When ye pray, say, Our Father which art in heaven, Hallowed be thy name. Thy kingdom come. Thy will be done, as in heaven, so in earth. Give us day by day our daily bread. And forgive us our sins; for we also forgive every one that is indebted to us. And lead us not into temptation; but deliver us from evil.*
>
> (Luke 11:1-4)

In the history of some of our forefathers of the United States of America, you will find that the nation was established on a foundation that is itself a mission. The founding mission of the United States of America, and its noble reason for continuation, is to present, to the world, a nation that shows forth the Kingdom of God. As with the Ten Commandments, the Lord's Prayer is also a part of the heritage, and a part of the building of the United States of America. But as of this writing, the Lord's Prayer does not receive the public esteem that is being given to the Ten Commandments.

Might it be that we have lost our courage? Might it be that we can no longer stomach truly revolutionary issues?

How much more could this country do if it petitioned God, as a whole, to bring about His kingdom in our midst? Might the Ten Commandments become, as Jesus Christ told us, necessary only in their summary form? Might we truly move to loving one another as God wills for us to do? Weren't we once, as a nation, at a time when this prayer was paramount to our existence? How far we have slipped!

Of my brethren in the Christian faith, those that spend such a great deal of time on this issue might want to take time out for a refreshing from God. When we display this face to the world, we are stepping heavily on the ground that brought about the condemnation of the religious leaders of Jesus' day. And this condemnation was not by the media or the government. This condemnation comes from Jesus Christ, the son of God, as he was speaking in the Father's authority.

> *Woe unto you, scribes and Pharisees, hypocrites! for ye pay tithe of mint and anise and cummin, and have omitted the weightier matters of the law, judgment, mercy, and faith: these ought ye to have done, and not to leave the other undone. Ye blind guides, which strain at a gnat, and swallow a camel.*
>
> (Matthew 23:23-24)

Might we, as Christians, be falling into the same pattern as some of the more vocal kinds of religious leaders of Jesus' day?

> *Then spake Jesus to the multitude, and to his disciples, Saying The scribes and the Pharisees sit in Moses' seat: All therefore whatsoever they bid you observe, that observe and do; but do not ye after their works: for they say, and do not. For they bind heavy burdens and grievous to be borne, and lay them on men's shoulders; but they themselves will not move them with one of their fingers. But all their works they do for to be seen of men: they make broad their phylacteries, and enlarge the borders of their garments, And love the uppermost rooms at feasts, and the chief seats in the synagogues, And greetings in the markets, and to be called of men, Rabbi, Rabbi.*
>
> (Matthew 23:1-7)

Please, let us get back to the message of the Son of God. Let us restore responsibility for the spiritual conversion of the country, adding to our ranks more servants of God and workers for the strengthening of mankind's presence in His Kingdom. Let us not depend on man to prop-up God's message—let us not depend on politicians, media, well-wishers, or any other source. Instead, let us, please, petition God for direction in this transformation; and, let us do so in the fashion that was requested of us by His Son.

> *And when thou prayest, thou shalt not be as the hypocrites are: for they love to pray standing in the synagogues and in the corners of the streets, that they may be seen of men. Verily I say unto you, They have their reward. But thou, when thou prayest, enter into thy closet, and when thou hast shut thy door, pray to thy Father which is in secret; and thy Father which seeth in secret shall reward thee openly.*
>
> (Matthew 6:5-6)

Let us be constant and diligent in praying to the Father for an extension of God's promise to the children of Israel. Let us ask Him to include all mankind in this great change of nature and practices. We need to return to the state of being in which the LORD speaks of us as the apostle Paul spoke of the Corinthian believers.

> *Ye are our epistle written in our hearts, known and read of all men: Forasmuch as ye are manifestly declared to be the epistle of Christ ministered by us, written not with ink, but with the Spirit of the living God; not in tables of stone, but in fleshly tables of the heart. And such trust have we through Christ to God-ward: Not that we are sufficient of ourselves to think any thing as of ourselves; but our sufficiency is of God; Who also hath made us able ministers of the new testament; not of the letter, but of the spirit: for the letter killeth, but the spirit giveth life.*
>
> (2 Corinthians 3:2-6)

Do not let satanic forces provide a handy diversion. Do not let these forces give mankind an out; which, once mankind has fulfilled, it will feel that it is let off the hook of required yearning for the perfect way of God. For, once this occurs; then mankind may conclude that it is no longer responsible to God for full righteousness, here and now. Mankind will create the conclusion that because it has met ***our*** requirements for righteous behavior, it has thus met God's.

We must keep them aware of the fact that ***our*** requirements are irrelevant: God's requirements are all that matter. The hook is set by Jesus Christ, the fisher of men. By him mankind will not be off the hook until he takes us off, and releases us in him. Christian, please keep these thoughts constantly before your eyes, and in your witness. The LORD God told us what His spiritual magnet is (and, it is not us).

And there shall come forth a rod out of the stem of Jesse, and a Branch shall grow out of his roots: And the spirit of the LORD shall rest upon him, the spirit of wisdom and understanding, the spirit of counsel and might, the spirit of knowledge and of the fear of the LORD; And shall make him of quick understanding in the fear of the LORD: and he shall not judge after the sight of his eyes, neither reprove after the hearing of his ears: But with righteousness shall he judge the poor, and reprove with equity for the meek of the earth: and he shall smite the earth with the rod of his mouth, and with the breath of his lips shall he slay the wicked. And righteousness shall be the girdle of his loins, and faithfulness the girdle of his reins.

The wolf also shall dwell with the lamb, and the leopard shall lie down with the kid; and the calf and the young lion and the fatling together; and a little child shall lead them. And the cow and the bear shall feed; their young ones shall lie down together: and the lion shall eat straw like the ox. And the sucking child shall play on the hole of the asp, and the weaned child shall put his hand on the cockatrice' den. They shall not hurt nor destroy in all my holy mountain: for the earth shall be full of the knowledge of the LORD, as the waters cover the sea.

And in that day there shall be a root of Jesse, which shall stand for an ensign of the people; to it shall the Gentiles seek: and his rest shall be glorious.

(Isaiah 11:1-10)

Speaking of hooks, we must not let one another off either: we are each a member of the cloud of witnesses that surround the actions of the saints. Wherefore let us revisit the words of Jesus, pertaining to the matter of service to masters. No, not that one: this one.

> *And they send unto him certain of the Pharisees and of the Herodians, to catch him in his words. And when they were come, they say unto him,*
>
> *Master, we know that thou art true, and carest for no man: for thou regardest not the person of men, but teachest the way of God in truth: Is it lawful to give tribute to Caesar, or not? Shall we give, or shall we not give?*
>
> *But he, knowing their hypocrisy, said unto them, Why tempt ye me? bring me a penny, that I may see it.*
>
> *And they brought it.*
>
> *And he saith unto them, Whose is this image and superscription?*
>
> *And they said unto him, Caesar's.*
>
> *And Jesus answering said unto them, Render to Caesar the things that are Caesar's, and to God the things that are God's.*
>
> *And they marvelled at him.*
>
> (Mark 12:13-17)

This can be a handy reminder when we start lamenting that the government will, for instance, take away our tax exempt status if we do thus and so. Let us return to our foundational principles.

> *The wicked flee when no man pursueth: but the righteous are bold as a lion.*
>
> (Proverbs 28:1)

Let us act as the apostles did, in a time when they were faced with difficult governmental demands. As an example, consider the action of the apostles when the leaders of their day raised this accusation, veiled in a question.

> *And it came to pass on the morrow, that their rulers, and elders, and scribes, And Annas the high priest, and Caiaphas, and John, and Alexander, and as many as were of the kindred of the high priest, were gathered together at Jerusalem. And when they had set them in the midst, they asked, By what power, or by what name, have ye done this?*
>
> (Acts 4:5-7)

At this point, the apostles had carnal options of behavior that they could have used, such as these: violent reaction; heaped on scorn; public groveling; or even, feigned ignorance. However, none of those options were exercised. Instead, the apostles, through their designated spokesman, projected their inner strength, outward to the religious leaders.

> *Then Peter, filled with the Holy Ghost, said unto them, Ye rulers of the people, and elders of Israel, If we this day be examined of the good deed done to the impotent man, by what means he is made whole; Be it known unto you all, and to all the people of Israel, that by the name of Jesus Christ of Nazareth, whom ye crucified, whom God raised from the dead, even by him doth this man stand here before you whole.*
>
> *This is the stone which was set at nought of you builders, which is become the head of the corner. Neither is there salvation in any other: for there is none other name under heaven given among men, whereby we must be saved.*
>
> (Acts 4:8-12)

The apostles' forthright behavior, and total reliance on the way that the LORD had put in place in the world, was more than enough to cause those leaders to rethink their confrontational, and somewhat arrogant, overbearing attitude.

> *Now when they saw the boldness of Peter and John, and perceived that they were unlearned and ignorant men, they marvelled; and*

they took knowledge of them, that they had been with Jesus. And beholding the man which was healed standing with them, they could say nothing against it.

But when they had commanded them to go aside out of the council, they conferred among themselves, Saying, What shall we do to these men? for that indeed a notable miracle hath been done by them is manifest to all them that dwell in Jerusalem; and we cannot deny it. But that it spread no further among the people, let us straitly threaten them, that they speak henceforth to no man in this name.

And they called them, and commanded them not to speak at all nor teach in the name of Jesus.

(Acts 4:13-18)

The leaders still had not learned with whom they were dealing. They had not perceived that the stance that the apostles took was not an optional one. Therefore, since it was not optional, no level of threat of man could change their course. In their slight ignorance, the leaders of that day needed further enlightenment. This is a situation of confrontation that we must be ready to face today. And our answer must be no less resolute than Peter's.

But Peter and John answered and said unto them, Whether it be right in the sight of God to hearken unto you more than unto God, judge ye. For we cannot but speak the things which we have seen and heard.

(Acts 4:19-20)

Additionally, remember this in matters of standing in the LORD, and yet living as a part of a group of people of mixed understanding and devotion: even Jesus did not hide behind a tax exempt status. When it came time to pay taxes, Jesus made sure that they were paid, and it is God that provided the funds.

And when they were come to Capernaum, they that received tribute money came to Peter, and said, Doth not your master pay tribute?

He saith, Yes.

And when he was come into the house, Jesus prevented him, saying, What thinkest thou, Simon? of whom do the kings of the earth take custom or tribute? of their own children, or of strangers?

Peter saith unto him, Of strangers.

Jesus saith unto him, Then are the children free. Notwithstanding, lest we should offend them, go thou to the sea, and cast an hook, and take up the fish that first cometh up; and when thou hast opened his mouth, thou shalt find a piece of money: that take, and give unto them for me and thee.

(Matthew 17:24-27)

Just as our fund raising efforts, and other outreaches, receive the support from God for the ministries for which we are charged by God; so, too, can it deliver any taxes that might be levied by the Caesars of this current age. If it ever becomes necessary to bypass tax exemption in order to do the will of God; then, bypass it in praise to God. God will provide your fish, and your coins; according to your need, and according to your faith. We have access to a power of blessing that is truly extraordinary.

Philip saith unto him, Lord, show us the Father, and it sufficeth us.

Jesus saith unto him, Have I been so long time with you, and yet hast thou not known me, Philip? he that hath seen me hath seen the Father; and how sayest thou then, Show us the Father? Believest thou not that I am in the Father, and the Father in me? the words that I speak unto you I speak not of myself: but the Father that dwelleth in me, he doeth the works. Believe me that I am in the Father, and the Father in me: or else believe me for the very works' sake.

Verily, verily, I say unto you, He that believeth on me, the works that I do shall he do also; and greater works than these shall he do; because I go unto my Father. And whatsoever ye shall ask in my name, that will I do, that the Father may be glorified in the Son. If ye shall ask any thing in my name, I will do it.

(John 14:8-14)

There are several other situations that the church of Christ is currently facing that require a fresh look at the power of God over the power of the government, but I will not explore that more here. It is my prayer that you refresh your dependence on God, in order to receive further clarification of how we will survive in spite of anything that the government tries to hold over our heads. I will, however, leave you with this.

Folks, if you truly believe that we are in the time of the Kingdom of God on earth, you have to know that God is the only set of rules that we must follow now. We must, more and more, trust in God for what we need; and for what we want. A slogan of the enabled is that "the difficult takes a little while, the impossible take a little longer." For God, and those immersed in Him, both are the same; and neither takes any time at all. When the Father's time comes, whatever is to be done is done.

> *But when ye pray, use not vain repetitions, as the heathen do: for they think that they shall be heard for their much speaking. Be not ye therefore like unto them: for your Father knoweth what things ye have need of, before ye ask him.*
>
> (Matthew 6:7-8)

Times are changing,
So they say that
This is definitely
A brand new day,

With some new rights,
Of this they are sure;
There is not any way
That we will endure

Anything that might
Take away our right
To speak for God,
As we fight the fight.

We must defend Him,
And let others know
That if we are crossed,
We will surely go

Before the judge
To stake our claim;
To have our say;
To clear our name.

Yes, we do have rights
That we can avail,
In our vain attempt,
Against man to prevail.

We seem to be acting
More like sinful man,
And still we claim,
This is God's plan?

Are we really in,
But not of, the world,
As all our rights
We forcefully hurl

At the courts of man,
To gain our due?
This is not the way
Evil to subdue?

Please, lean on God,
Whatever doth befall;
For, in our Saviour, alone,
We stand strong and tall.

CHAPTER 4A

Void of Humanistic Centrality

Rightly Dividing Scripture

Numbers 22:21-27

And Balaam rose up in the morning, and saddled his ass, and went with the princes of Moab. And God's anger was kindled because he went: and the angel of the LORD stood in the way for an adversary against him. Now he was riding upon his ass, and his two servants were with him. And the ass saw the angel of the LORD standing in the way, and his sword drawn in his hand: and the ass turned aside out of the way, and went into the field: and Balaam smote the ass, to turn her into the way.

But the angel of the LORD stood in a path of the vineyards, a wall being on this side, and a wall on that side. And when the ass saw the angel of the LORD, she thrust herself unto the wall, and crushed Balaam's foot against the wall: and he smote her again.

And the angel of the LORD went further, and stood in a narrow place, where was no way to turn either to the right hand or to the left. And when the ass saw the angel of the LORD, she fell down under Balaam: and Balaam's anger was kindled, and he smote the ass with a staff.

Definition
hu·man·ism (hym-nzm)

A system of thought that centers on humans and their values, capacities, and worth

Some of us, when we read the Bible, come away with the impression that it is instilling rights into our human existence. We may start to view humans as the center of the universe, or at least as the center of life on the earth. We look to God to provide us with the good life, in whatever manner we define it. And, therein is one of the major problems of this line of thinking: the good life is absolutely relative, from a human perspective.

Consider the fact that there were times in our history where the good life meant eating one meal a day. To get a picture of this, think, for a moment, about the depression that occurred in the United States of America. Then, there were times when just being healthy was considered to be the good life. Recall, if you will, the various plagues—such as, the bubonic plague—that have redefined satisfaction in health. Also, let your mind dwell on some of the famines—such as the potato famine—that have beset various areas of the world, and heightened the appreciation of even minimal sustenance. In times of plagues and famines, as at many other times in the history of the world, just surviving was the good life. However, now we have a tendency to think that the good life is having lots of material things.

But what is the position of God on this matter? Can we determine what the good life is, by reviewing relevant portions of the Bible? I hear a chorus of millions of Christians, and others who know the message of the Bible, saying, with one loud voice, "Of course we can." Then, they invoke the following passage from the Bible, as they try to project a measure of righteousness.

> *Ask, and it shall be given you; seek, and ye shall find; knock, and it shall be opened unto you: For every one that asketh receiveth; and he that seeketh findeth; and to him that knocketh it shall be opened. Or what man is there of you, whom if his son ask bread, will he give him a stone? Or if he ask a fish, will he give him a serpent? If ye then, being evil, know how to give good gifts*

unto your children, how much more shall your Father which is in heaven give good things to them that ask him?

Therefore all things whatsoever ye would that men should do to you, do ye even so to them: for this is the law and the prophets.
(Matthew 7:7-12)

But there is still the matter of, *things*. In order to more fully understand the good life, we have to go to the next step. For the student of the way of the LORD, things as a category of, well, things, is not a blanket that covers all that we could possibly search. Therefore, there must be some way of narrowing the field, and discovering what is the subset of things to seek. To get us started, let me fill in another part of the picture, with more insights and directives from the Bible.

Therefore I say unto you, Take no thought for your life, what ye shall eat, or what ye shall drink; nor yet for your body, what ye shall put on. Is not the life more than meat, and the body than raiment? Behold the fowls of the air: for they sow not, neither do they reap, nor gather into barns; yet your heavenly Father feedeth them. Are ye not much better than they?

Which of you by taking thought can add one cubit unto his stature? And why take ye thought for raiment? Consider the lilies of the field, how they grow; they toil not, neither do they spin: And yet I say unto you, That even Solomon in all his glory was not arrayed like one of these. Wherefore, if God so clothe the grass of the field, which to day is, and to morrow is cast into the oven, shall he not much more clothe you, O ye of little faith?

Therefore take no thought, saying, What shall we eat? or, What shall we drink? or, Wherewithal shall we be clothed? (For after all these things do the Gentiles seek:) for your heavenly Father knoweth that ye have need of all these things. But seek ye first the kingdom of God, and his righteousness; and all these things shall be added unto you. Take therefore no thought for the morrow: for the morrow shall take thought for the things of itself. Sufficient unto the day is the evil thereof.

(Matthew 6:25-34)

What, you mean we have to do some of that religious stuff before we can *feel good*?

Well, yes you do. So, let us fast forward, beyond the objection, and even beyond the acceptance. Let us say that you have absolutely followed the Scripture about the tithe and other associated passages related to supporting the elect of God and the mission of Jesus Christ. Oh, you say that you are not sure what this refers to. Let me share with you yet another insight from the Bible. This, too, is a precedent to demanding that the LORD release prosperity to you.

> *Bring ye all the tithes into the storehouse, that there may be meat in mine house, and prove me now herewith, saith the LORD of hosts, if I will not open you the windows of heaven, and pour you out a blessing, that there shall not be room enough to receive it.*
>
> *And I will rebuke the devourer for your sakes, and he shall not destroy the fruits of your ground; neither shall your vine cast her fruit before the time in the field, saith the LORD of hosts. And all nations shall call you blessed: for ye shall be a delightsome land, saith the LORD of hosts.*
>
> (Malachi 3:10-12)

Okay, I feel your frown. Here is a softening of the rigidity of the tithe. Do not worry, O church official; this has the potential to fill the LORD'S coffers with far more than a tithe.

> *Now concerning the collection for the saints, as I have given order to the churches of Galatia, even so do ye. Upon the first day of the week let every one of you lay by him in store, as God hath prospered him, that there be no gatherings when I come.*
>
> (1 Corinthians 16:1-2)

For those of you that noticed the words, *collection for the saints*, let us take the concept of giving beyond where this may seem to end. In the following Scripture, the freewill offering is stated as also being sufficient for the church, as a whole, or, as Paul designated it as being for: *the administration of this service.*

Therefore I thought it necessary to exhort the brethren, that they would go before unto you, and make up before hand your bounty, whereof ye had notice before, that the same might be ready, as a matter of bounty, and not as of covetousness. But this I say, He which soweth sparingly shall reap also sparingly; and he which soweth bountifully shall reap also bountifully.

Every man according as he purposeth in his heart, so let him give; not grudgingly, or of necessity: for God loveth a cheerful giver. And God is able to make all grace abound toward you; that ye, always having all sufficiency in all things, may abound to every good work: (As it is written, He hath dispersed abroad; he hath given to the poor: his righteousness remaineth for ever. Now he that ministereth seed to the sower both minister bread for your food, and multiply your seed sown, and increase the fruits of your righteousness;) Being enriched in every thing to all bountifulness, which causeth through us thanksgiving to God.

For the administration of this service not only supplieth the want of the saints, but is abundant also by many thanksgivings unto God; Whiles by the experiment of this ministration they glorify God for your professed subjection unto the gospel of Christ, and for your liberal distribution unto them, and unto all men; And by their prayer for you, which long after you for the exceeding grace of God in you.

Thanks be unto God for his unspeakable gift.
(2 Corinthians 9:5-15)

Let us say that we have done this, too; in that, we have given our tithes, or maybe we have given *as God hath prospered* us; or (thank God for a willing heart) we have done both in the church. Furthermore, let us say that, in support of a portion of the world, we have given a *liberal distribution unto them, and unto all men*. Then, aren't we entitled to the good life?

Yes, when we have done all that God requires in this regard, the good life will be available to you. No, you are not entitled to it. God has said that He will give it to you as a part of His grace. Therefore, after you have done all that is requested of you, according to righteousness; God will give you the good life. But there is still this demonstrative question: "Good life: what is the good life?"

The good life is to have the blessings of God.

I just heard someone say, "Then I am set!"

Well, wait just another minute! Do you fully understand what the blessing of God is? Do not translate "the blessing of God" into "everything that I ever wanted". Let us start this thing slowly. One thing we can say about the blessings of God is that it includes everything that you will need. Jesus Christ promised this, on behalf of the Father. However, your needs are not necessarily framed by your description of what you need; only by what God knows them to be. Therefore, our gifts that we set aside for the spread of God's message, and our requests from God, must both be done according to righteousness

> *Take heed that ye do not your alms before men, to be seen of them: otherwise ye have no reward of your Father which is in heaven. Therefore when thou doest thine alms, do not sound a trumpet before thee, as the hypocrites do in the synagogues and in the streets, that they may have glory of men. Verily I say unto you, They have their reward. But when thou doest alms, let not thy left hand know what thy right hand doeth: That thine alms may be in secret: and thy Father which seeth in secret himself shall reward thee openly.*
>
> *And when thou prayest, thou shalt not be as the hypocrites are: for they love to pray standing in the synagogues and in the corners of the streets, that they may be seen of men. Verily I say unto you, They have their reward. But thou, when thou prayest, enter into thy closet, and when thou hast shut thy door, pray to thy Father which is in secret; and thy Father which seeth in secret shall reward thee openly.*
>
> *But when ye pray, use not vain repetitions, as the heathen do: for they think that they shall be heard for their much speaking. Be not ye therefore like unto them: for your Father knoweth what things ye have need of, before ye ask him.*
>
> (Matthew 6:1-8)

God is very generous. Wants and needs are not fixed entities for all of mankind. That which is needed by one person is not necessarily what is needed by another. The separation of, need versus want, is not something that can be done by one person for another, except by those who are given custodial responsibility for the raising of another, such as parents.

One person may need to have good health in order to function and to do what God has assigned for their life. Another person may need poor health in order to move them to the next level in God. In another instance, one person may need to function in total isolation from other humans, while someone else may need to be a part of a community. Some may need to be married, while others need to be single. All our needs will be provided by God, in order to promote the full plan that He has for all creation. When we start to stack up the various potential needs against the various life situations, we see that, indeed it takes God to know how to manage this number of possibilities. God is a being of LARGE numbers. For instance, this number:

> *Hear, O my people, and I will speak; O Israel, and I will testify against thee: I am God, even thy God. I will not reprove thee for thy sacrifices or thy burnt offerings, to have been continually before me. I will take no bullock out of thy house, nor he goats out of thy folds. For every beast of the forest is mine, and the cattle upon a thousand hills. I know all the fowls of the mountains: and the wild beasts of the field are mine.*
>
> (Psalm 50:7-11)

Just thinking about the possible numbers of different humans that can be born on this earth is a large-number observation. In this, we are not just referring to the seven billion humans that were alive, as of this writing. We are referring to the genome's possibility for variation. There are some of us who understand the potential for variation that God has written into the human genome (it is some humongous number of possibilities that would probably take a whole page of zeros to write down, or at least a good part of a page). I am reminded of a statement that God made to Abraham. As you read this, realize the Abraham's household was a small community in the earth. At this time, Egypt and Assyria were far more populous communities.

> *And the angel of the LORD called unto Abraham out of heaven the second time, And said, By myself have I sworn, saith the LORD, for because thou hast done this thing, and hast not withheld thy son, thine only son: That in blessing I will bless thee, and in multiplying I will multiply thy seed as the stars of the heaven, and as the sand which is upon the sea shore; and thy seed shall possess the gate of his enemies; And in thy seed shall all the nations of the earth be blessed; because thou hast obeyed my voice.*
> (Genesis 22:15-18)

By understanding the human genome, we know that the various permutations of needs for each single human being will give us an equally astronomically large number. Something, or Someone, has to control the interplay of all those little genes, in all those little cells—and this must be done continually. This requires the intervention of God. There is none that can stand beside Him in this matter.

Even with the knowledge of the **extremely large** potential of reproduction (human and all other fruitful creations, as well as the cells that are their building blocks); some men still look at the Bible as if it is an owner's manual for the design of every human. As this thought is pushed to the next level, it is often thought good to look at Scripture as if we have ownership rights in it. There are so many stories about man, and about the condition of man, in the Bible. Doesn't this mean that the Bible is exclusively for the management of mankind? Doesn't this mean that it is only for the description of the relationship of men and women to God? Well, not totally.

Yes, the message of God to man, describing the mission of God for mankind, is contained in the Bible. However, it is not limited to the "care and feeding" of mankind. There is so much more that each individual needs to receive from God, in order to complete their life. There is much more that is needed by each person, in order to properly manage the Creation that God has given us. As we look into the Bible, we discover that man, in the person of Adam, was not the first of the things on earth that have communion with God. Let me share with you the first things to have communion with God.

> *And God said, Let the waters bring forth abundantly the moving creature that hath life, and fowl that may fly above the earth in*

the open firmament of heaven. And God created great whales, and every living creature that moveth, which the waters brought forth abundantly, after their kind, and every winged fowl after his kind: and God saw that it was good. And God blessed them, saying, Be fruitful, and multiply, and fill the waters in the seas, and let fowl multiply in the earth.

And the evening and the morning were the fifth day.

(Genesis 1:20-23)

Yes, folks, those poor creatures that are said to have no souls preceded mankind in their link with God. It was after the link was established by God between Himself and the creatures of the sea and air and earth, that mankind was created, and given its link with God.

And God said, Let the earth bring forth the living creature after his kind, cattle, and creeping thing, and beast of the earth after his kind: and it was so. And God made the beast of the earth after his kind, and cattle after their kind, and every thing that creepeth upon the earth after his kind: and God saw that it was good.

And God said, Let us make man in our image, after our likeness: and let them have dominion over the fish of the sea, and over the fowl of the air, and over the cattle, and over all the earth, and over every creeping thing that creepeth upon the earth. So God created man in his own image, in the image of God created he him; male and female created he them.

(Genesis 1:24-27)

And, yes, God did establish a unique type of link for the creatures with mankind.

And God said, Behold, I have given you every herb bearing seed, which is upon the face of all the earth, and every tree, in the which is the fruit of a tree yielding seed; to you it shall be for meat. And to every beast of the earth, and to every fowl of the air, and to every thing that creepeth upon the earth, wherein there is life, I have given every green herb for meat: and it was so.

(Genesis 1:29-30)

And, yes, God did give us a unique part, which He sent from Himself and placed in us. This gave us our eternal link with God; unlike the animals who only have the link with God as long as they remain alive on the earth, or at least that is the inference that can be made from the text of the Bible. (I, however, would not be unhappy if, in the eternity that exists after leaving this life and entering the next, I saw other creatures. I hope you would not be either.)

> *And the LORD God formed man of the dust of the ground, and breathed into his nostrils the breath of life; and man became a living soul.*
>
> (Genesis 2:7)

But none of this gives us exclusive rights to the message of the Bible; nor does any of this mean that we humans are the only concerns of God the Father. We are, as the creatures are, part of the whole Design of God for this portion of His Kingdom, which we call, our reality. The Design is directed toward His glory, not toward our survival; and especially, not toward our prosperity, as we define prosperity. Speaking for a moment from God's perspective, I believe that He would define prosperity as being able to carry out the commission that was given to us at the time of our creation.

> *And God blessed them, and God said unto them, Be fruitful, and multiply, and replenish the earth, and subdue it: and have dominion over the fish of the sea, and over the fowl of the air, and over every living thing that moveth upon the earth.*
>
> (Genesis 1:28)

Please note the word, *dominion*. We are God's custodians: the word, *dominion*, does not transfer ownership. God still owns all that is on the earth. As custodians, we have an obligation to take care of the Owner's belongings. In a discussion about that place of service, Jesus Christ gave us a measure of motivation to move more in the way of proper performance, as he described the kind of care that is given to one type of creature on God's earth.

> *I am the good shepherd: the good shepherd giveth his life for the sheep. But he that is an hireling, and not the shepherd, whose own the sheep are not, seeth the wolf coming, and leaveth the sheep, and fleeth: and the wolf catcheth them, and scattereth the sheep. The hireling fleeth, because he is an hireling, and careth not for the sheep. I am the good shepherd, and know my sheep, and am known of mine. As the Father knoweth me, even so know I the Father: and I lay down my life for the sheep.*
>
> *And other sheep I have, which are not of this fold: them also I must bring, and they shall hear my voice; and there shall be one fold, and one shepherd.*
>
> *Therefore doth my Father love me, because I lay down my life, that I might take it again. No man taketh it from me, but I lay it down of myself. I have power to lay it down, and I have power to take it again. This commandment have I received of my Father.*
>
> (John 10:11-18)

Thus, let me say that all creation is governed by the text of Scripture. Trees grow according to the directive of God. In a similar fashion creatures reproduce based on His directive. The directive for all is to *Be fruitful, and multiply*. The creatures fulfill their directive when they *fill the waters in the seas, and let fowl multiply in the earth*. However, humans have to go one step further. They have to *replenish the earth, and subdue it*. Wherefore humans will only fulfill their directive when they *have dominion over the fish of the sea, and over the fowl of the air, and over the cattle, and over all the earth, and over every creeping thing that creepeth upon the earth*. This is more than just nature conservation and husbandry; even scientific advancement is according to that same directive. This is also how we replenish the earth, and subdue it. Moreover, this is an area in which we must also exercise the vigilance of dominion. Otherwise, misuse can cause problems, as it did here.

> *O Timothy, keep that which is committed to thy trust, avoiding profane and vain babblings, and oppositions of science falsely so called: Which some professing have erred concerning the faith.*
>
> *Grace be with thee. Amen.*
>
> (1 Timothy 6:20-21)

For those who think that I am stretching Scripture beyond its bound and that I am thus taking honor away from man, let me give you two examples. The first example is that of the serpent. You might have heard about the serpent that had a conversation with Eve in the Garden of Eden. But did you think fully about what this revelation from God tells us about the serpent? If not, let me give you some insight about the time before their meeting in the garden.

In thinking about the time before the serpent communicated with Eve, consider this: the serpent came to Eve with more information than Eve had about the trees in the Garden. This serpent came to Eve with more information about the Design of God than Eve knew before she met the serpent. Have you ever wondered how the serpent had all this information? I did, and I was given some interesting, at least to me, insights.

The only way the serpent could have known this about the trees in the garden is if he had either been told it directly by God, or if he was just plain paying attention when God created the trees in the Garden. Third choice: the serpent was located in the area where this directive was pronounced.

> *And the LORD God took the man, and put him into the garden of Eden to dress it and to keep it. And the LORD God commanded the man, saying, Of every tree of the garden thou mayest freely eat: But of the tree of the knowledge of good and evil, thou shalt not eat of it: for in the day that thou eatest thereof thou shalt surely die.*
> (Genesis 2:15-17)

However, even if the serpent was lingering around the place of the directive, it still had to obtain other information about the capability of at least one of the trees. For without added information, the serpent could not have revealed this that was later proved true, in part.

> *And the serpent said unto the woman, Ye shall not surely die: For God doth know that in the day ye eat thereof, then your eyes shall be opened, and ye shall be as gods, knowing good and evil.*
> (Genesis 3:4-5)

However, if you look at the chronology of the equipping of the Garden of Eden, it is most likely that the serpent was created some time after Adam. Therefore, it seems that the serpent could not have been eavesdropping on any conversation which God may have had when the trees were being created. Remember, the trees were placed in the Garden before Adam was.

Now, I can imagine God telling the serpent about the trees, Personally; but, outside of my imagination, that does not seem to be too likely. I can, however, see where he told all the animals about the trees, and also told them to stay away from those special ones. To this day, certain creatures know that they must avoid certain trees, in order for them to stay alive and well. Humans know this too, about such things as poison ivy (though, not as widely about deadly mushrooms, growing in the wild). And the serpent, it seems, did just what God told him to do: he stayed away from eating of those trees.

However, the serpent had a special attribute that it had been given when it was created. This is described at the beginning of the account of the conversation with Eve.

> *Now the serpent was more subtle than any beast of the field which the LORD God had made. And he said unto the woman, Yea, hath God said, Ye shall not eat of every tree of the garden?*
> (Genesis 3:1)

But the serpent must not have held to the notion that mankind was the center of the universe. It must have felt that the being, known as mankind, was kind of deficient in that stuff known as the knowledge of good and evil. Did the serpent understand what good and evil is? I do not believe that, on this side of life, we will know the answer to that question. However, the serpent did know what the knowledge of good and evil is useful for. And it knew that God knew what the knowledge of good and evil would do. The serpent accurately quoted the state of affairs that would happen once the knowledge was acquired—well, almost. Yes, I know that you read this before, but it seems appropriate to repeat it here.

> *And the serpent said unto the woman, Ye shall not surely die: For God doth know that in the day ye eat thereof, then your eyes shall be opened, and ye shall be as gods, knowing good and evil.*
> (Genesis 3:4-5)

The serpent was not such a dumb creature after all, was it? Furthermore, the serpent was not a creature that was without cognizance of the God of the universe, and the worth of being like the LORD. Even so, the serpent also knew that there was no one who could be equal to God (he only referred to being as gods, not equal to God). It seems that this serpent knew some serious theology. This is a very potent link with the knowledge of the Creator. Yes, yes, I hear the voice saying, "But the serpent was Satan, or at least he was filled with Satan." This point I will not dispute, but I will note that the words came from the serpent.

Furthermore, there is another example of animal wisdom that cannot be linked with Satan. This example was designed to save a man's life. It is also recorded in the Bible. It was introduced at the start of the chapter, where we recounted the encounter between Balaam and the angel; with the creature in a supporting role. Read on to see the conclusion.

> *And the LORD opened the mouth of the ass, and she said unto Balaam, What have I done unto thee, that thou hast smitten me these three times?*
>
> *And Balaam said unto the ass, Because thou hast mocked me: I would there were a sword in mine hand, for now would I kill thee.*
>
> *And the ass said unto Balaam, Am not I thine ass, upon which thou hast ridden ever since I was thine unto this day? was I ever wont to do so unto thee?*
>
> *And he said, Nay.*
>
> *Then the LORD opened the eyes of Balaam, and he saw the angel of the LORD standing in the way, and his sword drawn in his hand: and he bowed down his head, and fell flat on his face.*
>
> *And the angel of the LORD said unto him, Wherefore hast thou smitten thine ass these three times? behold, I went out to withstand thee, because thy way is perverse before me: And the ass saw me, and turned from me these three times: unless she had turned from me, surely now also I had slain thee, and saved her alive.*
>
> (Numbers 22:28-33)

In this encounter we are given an expanded understanding of the purpose of God in creating the creatures. We could go on to list the passages that tell us of the creatures who came out, and did the works of God. Okay, we will share one more. One other such example is found with the prophet Elisha. There were some children who . . . Well, why don't I let you read it for yourself? (I warn you in advance that you might not like the outcome of this encounter by mankind and the creatures of God; however, it is still a message that includes creatures working according to God's requirement for mankind.)

> *And the men of the city said unto Elisha, Behold, I pray thee, the situation of this city is pleasant, as my lord seeth: but the water is nought, and the ground barren.*
>
> *And he said, Bring me a new cruse, and put salt therein.*
>
> *And they brought it to him.*
>
> *And he went forth unto the spring of the waters, and cast the salt in there, and said, Thus saith the LORD, I have healed these waters; there shall not be from thence any more death or barren land.*
>
> *So the waters were healed unto this day, according to the saying of Elisha which he spake.*
>
> *And he went up from thence unto Bethel: and as he was going up by the way, there came forth little children out of the city, and mocked him, and said unto him, Go up, thou bald head; go up, thou bald head.*
>
> *And he turned back, and looked on them, and cursed them in the name of the LORD. And there came forth two she bears out of the wood, and tare forty and two children of them.*
>
> (2 Kings 2:19-24)

To summarize: the Bible is not just an owner's manual for the human condition. It is the part of the Design of God, for all existence. The Design extends far beyond the part that the LORD has revealed to us in the Bible. No, the Bible is not the total blueprint of man's development; it is only part of it. Furthermore, the blueprint is only part of the Design. Therefore, no matter how noble is the way we wish to apply Scripture; its message cannot be limited to match only our *needs*. There is so much more that I could write about this, but I pray that God has given you enlightenment by what you have read.

Please; treat Scripture, and especially the message of the Gospel of Jesus Christ, which is a part of it, with the reverence that it deserves. And equally as important as that; let us honor the great gift of God given to us, in the Holy Ghost. This gift will take us beyond the limited amount of information that we have in the Bible: it will not replace the Bible. It will augment the Bible. Do not think that the warning about adding to the Bible applies to the Holy Ghost: it does not. This is the purpose of the Holy Ghost. It is the gift that, as they say, keeps on giving. Our part in the matter is this:

> *I charge thee therefore before God, and the Lord Jesus Christ, who shall judge the quick and the dead at his appearing and his kingdom; Preach the word; be instant in season, out of season; reprove, rebuke, exhort with all longsuffering and doctrine.*
>
> *For the time will come when they will not endure sound doctrine; but after their own lusts shall they heap to themselves teachers, having itching ears; And they shall turn away their ears from the truth, and shall be turned unto fables.*
>
> (2 Timothy 4:1-4)

Please, do not look to the Bible to fit into your mold of reality; rather, let it fit you into the mold of God's purpose for your life. Then, you will be able to seal these words of the apostle Paul into your life, as well.

> *But watch thou in all things, endure afflictions, do the work of an evangelist, make full proof of thy ministry. For I am now ready to be offered, and the time of my departure is at hand. I have fought a good fight, I have finished my course, I have kept the faith: Henceforth there is laid up for me a crown of righteousness, which the Lord, the righteous judge, shall give me at that day: and not to me only, but unto all them also that love his appearing.*
>
> (2 Timothy 4:5-8)

The Word from the Bible

Acts 17:22-31

Then Paul stood in the midst of Mars' hill, and said, Ye men of Athens, I perceive that in all things ye are too superstitious. For as I passed by, and beheld your devotions, I found an altar with this inscription, TO THE UNKNOWN GOD. Whom therefore ye ignorantly worship, him declare I unto you.

God that made the world and all things therein, seeing that he is Lord of heaven and earth, dwelleth not in temples made with hands; Neither is worshipped with men's hands, as though he needed any thing, seeing he giveth to all life, and breath, and all things; And hath made of one blood all nations of men for to dwell on all the face of the earth, and hath determined the times before appointed, and the bounds of their habitation; That they should seek the Lord, if haply they might feel after him, and find him, though he be not far from every one of us: For in him we live, and move, and have our being; as certain also of your own poets have said, For we are also his offspring.

Forasmuch then as we are the offspring of God, we ought not to think that the Godhead is like unto gold, or silver, or stone, graven by art and man's device. And the times of this ignorance God winked at; but now commandeth all men every where to repent: Because he hath appointed a day, in the which he will judge the world in righteousness by that man whom he hath ordained; whereof he hath given assurance unto all men, in that he hath raised him from the dead.

Romans 1:16-23

For I am not ashamed of the gospel of Christ: for it is the power of God unto salvation to every one that believeth; to the Jew first, and also to the Greek. For therein is the righteousness of God revealed from faith to faith: as it is written, The just shall live by faith.

For the wrath of God is revealed from heaven against all ungodliness and unrighteousness of men, who hold the truth in unrighteousness; Because that which may be known of God is manifest in them; for God hath showed it unto them. For the invisible things of him from the creation of the world are clearly seen, being understood by the things that are made, even his eternal power and Godhead; so that they are without excuse: Because that, when they knew God, they glorified him not as God, neither were thankful; but became vain in their imaginations, and their foolish heart was darkened. Professing themselves to be wise, they became fools, And changed the glory of the uncorruptible God into an image made like to corruptible man, and to birds, and fourfooted beasts, and creeping things.

Isaiah 9:2-10

The people that walked in darkness have seen a great light: they that dwell in the land of the shadow of death, upon them hath the light shined. Thou hast multiplied the nation, and not increased the joy: they joy before thee according to the joy in harvest, and as men rejoice when they divide the spoil. For thou hast broken the yoke of his burden, and the staff of his shoulder, the rod of his oppressor, as in the day of Midian. For every battle of the warrior is with confused noise, and garments rolled in blood; but this shall be with burning and fuel of fire.

For unto us a child is born, unto us a son is given: and the government shall be upon his shoulder: and his name shall be called Wonderful, Counsellor, The mighty God, The everlasting Father, The Prince of Peace. Of the increase of his government and peace there shall be no end, upon the throne of David, and upon his kingdom, to order it, and to establish it with judgment and with justice from henceforth even for ever. The zeal of the LORD of hosts will perform this.

The Lord sent a word into Jacob, and it hath lighted upon Israel. And all the people shall know, even Ephraim and the inhabitant of Samaria, that say in the pride and stoutness of heart, The bricks are fallen down, but we will build with hewn stones: the sycamores are cut down, but we will change them into cedars.

CHAPTER FIVE

Revelation

Clearing the way

John the Revelator delivered the message of Jesus Christ, in the book of Revelation, a long time ago. There is a portion of the book that is a part of John's history. This was included in the book to provide, for the reader, a perspective on what was to follow. Revelation also contains an account of the activities that went on in Heaven, to prepare, not just the earth, but also Heaven itself for the Kingdom of God in Christ Jesus. Key among these events is the birth, death and resurrection of Jesus of Nazareth. Satan tried to prevent the ministry of Christ from continuing. In this effort, Satan tried to affect reality in Heaven, as well as the flow of life on earth.

> *And there appeared a great wonder in heaven; a woman clothed with the sun, and the moon under her feet, and upon her head a crown of twelve stars: And she being with child cried, travailing in birth, and pained to be delivered.*
>
> *And there appeared another wonder in heaven; and behold a great red dragon, having seven heads and ten horns, and seven crowns upon his heads. And his tail drew the third part of the stars of heaven, and did cast them to the earth: and the dragon stood before the woman which was ready to be delivered, for to devour her child as soon as it was born. And she brought forth a man child, who was to rule all nations with a rod of iron: and her child was caught up unto God, and to his throne.*
>
> (Revelation 12:1-5)

Satan did not try to cause the woman to experience an abortion, because he knew that the child that was begotten is the Son of God. Therefore, Satan, not being stupid, did not want to get in the way of God's wrath against him, at that time. It is kind of like the demons who asked Jesus to allow them some relief.

> *And when he was come to the other side into the country of the Gergesenes, there met him two possessed with devils, coming out of the tombs, exceeding fierce, so that no man might pass by that way. And, behold, they cried out, saying, What have we to do with thee, Jesus, thou Son of God? art thou come hither to torment us before the time?*
>
> *And there was a good way off from them an herd of many swine feeding. So the devils besought him, saying, If thou cast us out, suffer us to go away into the herd of swine.*
>
> *And he said unto them, Go.*
>
> *And when they were come out, they went into the herd of swine: and, behold, the whole herd of swine ran violently down a steep place into the sea, and perished in the waters.*
>
> (Matthew 8:28-32)

Satan knows at least as much as all the demons in his domain. Actually, I am sure that he knows much more than they do. Therefore, he knew that the child would be born. The only thing left for him to do was to try to destroy the child once it was born. But in this attempt, he failed. This is the same failure that he experienced when he set out to tempt Jesus.

- As summarized in the gospel of Mark:

> *And it came to pass in those days, that Jesus came from Nazareth of Galilee, and was baptized of John in Jordan. And straightway coming up out of the water, he saw the heavens opened, and the Spirit like a dove descending upon him: And there came a voice*

from heaven, saying, Thou art my beloved Son, in whom I am well pleased.

And immediately the spirit driveth him into the wilderness. And he was there in the wilderness forty days, tempted of Satan; and was with the wild beasts; and the angels ministered unto him.

(Mark 1:9-13)

- As shared in its fullness in the gospel of Matthew:

Then was Jesus led up of the spirit into the wilderness to be tempted of the devil. And when he had fasted forty days and forty nights, he was afterward an hungred.

And when the tempter came to him, he said, If thou be the Son of God, command that these stones be made bread.

But he answered and said, It is written, Man shall not live by bread alone, but by every word that proceedeth out of the mouth of God.

Then the devil taketh him up into the holy city, and setteth him on a pinnacle of the temple, And saith unto him, If thou be the Son of God, cast thyself down: for it is written, He shall give his angels charge concerning thee: and in their hands they shall bear thee up, lest at any time thou dash thy foot against a stone.

Jesus said unto him, It is written again, Thou shalt not tempt the Lord thy God.

Again, the devil taketh him up into an exceeding high mountain, and sheweth him all the kingdoms of the world, and the glory of them; And saith unto him, All these things will I give thee, if thou wilt fall down and worship me.

Then saith Jesus unto him, Get thee hence, Satan: for it is written, Thou shalt worship the Lord thy God, and him only shalt thou serve.

Then the devil leaveth him, and, behold, angels came and ministered unto him.

(Matthew 4:1-11)

- As confirmed by the gospel of Luke:

And Jesus being full of the Holy Ghost returned from Jordan, and was led by the Spirit into the wilderness, Being forty days tempted of the devil. And in those days he did eat nothing: and when they were ended, he afterward hungered.

And the devil said unto him, If thou be the Son of God, command this stone that it be made bread.

And Jesus answered him, saying, It is written, That man shall not live by bread alone, but by every word of God.

And the devil, taking him up into an high mountain, shewed unto him all the kingdoms of the world in a moment of time. And the devil said unto him, All this power will I give thee, and the glory of them: for that is delivered unto me; and to whomsoever I will I give it. If thou therefore wilt worship me, all shall be thine.

And Jesus answered and said unto him, Get thee behind me, Satan: for it is written, Thou shalt worship the Lord thy God, and him only shalt thou serve.

And he brought him to Jerusalem, and set him on a pinnacle of the temple, and said unto him, If thou be the Son of God, cast thyself down from hence: For it is written, He shall give his angels charge over thee, to keep thee: And in their hands they shall bear thee up, lest at any time thou dash thy foot against a stone.

And Jesus answering said unto him, It is said, Thou shalt not tempt the Lord thy God.

And when the devil had ended all the temptation, he departed from him for a season.

(Luke 4:1-13)

As Jesus had dismissed Satan from his presence on earth; so, too, in Heaven, Satan was evicted from God's presence. Then, with the eviction of Satan from Heaven, we have a shift in the writings of John the Revelator. At the shift, John tells us of the events that happened in the earth at the time of the destruction of Jerusalem. This ends with the prophetic statement of the sickle.

> *And the angel thrust in his sickle into the earth, and gathered the vine of the earth, and cast it into the great winepress of the wrath of God. And the winepress was trodden without the city, and blood came out of the winepress, even unto the horse bridles, by the space of a thousand and six hundred furlongs.*
>
> (Revelation 14:19-20)

Afterward, God continued the cleanup process. Those who had taken an adversarial position against God the Father, and against His Christ, were the next in line for judgment. Besides Israel, there was another nation that had to be chastised for its defiance of God.

> *And the seventh angel poured out his vial into the air; and there came a great voice out of the temple of heaven, from the throne, saying, It is done. And there were voices, and thunders, and lightnings; and there was a great earthquake, such as was not since men were upon the earth, so mighty an earthquake, and so great. And the great city was divided into three parts, and the cities of the nations fell: and great Babylon came in remembrance before God, to give unto her the cup of the wine of the fierceness of his wrath.*
>
> (Revelation 16:17-19)

In due time, retribution was delivered, by the will of God, to those who were walking in the way of the beast.

> *And every island fled away, and the mountains were not found. And there fell upon men a great hail out of heaven, every stone about the weight of a talent: and men blasphemed God because of the plague of the hail; for the plague thereof was exceeding great.*
>
> (Revelation 16:20-21)

This is the area where there is much delusion, among many; even among those who are in the ranks of the Christians. To clear up this delusion, we have to return to some simple grammatical rules. When a phrase talks in the present tense, it is referring to an event that is happening now. When a phrase is framed in the past tense, it is referring to an event, or to events, that have already passed. With this in mind, please read the following (the **highlighting** in it is mine, not John's).

> *And there came one of the seven angels which had the seven vials, and talked with me, saying unto me, Come hither; I will show unto thee the judgment of the great whore that sitteth upon many waters: With whom the kings of the earth* ***have committed*** *fornication, and the inhabitants of the earth have been made drunk with the wine of her fornication.*
>
> (Revelation 17:1-2)

Revelation 17:2 points us to a location that existed on the earth in the time of John the Revelator. There is no prior statement that this is a future *great whore*. There is, however, ample information to let us know that the *great whore* is a nation or an empire. If it were a prophecy for the future, the correct grammatical phrase would be "will have committed", or an equivalent expression denoting a future occurrence. It does not denote a future occurrence; rather, it is history that occurred in John's past, and that may be continuing into John's future. At the time of Jesus' Revelation and John's writing of it, there is no indication that the *fornication* has stopped.

The angel goes on to describe the beast that carries the nation. The beast is the support for the harlot, and the transport for its functions. Specifically, the beast spans *seven mountains.*

> *So he carried me away in the spirit into the wilderness: and I saw a woman sit upon a scarlet coloured beast, full of names of blasphemy, having seven heads and ten horns. And the woman was arrayed in purple and scarlet colour, and decked with gold and precious stones and pearls, having a golden cup in her hand full of abominations and filthiness of her fornication: And upon her forehead was a name written, MYSTERY, BABYLON THE GREAT, THE MOTHER OF HARLOTS AND ABOMINATIONS OF THE*

EARTH. And I saw the woman drunken with the blood of the saints, and with the blood of the martyrs of Jesus: and when I saw her, I wondered with great admiration.

And the angel said unto me, Wherefore didst thou marvel? I will tell thee the mystery of the woman, and of the beast that carrieth her, which hath the seven heads and ten horns.

The beast that thou sawest was, and is not; and shall ascend out of the bottomless pit, and go into perdition: and they that dwell on the earth shall wonder, whose names were not written in the book of life from the foundation of the world, when they behold the beast that was, and is not, and yet is.

And here is the mind which hath wisdom. The seven heads are seven mountains, on which the woman sitteth.

(Revelation 17:3-9)

I include the following for your later use. Please, for now, just store this in memory: or you can make the obvious attachment with the above, right now, if you are so inclined.

The Seven Hills of Rome

Of Early Rome:	***Of Later Rome:***
Cermalus	Aventinus (Aventine)
Cispius	Caelius (Caelian)
Fagutal	Capitolium (Capitoline)
Oppius	Esquiliae (Esquiline)
Palatium	Palatium (Palatine)
Sucusa	Quirinalis (Quirinal)
Velia	Viminalis (Viminal)

We will not string this out, as a mystery. The evidence of the prophecy points to the destruction of the Roman Empire. At the time of the receipt of the Revelation by John, this empire is in existence. It was the center of much commerce. All nations did do business with it. And it had seven mountains, which were at the center of the empire. This leads us to say that the authority, and practices, of the, then, Roman Empire is *the great whore* as described in Revelation 17:1-2. This would also fit well with prophecy of Daniel.

In Daniel's prophecy, he is told of an empire that would be the one in existence at the time of the establishment of the Kingdom of God on the earth.

> *After this I saw in the night visions, and behold a fourth beast, dreadful and terrible, and strong exceedingly; and it had great iron teeth: it devoured and brake in pieces, and stamped the residue with the feet of it: and it was diverse from all the beasts that were before it; and it had ten horns*
>
> (Daniel 7:7)

> *And in the days of these kings shall the God of heaven set up a kingdom, which shall never be destroyed: and the kingdom shall not be left to other people, but it shall break in pieces and consume all these kingdoms, and it shall stand for ever.*
>
> (Daniel 2:44)

This is the sort of warfare that was going on in the time of John the Revelator. There are, too, other passages that are even more specific about placing the Greek and Roman Empire in the action that would occur in the time of the replacement—or end—of that world order. Therefore, since the Roman Empire is identified as the earthly kingdom that is to be destroyed; then, this is the era of the establishment of the eternal Kingdom of God among men. This was quietly introduced into the world of that day, to Daniel, first, and then passed on to us, in Daniel 2:44. This was broadcast at the death of Jesus Christ. Recall, if you will, the conversation between Jesus and the thief, as they hung on their crosses.

> *And one of the malefactors which were hanged railed on him, saying, If thou be Christ, save thyself and us.*

> *But the other answering rebuked him, saying, Dost not thou fear God, seeing thou art in the same condemnation? And we indeed justly; for we receive the due reward of our deeds: but this man hath done nothing amiss.*

And he said unto Jesus, Lord, remember me when thou comest into thy kingdom.

And Jesus said unto him, Verily I say unto thee, To day shalt thou be with me in paradise.

(Luke 23:39-43)

Jesus Christ, by answering the repentant thief's request, stated, for us, where his kingdom is. The thief asked Jesus, the *Lord*, to remember him when Jesus came into his kingdom. Jesus then stated, by implication, that his kingdom is paradise. For further understanding, let us look at the Scripture where Jesus describes the nature of his kingdom.

Jesus answered, My kingdom is not of this world: if my kingdom were of this world, then would my servants fight, that I should not be delivered to the Jews: but now is my kingdom not from hence.

Pilate therefore said unto him, Art thou a king then?

Jesus answered, Thou sayest that I am a king. To this end was I born, and for this cause came I into the world, that I should bear witness unto the truth. Every one that is of the truth heareth my voice.

(John 18:36-37)

Look back, with me, at the transformation that God accomplished in paradise. And also remember that the Garden of Eden is where the tree of life still sits, to this day—at least, there is no Scripture that indicates that God moved it from there.

And the LORD God said, Behold, the man is become as one of us, to know good and evil: and now, lest he put forth his hand, and take also of the tree of life, and eat, and live for ever: Therefore the LORD God sent him forth from the garden of Eden, to till the ground from whence he was taken. So he drove out the man; and he placed at the east of the garden of Eden Cherubims, and a flaming sword which turned every way, to keep the way of the tree of life.

(Genesis 3:22-24)

By this action, it seems apparent that God removed the Garden of Eden from ownership by, and availability to, this physical world; whereby He made it exclusively His own. And since the Garden of Eden was made a part of God's exclusive things, it is also a part of the things of the Son of God: *thine are mine.*

> *And now, O Father, glorify thou me with thine own self with the glory which I had with thee before the world was. I have manifested thy name unto the men which thou gavest me out of the world: thine they were, and thou gavest them me; and they have kept thy word. Now they have known that all things whatsoever thou hast given me are of thee. For I have given unto them the words which thou gavest me; and they have received them, and have known surely that I came out from thee, and they have believed that thou didst send me.*
>
> *I pray for them: I pray not for the world, but for them which thou hast given me; for they are thine. And all mine are thine, and thine are mine; and I am glorified in them.*
>
> (John 17:5-10)

And finally; the kingdom of God in Christ Jesus is an everlasting kingdom. Please turn your attention to the following two portions of Scripture, so *that in the mouth of two or three witnesses every word may be established.* First, according to the prophecy revealed to Daniel, from God: *an everlasting kingdom.*

> *I beheld, and the same horn made war with the saints, and prevailed against them; Until the Ancient of days came, and judgment was given to the saints of the most High; and the time came that the saints possessed the kingdom.*

> *Thus he said, The fourth beast shall be the fourth kingdom upon earth, which shall be diverse from all kingdoms, and shall devour the whole earth, and shall tread it down, and break it in pieces. And the ten horns out of this kingdom are ten kings that shall arise: and another shall rise after them; and he shall be diverse from the first, and he shall subdue three kings. And he shall speak great words against the most High, and shall wear out the saints of*

> *the most High, and think to change times and laws: and they shall be given into his hand until a time and times and the dividing of time.*
>
> *But the judgment shall sit, and they shall take away his dominion, to consume and to destroy it unto the end. And the kingdom and dominion, and the greatness of the kingdom under the whole heaven, shall be given to the people of the saints of the most High, whose kingdom is an everlasting kingdom, and all dominions shall serve and obey him.*
>
> (Daniel 7:21-27)

Second, as recorded in the Gospel, that was given, by God, to the apostle Peter: *everlasting kingdom of our Lord and Saviour Jesus Christ.*

> *Grace and peace be multiplied unto you through the knowledge of God, and of Jesus our Lord, According as his divine power hath given unto us all things that pertain unto life and godliness, through the knowledge of him that hath called us to glory and virtue: Whereby are given unto us exceeding great and precious promises: that by these ye might be partakers of the divine nature, having escaped the corruption that is in the world through lust.*
>
> *And beside this, giving all diligence, add to your faith virtue; and to virtue knowledge; And to knowledge temperance; and to temperance patience; and to patience godliness; And to godliness brotherly kindness; and to brotherly kindness charity. For if these things be in you, and abound, they make you that ye shall neither be barren nor unfruitful in the knowledge of our Lord Jesus Christ. But he that lacketh these things is blind, and cannot see afar off, and hath forgotten that he was purged from his old sins.*
>
> *Wherefore the rather, brethren, give diligence to make your calling and election sure: for if ye do these things, ye shall never fall: For so an entrance shall be ministered unto you abundantly into the everlasting kingdom of our Lord and Saviour Jesus Christ.*
>
> (2 Peter 1:2-11)

We will pause at this point in clearing the way. Our purpose was to isolate, for understanding, those parts of the Revelation of John that had been done or that were a continuation of things already started. When we continue, we will explore those things that remained to be done after the time of the writing of the book of Revelation. Some of these may be events that would not occur until after the death of the Revelator. When we resume, we will continue with Revelation 17:10.

Before we pause, however, we will provide some more foundational support for where we will begin anew. To prepare you for what is to come in a later portion of this work, we begin with these words of the Psalmist.

> *A Psalm of David.*
>
> *The LORD said unto my Lord, Sit thou at my right hand, until I make thine enemies thy footstool.*
>
> *The LORD shall send the rod of thy strength out of Zion: rule thou in the midst of thine enemies. Thy people shall be willing in the day of thy power, in the beauties of holiness from the womb of the morning: thou hast the dew of thy youth. The LORD hath sworn, and will not repent, Thou art a priest for ever after the order of Melchizedek.*
>
> *The Lord at thy right hand shall strike through kings in the day of his wrath. He shall judge among the heathen, he shall fill the places with the dead bodies; he shall wound the heads over many countries. He shall drink of the brook in the way: therefore shall he lift up the head.*
>
> (Psalm 110:1-7)

The Scripture in Psalm 110:1-7 is being fulfilled in the day of John, by events in the Roman Empire. Originally, the citizens of Rome were just ignorant bystanders. Originally, Rome did not understand the things that were going on with the Messiah. One of their officials, Pilate, gave us a look at their ignorance, relative to this matter.

> *Then Pilate entered into the judgment hall again, and called Jesus, and said unto him, Art thou the King of the Jews?*
>
> *Jesus answered him, Sayest thou this thing of thyself, or did others tell it thee of me?*

> *Pilate answered, Am I a Jew? Thine own nation and the chief priests have delivered thee unto me: what hast thou done?*
>
> (John 18:33-35)

But later, there are certain folks that received, what is called, the Great Commission: *Go ye into all the world.*

> *Afterward he appeared unto the eleven as they sat at meat, and upbraided them with their unbelief and hardness of heart, because they believed not them which had seen him after he was risen. And he said unto them, Go ye into all the world, and preach the gospel to every creature. He that believeth and is baptized shall be saved; but he that believeth not shall be damned.*
>
> (Mark 16:14-16)

The people elected to perform the Commission were so fired up for the Lord that it was, over the course of time and in that day, possible for them to reach the entire world. This was declared by the apostle Paul.

> *For whosoever shall call upon the name of the Lord shall be saved.*
>
> *How then shall they call on him in whom they have not believed? and how shall they believe in him of whom they have not heard? and how shall they hear without a preacher? And how shall they preach, except they be sent? as it is written, How beautiful are the feet of them that preach the gospel of peace, and bring glad tidings of good things! But they have not all obeyed the gospel. For Esaias saith, Lord, who hath believed our report? So then faith cometh by hearing, and hearing by the word of God.*
>
> *But I say, Have they not heard? Yes verily, their sound went into all the earth, and their words unto the ends of the world.*
>
> (Romans 10:13-18)

During this time in our history, it was much easier to spread the Gospel to the world than it would have been if God had waited until now. This is true because, during this time all nations had commerce with the Roman Empire. As one thinks about it, further: commerce was not the only thing that Rome shared with the world; Rome also shared information. Knowing this—of course He does—God directed the apostle Paul to go directly to the source of all information for the world. This is how that happened. Please note the LORD'S Hand moving in the disposition of Paul to send him to the Gentiles, in that even his judges had to say, *if he had not appealed unto Caesar.*

> *And as he thus spake for himself, Festus said with a loud voice, Paul, thou art beside thyself; much learning doth make thee mad.*
>
> *But he said, I am not mad, most noble Festus; but speak forth the words of truth and soberness. For the king knoweth of these things, before whom also I speak freely: for I am persuaded that none of these things are hidden from him; for this thing was not done in a corner.*
>
> *King Agrippa, believest thou the prophets? I know that thou believest.*
>
> *Then Agrippa said unto Paul, Almost thou persuadest me to be a Christian.*
>
> *And Paul said, I would to God, that not only thou, but also all that hear me this day, were both almost, and altogether such as I am, except these bonds.*
>
> *And when he had thus spoken, the king rose up, and the governor, and Bernice, and they that sat with them: And when they were gone aside, they talked between themselves, saying, This man doeth nothing worthy of death or of bonds.*
>
> *Then said Agrippa unto Festus, This man might have been set at liberty, if he had not appealed unto Caesar.*
>
> (Acts 26:24-32)

Let us take a brief detour here, and look at the extensive resources that the LORD brought to bear in Paul for the spread of the Gospel to the Gentiles. These are just the first of the resources that were made available for the spread of the Gospel through the apostle Paul, as marshaled by the command of the chief captain.

And he called unto him two centurions, saying, Make ready two hundred soldiers to go to Caesarea, and horsemen threescore and ten, and spearmen two hundred, at the third hour of the night; And provide them beasts, that they may set Paul on, and bring him safe unto Felix the governor.

And he wrote a letter after this manner:
Claudius Lysias unto the most excellent governor Felix sendeth greeting. This man was taken of the Jews, and should have been killed of them: then came I with an army, and rescued him, having understood that he was a Roman. And when I would have known the cause wherefore they accused him, I brought him forth into their council: Whom I perceived to be accused of questions of their law, but to have nothing laid to his charge worthy of death or of bonds. And when it was told me how that the Jews laid wait for the man, I sent straightway to thee, and gave commandment to his accusers also to say before thee what they had against him. Farewell.

Then the soldiers, as it was commanded them, took Paul, and brought him by night to Antipatris. On the morrow they left the horsemen to go with him, and returned to the castle: Who, when they came to Caesarea, and delivered the epistle to the governor, presented Paul also before him.

(Acts 23:23-33)

Through the record of the Bible, we know of Paul's travel in the world, to spread the Gospel to the Gentiles; travel that was extensive, comprehensive for him and the Gentiles, and exhaustive for both, as well. This means that the message of the Gospel was being spread throughout the world, with the unintended help of Rome. That is to say, it was unintended by Rome, but not unintended by God. Paul's extensive travel was a key part of the ordinance of God for the redemption of the world, to Himself. It was all part of God's will for mankind.

Then Paul and Barnabas waxed bold, and said, It was necessary that the word of God should first have been spoken to you: but seeing ye put it from you, and judge yourselves unworthy of everlasting life, lo, we turn to the Gentiles. For so hath the Lord commanded

> *us, saying, I have set thee to be a light of the Gentiles, that thou shouldest be for salvation unto the ends of the earth.*
>
> *And when the Gentiles heard this, they were glad, and glorified the word of the Lord: and as many as were ordained to eternal life believed. And the word of the Lord was published throughout all the region.*
>
> (Acts 13:46-49)

Now, we must admit that the Gospel was not being spread in the fashion that we, today, would have liked it to be spread. In that day, it was not being spread by the delicate things of quiet church service. On the contrary, in that day, the Gospel was being spread by every act of persecution, every public execution, every treatise issued against worship, and by all the things that Rome did to suppress the spread of the gospel of Jesus Christ. God was mightily using the harlot and the beast to spread His message to the world. And in this regard, God is absolutely successful, as His glory shines even over the noise of the slander and persecution of His servants, among which Paul is one.

> *But I would ye should understand, brethren, that the things which happened unto me have fallen out rather unto the furtherance of the gospel; So that my bonds in Christ are manifest in all the palace, and in all other places; And many of the brethren in the Lord, waxing confident by my bonds, are much more bold to speak the word without fear.*
>
> *Some indeed preach Christ even of envy and strife; and some also of good will: The one preach Christ of contention, not sincerely, supposing to add affliction to my bonds: But the other of love, knowing that I am set for the defence of the gospel. What then? notwithstanding, every way, whether in pretence, or in truth, Christ is preached; and I therein do rejoice, yea, and will rejoice. For I know that this shall turn to my salvation through your prayer, and the supply of the Spirit of Jesus Christ, According to my earnest expectation and my hope, that in nothing I shall be ashamed, but that with all boldness, as always, so now also Christ shall be magnified in my body, whether it be by life, or by death. For to me to live is Christ, and to die is gain.*
>
> (Philippians 1:12-21)

Therefore, once the world knew of the Gospel, and, especially, the authority behind, and the practices of, the Roman Empire; it was obvious to al mankind that Rome had joined the ranks of the enemies of Christ. Jesus Christ described how the transformation is made from innocent bystander to the state of being an active adversarial participant.

> *If I had not come and spoken unto them, they had not had sin: but now they have no cloak for their sin. He that hateth me hateth my Father also.*
>
> *If I had not done among them the works which none other man did, they had not had sin: but now have they both seen and hated both me and my Father.*
>
> (John 15:22-24)

By a very simple statement, the leaders of Israel had already established their place as being in the enemy camp: *His blood be on us, and on our children.*

> *The governor answered and said unto them, Whether of the twain will ye that I release unto you?*
>
> *They said, Barabbas.*
>
> *Pilate saith unto them, What shall I do then with Jesus which is called Christ?*
>
> *They all say unto him, Let him be crucified.*
>
> *And the governor said, Why, what evil hath he done?*
>
> *But they cried out the more, saying, Let him be crucified.*
>
> *When Pilate saw that he could prevail nothing, but that rather a tumult was made, he took water, and washed his hands before the multitude, saying, I am innocent of the blood of this just person: see ye to it.*
>
> *Then answered all the people, and said, His blood be on us, and on our children.*
>
> (Matthew 27:21-25)

We know what God had prepared for the nation of Israel, and what the Father did set against them. The rebellious Israel took its place as a portion of the footstool referred to in Psalm 110:1, which was referenced above. It is now consistent with God's promise to His Son that He made the Roman Empire, and its offshoot, a part of the footstool of His Son. When we continue, we will search for the judgment that either has been issued against the Roman Empire, or that is prepared to be issued on this newly identified enemy of Christ Jesus the Lord, who is, too, the Son of God. And why do we say that they are his new enemies. We'll let the Scripture give you the answer.

> *Then shall he say also unto them on the left hand, Depart from me, ye cursed, into everlasting fire, prepared for the devil and his angels: For I was an hungred, and ye gave me no meat: I was thirsty, and ye gave me no drink: I was a stranger, and ye took me not in: naked, and ye clothed me not: sick, and in prison, and ye visited me not.*
>
> *Then shall they also answer him, saying, Lord, when saw we thee an hungred, or athirst, or a stranger, or naked, or sick, or in prison, and did not minister unto thee?*
>
> *Then shall he answer them, saying, Verily I say unto you, Inasmuch as ye did it not to one of the least of these, ye did it not to me.*
>
> *And these shall go away into everlasting punishment: but the righteous into life eternal.*
>
> (Matthew 25:41-46)

Many thing happen,
From day to day;
Things God sends
To point the way

To a message that is
Most holy and divine;
Revealing, to us,
Our destined line.

This is the line set
To show us, quite clear,
The mission that our
Soul must bear;

With places to see,
And what we must be,
So that we can, now,
His way clearly see.

This is that which was
In prophecy, concealed
As future pointers,
In its time revealed;

Showing actions of God
In our particular world,
As designed by the Father
To progressively unfurl.

These mysterious things
That make up our destiny
Are steadily revealed,
Becoming, for us, history.

Thus, they cease to be
Mysteries of our life;
Now, they show ways
To avoid needless strife.

But when, these mysteries,
We force their retention;
We have moved beyond
The Father's intention.

So, let fulfillment flow,
We must move along,
So that we, in God,
Will for ever stand strong.

CHAPTER 5A

No dilution

Rightly Dividing Scripture

James 5:13-20

Is any among you afflicted? let him pray. Is any merry? let him sing psalms. Is any sick among you? let him call for the elders of the church; and let them pray over him, anointing him with oil in the name of the Lord: And the prayer of faith shall save the sick, and the Lord shall raise him up; and if he have committed sins, they shall be forgiven him.

Confess your faults one to another, and pray one for another, that ye may be healed. The effectual fervent prayer of a righteous man availeth much. Elias was a man subject to like passions as we are, and he prayed earnestly that it might not rain: and it rained not on the earth by the space of three years and six months. And he prayed again, and the heaven gave rain, and the earth brought forth her fruit.

Brethren, if any of you do err from the truth, and one convert him; Let him know, that he which converteth the sinner from the error of his way shall save a soul from death, and shall hide a multitude of sins.

Dilution is the act of weakening a substance from its full strength. In the context of the Scripture, this may be seen as the act of taking away the full impact of the words. To begin to understand this process, think about how dilution is accomplished in liquids. Dilution in liquids is accomplished by adding other substances to the liquid. We dilute concentrated orange juice by adding water to it. The act of taking away water from juice, for instance, is the act of concentration. We need to be wary of dilution of the Scripture.

The attempt to dilute Scripture is the act of placing additional facts into the text of the Scripture. The additional facts are designed to reduce, or sometimes, eliminate the power of the written word. This is a thing that must not be done. There is a stern biblical condemnation of those who add anything to the word of God in the Bible.

> *For I testify unto every man that heareth the words of the prophecy of this book, If any man shall add unto these things, God shall add unto him the plagues that are written in this book: And if any man shall take away from the words of the book of this prophecy, God shall take away his part out of the book of life, and out of the holy city, and from the things which are written in this book.*
>
> (Revelation 22:18-19)

There is a song that has a phrase which says: "Just as I am, without one plea". This was written to describe the way we come to God through Jesus Christ the Lord. It is a very appropriate thought to store as we begin this presentation.

As you look through the Bible, especially as you look among the first few kings of Israel, you see that God chose ordinary people to reign over the nation, in several pioneering stages of Israel's development. The people were ordinary in the sense of not being persons of notoriety prior to their selection. Neither Moses, nor Saul, nor David, were dignitaries prior to their call. In beginning new processes, it seems that God purposely looked for the unrecognized among His people, in order to bestow great honor on them. And, if this is the case, then the LORD must have been sending a message to us about our own selection process. And I think that it is the case.

> *The wolf also shall dwell with the lamb, and the leopard shall lie down with the kid; and the calf and the young lion and the fatling together; and a little child shall lead them.*
>
> (Isaiah 11:6)

It is an astonishing thing to think about these creatures, mentioned above in Isaiah 11:6, co-existing in the same space. There is at least one really dangerous critters mentioned there: two, if the lion isn't very young. It is an extremely glorious thing to think that *a little child shall lead them*. Too often, we look only to the great to illustrate the richness of God's glory.

Sometimes, though, it seems that we are no longer given a choice. In this world, it is only the *connected* that get the publicity—except where God decides to bring forth someone, or something, ordinary into the light of the extraordinary. But for the most part, in the secular world, it is true that power rules. Fortunately, God is not restrained by the secular world.

I would love to be able to say that the legal organization known as "the church" is not constrained by the secular world. However, it is becoming more and more difficult to see where the secular world ends and the organizational church begins. This is a state of worship that was foretold, long ago, in Scripture.

> *Then if any man shall say unto you, Lo, here is Christ, or there; believe it not. For there shall arise false Christs, and false prophets, and shall shew great signs and wonders; insomuch that, if it were possible, they shall deceive the very elect. Behold, I have told you before.*
>
> *Wherefore if they shall say unto you, Behold, he is in the desert; go not forth: behold, he is in the secret chambers; believe it not. For as the lightning cometh out of the east, and shineth even unto the west; so shall also the coming of the Son of man be.*
>
> (Matthew 24:23-27)

I am not saying that we should go out of our way to find the obscure individual, just so that we can say that we are imitating God: He will take care of that; and, He has taken care of that. The great are only, the great, because God has chosen them for greatness, which is true regardless of how, the great, may be defined: All power is God's. This includes all power in Heaven and earth, which He has shared with His Son, Jesus Christ, as a gift of empowering authority.

Then the eleven disciples went away into Galilee, into a mountain where Jesus had appointed them. And when they saw him, they worshipped him: but some doubted.

And Jesus came and spake unto them, saying, All power is given unto me in heaven and in earth.

(Matthew 28:16-18)

As Christians, however, we must be careful (or as any other servant of God, for that matter). We must not place our trust in humanity, in a vacuum. In *The Revelation of Jesus Christ, which God gave unto him, to show unto his servants things which must shortly come to pass*, Jesus told his angel, John, to be vigilant in his worship, in this area of dilution.

And I fell at his feet to worship him. And he said unto me, See thou do it not: I am thy fellowservant, and of thy brethren that have the testimony of Jesus: worship God: for the testimony of Jesus is the spirit of prophecy.

(Revelation 19:10)

Spiritual exaltation of the human condition—including spiritual exhalation of ones that are divinely inspired—is a problem that arises even among some of the elect of God. There is a tendency to look at human situations, and then to modify the thrust of the Scripture to fit the human condition. This is the philosophy that holds that theology must change with the times. I must admit that this is a difficult one for me to accept; however, for now, I will ask God to allow me to look at the issue through the eyes of those who are embedded therein. To make the topic much clearer, let us look at an example from the Bible. This is one of my most read examples from the Bible; because it has so many applications. Let us look again at the first king of Israel, Saul.

As we turn our attention to king Saul, we must warn you that this is a somewhat hard example for modern times. The hardness is in the fact that it is an example from the early period of mankind, when God had to use the rod heavily in our life, in order to promote progress among mankind. Do not worry: later, we will look at a less vigorous example from the time of Jesus of Nazareth. That time is less rigorous because, starting with the era of the Son; God gave us the tools of persuasion and of reason, to propel us to Him. This is the period of freewill offerings and grace. However, we must delay our evaluation of that time; for, even though the example of king Saul is from a much harder time in the history of our walk with God, it still has lessons that we need to learn.

A key lesson from the life of Saul begins with this recap of his unproductive behavior, which he claimed as being in support of the glory of the LORD.

> *And when Samuel rose early to meet Saul in the morning, it was told Samuel, saying, Saul came to Carmel, and, behold, he set him up a place, and is gone about, and passed on, and gone down to Gilgal.*
>
> *And Samuel came to Saul: and Saul said unto him, Blessed be thou of the LORD: I have performed the commandment of the LORD.*
>
> *And Samuel said, What meaneth then this bleating of the sheep in mine ears, and the lowing of the oxen which I hear?*
>
> *And Saul said, They have brought them from the Amalekites: for the people spared the best of the sheep and of the oxen, to sacrifice unto the LORD thy God; and the rest we have utterly destroyed.*
>
> *Then Samuel said unto Saul, Stay, and I will tell thee what the LORD hath said to me this night.*
>
> *And he said unto him, Say on.*
>
> *And Samuel said, When thou wast little in thine own sight, wast thou not made the head of the tribes of Israel, and the LORD anointed thee king over Israel? And the LORD sent thee on a journey, and said, Go and utterly destroy the sinners the Amalekites, and fight against them until they be consumed. Wherefore then didst thou not obey the voice of the LORD, but didst fly upon the spoil, and didst evil in the sight of the LORD?*
>
> *And Saul said unto Samuel, Yea, I have obeyed the voice of the LORD, and have gone the way which the LORD sent me, and have brought Agag the king of Amalek, and have utterly destroyed*

the Amalekites. But the people took of the spoil, sheep and oxen, the chief of the things which should have been utterly destroyed, to sacrifice unto the LORD thy God in Gilgal.

(1 Samuel 15:12-21)

During the process of uncovering Saul's error, Samuel gave us a lesson in prioritization of areas of service. The prioritization will help us avoid conflicts of devotion. These conflicts may occur both between competing things that are, both of them, interpretations of God's Law, and between God Law and the expectations of our world systems.

And Samuel said, Hath the LORD as great delight in burnt offerings and sacrifices, as in obeying the voice of the LORD? Behold, to obey is better than sacrifice, and to hearken than the fat of rams. For rebellion is as the sin of witchcraft, and stubbornness is as iniquity and idolatry. Because thou hast rejected the word of the LORD, he hath also rejected thee from being king.

And Saul said unto Samuel, I have sinned: for I have transgressed the commandment of the LORD, and thy words: because I feared the people, and obeyed their voice.

(1 Samuel 15:22-24)

In this example, king Saul was given responsibility in two directions. He had a responsibility to God and a responsibility to the nation of Israel. Of course, his responsibility to God should have been the first one on his mind and in his heart. You read which responsibility king Saul held as primary, in this instance. This is where we get into the example for us today. This is what faces many of religious leaders, today. They know that God has been very precise in His statements in the Bible, through his prophets and apostles; however, they find that the people whom they are serving want to move in a different direction. So, they come to a point of decision.

It is not a situation where the people want to do things that are against God. No, it is not that at all. In such cases, the people have actually framed the actions as being for the enhancement of God's mission on the earth. This can be things such as, providing God with resources from questionable sources. It can be things like, accepting the behavior of certain unrepentant individuals because they have a skill that is useful to the ministry that is being served to the people. It can also be things like, communing with certain non-aligned individuals in an effort to show the accepting nature of God. However, in each of these cases, there is a specific passage of Scripture that tells us not to indulge in the activity, even though it may seem to give benefit to the mission of God.

Okay, since you asked, I will give a Scripture that is an illustration of the avoidance of each one.

- Resources from questionable sources:

For it seemed good to the Holy Ghost, and to us, to lay upon you no greater burden than these necessary things; That ye abstain from meats offered to idols, and from blood, and from things strangled, and from fornication: from which if ye keep yourselves, ye shall do well. Fare ye well.

(Acts 15:28-29)

- Accepting behavior of unrepentant individuals:

This charge I commit unto thee, son Timothy, according to the prophecies which went before on thee, that thou by them mightest war a good warfare; Holding faith, and a good conscience; which some having put away concerning faith have made shipwreck: Of whom is Hymenaeus and Alexander; whom I have delivered unto Satan, that they may learn not to blaspheme.

(1 Timothy 1:18-20)

- Communing with certain non-aligned individuals:

Be ye not unequally yoked together with unbelievers: for what fellowship hath righteousness with unrighteousness? and what communion hath light with darkness? And what concord hath Christ with Belial? or what part hath he that believeth with an infidel? And what agreement hath the temple of God with idols? for ye are the temple of the living God; as God hath said, I will dwell in them, and walk in them; and I will be their God, and they shall be my people.

> *Wherefore come out from among them, and be ye separate, saith the Lord, and touch not the unclean thing; and I will receive you, And will be a Father unto you, and ye shall be my sons and daughters, saith the Lord Almighty.*
>
> (2 Corinthians 6:14-18)

There are many other examples of cautions that we have been given by God; and these examples must be incorporated into our ministries. Let me be very clear here: this does not mean that we do not associate, at all, with those who are not of the faith. We are definitely called to associate with everyone; those of the faith, and those not of the faith. In fact, when our life is lived as an example of the love of God in Christ Jesus, it is imperative that we associate with non-believers.

> *And it came to pass, that, as Jesus sat at meat in his house, many publicans and sinners sat also together with Jesus and his disciples: for there were many, and they followed him. And when the scribes and Pharisees saw him eat with publicans and sinners, they said unto his disciples, How is it that he eateth and drinketh with publicans and sinners?*
>
> *When Jesus heard it, he saith unto them, They that are whole have no need of the physician, but they that are sick: I came not to call the righteous, but sinners to repentance.*
>
> (Mark 2:15-17)

I must stress the caution that our lives must be lived according to the example of the love of God in Christ Jesus, and explain it a little more. This does not mean that we have achieved perfection: that will not happen on this side of life. It does means that we must have a consistent devotion time with God; and whatever happens—being in sin or being whole in God—we must be constant in recognizing that we belong to God. We are all sinners saved by grace; and we, on this side of life, will always be sinners saved by grace. It is the light of the Holy Ghost shining through our insufficiencies that produces the illumination that is needed by the world, so that it may see Christ in us--our words are only the smallest fraction of the message of God. Even the man who cannot speak, or, even, who does not speak, can still illustrate the love of God in Christ Jesus as it branches out into the world. For instance, as a result of a somewhat irritating physical condition of his, the apostle Paul was able to send a potent message to the world; and this, even when he was not speaking.

> *And lest I should be exalted above measure through the abundance of the revelations, there was given to me a thorn in the flesh, the messenger of Satan to buffet me, lest I should be exalted above measure. For this thing I besought the Lord thrice, that it might depart from me.*
>
> *And he said unto me, My grace is sufficient for thee: for my strength is made perfect in weakness.*
>
> *Most gladly therefore will I rather glory in my infirmities, that the power of Christ may rest upon me. Therefore I take pleasure in infirmities, in reproaches, in necessities, in persecutions, in distresses for Christ's sake: for when I am weak, then am I strong.*
> (2 Corinthians 12:7-10)

I do not want anyone to fixate on this level of behavior as being a necessity, or even a capability at all levels; we must wait, patiently, for the LORD'S empowerment. We must wait, patiently, for the LORD'S empowerment. It is not a nice thing when anyone has burdens placed on them that they cannot bear; nor is it productive, for us to place on others, burdens that they cannot bear. The burden of being perfect is not something that we should ever expect from any human with whom we associate. Yes, we must strive for perfection, but, too, we must not grieve because we are not yet perfect. All good things come to the child of God, in time. The apostle Paul gave us further edification about this, as it was given to us by Jesus, when he gave us our marching orders, if you will.

> *Yea doubtless, and I count all things but loss for the excellency of the knowledge of Christ Jesus my Lord: for whom I have suffered the loss of all things, and do count them but dung, that I may win Christ, And be found in him, not having mine own righteousness, which is of the law, but that which is through the faith of Christ, the righteousness which is of God by faith: That I may know him, and the power of his resurrection, and the fellowship of his*

> *sufferings, being made conformable unto his death; If by any means I might attain unto the resurrection of the dead. Not as though I had already attained, either were already perfect: but I follow after, if that I may apprehend that for which also I am apprehended of Christ Jesus.*
>
> *Brethren, I count not myself to have apprehended: but this one thing I do, forgetting those things which are behind, and reaching forth unto those things which are before, I press toward the mark for the prize of the high calling of God in Christ Jesus.*
>
> (Philippians 3:8-14)

This is the mark of being fully equipped for the calling which God has given us; it does not matter how *small* or *large* it may be, from a human perspective. To God, the calling that He has placed on us is as big as the world; for it is my world.

There is no, small, in the calling of God. Even the tallest office building needs someone smaller to keep it clean. Without the services of the cleaning crew, the greatest of monuments would be no more than a slum. The mechanism that flushes the toilet is no less important than the one that runs the elevators. Size is irrelevant. Right performance of the assigned task is everything.

The religious leader of Jesus' day were really good about that "small-large, others burden" thing. Think about the condemnation that Jesus placed on the scribes and Pharisees, based on the burden placed on others by them.

> *But woe unto you, scribes and Pharisees, hypocrites! for ye shut up the kingdom of heaven against men: for ye neither go in yourselves, neither suffer ye them that are entering to go in.*
>
> *Woe unto you, scribes and Pharisees, hypocrites! for ye devour widows' houses, and for a pretence make long prayer: therefore ye shall receive the greater damnation.*
>
> *Woe unto you, scribes and Pharisees, hypocrites! for ye compass sea and land to make one proselyte, and when he is made, ye make him twofold more the child of hell than yourselves.*
>
> (Matthew 23:13-15)

Now, the unbalanced approach of the scribes and Pharisees was not limited to other people; they also extended their reach to other creatures, and even architectural structures.

> *Woe unto you, ye blind guides, which say, Whosoever shall swear by the temple, it is nothing; but whosoever shall swear by the gold of the temple, he is a debtor! Ye fools and blind: for whether is greater, the gold, or the temple that sanctifieth the gold? And, Whosoever shall swear by the altar, it is nothing; but whosoever sweareth by the gift that is upon it, he is guilty. Ye fools and blind: for whether is greater, the gift, or the altar that sanctifieth the gift?*
>
> *Whoso therefore shall swear by the altar, sweareth by it, and by all things thereon. And whoso shall swear by the temple, sweareth by it, and by him that dwelleth therein. And he that shall swear by heaven, sweareth by the throne of God, and by him that sitteth thereon.*
>
> (Matthew 23:16-22)

There are more woes spoken against the scribes and Pharisees, which are written in Matthew 23:23-35, but you get the idea—I pray. The religious leaders had added so much man-made doctrine to the text of the law of Moses, so that their law had been rendered impotent for the purposes for which it was designed. By the teaching of their revised form of the Law; they were making devils, by using struggling individuals. These were individuals who would have been very glad to hear the true word of the Law, and to follow it. In reaction to the man-centered behavior of the scribes and Pharisees, Jesus told his disciples to discard the behavior of these leaders, and to only obey their call to worship, as this was in accordance with the requirement of God that tells us to obey leaders. The scribes and Pharisees were no longer to be viewed as examples of righteous living, in God. Jesus set the standard for them, and for us. Wherefore the disciples need only look to the example of Jesus for the direction for life.

> *Then spake Jesus to the multitude, and to his disciples, Saying The scribes and the Pharisees sit in Moses' seat: All therefore whatsoever they bid you observe, that observe and do; but do not ye after their works: for they say, and do not. For they bind heavy burdens and*

> *grievous to be borne, and lay them on men's shoulders; but they themselves will not move them with one of their fingers.*
>
> *But all their works they do for to be seen of men: they make broad their phylacteries, and enlarge the borders of their garments, And love the uppermost rooms at feasts, and the chief seats in the synagogues, And greetings in the markets, and to be called of men, Rabbi, Rabbi.*
>
> (Matthew 23:1-7)

It was for this reason and many others that God sent His Son to the earth. It was time for the world to have a refreshing; like unto that done at the time of Noah and the flood. The examples that the children of the world had before them, at that time, were not anywhere near sufficient for the well-being of the nation of Israel, nor were they sufficient for the other nations of the world. In Israel, the revised compendium of man-logic based laws was in no way appropriate for the children to follow. These man-derived things could not serve as the way to lead the world-stretching that had to happen *in Jerusalem, and in all Judaea, and in Samaria, and unto the uttermost part of the earth*, and then bring the redeemed back to God. And yet, that stretch is precisely what the world needed. Moreover, this is what the remnant of Israel was charged, by God in Christ, to do.

> *And he said unto them, It is not for you to know the times or the seasons, which the Father hath put in his own power. But ye shall receive power, after that the Holy Ghost is come upon you: and ye shall be witnesses unto me both in Jerusalem, and in all Judaea, and in Samaria, and unto the uttermost part of the earth.*
>
> (Acts 1:7-8)

God will protect all his children, whether they are his children-sealed, children-to-be, children-in-rebellion, or any other type of children-to-something. All children are headed toward God, and all children are God's; and before God, all humans are children. Moreover, God is very protective of His children; starting with the littlest ones that need His protection the most.

> *At the same time came the disciples unto Jesus, saying, Who is the greatest in the kingdom of heaven?*

> *And Jesus called a little child unto him, and set him in the midst of them, And said, Verily I say unto you, Except ye be converted, and become as little children, ye shall not enter into the kingdom of heaven.*
>
> *Whosoever therefore shall humble himself as this little child, the same is greatest in the kingdom of heaven. And whoso shall receive one such little child in my name receiveth me. But whoso shall offend one of these little ones which believe in me, it were better for him that a millstone were hanged about his neck, and that he were drowned in the depth of the sea.*
>
> (Matthew 18:1-6)

> *Take heed that ye despise not one of these little ones; for I say unto you, That in heaven their angels do always behold the face of my Father which is in heaven.*
>
> (Matthew 18:10)

The word of God, in the Gospel of the Kingdom of God, as brought to us by Jesus Christ, is the fulfillment of components of the law of Moses; particularly, the part that is for righteousness sake.

> *Brethren, my heart's desire and prayer to God for Israel is, that they might be saved. For I bear them record that they have a zeal of God, but not according to knowledge. For they being ignorant of God's righteousness, and going about to establish their own righteousness, have not submitted themselves unto the righteousness of God. For Christ is the end of the law for righteousness to every one that believeth.*
>
> (Romans 10:1-4)

The remainder of the law of Moses is for memory sake. Much of it is designed to prod the memory of the nation of Israel, and to serve as an example to the remainder of the world. This memory jogging, in its projection of motivating examples, is sent into us to call to mind the power of God to deliver and to judge. A powerful motivation for the Old Testament world was sent into it when the LORD delivered Israel from oppressive bondage, in a delivery of a stern judgment to the nation of Egypt.

Both deliverance and judgment are contained in the observances in the law of Moses. And, these observances should still be made. They need not be made by a narrow interpretation of that which is written in the Law (it gets really difficult to sacrifice animals in the United States of America, for instance). By taking a comprehensive view of the law of Moses, we notice that there are alternatives; such as this one for substituting something else for the living thing, in the process of redeeming it.

> *And if it be any unclean beast, of which they do not offer a sacrifice unto the LORD, then he shall present the beast before the priest: And the priest shall value it, whether it be good or bad: as thou valuest it, who art the priest, so shall it be. But if he will at all redeem it, then he shall add a fifth part thereof unto thy estimation.*
>
> (Leviticus 27:11-13)

In the time of transition, the law of Moses was internalized in each one of us, to be observed in the heart of man. This is the change that God instituted at the establishment of the eternal kingdom of Christ Jesus. This is the form of worship that is exempt from legislative interference, or intervention.

> *Behold, the days come, saith the LORD, that I will make a new covenant with the house of Israel, and with the house of Judah: Not according to the covenant that I made with their fathers in the day that I took them by the hand to bring them out of the land of Egypt; which my covenant they brake, although I was an husband unto them, saith the LORD: But this shall be the covenant that I will make with the house of Israel; After those days, saith the LORD, I will put my law in their inward parts, and write it in their hearts; and will be their God, and they shall be my people.*
>
> *And they shall teach no more every man his neighbour, and every man his brother, saying, Know the LORD: for they shall all know me, from the least of them unto the greatest of them, saith the LORD: for I will forgive their iniquity, and I will remember their sin no more.*
>
> (Jeremiah 31:31-34)

Along with the observance of the power and strength of God, as illustrated in the law of Moses and all that is the background of the Law, there is another law. The other law is the Law of Love, and it is contained in the Gospel, which is of the Kingdom of God in Christ Jesus, the Son of God. The words of this law are stated throughout what we call the New Testament of the Bible; they had already been introduced, by example, in the Old Testament. There is no other source for the message of the Kingdom of God in Christ Jesus. By the authority of these Testaments, one must not, ever, imitate the self-centric knowledge of the scribes and Pharisees, and add information or doctrine that is not contained in these Testaments. Most forcefully, I say that we must not dilute the message of Jesus Christ that is in the testimony of his life and the record of the admonitions, exhortations and preaching of the apostles.

> *All scripture is given by inspiration of God, and is profitable for doctrine, for reproof, for correction, for instruction in righteousness: That the man of God may be perfect, thoroughly furnished unto all good works.*
>
> (2 Timothy 3:16-17)

Know this, that any addition to the text of the Bible will be the addition of man-derived philosophical water to the strong solution of God. It is the water of man that leaves behind a thing which is too weak to provide sufficient sustenance for the child of God. This is why God commands that we not try to weaken His message by dilution.

> *Now therefore hearken, O Israel, unto the statutes and unto the judgments, which I teach you, for to do them, that ye may live, and go in and possess the land which the LORD God of your fathers giveth you. Ye shall not add unto the word which I command you, neither shall ye diminish ought from it, that ye may keep the commandments of the LORD your God which I command you.*
>
> (Deuteronomy 4:1-2)

The message must provide sustenance to all God's children, not just to those that are served by a particular minister, priest, pastor or any other servant of God. Nothing that we can invent will ever have the potency necessary to meet the mark of the high calling in Christ Jesus. For the child of God, it is the same as would be the case with adding water to the required milk of an infant. Over the course of time the infant may die from such addition. And if we fed the infant a double portion of this diluted milk, then the body will have to work harder to remove the water and utilize the nutrients of the milk. With such a double feeding, if we forced the fluids into the child, we may still cause the death of the child, by over hydration. This is the sort of force that the world uses to get its philosophical water into both our soul, and into our worship. It seems so much easier to follow the true way of the LORD, and to feed one another as the LORD taught Israel, through Moses.

> *When thou shalt beget children, and children's children, and ye shall have remained long in the land, and shall corrupt yourselves, and make a graven image, or the likeness of any thing, and shall do evil in the sight of the LORD thy God, to provoke him to anger: I call heaven and earth to witness against you this day, that ye shall soon utterly perish from off the land whereunto ye go over Jordan to possess it; ye shall not prolong your days upon it, but shall utterly be destroyed. And the LORD shall scatter you among the nations, and ye shall be left few in number among the heathen, whither the LORD shall lead you. And there ye shall serve gods, the work of men's hands, wood and stone, which neither see, nor hear, nor eat, nor smell.*
>
> *But if from thence thou shalt seek the LORD thy God, thou shalt find him, if thou seek him with all thy heart and with all thy soul. When thou art in tribulation, and all these things are come upon thee, even in the latter days, if thou turn to the LORD thy God, and shalt be obedient unto his voice; (For the LORD thy God is a merciful God;) he will not forsake thee, neither destroy thee, nor forget the covenant of thy fathers which he sware unto them.*
> (Deuteronomy 4:25-31)

It would be considered ridiculous for a nursing mother to inject water into her breast to dilute the natural milk before it entered the child. The milk of the mother is constituted in the fashion that is to be given to the infant of that mother. So it is with the word. We do not need to add any man-made water to the natural milk of God's word. And for those who are still infants, they should not attempt by themselves, nor be forced by other, to partake of the meat of the word. God made the message of the Gospel just the way He wanted it to be, and it is He THAT will introduce it to the child of God; delivering it at the rate that He knows is required for growth. To steep your heart in understanding, please, with an open heart, read these words of Jesus Christ, our Lord.

> *Come unto me, all ye that labour and are heavy laden, and I will give you rest. Take my yoke upon you, and learn of me; for I am meek and lowly in heart: and ye shall find rest unto your souls. For my yoke is easy, and my burden is light.*
>
> (Matthew 11:28-30)

If we either do not want to do it God's way or we have people who persuade us that we cannot do it God way; then, we must be honest with God about our insufficiency. Paul recognized that the thorn in the flesh was something that he could not change. So, Paul petitioned God for release from it. But, instead of removing the annoyance, God told the apostle to live with it. Through Paul's admission of his weakness, God gave him the power to be strong. This is the same power that is available to raise us above our inability to follow what appears to be a strong message from God. In some cases, rather than forcing our self to victory, we may have to live with not overcoming. However, if we are ever to overcome, then we must know that the power to achieve the goals that God has set before us does not come from man. Rather, we must believe that this power comes from God; and from God alone. In either place in life, the living water that nourishes our soul, as flowing from the word of God, must be consumed as it is given: without dilution.

> *When they therefore were come together, they asked of him, saying, Lord, wilt thou at this time restore again the kingdom to Israel?*
>
> *And he said unto them, It is not for you to know the times or the seasons, which the Father hath put in his own power. But ye shall receive power, after that the Holy Ghost is come upon you: and ye shall be witnesses unto me both in Jerusalem, and in all Judaea, and in Samaria, and unto the uttermost part of the earth.*

And when he had spoken these things, while they beheld, he was taken up; and a cloud received him out of their sight.

And while they looked stedfastly toward heaven as he went up, behold, two men stood by them in white apparel; Which also said, Ye men of Galilee, why stand ye gazing up into heaven? this same Jesus, which is taken up from you into heaven, shall so come in like manner as ye have seen him go into heaven.

(Acts 1:6-11)

The Word from the Bible

Psalm 2:7-12

I will declare the decree: the LORD hath said unto me, Thou art my Son; this day have I begotten thee. Ask of me, and I shall give thee the heathen for thine inheritance, and the uttermost parts of the earth for thy possession. Thou shalt break them with a rod of iron; thou shalt dash them in pieces like a potter's vessel.

Be wise now therefore, O ye kings: be instructed, ye judges of the earth. Serve the LORD with fear, and rejoice with trembling. Kiss the Son, lest he be angry, and ye perish from the way, when his wrath is kindled but a little. Blessed are all they that put their trust in him.

CHAPTER SIX

Revelation

Era of the Revelator

Before we continue our exploration of The Revelation of Jesus Christ, as recorded in the Bible in The Revelation of Saint John the divine, let us look back at what we have learned, up to this point. We have studied the book of Revelation from the beginning to about the middle of chapter seventeen. We have shown that, up to this point, the bulk of the information given in the book is for admonition to excellence.

The book of Revelation starts with recognition of the various forms of congregations. This is necessary information for us, as we serve God in congregations. It lets us see the view that God has of the various worship practices in the churches of the world. Though it is directed at the churches in Asia, it is also useful for all churches.

As you review the Scripture given in The Revelation, you will understand that these forms of worship still exist today. Moreover, as you peek into other religions' practices, you will note that the practices in Revelation occur in other religions; for instance, they can be seen in the worship of the Hebrews, in Islamic worship, as well as in Christianity. The warnings that are in Revelation are for all peoples assembling in congregations. Also available to all peoples are the blessing of Revelation, including inspiration from the seven Spirits of God. These Spirits are a necessary part of the Christian experience, as they are at the center of the source of The Revelation.

And I beheld, and, lo, in the midst of the throne and of the four beasts, and in the midst of the elders, stood a Lamb as it had

been slain, having seven horns and seven eyes, which are the seven Spirits of God sent forth into all the earth.
(Revelation 5:6)

The recognition of the *Lamb* provides us a welcome contrast to some of the scary explanations of that time, the day of the LORD, which is the frame for the Revelation. As it gives us greater knowledge of the Lamb, the Revelation gives us a beautiful view of the time from the start of the designation of the Messiah, to the period of his death and resurrection. Satan is shown to be the antagonist of the people of God, and much of his fearfulness is removed; indeed, in the course of the Revelation, Satan is eliminated, together with his empire. The terror that Satan works to instigates is pushed to its peek in that day, as he realizes that he cannot stop Jesus Christ from doing that which God assigned him. Then, because he cannot touch the forward momentum of the Lamb, the devil greatly increases the effort to persecute those who dared to believe in him. In our written history, this is clearly seen in the era following the death and resurrection of Jesus Christ.

The time of the presentation of The Revelation is a period of extreme persecution of the church of Christ, but the church has always been destined to survive through such periods. The church was, then, and is still now, equipped by God so that it continually shows the perseverance of God's Gospel among men. This is what it did even during that dark period; and this is what it continues to do, up to this day, and beyond, as Jesus said it will.

When Jesus came into the coasts of Caesarea Philippi, he asked his disciples, saying, Whom do men say that I the Son of man am?

And they said, Some say that thou art John the Baptist: some, Elias; and others, Jeremias, or one of the prophets.

He saith unto them, But whom say ye that I am?

And Simon Peter answered and said, Thou art the Christ, the Son of the living God.

And Jesus answered and said unto him, Blessed art thou, Simon Barjona: for flesh and blood hath not revealed it unto thee, but my Father which is in heaven. And I say also unto thee, That thou art

Peter, and upon this rock I will build my church; and the gates of hell shall not prevail against it.

(Matthew 16:13-18)

In the time of the initial presentation of The Revelation; in addition to reshaping Israel, God was also moving terribly and mightily among the peoples of the world of that time. As pertains to the world, in general, a time of cleansing had been prophesied, to occur in a time that was near the days of Jesus and his apostles. God's prophet had said that the LORD would vigorously cleanse the nation of Israel, as God scattered it to the nations of the earth. In an attempt to bypass this judgment, there was a fierce struggle in Jerusalem by the people of the city. The people tried to preserve the form of religion that they had built; however, God was not swayed by their desire to maintain the status quo. The outcome for Israel was sealed; because, in a former time the LORD sent forth a promise that would not be taken back. The first part of the promise involved the separation of a major portion of Israel from being favored by God.

Go, tell Jeroboam, Thus saith the LORD God of Israel, Forasmuch as I exalted thee from among the people, and made thee prince over my people Israel, And rent the kingdom away from the house of David, and gave it thee: and yet thou hast not been as my servant David, who kept my commandments, and who followed me with all his heart, to do that only which was right in mine eyes; But hast done evil above all that were before thee: for thou hast gone and made thee other gods, and molten images, to provoke me to anger, and hast cast me behind thy back: Therefore, behold, I will bring evil upon the house of Jeroboam, and will cut off from Jeroboam him that pisseth against the wall, and him that is shut up and left in Israel, and will take away the remnant of the house of Jeroboam, as a man taketh away dung, till it be all gone. Him that dieth of Jeroboam in the city shall the dogs eat; and him that dieth in the field shall the fowls of the air eat: for the LORD hath spoken it.

Arise thou therefore, get thee to thine own house: and when thy feet enter into the city, the child shall die. And all Israel shall mourn for him, and bury him: for he only of Jeroboam shall come to the grave, because in him there is found some good thing toward the LORD God of Israel in the house of Jeroboam.

Moreover the LORD shall raise him up a king over Israel, who shall cut off the house of Jeroboam that day: but what? even now.

For the LORD shall smite Israel, as a reed is shaken in the water, and he shall root up Israel out of this good land, which he gave to their fathers, and shall scatter them beyond the river, because they have made their groves, provoking the LORD to anger. And he shall give Israel up because of the sins of Jeroboam, who did sin, and who made Israel to sin.

(1 Kings 14:7-16)

The second part of the promise of cleansing for Israel was accomplished by the separation of the remaining portion of the tribes of Israel from being favored by God. This is the portion of the tribes that were consolidated with Judah, where Jerusalem is. This was the separation of the first remnant from its position of grace in the sight of the LORD.

And the LORD spake by his servants the prophets, saying, Because Manasseh king of Judah hath done these abominations, and hath done wickedly above all that the Amorites did, which were before him, and hath made Judah also to sin with his idols: Therefore thus saith the LORD God of Israel,

Behold, I am bringing such evil upon Jerusalem and Judah, that whosoever heareth of it, both his ears shall tingle. And I will stretch over Jerusalem the line of Samaria, and the plummet of the house of Ahab: and I will wipe Jerusalem as a man wipeth a dish, wiping it, and turning it upside down.

And I will forsake the remnant of mine inheritance, and deliver them into the hand of their enemies; and they shall become a prey and a spoil to all their enemies; Because they have done that which was evil in my sight, and have provoked me to anger, since the day their fathers came forth out of Egypt, even unto this day.

Moreover Manasseh shed innocent blood very much, till he had filled Jerusalem from one end to another; beside his sin wherewith he made Judah to sin, in doing that which was evil in the sight of the LORD.

(2 Kings 21:10-16)

The LORD'S promise was that Jerusalem, and the kingdom of Judah would cease to be the center of worship of the Living God, in that world. Even so, there would still be a portion of the congregation of Israel that persisted in true worship, as a remnant of the people. These remaining people would, one day, form the seed of the re-establishment of the whole nation of Israel.

Since the days of our fathers have we been in a great trespass unto this day; and for our iniquities have we, our kings, and our priests, been delivered into the hand of the kings of the lands, to the sword, to captivity, and to a spoil, and to confusion of face, as it is this day. And now for a little space grace hath been showed from the LORD our God, to leave us a remnant to escape, and to give us a nail in his holy place, that our God may lighten our eyes, and give us a little reviving in our bondage. For we were bondmen; yet our God hath not forsaken us in our bondage, but hath extended mercy unto us in the sight of the kings of Persia, to give us a reviving, to set up the house of our God, and to repair the desolations thereof, and to give us a wall in Judah and in Jerusalem.

(Ezra 9:7-9)

During the history of Israel, there were many righteous men and some righteous kings that sought to have the judgment of God removed from the nation; however, the judgment stayed. Howbeit, for the sake of the righteous behavior of certain ones of His servants, God told them just what He would do and why He would do it. One of these messages was delivered in the time of king Josiah of Judah.

And it came to pass, when the king had heard the words of the book of the law, that he rent his clothes. And the king commanded Hilkiah the priest, and Ahikam the son of Shaphan, and Achbor the son of Michaiah, and Shaphan the scribe, and Asahiah a servant of the king's, saying, Go ye, inquire of the LORD for me, and for the people, and for all Judah, concerning the words of this book that is found: for great is the wrath of the LORD that is kindled against us, because our fathers have not hearkened unto the words of this book, to do according unto all that which is written concerning us.

So Hilkiah the priest, and Ahikam, and Achbor, and Shaphan, and Asahiah, went unto Huldah the prophetess, the wife of Shallum the son of Tikvah, the son of Harhas, keeper of the wardrobe; (now she dwelt in Jerusalem in the college;) and they communed with her.

And she said unto them, Thus saith the LORD God of Israel, Tell the man that sent you to me, Thus saith the LORD, Behold, I will bring evil upon this place, and upon the inhabitants thereof, even all the words of the book which the king of Judah hath read: Because they have forsaken me, and have burned incense unto other gods, that they might provoke me to anger with all the works of their hands; therefore my wrath shall be kindled against this place, and shall not be quenched.

But to the king of Judah which sent you to inquire of the LORD, thus shall ye say to him, Thus saith the LORD God of Israel, As touching the words which thou hast heard; Because thine heart was tender, and thou hast humbled thyself before the LORD, when thou heardest what I spake against this place, and against the inhabitants thereof, that they should become a desolation and a curse, and hast rent thy clothes, and wept before me; I also have heard thee, saith the LORD. Behold therefore, I will gather thee unto thy fathers, and thou shalt be gathered into thy grave in peace; and thine eyes shall not see all the evil which I will bring upon this place.

And they brought the king word again.

(2 Kings 22:11-20)

The cleansing of Israel was repeated through several iterations, each with the removal of Jerusalem and the temple in Jerusalem. This continued to the time of the Son. The cleansing of Israel that occurred in the time of the Son was the fulfillment of the prophecy of king David. However, in the time of the Son, the fulfillment was not accomplished by an earthly nation-son, but rather, by the only begotten Son of God. For, the prophecy said that God would make that world's Lord's enemies his footstool. This is one of the many prophecies that pointed to the time of the Christ, the Son of God, who is called Jesus of Nazareth, the one that was sent by God the Father, for Israel's redemption.

> *A Psalm of David.*
>
> *The LORD said unto my Lord, Sit thou at my right hand, until I make thine enemies thy footstool. The LORD shall send the rod of thy strength out of Zion: rule thou in the midst of thine enemies. Thy people shall be willing in the day of thy power, in the beauties of holiness from the womb of the morning: thou hast the dew of thy youth. The LORD hath sworn, and will not repent, Thou art a priest for ever after the order of Melchizedek. The Lord at thy right hand shall strike through kings in the day of his wrath.*
>
> *He shall judge among the heathen, he shall fill the places with the dead bodies; he shall wound the heads over many countries. He shall drink of the brook in the way: therefore shall he lift up the head.*
>
> (Psalm 110:1-7)

However, in spite of the Father's outstretched Hand of Peace, as seen in the life of the Prince of Peace, the Son of God; still, there was much resistance by the nation. Therefore, it was obvious to both the Son and his true disciples that it would be a little while longer before God was fully honored in their midst, by the acceptance of the Messiah. But God has promised that it will happen. He even showed us a preview of it. In that day, even though there was much resistance, there were many who believed. The Bible tells us about the 144,000 servants who were devoted to the Lord Jesus Christ. These were sealed to do the work of the God, in the name of the Christ.

> *And after these things I saw four angels standing on the four corners of the earth, holding the four winds of the earth, that the wind should not blow on the earth, nor on the sea, nor on any tree. And I saw another angel ascending from the east, having the seal of the living God: and he cried with a loud voice to the four angels,*

to whom it was given to hurt the earth and the sea, Saying, Hurt not the earth, neither the sea, nor the trees, till we have sealed the servants of our God in their foreheads.

And I heard the number of them which were sealed: and there were sealed an hundred and forty and four thousand of all the tribes of the children of Israel.

Of the tribe of Juda were sealed twelve thousand.
Of the tribe of Reuben were sealed twelve thousand.
Of the tribe of Gad were sealed twelve thousand.
Of the tribe of Aser were sealed twelve thousand.
Of the tribe of Nephthalim were sealed twelve thousand.
Of the tribe of Manasses were sealed twelve thousand.
Of the tribe of Simeon were sealed twelve thousand.
Of the tribe of Levi were sealed twelve thousand.
Of the tribe of Issachar were sealed twelve thousand.
Of the tribe of Zabulon were sealed twelve thousand.
Of the tribe of Joseph were sealed twelve thousand.
Of the tribe of Benjamin were sealed twelve thousand.

(Revelation 7:1-8)

As we resume our studies in Revelation, at the, then, contemporary world, we see the oppressor trying to destroy the remnant of God, in Israel. These are the sealed ones that are spreading the Gospel of the Kingdom of God, in the name of the Lord Jesus Christ. The oppression is being done by the power that controlled the world of that time: this is the Roman Empire. This is a kingdom that was prophesied by Daniel as being the continuation of the abomination of the fourth kingdom. Here is the historical progression that flows to that point.

This is the dream; and we will tell the interpretation thereof before the king. Thou, O king, art a king of kings: for the God of heaven hath given thee a kingdom, power, and strength, and glory. And wheresoever the children of men dwell, the beasts of the field and the fowls of the heaven hath he given into thine hand, and hath made thee ruler over them all. Thou art this head of gold.

And after thee shall arise another kingdom inferior to thee,

and another third kingdom of brass, which shall bear rule over all the earth.

And the fourth kingdom shall be strong as iron: forasmuch as iron breaketh in pieces and subdueth all things: and as iron that breaketh all these, shall it break in pieces and bruise. And whereas thou sawest the feet and toes, part of potters' clay, and part of iron, the kingdom shall be divided; but there shall be in it of the strength of the iron, forasmuch as thou sawest the iron mixed with miry clay. And as the toes of the feet were part of iron, and part of clay, so the kingdom shall be partly strong, and partly broken. And whereas thou sawest iron mixed with miry clay, they shall mingle themselves with the seed of men: but they shall not cleave one to another, even as iron is not mixed with clay.

And in the days of these kings shall the God of heaven set up a kingdom, which shall never be destroyed: and the kingdom shall not be left to other people, but it shall break in pieces and consume all these kingdoms, and it shall stand for ever.

(Daniel 2:36-44)

The book of Revelation tells us about the events that happened in that kingdom, up to the point of the writing of the book of Revelation. It also gives us a preview of things to come. These are things that lead up to the installation of the eternal Kingdom of God, in Christ; abiding in a renewed human world sphere.

And there are seven kings: five are fallen, and one is, and the other is not yet come; and when he cometh, he must continue a short space. And the beast that was, and is not, even he is the eighth, and is of the seven, and goeth into perdition. And the ten horns which thou sawest are ten kings, which have received no kingdom as yet; but receive power as kings one hour with the beast. These have one mind, and shall give their power and strength unto the beast. These shall make war with the Lamb, and the Lamb shall overcome them: for he is Lord of lords, and King of kings: and they that are with him are called, and chosen, and faithful.

And he saith unto me, The waters which thou sawest, where the whore sitteth, are peoples, and multitudes, and nations, and tongues.

And the ten horns which thou sawest upon the beast, these shall hate the whore, and shall make her desolate and naked, and shall eat her flesh, and burn her with fire. For God hath put in their hearts to fulfil his will, and to agree, and give their kingdom unto the beast, until the words of God shall be fulfilled.

And the woman which thou sawest is that great city, which reigneth over the kings of the earth.

(Revelation 17:10-18)

The following information was extracted from a search about the ancient Roman Empire. It might be helpful for your understanding of the horns of the beast.

The ten nations which were most instrumental in breaking up the Roman empire, and which at some time in their history held respectively portions of Roman territory as separate and independent kingdoms, may be enumerated . . . as follows: The Huns, Ostrogoths, Visigoths, Franks, Vandals, Suevi, Burgundians, Heruli, Anglo-Saxons, and Lombards.

Huns or Alemani	*Germany*
Visigoths	*Spain*
Franks	*France*
Suevi	*Portugal*
Burgundians	*Switzerland*
Anglo-Saxons	*England*
Lombards or Bavarians	*Italy*
Ostrogoths	*Wiped Out*
Vandals	*Wiped Out*
Heruli	*Wiped Out*

Let us see what happened between the time of the writing of the book of Revelation and our current time. Today, we know that the Roman Empire was indeed destroyed. We know also that it was the central antagonist and adversary in the persecution of the Christian, and that it still could not stop the flow of Christianity throughout the world, in spite of its vigorous persecution. We have already read about the identification of the Roman Empire in the seven heads of the beast, on which the whore sat. This is the beast that did indeed seduce and deceive the world, to draw it away from God. Additionally, we know that the *woman* failed, and that its disposition was as the Revelation said it would be.

> *And after these things I saw another angel come down from heaven, having great power; and the earth was lightened with his glory. And he cried mightily with a strong voice, saying, Babylon the great is fallen, is fallen, and is become the habitation of devils, and the hold of every foul spirit, and a cage of every unclean and hateful bird. For all nations have drunk of the wine of the wrath of her fornication, and the kings of the earth have committed fornication with her, and the merchants of the earth are waxed rich through the abundance of her delicacies.*
>
> *And I heard another voice from heaven, saying, Come out of her, my people, that ye be not partakers of her sins, and that ye receive not of her plagues. For her sins have reached unto heaven, and God hath remembered her iniquities. Reward her even as she rewarded you, and double unto her double according to her works: in the cup which she hath filled fill to her double. How much she hath glorified herself, and lived deliciously, so much torment and sorrow give her: for she saith in her heart, I sit a queen, and am no widow, and shall see no sorrow. Therefore shall her plagues come in one day, death, and mourning, and famine; and she shall be utterly burned with fire: for strong is the Lord God who judgeth her.*
>
> (Revelation 18:1-8)

We also know that the fall of the Roman Empire is an event that was prophesied as being for a time after the book of Revelation. The tense of the following lets us know that this is the case: *with violence shall that great city Babylon be thrown down.*

> *And a mighty angel took up a stone like a great millstone, and cast it into the sea, saying, Thus with violence shall that great city Babylon be thrown down, and shall be found no more at all. And the voice of harpers, and musicians, and of pipers, and trumpeters, shall be heard no more at all in thee; and no craftsman, of whatsoever craft he be, shall be found any more in thee; and the sound of a millstone shall be heard no more at all in thee; And the light of a candle shall shine no more at all in thee; and the voice of the bridegroom and of the bride shall be heard no more at all in thee: for thy merchants were the great men of the earth; for by thy sorceries were all nations deceived. And in her was found the blood of prophets, and of saints, and of all that were slain upon the earth.*
>
> (Revelation 18:21-24)

We know now that the fall of the Roman Empire did happen: the timeframe was around 476 AD. Furthermore, we know that there was a mighty hand against the Roman Empire that caused its destruction. We know now that this was done at the same intensity as the judgment of God.

> *And after these things I heard a great voice of much people in heaven, saying, Alleluia; Salvation, and glory, and honour, and power, unto the Lord our God: For true and righteous are his judgments: for he hath judged the great whore, which did corrupt the earth with her fornication, and hath avenged the blood of his servants at her hand. And again they said, Alleluia.*
>
> *And her smoke rose up for ever and ever.*
>
> *And the four and twenty elders and the four beasts fell down and worshipped God that sat on the throne, saying, Amen; Alleluia.*
>
> (Revelation 19:1-4)

At this point, we have to pause in our presentation of the visible, historical aspects of this study. The next few chapters start to describe the events that were to occur as driven from the Heavens, and in the spiritual world. We will start with them when we continue with the chapter on the Heaven-centric portion of the book of Revelation. This is where we exit history, and re-enter mystery. That is not to say that the remaining chapters and verses are a mystery, anymore; however, we do say that only those who were (or who will be) a part of these events can fully confirm what is written here; that is, where confirmation is sought from the natural point of view.

In our search for that which is of the seven, we will continue our journey in Revelation in chapter seven: *Just Doing God's Will.* This is the place that follows the connecting thoughts that are titled, *Full Depth*

The next portion of The Revelation of Jesus Christ requires a dependence on the teaching of the Holy Ghost. There are no man-made historical records that can be compared with the writing in Revelation that follows. This must be revealed to those whom God selects for such information. It can then be told to others. But, those others will still have to rely on the Holy Ghost, in them, in order to confirm, or deny, the knowledge that anyone—including this one, your present scribe of logic—says they have received about the meaning of these chapters and verses. Therefore, let me leave you to ready your self, by having your soul absorb this promise that we received from the Lord and Saviour, Jesus Christ.

> *If ye love me, keep my commandments. And I will pray the Father, and he shall give you another Comforter, that he may abide with you for ever; Even the Spirit of truth; whom the world cannot receive, because it seeth him not, neither knoweth him: but ye know him; for he dwelleth with you, and shall be in you. I will not leave you comfortless: I will come to you.*
>
> *Yet a little while, and the world seeth me no more; but ye see me: because I live, ye shall live also. At that day ye shall know that I am in my Father, and ye in me, and I in you. He that hath my commandments, and keepeth them, he it is that loveth me: and he that loveth me shall be loved of my Father, and I will love him, and will manifest myself to him.*
>
> *Judas saith unto him, not Iscariot, Lord, how is it that thou wilt manifest thyself unto us, and not unto the world?*

Jesus answered and said unto him, If a man love me, he will keep my words: and my Father will love him, and we will come unto him, and make our abode with him. He that loveth me not keepeth not my sayings: and the word which ye hear is not mine, but the Father's which sent me.

These things have I spoken unto you, being yet present with you. But the Comforter, which is the Holy Ghost, whom the Father will send in my name, he shall teach you all things, and bring all things to your remembrance, whatsoever I have said unto you.

Peace I leave with you, my peace I give unto you: not as the world giveth, give I unto you. Let not your heart be troubled, neither let it be afraid.

(John 14:15-27)

As we walk the paths
Of two views of reality,
There is the one we know,
And the one we cannot see.

The lessons of history,
We have been shown,
And their message
Can be clearly known.

From history's message,
We know that the Lord
Gave us a precious gift
That shows how adored

Are those who walk
In his blessed way,
And from God's path
Refuse to stray.

There, early Christians
Suffered great strife;
Some, even giving
The offering of their life

Because the Lord
Sent this command:
Children, take My Gospel
Throughout every land.

The rulers of the day,
On the Gospel did frown:
They had no intention
To simply lie down

And let this message
Rule in their world,
Or God's Kingdom
To quietly unfurl.

But killing the messenger
To quench the glow,
They only succeeded
In increasing the flow:

Ever shining brightly
In the darkest hour,
In heaven and in earth,
It possesses All Power.

CHAPTER 6A

Full depth

Rightly Dividing Scripture

The Bible is not a book that you understand. This is not just referring to one particular you, or even one particular type of you (such as the unsaved). This is referring to all *you's*. The Bible is not a book that you understand: the Bible is a book that you accept. Let's travel!

Probably one of the most common verses of Scripture that tells us how to handle the Bible was written to Timothy by the apostle Paul.

> *Study to show thyself approved unto God, a workman that needeth not to be ashamed, rightly dividing the word of truth.*
>
> (2 Timothy 2:15)

This is often portrayed as being a reason to push our self to obtain mastery of Scripture. However, before you start pushing, it might be helpful to read the preceding and the following verses.

> *Of these things put them in remembrance, charging them before the Lord that they strive not about words to no profit, but to the subverting of the hearers.*
>
> (2 Timothy 2:14)

> *But shun profane and vain babblings: for they will increase unto more ungodliness.*
>
> (2 Timothy 2:16)

In the second epistle of Paul the apostle to Timothy, chapter two, verse fourteen, the apostle Paul writes about *remembrance,* and tells us to *strive not about words to no profit.* This is one of the problems that can arise when we get the impression that we, having studied, thereby have mastery of Scripture and that we fully understand it. The problem is this: once we understand something, we are inclined to take a kind of ownership of it. We feel that we have the right to tell others precisely what it means, and what they must believe about it. We must keep our self from this attitude.

In the second epistle of Paul the apostle to Timothy, chapter two, verse sixteen, the apostle Paul teaches us the proper way to do our study of Scripture into the world. This is the verse where Paul talks about shunning *profane and vain babblings.* Of course, no Christian in his right mind would ever consider uttering *profane* statements. However, what about the *vain babblings*?

Consider this: when I am speaking to a person who does not understand my language; might not that person consider what I am saying as being babblings? And if I expect that person to perform some act or to stop doing something, based on what I am telling him; might this not be a hopeless cause? This is what often happens when those of us that think we know the Bible come upon someone who we think is in need of our wisdom. We often come to them with the notion that our truth is the truth that must be immediately understood and then unconditionally accepted. I, too, lived through such a period of my custody of knowledge; a period of acting as if I had ownership of truth.

Now, do not take this the wrong way; there is no such thing as relative truth: truth is always absolute. On the other hand, the understanding of truth is all too relative. It is for this reason that God does not tell us to understand, absolutely, the words of the Bible. Please, do not tamper with the line that exists separating understanding and knowledge, as pertains to the works of Scripture. For instance, here is something that you need to know, even though you cannot claim to have complete understanding: *that ye have eternal life.* The apostle John spoke of how we achieve that level of knowledge.

> *If we receive the witness of men, the witness of God is greater: for this is the witness of God which he hath testified of his Son. He that believeth on the Son of God hath the witness in himself: he*

that believeth not God hath made him a liar; because he believeth not the record that God gave of his Son. And this is the record, that God hath given to us eternal life, and this life is in his Son. He that hath the Son hath life; and he that hath not the Son of God hath not life.

These things have I written unto you that believe on the name of the Son of God; that ye may know that ye have eternal life, and that ye may believe on the name of the Son of God. And this is the confidence that we have in him, that, if we ask any thing according to his will, he heareth us: And if we know that he hear us, whatsoever we ask, we know that we have the petitions that we desired of him.

(1 John 5:9-15)

However, even without full understanding of it, there is a topic in the Bible that we do need to absorb; for, God has revealed to us this that we must understand of the topic of, *the fear of the Lord.*

And unto man he said, Behold, the fear of the Lord, that is wisdom; and to depart from evil is understanding.

(Job 28:28)

The fear of the LORD is the beginning of wisdom: and the knowledge of the holy is understanding.

(Proverbs 9:10)

Is that it for understanding: *the knowledge of the holy is understanding*? Is this where we stop, in our mastery of the Scripture, so that we can forcefully present it to the world? What does this mean? Doesn't God want us to have Scripture memorized, and, thereby, to be ready to tell others about what we know? What about the passage that tells us to be ready?

But sanctify the Lord God in your hearts: and be ready always to give an answer to every man that asketh you a reason of the hope that is in you with meekness and fear: Having a good conscience;

> *that, whereas they speak evil of you, as of evildoers, they may be ashamed that falsely accuse your good conversation in Christ.*
> (1 Peter 3:15-16)

Good thought; but this does not change the point about understanding. We are not called to strive to understand Scripture. We are, however, called to share it. Understanding is something that is given to us by teachers. But God said that the time would come when we would have no need of teachers.

> *Behold, the days come, saith the LORD, that I will make a new covenant with the house of Israel, and with the house of Judah: Not according to the covenant that I made with their fathers in the day that I took them by the hand to bring them out of the land of Egypt; which my covenant they brake, although I was an husband unto them, saith the LORD: But this shall be the covenant that I will make with the house of Israel;*
>
> *After those days, saith the LORD, I will put my law in their inward parts, and write it in their hearts; and will be their God, and they shall be my people. And they shall teach no more every man his neighbour, and every man his brother, saying, Know the LORD: for they shall all know me, from the least of them unto the greatest of them, saith the LORD: for I will forgive their iniquity, and I will remember their sin no more.*
> (Jeremiah 31:31-34)

Furthermore, that time—the time that is *After those days*—has come: it is the time of the Messiah. At the dawn of this time, the Messiah, Jesus Christ, told us just how God was going to accomplish the *new covenant*. By the way, the LORD did not say that it would be done by way of human understanding. It is done, now, and will continue to be done, into the future, by the transformation of human understanding; by the infusion of Higher knowledge from the Spirit of truth.

> *But the Comforter, which is the Holy Ghost, whom the Father will send in my name, he shall teach you all things, and bring all things to your remembrance, whatsoever I have said unto you.*
>
> (John 14:26)

Jesus is a very capable teacher. Jesus has the power to teach his followers anything that they need to know. As Christ, Jesus can teach anyone who will listen all that they should ever know. And there is the small complication: anyone who will listen. We are not ready to listen. This does not just mean that there are days when we are not ready to listen. This means that for our entire lifetime, we will not be ready to listen. There is just so much in the glory of God; it cannot be contained in the human frame, in the original equipment. As God said to the nation of Israel, by little and little; this is how we, too, will receive our specific Promised Land, as we yield to God.

Reaching out to us, in the image of the Father, Jesus also taught his disciples about the increase in their knowledge of the holy by stages; for, the staging of knowledge is what builds our understanding.

> *I have yet many things to say unto you, but ye cannot bear them now. Howbeit when he, the Spirit of truth, is come, he will guide you into all truth: for he shall not speak of himself; but whatsoever he shall hear, that shall he speak: and he will shew you things to come.*
>
> (John 16:12-13)

When it comes to the fullness of God, many times we think that we have taken a scuba dive into the word. However, if we look closely at ourselves, and truly evaluate our position in Christ; we will see that we are just wading in the water. This is the way it is; we are, after all, human: after all, we do have a limited recognized potential. We are prone, too often, to telling ourselves that we can't. And so we don't. And eventually, we really can't.

Though the limited recognition of our potential may be a natural limitation, it is not a spiritual limitation. In the way of the Spirit, the limited recognition of our potential is a benefit. Furthermore, it is a benefit that we must accept as being an attribute of all our fellow humans, on this earth. When you look at someone who you think is not a part of the Christian family (a thought which you should never have upon first observation), you might feel the urge to make them understand. I also used to feel those kinds of urges. Then, God revealed to me what had always been in the Bible. I had read it many times, and quoted it to many people; but I had not listened to the Holy Ghost reading it to me.

> *For while one saith, I am of Paul; and another, I am of Apollos; are ye not carnal? Who then is Paul, and who is Apollos, but ministers by whom ye believed, even as the Lord gave to every man? I have planted, Apollos watered; but God gave the increase. So then neither is he that planteth any thing, neither he that watereth; but God that giveth the increase.*
>
> *Now he that planteth and he that watereth are one: and every man shall receive his own reward according to his own labour. For we are labourers together with God: ye are God's husbandry, ye are God's building. According to the grace of God which is given unto me, as a wise masterbuilder, I have laid the foundation, and another buildeth thereon. But let every man take heed how he buildeth thereupon. For other foundation can no man lay than that is laid, which is Jesus Christ.*
>
> (1 Corinthians 3:4-11)

Finally, one day, God inspired me to ask Him why this was so. So, I did. I asked, "God, why can't we convert people to Your ways? Why didn't You give us the power to look people in the eye, and say to them, 'You will believe?' Why didn't You allow the prophets to cause the children of Israel to 'drop those idols, and follow the LORD? Why did You make the prophet so impotent as to have to, basically, ask the people to give them permission to present Your message to them? These are Your people; a nation begotten of You: You called him son. Why didn't You **make** Your son behave?"

You know something; the Holy Ghost answered it—he truly does teach all things. The Holy Ghost, the Spirit of truth, said, simply, "Because the Father loves them." And I am happy to tell you that because the Spirit of truth spoke directly to my spirit, and because, on this occasion, I was not able to raise my resistive guard fast enough; therefore, I perceived the answer. To love is not, to force. To love has a lot of ***allow*** in it. This is what is termed tolerance in the Bible. It is not an easy thing for humans to do.

God, however, has this love thing down to much more than a science, since that is what He Is. And all the Spirits that come from God are bestowed with the same measure of His love, to work with whatever charges they are given. The Spirit of Jesus Christ is one of the Spirits that is of God. Therefore, from observation of Jesus Christ's ministry, we can learn much about God the Father. As you read this portion of the ministry of Jesus, please notice the absence of force . . .

> *Come unto me, all ye that labour and are heavy laden, and I will give you rest. Take my yoke upon you, and learn of me; for I am meek and lowly in heart: and ye shall find rest unto your souls. For my yoke is easy, and my burden is light.*
>
> (Matthew 11:28-30)

The Spirit of God was included in the angel that came to Hagar, and comforted her. It was also in the angel that came to Sarai, and gave her the news—and to Abram, too, to let him know that an almost unimaginable thing was about to happen. In these, and many other cases of angels receiving an assignment from God, they came with the full power of the love of God. So powerful and obvious is the presence of the love of God in His true representatives—in this case, the angels—that those who receive the fruit of their delivery only see God. It is for this reason that many of them had the fear of death. What they feared was that they had seen God face to face. Indeed, life ceases if that occurs; the truth of that is as the LORD told Moses.

> *And he said, I will make all my goodness pass before thee, and I will proclaim the name of the LORD before thee; and will be gracious to whom I will be gracious, and will shew mercy on whom I will shew mercy. And he said, Thou canst not see my face: for there shall no man see me, and live.*
>
> (Exodus 33:19-20)

Given the observer's attribution of God's Spirit to the angels, as if they were, in fact, in the presence of God, it is no wonder that they were afraid. The reverence that was shown to the angels of God is the same sort of reverence for Scripture; for, in a real sense, it is too an angel of the LORD. Therefore, in reverence to this particular angel, we must apply its words of caution and reservation to any attempt to persuade us that we must, through our complete understanding of Scripture, see the face of God in it. To see God's face would be, for a natural human, an overwhelming spiritual encounter that would absorb the entire essence of a person. No one has done this, except the Son of man; who is, *he which is of God*. In all other cases, the person on the other end of the blessed sighting of the incarnate love of God was conversing with a representative of God; an angel. By the way; Jesus, too, is an angel—**the** Angel—of God.

> *Jesus therefore answered and said unto them, Murmur not among yourselves. No man can come to me, except the Father which hath sent me draw him: and I will raise him up at the last day. It is written in the prophets, And they shall be all taught of God.*
>
> *Every man therefore that hath heard, and hath learned of the Father, cometh unto me.*
>
> *Not that any man hath seen the Father, save he which is of God, he hath seen the Father.*
>
> (John 6:43-46)

This is where we go when we need to go deep into the mission of the Bible, which is portrayed in the text of the Bible: we immerse ourselves in the love of God; and, this love will pull us on a scuba dive into the depths of the richness of God. Then, when we are sent to appear before any other citizen of God's Creation, we will do so in God's way. As we handle our ministering, in the LORD, we will not go out, or come in, to others carrying with us a weight of determination to show them **THE WAY**. We will come only with the determination to love God first, and to share this love with anyone who crosses our path.

> *And we have known and believed the love that God hath to us. God is love; and he that dwelleth in love dwelleth in God, and God in him. Herein is our love made perfect, that we may have boldness in the day of judgment: because as he is, so are we in this world. There is no fear in love; but perfect love casteth out fear: because fear hath torment. He that feareth is not made perfect in love.*

We love him, because he first loved us. If a man say, I love God, and hateth his brother, he is a liar: for he that loveth not his brother whom he hath seen, how can he love God whom he hath not seen? And this commandment have we from him, That he who loveth God love his brother also.

(1 John 4:16-21)

We must also honor the Scripture that tells us how to give an answer. Yes, the Bible does tell us how we must give an answer to those who ask of us. Many think that they have to have a repertoire of Bible verses to throw at the person to whom they are witnessing of the things of God; especially, when witnessing in Christ of the things of God. Then, when the person starts to show resistance, we throw some more Bible verses at them. And if the person should dare indicate that they do not believe what we are saying, we throw what is considered to be the ultimate type of Bible verses: we tell them that they are *lost*. Well, unfortunately, the matter of being *lost* is not something that is allowed to us to know.

Brethren, my heart's desire and prayer to God for Israel is, that they might be saved. For I bear them record that they have a zeal of God, but not according to knowledge. For they being ignorant of God's righteousness, and going about to establish their own righteousness, have not submitted themselves unto the righteousness of God. For Christ is the end of the law for righteousness to every one that believeth.

For Moses describeth the righteousness which is of the law, That the man which doeth those things shall live by them.

But the righteousness which is of faith speaketh on this wise, Say not in thine heart, Who shall ascend into heaven? (that is, to bring Christ down from above:) Or, Who shall descend into the deep? (that is, to bring up Christ again from the dead.) But what saith it?

The word is nigh thee, even in thy mouth, and in thy heart: that is, the word of faith, which we preach; That if thou shalt confess with thy mouth the Lord Jesus, and shalt believe in thine heart that God hath raised him from the dead, thou shalt be saved.

(Romans 10:1-9)

Yes, it is true that we can know when a person is not living a life according to the righteousness of God . . .

> *Beware of false prophets, which come to you in sheep's clothing, but inwardly they are ravening wolves. Ye shall know them by their fruits. Do men gather grapes of thorns, or figs of thistles? Even so every good tree bringeth forth good fruit; but a corrupt tree bringeth forth evil fruit. A good tree cannot bring forth evil fruit, neither can a corrupt tree bring forth good fruit. Every tree that bringeth not forth good fruit is hewn down, and cast into the fire. Wherefore by their fruits ye shall know them.*
>
> *Not every one that saith unto me, Lord, Lord, shall enter into the kingdom of heaven; but he that doeth the will of my Father which is in heaven.*
>
> (Matthew 7:15-21)

. . . But, this knowledge of behavior-seen does not give us the right, or the responsibility, to proclaim others final destination; as based on some incident that has happened at a time of our meeting with them. Such focused declarations of final destination are outside of the love of God, and they violate the teaching that Jesus sent to us through his apostle, Paul.

> *Brethren, if a man be overtaken in a fault, ye which are spiritual, restore such an one in the spirit of meekness; considering thyself, lest thou also be tempted. Bear ye one another's burdens, and so fulfil the law of Christ.*
>
> (Galatians 6:1-2)

It is not meek to say to a person, "So you won't listen to me. Well, I'm going to Heaven; and I won't see you there!" No, that is not meek, at all. And in most cases, it does not restore the person.

Oh, you thought that Galatians 6:1-2 only governs our relationships with those who believe? Think about it; what is the biggest error that anyone can ever make? What is the greatest fault in which one can be overtaken? Isn't it, to not accept the pull of God on their life? Those who saw the works of God in the nation of Israel, at this time in its history, would tell you that it is.

> *Behold, ye trust in lying words, that cannot profit. Will ye steal, murder, and commit adultery, and swear falsely, and burn incense unto Baal, and walk after other gods whom ye know not; And come and stand before me in this house, which is called by my name, and say, We are delivered to do all these abominations? Is this house, which is called by my name, become a den of robbers in your eyes? Behold, even I have seen it, saith the LORD. But go ye now unto my place which was in Shiloh, where I set my name at the first, and see what I did to it for the wickedness of my people Israel.*
>
> *And now, because ye have done all these works, saith the LORD, and I spake unto you, rising up early and speaking, but ye heard not; and I called you, but ye answered not; Therefore will I do unto this house, which is called by my name, wherein ye trust, and unto the place which I gave to you and to your fathers, as I have done to Shiloh. And I will cast you out of my sight, as I have cast out all your brethren, even the whole seed of Ephraim.*
>
> (Jeremiah 7:8-15)

So, when we are introduced to someone, by the Spirit of truth, and we are given the push to speak to them of the Gospel; then, we must take some time to understand what is happening. When the Holy Ghost pushes us to communicate with someone on a matter of the Gospel, it is because something is missing. There is an error of omission somewhere. Now, you may think that it is always an error in the person to whom you are directed. This may or may not be the case. It may be an error of omission in you.

What you are led to share with another blessed human offspring of Creation—whether person or group—may be the very message that you have been resisting. Do you see now how this matter of trying to diagnose the status of someone else, in God, can become really complex? If not, then notice the perplexity that Peter experienced when he was sent to this group of people that needed the message he had been given.

> *Now Peter sat without in the palace: and a damsel came unto him, saying, Thou also wast with Jesus of Galilee. But he denied before them all, saying, I know not what thou sayest.*
>
> *And when he was gone out into the porch, another maid saw him, and said unto them that were there, This fellow was also with Jesus of Nazareth. And again he denied with an oath, I do not know the man.*
>
> *And after a while came unto him they that stood by, and said to Peter, Surely thou also art one of them; for thy speech bewrayeth thee. Then began he to curse and to swear, saying, I know not the man.*
>
> *And immediately the cock crew.*
>
> *And Peter remembered the word of Jesus, which said unto him, Before the cock crow, thou shalt deny me thrice. And he went out, and wept bitterly.*
>
> (Matthew 26:69-75)

The perplexed state of Peter's being arose because he did not understand that, first he needed to receive the message that he carried. In the time before his period of perplexity and drift, Peter had been told of his need. Jesus himself told Peter that he was in a time of a need for deeper understanding and direction.

> *And the Lord said, Simon, Simon, behold, Satan hath desired to have you, that he may sift you as wheat: But I have prayed for thee, that thy faith fail not: and when thou art converted, strengthen thy brethren.*
>
> *And he said unto him, Lord, I am ready to go with thee, both into prison, and to death.*
>
> *And he said, I tell thee, Peter, the cock shall not crow this day, before that thou shalt thrice deny that thou knowest me.*
>
> (Luke 22:31-34)

This complexity is present, especially, when we try to diagnose its nature in the audience; and then, based on our being sent to talk to them of the Gospel, we insist that they are the only ones with deficiencies. When we walk in the LORD, among our greatest strength is our openness to the situation to which we are sent. For, when we are open to other perspectives, we know that our best, and only successful, way of rightly dividing the word of truth, at the deeper levels, is to do so in the love of God. This does not mean that we have a pliable philosophy of life: we are listening; not necessarily, absorbing. We may only need to catalog what we hear. Scripture tells us where our mind needs to abide.

> *Behold, I send you forth as sheep in the midst of wolves: be ye therefore wise as serpents, and harmless as doves. But beware of men: for they will deliver you up to the councils, and they will scourge you in their synagogues; And ye shall be brought before governors and kings for my sake, for a testimony against them and the Gentiles.*
>
> (Matthew 10:16-18)

Understand this: when we are talking with our children, it may be sufficient to wade in the water. It is not always required that we present the Gospel in its richest form to those who are given to us as children. When they are children, they will believe because they see it in us. We can, therefore, tell them the stories of what we read in the Bible, and this will be sufficient for the child.

However, when one grows up; then, one has a need for different treatment. When we are interacting with such a person, we must discard all pressuring that may creep into our attempts to share the Gospel. When we are speaking to a more mature one, we need to settle into a more relaxed communion with them, in our speech about the things of God. This may mean that we do not, then, know precisely what must be said. No, we are not held responsible for not knowing what to say when we come to someone. We study to be approved of God: we study because this pleases God: we do not study so that we can convince man.

To say that our objective is not, to explain until conversion, may offend some of those folks who call themselves apologists. We do not have to apologize for God. We do not have to explain God. We do not have to defend God. Moreover, we do not have to convince anyone that the

LORD God is. We have only to present God: for extra-us communions' sake, this is the depth to which we need to go.

For the sake of all our times of service to the LORD that is done for the sake of our soul as we abide in our closet of worship, we many need to go much deeper. How we do this is clearly laid out for us in the Bible: we go deep in the word by going deep in the Spirit of truth. Jesus said it clearly.

> *When they therefore were come together, they asked of him, saying, Lord, wilt thou at this time restore again the kingdom to Israel?*
>
> *And he said unto them, It is not for you to know the times or the seasons, which the Father hath put in his own power. But ye shall receive power, after that the Holy Ghost is come upon you: and ye shall be witnesses unto me both in Jerusalem, and in all Judaea, and in Samaria, and unto the uttermost part of the earth.*
>
> (Acts 1:6-8)

Moses is another living example of the way one goes deeply into the Spirit of truth. Moses was immersed in the Spirit to such a depth that his experience in the LORD was given to others, to serve in them as the power of their service to the LORD. Moreover, the transfer from Moses to the others was done with no strain or stress, on either side. This "battle" belonged, then, as it still does, now, to the LORD.

> *And the LORD said unto Moses, Gather unto me seventy men of the elders of Israel, whom thou knowest to be the elders of the people, and officers over them; and bring them unto the tabernacle of the congregation, that they may stand there with thee. And I will come down and talk with thee there: and I will take of the spirit which is upon thee, and will put it upon them; and they shall bear the burden of the people with thee, that thou bear it not thyself alone.*
>
> (Numbers 11:16-17)

So when you find yourself face to face with someone, or *some ones*, to whom God has told you to present His Gospel; just follow the Scripture. Though the following Scripture tells us how to stand in the face of confrontation, its admonition is also appropriate for all situations in which we share the word of God.

> *But when they deliver you up, take no thought how or what ye shall speak: for it shall be given you in that same hour what ye shall speak. For it is not ye that speak, but the Spirit of your Father which speaketh in you.*
>
> (Matthew 10:19-20)

For, in some sense, everyone you meet will try to *deliver you up*, to a certain degree. Moreover, as they deliver you up, they will also try to tear God down, as they judge Him. (Yes, they do have the audacity to do this.) They may not be judging God on His righteousness, but instead, they may be judging God by you. This is why God, being jealous to protect His reputation, tells us to let the Spirit of truth, sent from Him, deliver the message. As we do this, we will avoid any temptation to shift into the role of judge of others; possibly doing so in an unnecessary spirit of defense of God. We must not judge others unless the LORD has called us to sit as a judge in the land. The prophet Elijah was taught about the lack of need for such defenses, by way of words of encouragement from the LORD.

> *And he came thither unto a cave, and lodged there; and, behold, the word of the LORD came to him, and he said unto him, What doest thou here, Elijah?*
>
> *And he said, I have been very jealous for the LORD God of hosts: for the children of Israel have forsaken thy covenant, thrown down thine altars, and slain thy prophets with the sword; and I, even I only, am left; and they seek my life, to take it away.*
>
> *And he said, Go forth, and stand upon the mount before the LORD.*
>
> *And, behold, the LORD passed by, and a great and strong wind rent the mountains, and brake in pieces the rocks before the LORD; but the LORD was not in the wind: and after the wind an earthquake; but the LORD was not in the earthquake:*

> *And after the earthquake a fire; but the LORD was not in the fire: and after the fire a still small voice.*
>
> *And it was so, when Elijah heard it that he wrapped his face in his mantle, and went out, and stood in the entering in of the cave.*
>
> *And, behold, there came a voice unto him, and said, What doest thou here, Elijah?*
>
> *And he said, I have been very jealous for the LORD God of hosts: because the children of Israel have forsaken thy covenant, thrown down thine altars, and slain thy prophets with the sword; and I, even I only, am left; and they seek my life, to take it away.*
>
> *And the LORD said unto him, Go, return on thy way to the wilderness of Damascus: and when thou comest, anoint Hazael to be king over Syria: And Jehu the son of Nimshi shalt thou anoint to be king over Israel: and Elisha the son of Shaphat of Abelmeholah shalt thou anoint to be prophet in thy room. And it shall come to pass, that him that escapeth the sword of Hazael shall Jehu slay: and him that escapeth from the sword of Jehu shall Elisha slay. Yet I have left me seven thousand in Israel, all the knees which have not bowed unto Baal, and every mouth which hath not kissed him.*
>
> (1 Kings 19:9-18)

The LORD declared His ability to take care of Himself. And the way that God takes care of Himself is in a fashion that is similar to his revelation of Elijah: *Yet I have left me seven thousand in Israel.* Among the people of God, the LORD has no need for our judgment skills; the breadth of His judgment is sufficient for all things. (Also note that the LORD sent His judgment to other kings of the world of that day, besides Israel.) In the church, there is no one that can sit as a judge; the Spirit of truth is the only judge that is needed. In the church, the Spirit of truth is the ambassador of the Father that is empowered to know us, and, thereby, to know when we, both in the church and out in the wider world, need to be judged. Wherefore even if we are authorized as a judge in government, we must not arbitrarily judge others; and we must not give others the opportunity to, with presumed justification, judge God, based on our actions.

Of course, there will be some people who will, even if we do no more than sneeze in their presence, judge God as based on our actions. These are the ones that God will move, through the intervention of His Spirit in their lives, when it is their time. We are not responsible for such ones; they are not exempt, and they are not hopeless. Their knee too will bow; for, every knee will bow; in the LORD'S time, He will require it. An example of this is the lesson of the wicked judge.

> *And he spake a parable unto them to this end, that men ought always to pray, and not to faint; Saying, There was in a city a judge, which feared not God, neither regarded man: And there was a widow in that city; and she came unto him, saying, Avenge me of mine adversary.*
>
> *And he would not for a while: but afterward he said within himself, Though I fear not God, nor regard man; Yet because this widow troubleth me, I will avenge her, lest by her continual coming she weary me.*
>
> *And the Lord said, Hear what the unjust judge saith. And shall not God avenge his own elect, which cry day and night unto him, though he bear long with them?*
>
> (Luke 18:1-7)

In this message, Jesus let us know that there is a very powerful force that has been given to us. This force is the power of prayer. The parable Jesus told did not mean that we could talk face-to-face with God, as the woman did with the judge; but only that we can present our case before Him. Our starting point should be the Lord's Prayer; for in starting there, we have raised the awareness of our availability for service to God. What; you did not know that the Lord's Prayer was a message from a volunteer? Well, I think you ought to look at it one more time. Who do you think God is calling into action in order to bring the Father's Kingdom to this earth as described in the Prayer?

> *After this manner therefore pray ye: Our Father which art in heaven, Hallowed be thy name. Thy kingdom come, Thy will be done in earth, as it is in heaven. Give us this day our daily bread. And forgive us our debts, as we forgive our debtors. And lead us not*

> *into temptation, but deliver us from evil: For thine is the kingdom, and the power, and the glory, for ever. Amen.*
> (Matthew 6:9-13)

We can always pray in this fashion; even if our life has degenerated to the point where God has to put on His Angry Face, we still can approach Him. Even when we deserve the Angry Face of God, because we think that we must say something volatile to someone, whether God likes it or not; we may still ask the Father for aid. We can go to Him and ask for His intervention with those who are causing us to want to grab them and shake them, and make them believe. We can call a personal timeout for us, and then we can meet with God in our private closet, when we want to just ***slap someone with the word.***

To we, who believe, these non-listeners, these unbelievers, may be seen as our adversaries. We raise this (as a matter of our opinion) because they just do not seem to want to accept what we believe to be true, and, too, they often criticize us for our beliefs. When this happens, we find ourselves entertaining a thought that is similar to this one:

> God, we want you to avenge us of our adversary. God, we want you to convert them. And if you want ***me*** to slap them—with the word of truth—then here am I, LORD, send me. God, maybe you want to rest your arm, or maybe there's a bigger fish for you to fry. LORD, please just let me take care of this.

In its own way, this pattern of thought promotes the message of the Gospel. In a warped kind of way, we are still expressing the desire of the Lord's Prayer. Though, for now let us just calm down a bit, and, with love, go into the world to fulfill what was given to us to do. Let us honor the Lord Jesus Christ by accepting our commission to the world; performing it, one person at a time. We do this even when each of these individuals is a part of a ten thousand member group. The message that goes forth, from the words that we say, still flows through the group to one person at a time.

> *Now when Jesus was risen early the first day of the week, he appeared first to Mary Magdalene, out of whom he had cast seven devils.*

And she went and told them that had been with him, as they mourned and wept.

And they, when they had heard that he was alive, and had been seen of her, believed not.

After that he appeared in another form unto two of them, as they walked, and went into the country.

And they went and told it unto the residue:
neither believed they them.

Afterward he appeared unto the eleven as they sat at meat, and upbraided them with their unbelief and hardness of heart, because they believed not them which had seen him after he was risen. And he said unto them,

Go ye into all the world, and preach the gospel to every creature. He that believeth and is baptized shall be saved; but he that believeth not shall be damned.

And these signs shall follow them that believe; In my name shall they cast out devils; they shall speak with new tongues; They shall take up serpents; and if they drink any deadly thing, it shall not hurt them; they shall lay hands on the sick, and they shall recover.

So then after the Lord had spoken unto them, he was received up into heaven, and sat on the right hand of God.

And they went forth, and preached every where, the Lord working with them, and confirming the word with signs following. Amen.

(Mark 16:9-20)

THE WORD FROM THE BIBLE

Revelation 19:5-21

And a voice came out of the throne, saying, Praise our God, all ye his servants, and ye that fear him, both small and great. And I heard as it were the voice of a great multitude, and as the voice of many waters, and as the voice of mighty thunderings, saying, Alleluia: for the Lord God omnipotent reigneth. Let us be glad and rejoice, and give honour to him: for the marriage of the Lamb is come, and his wife hath made herself ready. And to her was granted that she should be arrayed in fine linen, clean and white: for the fine linen is the righteousness of saints.

And he saith unto me, Write, Blessed are they which are called unto the marriage supper of the Lamb. And he saith unto me, These are the true sayings of God. And I fell at his feet to worship him. And he said unto me, See thou do it not: I am thy fellowservant, and of thy brethren that have the testimony of Jesus: worship God: for the testimony of Jesus is the spirit of prophecy.

And I saw heaven opened, and behold a white horse; and he that sat upon him was called Faithful and True, and in righteousness he doth judge and make war. His eyes were as a flame of fire, and on his head were many crowns; and he had a name written, that no man knew, but he himself. And he was clothed with a vesture dipped in blood: and his name is called The Word of God. And the armies which were in heaven followed him upon white horses, clothed in fine linen, white and clean. And out of his mouth goeth a sharp sword, that with it he should smite the nations: and he shall rule them with a rod of iron: and he treadeth the winepress of the fierceness and wrath of Almighty

God. And he hath on his vesture and on his thigh a name written, KING OF KINGS, AND LORD OF LORDS.

And I saw an angel standing in the sun; and he cried with a loud voice, saying to all the fowls that fly in the midst of heaven, Come and gather yourselves together unto the supper of the great God; That ye may eat the flesh of kings, and the flesh of captains, and the flesh of mighty men, and the flesh of horses, and of them that sit on them, and the flesh of all men, both free and bond, both small and great.

And I saw the beast, and the kings of the earth, and their armies, gathered together to make war against him that sat on the horse, and against his army. And the beast was taken, and with him the false prophet that wrought miracles before him, with which he deceived them that had received the mark of the beast, and them that worshipped his image. These both were cast alive into a lake of fire burning with brimstone.

And the remnant were slain with the sword of him that sat upon the horse, which sword proceeded out of his mouth: and all the fowls were filled with their flesh.

Chapter Seven

Revelation

Just Doing God's Will

Here is another one of those obvious statements: The Word of God accomplishes the will of God. What may not be obvious is how the Word of God accomplishes the will of God. The most common view of this process is that it is done by smiting individuals, and clearing their way for the righteous to live in political peace. This is not the way God operates. There are a number of individuals who are mentioned in the Bible, who did some pretty terrible things, but God did not smite them. To find a list of them, read the books 1 Kings and 2 Kings. Among the kings of Israel there were many really bad men. They turned away from God, they killed their own people, they sent the property of God from the temple to others to protect themselves; and many other things that did not please God; but still, God did not smite them all. In many cases, God did not smite them, at all; rather, God smote the nation. Here is an example: *Manasseh king of Judah.*

> *And Hezekiah slept with his fathers: and Manasseh his son reigned in his stead.*
>
> (2 Kings 20:21)

> *Manasseh was twelve years old when he began to reign, and reigned fifty and five years in Jerusalem. And his mother's name was Hephzibah. And he did that which was evil in the sight of the LORD, after the abominations of the heathen, whom the LORD cast out before the children of Israel.*
>
> (2 Kings 21:1-2)

> *And the LORD spake by his servants the prophets, saying, Because Manasseh king of Judah hath done these abominations, and hath done wickedly above all that the Amorites did, which were before him, and hath made Judah also to sin with his idols: Therefore thus saith the LORD God of Israel, Behold, I am bringing such evil upon Jerusalem and Judah, that whosoever heareth of it, both his ears shall tingle. And I will stretch over Jerusalem the line of Samaria, and the plummet of the house of Ahab: and I will wipe Jerusalem as a man wipeth a dish, wiping it, and turning it upside down. And I will forsake the remnant of mine inheritance, and deliver them into the hand of their enemies; and they shall become a prey and a spoil to all their enemies; Because they have done that which was evil in my sight, and have provoked me to anger, since the day their fathers came forth out of Egypt, even unto this day.*
>
> *Moreover Manasseh shed innocent blood very much, till he had filled Jerusalem from one end to another; beside his sin wherewith he made Judah to sin, in doing that which was evil in the sight of the LORD.*
>
> *Now the rest of the acts of Manasseh, and all that he did, and his sin that he sinned, are they not written in the book of the chronicles of the kings of Judah? And Manasseh slept with his fathers, and was buried in the garden of his own house, in the garden of Uzza: and Amon his son reigned in his stead.*
>
> (2 Kings 21:10-18)

The LORD did not say that he was directing his judgment at the king: God directed the judgment at the nation. Manasseh king of Judah lived for a fairly long time—long, in relation to other kings of that day. Manasseh was twelve when he started in office, and he reigned for 55 more years. Then, at the end of Manasseh's life, he *slept with his fathers.* There were several more kings of Judah after king Manasseh.

King	Type of rule	Reign, in years
Manasseh	evil	55 years
Amon	evil	02 years
Josiah	righteous	31 years
Jehoahaz	evil	03 months
Eliakim	evil	11 years
Jehoiachin	evil	03 months
Mattaniah (name changed to Zedekiah)		
	evil	11 years

During all the time of those kings, God sent his prophets to plead for repentance from the nation of Israel.

> *Since the day that your fathers came forth out of the land of Egypt unto this day I have even sent unto you all my servants the prophets, daily rising up early and sending them: Yet they hearkened not unto me, nor inclined their ear, but hardened their neck: they did worse than their fathers.*
>
> (Jeremiah 7:25-26)

This is the way God does things: He sends His Word to accomplish His will. In the case of the prophets, this word was not a command to make anything for God, but a request for the nation to return to God. In that statement, please note that the stress was on the request, not on the command. The commandments of God had already been given, in the law of Moses. The request was that Israel would return to its peculiar place of service, as the LORD'S peculiar treasure. Had God given a command to return, there would have been no option but for it to be obeyed.

> *For my thoughts are not your thoughts, neither are your ways my ways, saith the LORD. For as the heavens are higher than the earth, so are my ways higher than your ways, and my thoughts than your thoughts. For as the rain cometh down, and the snow from heaven, and returneth not thither, but watereth the earth, and maketh it bring forth and bud, that it may give seed to the sower, and bread to the eater: So shall my word be that goeth forth out of my mouth: it shall not return unto me void, but it shall*

accomplish that which I please, and it shall prosper in the thing whereto I sent it.

(Isaiah 55:8-11)

God did not create man so that He can control Him. God created man so that mankind can learn His ways. One of the ways of God is that those who know Him, and who love Him, will give worship to Him. Worship is not just saying "at a boy" to God. To worship is to understand that our best state is achieved when we are encased in God. Worship is a result of our moving closer to God. When we move closer to God, then we observe all that He has prepared for our well-being.

For since the beginning of the world men have not heard, nor perceived by the ear, neither hath the eye seen, O God, beside thee, what he hath prepared for him that waiteth for him. Thou meetest him that rejoiceth and worketh righteousness, those that remember thee in thy ways: behold, thou art wroth; for we have sinned: in those is continuance, and we shall be saved.

But we are all as an unclean thing, and all our righteousnesses are as filthy rags; and we all do fade as a leaf; and our iniquities, like the wind, have taken us away. And there is none that calleth upon thy name, that stirreth up himself to take hold of thee: for thou hast hid thy face from us, and hast consumed us, because of our iniquities.

But now, O LORD, thou art our father; we are the clay, and thou our potter; and we all are the work of thy hand. Be not wroth very sore, O LORD, neither remember iniquity for ever: behold, see, we beseech thee, we are all thy people.

(Isaiah 64:4-9)

As we move closer to God and we see all that He has done to order our lives, we find ourselves repeating these words of the Israelites, but in a childlike tone, rather than in the intensity that prompted their response.

And Elijah said unto all the people, Come near unto me.

And all the people came near unto him. And he repaired the altar of the LORD that was broken down.

And Elijah took twelve stones, according to the number of the tribes of the sons of Jacob, unto whom the word of the LORD came, saying, Israel shall be thy name: And with the stones he built an altar in the name of the LORD: and he made a trench about the altar, as great as would contain two measures of seed. And he put the wood in order, and cut the bullock in pieces, and laid him on the wood, and said, Fill four barrels with water, and pour it on the burnt sacrifice, and on the wood.

And he said, Do it the second time.

And they did it the second time.

And he said, Do it the third time.

And they did it the third time.

And the water ran round about the altar; and he filled the trench also with water.

And it came to pass at the time of the offering of the evening sacrifice, that Elijah the prophet came near, and said, LORD God of Abraham, Isaac, and of Israel, let it be known this day that thou art God in Israel, and that I am thy servant, and that I have done all these things at thy word. Hear me, O LORD, hear me, that this people may know that thou art the LORD God, and that thou hast turned their heart back again.

Then the fire of the LORD fell, and consumed the burnt sacrifice, and the wood, and the stones, and the dust, and licked up the water that was in the trench.

And when all the people saw it, they fell on their faces: and they said, The LORD, he is the God; the LORD, he is the God.

(1 Kings 18:30-39)

This is worship. To not just say, "*The LORD, he is the God; the LORD, he is the God*," but to say so in sincerity and in truth, and because we understand that even though the LORD God is well above any man, there is no word that we can use to describe the wonder that we behold. In the time of Joshua, Israel was in that place, as Joshua issued the challenge to serve.

> *Now therefore fear the LORD, and serve him in sincerity and in truth: and put away the gods which your fathers served on the other side of the flood, and in Egypt; and serve ye the LORD. And if it seem evil unto you to serve the LORD, choose you this day whom ye will serve; whether the gods which your fathers served that were on the other side of the flood, or the gods of the Amorites, in whose land ye dwell: but as for me and my house, we will serve the LORD.*
>
> *And the people answered and said, God forbid that we should forsake the LORD, to serve other gods; For the LORD our God, he it is that brought us up and our fathers out of the land of Egypt, from the house of bondage, and which did those great signs in our sight, and preserved us in all the way wherein we went, and among all the people through whom we passed: And the LORD drave out from before us all the people, even the Amorites which dwelt in the land: therefore will we also serve the LORD; for he is our God.*
>
> *And Joshua said unto the people, Ye cannot serve the LORD: for he is an holy God; he is a jealous God; he will not forgive your transgressions nor your sins. If ye forsake the LORD, and serve strange gods, then he will turn and do you hurt, and consume you, after that he hath done you good.*
>
> *And the people said unto Joshua, Nay; but we will serve the LORD.*
>
> *And Joshua said unto the people, Ye are witnesses against yourselves that ye have chosen you the LORD, to serve him.*
>
> *And they said, We are witnesses.*
>
> *Now therefore put away, said he, the strange gods which are among you, and incline your heart unto the LORD God of Israel.*
>
> *And the people said unto Joshua, The LORD our God will we serve, and his voice will we obey.*
>
> (Joshua 24:14-24)

Even as majestic as the LORD is, the marvel of existence is that God still allows us to speak to Him. We do so in our personal devotions, in words of wonder that come from the heart of our human condition. This is the grace of God, extended to each of us. And, if you truly place yourself in the childlike mindset, you will understand just how big this allowance is to a child. Remember, though; it is in this manner that we must come to God, as a child, to truly accept the best that He has to offer . . .

> *At the same time came the disciples unto Jesus, saying, Who is the greatest in the kingdom of heaven?*
>
> *And Jesus called a little child unto him, and set him in the midst of them, And said, Verily I say unto you, Except ye be converted, and become as little children, ye shall not enter into the kingdom of heaven. Whosoever therefore shall humble himself as this little child, the same is greatest in the kingdom of heaven. And whoso shall receive one such little child in my name receiveth me. But whoso shall offend one of these little ones which believe in me, it were better for him that a millstone were hanged about his neck, and that he were drowned in the depth of the sea.*
>
> (Matthew 18:1-6)

We also must understand that God did not create man for the purpose of destroying him. He made this clear when he *loaded* Jesus of Nazareth, the Christ, the Son of God (and many other titles), with the prophecy about the destruction in Jerusalem. When God executed this judgment, He did not wait until the evil ones had prevailed against the saints of God, and eliminated them. To give them time to prepare for, and, thereby, evade, the attempt to destroy them; the representative of God, the Son of God, gave a warning to the righteous, so that they might be saved from the destruction.

> *When ye therefore shall see the abomination of desolation, spoken of by Daniel the prophet, stand in the holy place, (whoso readeth, let him understand:) Then let them which be in Judaea flee into the mountains: Let him which is on the housetop not come down to take any thing out of his house: Neither let him which is in the*

> *field return back to take his clothes. And woe unto them that are with child, and to them that give suck in those days!*
>
> *But pray ye that your flight be not in the winter, neither on the sabbath day: For then shall be great tribulation, such as was not since the beginning of the world to this time, no, nor ever shall be.*
>
> (Matthew 24:15-21)

If God had waited, this would have allowed all the evil ones to consume everyone else. The desire of the evil one was to consume his perceived adversary, if they could, before they were consumed. However, if they could not prevent their own destruction, the evil ones were content to bring about the destruction of everybody, and, if necessary, everything. "Misery loves company. If I gotta go, I'm taking you out with me. Cut off their nose to spite their face." These and many other, very well used, threats would have been put into active use by those in control.

You have probably heard the story about emperor Nero, who is reputed to have given a recital, of sorts, while Rome was burning. In this story, Nero, an emperor, amused himself while folks around him died. This is the character flaw that is, too often, in those who do not honor God, and yet are in power. Though, in spite of their portion of power, God will not let them destroy the human race. This limitation of damage was activated in the time of assault on the newly collected Christian family.

> *And except those days should be shortened, there should no flesh be saved: but for the elect's sake those days shall be shortened.*
>
> (Matthew 24:22)

This brings us to the lesson that is being taught back to the world of the time of *The Revelation of Jesus Christ, which God gave unto him, to show unto his servants things which must shortly come to pass.* In that day, the major burst of power in the lesson was delivered by the *KING OF KINGS, AND LORD OF LORDS*, when he came to set things straight on the earth. God's will is that the human race continues, until such time as He has designated that it has continued long enough; and this time may never come. God will not let any earthly individual, or nation, destroy what He has made, before the time (and there may not be a time set). This is especially true of those whom He has made, known as humans. Every soul of every human belongs to him.

> *The word of the LORD came unto me again, saying, What mean ye, that ye use this proverb concerning the land of Israel, saying, The fathers have eaten sour grapes, and the children's teeth are set on edge?*
>
> *As I live, saith the Lord GOD, ye shall not have occasion any more to use this proverb in Israel. Behold, all souls are mine; as the soul of the father, so also the soul of the son is mine: the soul that sinneth, it shall die.*
>
> (Ezekiel 18:1-4)

Each time the *KING OF KINGS, AND LORD OF LORDS* has come, he has come in the full power of God. The power of God is contained in *The Word of God*; but, not limited by it. *The Word of God* is fully expressed in the Lamb of God, who is, the Son of God. And, the Son of God is Jesus of Nazareth, the Christ, who is, the Messiah. But you already knew that, didn't you? (By the way, he is also the Son of man.) Those souls that have yielded themselves to the righteousness of God receive a rich blessing from God, as declared by *The Word of God.*

> *But if a man be just, and do that which is lawful and right, And hath not eaten upon the mountains, neither hath lifted up his eyes to the idols of the house of Israel, neither hath defiled his neighbour's wife, neither hath come near to a menstruous woman, And hath not oppressed any, but hath restored to the debtor his pledge, hath spoiled none by violence, hath given his bread to the hungry, and hath covered the naked with a garment; He that hath not given forth upon usury, neither hath taken any increase, that hath withdrawn his hand from iniquity, hath executed true judgment between man and man, Hath walked in my statutes, and hath kept my judgments, to deal truly; he is just, he shall surely live, saith the Lord GOD.*
>
> (Ezekiel 18:5-9)

Let us go further. Jesus said that the Father had given him everything that He has. Among those things that were opened up to Jesus Christ, by God the Father, is all power in Heaven and in earth.

> *Then the eleven disciples went away into Galilee, into a mountain where Jesus had appointed them. And when they saw him, they worshipped him: but some doubted.*
>
> *And Jesus came and spake unto them, saying, All power is given unto me in heaven and in earth.*
>
> (Matthew 28:16-18)

This is a power beyond the energy sources that we have directly experienced. Jesus was not topping out this at the level of all the earth's nuclear power; that is too weak. Jesus was not limiting this to the power of the sun; it is not intense enough. Nor was Jesus limiting it to the pull in a black hole, so called by scientists; that would not be attractive enough. Jesus was talking about the power of the LORD of hosts: This is the power of the Spirit. The power of the Spirit is a force that makes a dwarf star's effect as intensive as a floating piece of dust, by comparison. It has power that makes anti-matter seem as a drop of rain. The Spirit is the power that can makes a positron, as well as any other subatomic particle, submit. To those who are deep into science, we say, the power of the Spirit is the essence that, if they truly exist, builds the quarks, including the one that is, at this time, still eluding us. This massive and expansive force is the power of *The Word of God.* This is the power that was given unto Jesus of Nazareth.

> *And the Word was made flesh, and dwelt among us, (and we beheld his glory, the glory as of the only begotten of the Father,) full of grace and truth. John bare witness of him, and cried, saying, This was he of whom I spake, He that cometh after me is preferred before me: for he was before me. And of his fulness have all we received, and grace for grace. For the law was given by Moses, but grace and truth came by Jesus Christ.*
>
> (John 1:14-17)

Now, you have to understand the power of *The Word of God.* It is not a power that you hold; it is a power that you become. As promised by the Son, who holds all power *in heaven and in earth*; at Pentecost, the disciples got a little taste of what this means.

> *When they therefore were come together, they asked of him, saying, Lord, wilt thou at this time restore again the kingdom to Israel?*
>
> *And he said unto them, It is not for you to know the times or the seasons, which the Father hath put in his own power. But ye shall receive power, after that the Holy Ghost is come upon you: and ye shall be witnesses unto me both in Jerusalem, and in all Judaea, and in Samaria, and unto the uttermost part of the earth.*
>
> (Acts 1:6-8)

> *And when the day of Pentecost was fully come, they were all with one accord in one place. And suddenly there came a sound from heaven as of a rushing mighty wind, and it filled all the house where they were sitting. And there appeared unto them cloven tongues like as of fire, and it sat upon each of them. And they were all filled with the Holy Ghost, and began to speak with other tongues, as the Spirit gave them utterance.*
>
> (Acts 2:1-4)

We do not say that the power of the incarnate Word of God was first introduced to the world with the arrival of the Christ; for, it was in use throughout the righteous lives of the men of the Old Testament. Moses was introduced to it at the burning bush. Joshua was introduced to it when he met the captain of the host of the LORD. It is the power that was delivered to, and that worked through all the prophets of God. And it is the power that is resident in the testimony of Jesus. For, the Scripture reveals that *the testimony of Jesus is the spirit of prophecy*. In all these cases, it is brought to bear in order to present, or to perform, the will of God. *The Word of God* is the power that is born of God; therefore, it is Spirit. Moreover, it is Spirit in which we must be immersed.

> *Nicodemus saith unto him, How can a man be born when he is old? can he enter the second time into his mother's womb, and be born?*

> *Jesus answered, Verily, verily, I say unto thee, Except a man be born of water and of the Spirit, he cannot enter into the kingdom of God. That which is born of the flesh is flesh; and that which is born of the Spirit is spirit.*
>
> (John 3:4-6)

At the beginning of the establishment of the framework for human existence, *The Word of God* was brought into effectual interaction with the entire kingdom of man. It is the power behind Creation, and the power within the establishment of the kingdom of man. This is described by the apostle John.

> *In the beginning was the Word, and the Word was with God, and the Word was God. The same was in the beginning with God. All things were made by him; and without him was not any thing made that was made. In him was life; and the life was the light of men.*
>
> (John 1:1-4)

The Word of God: doing the will of God. It is no wonder then that Jesus could proclaim that life in the Father, through the Son, is easy.

> *All things are delivered unto me of my Father: and no man knoweth the Son, but the Father; neither knoweth any man the Father, save the Son, and he to whomsoever the Son will reveal him.*
>
> *Come unto me, all ye that labour and are heavy laden, and I will give you rest. Take my yoke upon you, and learn of me; for I am meek and lowly in heart: and ye shall find rest unto your souls. For my yoke is easy, and my burden is light.*
>
> (Matthew 11:27-30)

It is very easy indeed. All we have to do is to do the will of God. We do not have to create it. We do not have to analyze it. We do not have to defend it. Oh, and by he way, though God may give us full understanding of the why about our mission for Him; actually, we do not have to understand it. All we have to do is to do it. But to do it, we have to know it. This is where two Scripture provides assistance.

*Of these things put them in remembrance, charging them before the Lord that they strive not about words to no profit, but to the subverting of the hearers. *

Study to show thyself approved unto God, a workman that needeth not to be ashamed, rightly dividing the word of truth. But shun profane and vain babblings: for they will increase unto more ungodliness.

(2 Timothy 2:14-16)

Rejoice evermore.
Pray without ceasing.
In every thing give thanks: for this is the will of God in Christ Jesus concerning you.
Quench not the Spirit.
Despise not prophesyings.
Prove all things; hold fast that which is good.
Abstain from all appearance of evil.

And the very God of peace sanctify you wholly; and I pray God your whole spirit and soul and body be preserved blameless unto the coming of our Lord Jesus Christ.

(1 Thessalonians 5:16-23)

For those of you who are just doing God's will; wonder at this, for a while. For, when you do, you will begin to understand just how great the gift is that God has given us at the request of His Son. I repeat:

But ye shall receive power, after that the Holy Ghost is come upon you: and ye shall be witnesses unto me both in Jerusalem, and in all Judaea, and in Samaria, and unto the uttermost part of the earth.

(Acts 1:8)

We, who have been moved to receive the gift of the Holy Ghost, have received a part of God. This part is not just the knowledge of truth; this part is also a portion of God's power. This happened to the disciples in the time of Pentecost. We too are heirs to the promise, and some of us have already received the inheritance. This means that the Word of God (*ye shall receive power*) comes to reside within us, carried on the transport of the Spirit of truth, the Comforter (*after that the Holy Ghost is come upon you*), which has been sent to us by the Father. Wow! This is indeed neat!

Here, take a look at the power of our inheritance, and know that this is only the beginning.

> *And there were dwelling at Jerusalem Jews, devout men, out of every nation under heaven. Now when this was noised abroad, the multitude came together, and were confounded, because that every man heard them speak in his own language. And they were all amazed and marvelled, saying one to another, Behold, are not all these which speak Galilaeans? And how hear we every man in our own tongue, wherein we were born?*
>
> *Parthians, and Medes, and Elamites, and the dwellers in Mesopotamia, and in Judaea, and Cappadocia, in Pontus, and Asia, Phrygia, and Pamphylia, in Egypt, and in the parts of Libya about Cyrene, and strangers of Rome, Jews and proselytes, Cretes and Arabians, we do hear them speak in our tongues the wonderful works of God.*
>
> *And they were all amazed, and were in doubt, saying one to another, What meaneth this?*
>
> (Acts 2:5-12)

> *And by the hands of the apostles were many signs and wonders wrought among the people; (and they were all with one accord in Solomon's porch. And of the rest durst no man join himself to them: but the people magnified them. And believers were the more added to the Lord, multitudes both of men and women.) Insomuch that they brought forth the sick into the streets, and laid them on beds and couches, that at the least the shadow of Peter passing by might overshadow some of them. There came also a multitude out of the cities round about unto Jerusalem, bringing sick folks, and them which were vexed with unclean spirits: and they were healed every one.*
>
> (Acts 5:12-16)

> *And when Paul had laid his hands upon them, the Holy Ghost came on them; and they spake with tongues, and prophesied. And all the men were about twelve.*

And he went into the synagogue, and spake boldly for the space of three months, disputing and persuading the things concerning the kingdom of God. But when divers were hardened, and believed not, but spake evil of that way before the multitude, he departed from them, and separated the disciples, disputing daily in the school of one Tyrannus. And this continued by the space of two years; so that all they which dwelt in Asia heard the word of the Lord Jesus, both Jews and Greeks.

And God wrought special miracles by the hands of Paul: So that from his body were brought unto the sick handkerchiefs or aprons, and the diseases departed from them, and the evil spirits went out of them.

(Acts 19:6-12)

For all that, for me,
God has made,
I think He really
Should be repaid.

But what do you give
The omnipotent One,
Who gave His highest,
His blessed Son,

To save mankind
From deep-set sin?
(I really wish all
Would let him in.)

What do you show One
Who will always see
All that ever was and
That will ever be?

Rest, in a hammock
In a place in the shade?
Nah, He has been there,
Before it was made.

What in the world
Do you get for God?
Maybe he needs
A new chastening rod:

With the way mankind,
His way doth abuse;
The one He wields
Must be well used.

No! With my willfulness
And stubborn pride,
He'd wear that out
On just my backside.

I search for ideas:
I am not going to win.
I think so hard,
My head starts to spin.

If I keep this up,
I might become ill.
Ah, I know what I'll do:
I will do His will.

CHAPTER 7A

Broad Scope Rightly Dividing Scripture

Ephesians 2:13-22

But now in Christ Jesus ye who sometimes were far off are made nigh by the blood of Christ. For he is our peace, who hath made both one, and hath broken down the middle wall of partition between us; Having abolished in his flesh the enmity, even the law of commandments contained in ordinances; for to make in himself of twain one new man, so making peace; And that he might reconcile both unto God in one body by the cross, having slain the enmity thereby: And came and preached peace to you which were afar off, and to them that were nigh. For through him we both have access by one Spirit unto the Father.

Now therefore ye are no more strangers and foreigners, but fellowcitizens with the saints, and of the household of God; And are built upon the foundation of the apostles and prophets, Jesus Christ himself being the chief corner stone; In whom all the building fitly framed together groweth unto an holy temple in the Lord: In whom ye also are builded together for an habitation of God through the Spirit.

Romans 12:1-2

I beseech you therefore, brethren, by the mercies of God, that ye present your bodies a living sacrifice, holy, acceptable unto God, which is your reasonable service. And be not conformed to this world: but be ye transformed by the renewing of your mind, that ye may prove what is that good, and acceptable, and perfect, will of God.

Ephesians 3:14-19

For this cause I bow my knees unto the Father of our Lord Jesus Christ, Of whom the whole family in heaven and earth is named, That he would grant you, according to the riches of his glory, to be strengthened with might by his Spirit in the inner man; That Christ may dwell in your hearts by faith; that ye, being rooted and grounded in love, May be able to comprehend with all saints what is the breadth, and length, and depth, and height; And to know the love of Christ, which passeth knowledge, that ye might be filled with all the fulness of God.

We have explored the matter of going deep into the word of God; this does not mean, learning a lot about the Bible. Rather, going deep into the word of God is the lifetime process of yielding to the Holy Ghost and allowing him to take us deep into the truth of God. For, this is what the Holy Ghost is: the Holy Ghost is the Spirit of truth, and the truth of God is very deep. Thus, having readied ourselves to be taken deep into the goodness of God, we must now prepare for our expansion into the next dimension: Breadth. The breadth of God's Word is the church of Christ.

Let us get our bearing about the church of Christ; what is expected of us, and what we can expect from it. The church is established for the mutual benefit of the author of the church and those who participate in it. In the church there are a series of bi-lateral (two-way) relationship going on. For purposes of this thought, think of the born again believer as a series of walking bi-lateral contracts. Among the clauses that are in our bi-lateral contracts is this one:

Brethren, if a man be overtaken in a fault, ye which are spiritual, restore such an one in the spirit of meekness; considering thyself, lest thou also be tempted. Bear ye one another's burdens, and so fulfil

> *the law of Christ. For if a man think himself to be something, when he is nothing, he deceiveth himself.*
>
> (Galatians 6:1-3)

For each Christian, there are many contracts with other individuals on this earth; however, the most important contract is what I will refer to as, the first one. Our first contract is the one in which the Holy Ghost negotiates for control with our spirit; while our spirit negotiates for control with the Holy Ghost. It is not a simple bi-lateral contract because others are involved.

> *For we know that the whole creation groaneth and travaileth in pain together until now. And not only they, but ourselves also, which have the firstfruits of the Spirit, even we ourselves groan within ourselves, waiting for the adoption, to wit, the redemption of our body. For we are saved by hope: but hope that is seen is not hope: for what a man seeth, why doth he yet hope for? But if we hope for that we see not, then do we with patience wait for it.*
>
> *Likewise the Spirit also helpeth our infirmities: for we know not what we should pray for as we ought: but the Spirit itself maketh intercession for us with groanings which cannot be uttered. And he that searcheth the hearts knoweth what is the mind of the Spirit, because he maketh intercession for the saints according to the will of God.*
>
> (Romans 8:22-27)

When we first start out, in our first contract, our spirit is asking that it have exclusive control and the Holy Ghost is asking for the same. As time goes on, and as we really understand the priceless gift we have been given, then the negotiation changes. Actually, that is too rosy a picture of our natures. What really happens is that as time goes on we see all the pitfalls that lay in our path, and then the negotiation changes. Our spirit, by little and little, start to ask the Holy Ghost, "Won't you please take control of this piece; but not of ***that*** one." Then, slowly over time, the excluded pieces are released to the Spirit of truth. This happens as God continues to stir the Spirit of truth, in us. Finally, somewhere on this side of life on earth or the other, we say, "You, Holy Ghost, are worthy of full control." Then, the Holy Ghost can express itself in its fullness. This transformation that comes over us is illustrated by John the Baptist. John the Baptist passed the point of release very early in his life, in the manner that the angel revealed to his soon-to-be father.

> *But the angel said unto him, Fear not, Zacharias: for thy prayer is heard; and thy wife Elisabeth shall bear thee a son, and thou shalt call his name John. And thou shalt have joy and gladness; and many shall rejoice at his birth. For he shall be great in the sight of the Lord, and shall drink neither wine nor strong drink; and he shall be filled with the Holy Ghost, even from his mother's womb.*
>
> (Luke 1:13-15)

The very early process that John experienced is this: *he shall be filled with the Holy Ghost.* Jesus took care of this negotiation as he was being conceived—if you can call that a negotiation; Jesus never put up any resistance, he just submitted. In fact, according to God's Design, Jesus Christ had submitted from before the foundation of the world. So the Holy Ghost was delivering this submitted soul to the womb of the Virgin Mary.

> *And the angel said unto her, Fear not, Mary: for thou hast found favour with God. And, behold, thou shalt conceive in thy womb, and bring forth a son, and shalt call his name JESUS. He shall be great, and shall be called the Son of the Highest: and the Lord God shall give unto him the throne of his father David: And he shall reign over the house of Jacob for ever; and of his kingdom there shall be no end.*
>
> *Then said Mary unto the angel, How shall this be, seeing I know not a man?*
>
> *And the angel answered and said unto her, The Holy Ghost shall come upon thee, and the power of the Highest shall overshadow thee: therefore also that holy thing which shall be born of thee shall be called the Son of God.*
>
> (Luke 1:30-35)

When he was older, Jesus of Nazareth showed us how the negotiation process can begin in every one of us.

> *Then cometh Jesus from Galilee to Jordan unto John, to be baptized of him. But John forbad him, saying, I have need to be baptized of thee, and comest thou to me?*
>
> *And Jesus answering said unto him, Suffer it to be so now: for thus it becometh us to fulfil all righteousness.*
> *Then he suffered him.*
>
> *And Jesus, when he was baptized, went up straightway out of the water: and, lo, the heavens were opened unto him, and he saw the Spirit of God descending like a dove, and lighting upon him: And lo a voice from heaven, saying, This is my beloved Son, in whom I am well pleased.*
>
> (Matthew 3:13-17)

This was our introduction to what the church was going to be like. When Jesus was ministering on earth, there was not an organizational church of Christ; except, for a very short period of time. While John the Baptist was alive and ministering, the church of Christ was active in him, but this was only a church of one. We do not count Jesus as a member of the church; he has a totally different function in the church, which we will see shortly. Even though Jesus is not a member of the early church, we can still explore one of his duties relative to the church. Relative to church planting, Jesus had the responsibility of proclaiming the good news of the church arising. In this, he had some help from the apostle Peter, the vessel for the following revelation from God: *Thou art the Christ.*

> *When Jesus came into the coasts of Caesarea Philippi, he asked his disciples, saying, Whom do men say that I the Son of man am?*
> *And they said, Some say that thou art John the Baptist: some, Elias; and others, Jeremias, or one of the prophets.*
>
> *He saith unto them, But whom say ye that I am?*
> *And Simon Peter answered and said, Thou art the Christ, the Son of the living God.*

And Jesus answered and said unto him, Blessed art thou, Simon Barjona: for flesh and blood hath not revealed it unto thee, but my Father which is in heaven. And I say also unto thee, That thou art Peter, and upon this rock I will build my church; and the gates of hell shall not prevail against it.

(Matthew 16:13-18)

Peter's revelation is our pointer to the foundation of the church of Jesus Christ, which was to support church planting. It is as Jesus said, *upon this rock I will build my church*. Now, there is some contention about this matter of *this rock*. Therefore, let us go through a few thoughts. As you read further, keep this thought in mind: for Jesus to single out Peter as the foundation of the church would have been either a contradiction to or an adulteration of the message of Jesus' as given in the following Scripture, or both. Jesus Christ does not contradict his own words; therefore, the following Scripture is still active, throughout all the church of Jesus Christ.

Then came to him the mother of Zebedees children with her sons, worshipping him, and desiring a certain thing of him. And he said unto her, What wilt thou?

She saith unto him, Grant that these my two sons may sit, the one on thy right hand, and the other on the left, in thy kingdom.

But Jesus answered and said, Ye know not what ye ask. Are ye able to drink of the cup that I shall drink of, and to be baptized with the baptism that I am baptized with?

They say unto him, We are able.

And he saith unto them, Ye shall drink indeed of my cup, and be baptized with the baptism that I am baptized with: but to sit on my right hand, and on my left, is not mine to give, but it shall be given to them for whom it is prepared of my Father.

And when the ten heard it, they were moved with indignation against the two brethren. But Jesus called them unto him, and said,

Ye know that the princes of the Gentiles exercise dominion over them, and they that are great exercise authority upon them. But

> *it shall not be so among you: but whosoever will be great among you, let him be your minister; And whosoever will be chief among you, let him be your servant: Even as the Son of man came not to be ministered unto, but to minister, and to give his life a ransom for many.*
>
> (Matthew 20:20-28)

Some say that it was Peter to which Jesus shifted all earthly authority, as well as all primary recognition of responsibility. We do not think so. We do believe that such thoughts produce an environment in the church that is insufficient for faithful and true worship of the Living God, as we are commanded to do, by Jesus. If such were the case, this would be a repetition of the house that was built on sand, which Jesus warned us about accepting.

> *And every one that heareth these sayings of mine, and doeth them not, shall be likened unto a foolish man, which built his house upon the sand: And the rain descended, and the floods came, and the winds blew, and beat upon that house; and it fell: and great was the fall of it.*
>
> (Matthew 7:26-27)

Some may point to the change that came over Peter, as he matured in the Gospel. Let us look at that, in stages. At the time of this declaration by Jesus, the Holy Ghost was not resident in Peter. Therefore, the Peter who was listening to the message could not have been the foundation for anything of God. Furthermore, at a later time, Peter demonstrated that he was having a really difficult time keeping the gates of hell from prevailing against him. At that time, there was not much hope that Peter could build a structure that would withstand the onslaught of the gates of hell; considering the state that he was in, at that time. Then, Jesus prayed for him.

> *And the Lord said, Simon, Simon, behold, Satan hath desired to have you, that he may sift you as wheat: But I have prayed for thee, that thy faith fail not: and when thou art converted, strengthen thy brethren.*

And he said unto him, Lord, I am ready to go with thee, both into prison, and to death.

And he said, I tell thee, Peter, the cock shall not crow this day, before that thou shalt thrice deny that thou knowest me.
(Luke 22:31-34)

At this time, the Holy Ghost had still not come upon Peter, in its fullness. I hope that we can all agree that any human, including the Son of man, would absolutely and positively have to have the indwelling of the Holy Ghost to build anything of God. Okay, now that we have that portion of agreement, let us slip past the overconfidence of Peter, his running away at the time Jesus was taken to be crucified, his denial of Jesus, and his slight skepticism about the news of Jesus' resurrection. Let us go all the way to where the Holy Ghost has come upon him.

When we get to the time where the Holy Ghost has come upon him, Peter was no longer the formerly-a-fisherman Peter. Peter was, then, a Spirit filled servant of God. Therefore, anything that he built would be owned by God. Thus, even if he were somehow related to the rock that was to build the church, it could only be because he was standing on it. You see, Peter was solidly standing in the Spirit of truth. The one time he moved away from it (and this was after he had already received the Holy Ghost) was that time when Peter had to be pushed back to his place on rock of his ministry by the apostle Paul.

And when James, Cephas, and John, who seemed to be pillars, perceived the grace that was given unto me, they gave to me and Barnabas the right hands of fellowship; that we should go unto the heathen, and they unto the circumcision. Only they would that we should remember the poor; the same which I also was forward to do.

But when Peter was come to Antioch, I withstood him to the face, because he was to be blamed. For before that certain came from James, he did eat with the Gentiles: but when they were come, he withdrew and separated himself, fearing them which were of the circumcision. And the other Jews dissembled likewise with him; insomuch that Barnabas also was carried away with their dissimulation.

> *But when I saw that they walked not uprightly according to the truth of the gospel, I said unto Peter before them all, If thou, being a Jew, livest after the manner of Gentiles, and not as do the Jews, why compellest thou the Gentiles to live as do the Jews? We who are Jews by nature, and not sinners of the Gentiles, Knowing that a man is not justified by the works of the law, but by the faith of Jesus Christ, even we have believed in Jesus Christ, that we might be justified by the faith of Christ, and not by the works of the law: for by the works of the law shall no flesh be justified. But if, while we seek to be justified by Christ, we ourselves also are found sinners, is therefore Christ the minister of sin? God forbid.*
>
> (Galatians 2:9-17)

So, by act of logic, even if Peter were involved in the foundation of the church, it would only be as one who is standing in the Holy Ghost; thus, the Holy Ghost would be the rock. I think this is enough preparatory logic, so I will tell you who the Holy Ghost revealed as the foundation of the church. The foundation is Jesus Christ. And this is why Jesus cannot be limited in the church, in any fashion; especially, as being a member is limited.

> *For we are labourers together with God: ye are God's husbandry, ye are God's building. According to the grace of God which is given unto me, as a wise masterbuilder, I have laid the foundation, and another buildeth thereon. But let every man take heed how he buildeth thereupon. For other foundation can no man lay than that is laid, which is Jesus Christ.*
>
> (1 Corinthians 3:9-11)

So, you wonder why I took such a long route to identify the rock on which the church is built. Well, maybe it is because I am a long-winded person. Or, maybe it is because I think you need to fully understand the power source for everything that is done in the church. And, maybe it is also because I want you to understand the limits of the responsibility that God has given to man, in our custodianship of the things of the church.

Man is not to have any control over the church: God has all control of the church. Man is not the reason for the church: God is.

> *Now the God of patience and consolation grant you to be likeminded one toward another according to Christ Jesus: That ye may with one mind and one mouth glorify God, even the Father of our Lord Jesus Christ.*
>
> (Romans 15:5-6)

One of the best evidences of the supremacy of God over everything in the church is what happened with the first church. The first church is the best example that we will ever have of how the church should operate. There are few institutions—calling themselves churches or anything else relating to Christ—that exists today that has the closeness to God, and to Christ, as did the first church. This place was filled with men who had walked with Jesus. This place was filled with those who received thrones, to judge the twelve tribes of Israel.

Now, even though Peter was still human, and not eligible for the position of being the foundation of the church, he was still a quite powerful Spirit-filled man. According to the Bible, people gathered so that they could have a chance to be healed by his shadow.

> *And by the hands of the apostles were many signs and wonders wrought among the people; (and they were all with one accord in Solomon's porch. And of the rest durst no man join himself to them: but the people magnified them. And believers were the more added to the Lord, multitudes both of men and women.) Insomuch that they brought forth the sick into the streets, and laid them on beds and couches, that at the least the shadow of Peter passing by might overshadow some of them. There came also a multitude out of the cities round about unto Jerusalem, bringing sick folks, and them which were vexed with unclean spirits: and they were healed every one.*
>
> (Acts 5:12-16)

This is God working in man, in Power. You might say that it is something that Jesus, when he was on earth, did not choose to demonstrate. Though, Jesus' works did include the woman who touched the hem of his garment, but I do not remember anything about shadows. Oh yes, he did heal that boy from some unknown distance away; so, I guess he still holds the *record* for most outstanding miracle. But Peter was no slouch in that category. Peter expressed power in a fashion as the Lord Jesus Christ said key believers (of which Peter was one, among many) would express in, and to, the world: *greater works than these shall he do.*

> *Believest thou not that I am in the Father, and the Father in me? the words that I speak unto you I speak not of myself: but the Father that dwelleth in me, he doeth the works. Believe me that I am in the Father, and the Father in me: or else believe me for the very works' sake.*
>
> *Verily, verily, I say unto you, He that believeth on me, the works that I do shall he do also; and greater works than these shall he do; because I go unto my Father. And whatsoever ye shall ask in my name, that will I do, that the Father may be glorified in the Son.*
>
> *If ye shall ask any thing in my name, I will do it.*
>
> *If ye love me, keep my commandments.*
>
> (John 14:10-15)

However, even considering all those miraculous things that were done, there is one, more overwhelming, miracle that tells me more than anything else that this church is the example for all churches. I have not seen one like it in this day; at least, not any in areas in which I have lived or visited. The thing that really impresses me about this church is that God moved, through the power of the Holy Ghost, with such force that the people of the church actually all got along. They even went beyond getting along; I will let you read it, for yourself.

> *Then they that gladly received his word were baptized: and the same day there were added unto them about three thousand souls. And they continued stedfastly in the apostles' doctrine and fellowship, and in breaking of bread, and in prayers.*
>
> *And fear came upon every soul: and many wonders and signs were done by the apostles. And all that believed were together, and*

> *had all things common; And sold their possessions and goods, and parted them to all men, as every man had need.*
>
> (Acts 2:41-45)

These early followers of Christ (disciples, apostles, ordinary people and just plain seekers) were given one of the highest honors that can be given to any group. Remember back when the nation of Israel was being formed, and God gave them a great honor; He called them the people who were called by His name? Well, Jesus gave these folks the same honor relative to his name; and his name is a name that has been placed, by God, above every other name. Let your heart pause, and really appreciate the honor that was given to those early believers. They were given the honor of being called, uniquely and exclusively, by the name of Christ.

> *Now they which were scattered abroad upon the persecution that arose about Stephen travelled as far as Phenice, and Cyprus, and Antioch, preaching the word to none but unto the Jews only. And some of them were men of Cyprus and Cyrene, which, when they were come to Antioch, spake unto the Grecians, preaching the Lord Jesus. And the hand of the Lord was with them: and a great number believed, and turned unto the Lord.*
>
> *Then tidings of these things came unto the ears of the church which was in Jerusalem: and they sent forth Barnabas, that he should go as far as Antioch. Who, when he came, and had seen the grace of God, was glad, and exhorted them all, that with purpose of heart they would cleave unto the Lord. For he was a good man, and full of the Holy Ghost and of faith: and much people was added unto the Lord.*
>
> *Then departed Barnabas to Tarsus, for to seek Saul: And when he had found him, he brought him unto Antioch. And it came to pass, that a whole year they assembled themselves with the church, and taught much people. And the disciples were called Christians first in Antioch.*
>
> (Acts 11:19-26)

Okay, as we pause on the ethereal, let us get back to everyday life. What are the provisions for the Christians to survive in this world? Well, again we go back to the nation of Israel. God had already established the mechanism for survival of the priesthood, and this was extended to the church of Christ. No, it was not discarded as part of the fulfillment of the law of Moses for righteousness sake. It is still highly active, and it still provides a constant tug on those who want to, but just do not know how they are going to participate in building the church, as it grows into its place of witness to the world. Moreover, it still provides tremendous blessings for those who are doing it. The LORD God provided these words of motivation, to inspire our participation. The LORD'S motivation begins with a question that was taken from the mind of a self-satisfied man, and culture: *Will a man rob God?*

> *Will a man rob God?*
>
> *Yet ye have robbed me. But ye say,*
> *Wherein have we robbed thee?*
>
> *In tithes and offerings. Ye are cursed with a curse: for ye have robbed me, even this whole nation.*
>
> *Bring ye all the tithes into the storehouse, that there may be meat in mine house, and prove me now herewith, saith the LORD of hosts, if I will not open you the windows of heaven, and pour you out a blessing, that there shall not be room enough to receive it.*
> *And I will rebuke the devourer for your sakes, and he shall not destroy the fruits of your ground; neither shall your vine cast her fruit before the time in the field, saith the LORD of hosts. And all nations shall call you blessed: for ye shall be a delightsome land, saith the LORD of hosts.*
>
> (Malachi 3:8-12)

Firstly, the tithe is the method provided, by God, for the church to fulfill its fiscal responsibility in the world. This is how the church can be in the world, but not of the world. Additionally, there is another level; it is the one that flows from the fact that God, in accord with His great generosity, added another level of blessing that can be achieved by

Christians. The additional level of blessing is that we can be endowed with substance beyond our needs and have a goodly surplus.

When we are endowed with substance beyond our needs and have a goodly surplus, then we have the opportunity to give a boost to the fiscal possibilities of the church. We can follow the words of Scripture as pertains to generous giving; words that were, undoubtedly, well known by the widow who gave her mite. This is true whether she knew them in her mind, or in her spirit, only; or in both.

> *And he looked up, and saw the rich men casting their gifts into the treasury. And he saw also a certain poor widow casting in thither two mites. And he said, Of a truth I say unto you, that this poor widow hath cast in more than they all: For all these have of their abundance cast in unto the offerings of God: but she of her penury hath cast in all the living that she had.*
>
> (Luke 21:1-4)

But, we cannot just wait for either overwhelming materials means or earth-shaking spiritual insight. For those of us who are just getting our spiritual wings, we have to start somewhere, which can be in giving the tithe. However, as you stretch those wings, and when are able to do so, why not continue beyond the tithe, in accordance with the Scripture that is written below?

> *Therefore I thought it necessary to exhort the brethren, that they would go before unto you, and make up before hand your bounty, whereof ye had notice before, that the same might be ready, as a matter of bounty, and not as of covetousness. But this I say, He which soweth sparingly shall reap also sparingly; and he which soweth bountifully shall reap also bountifully. Every man according as he purposeth in his heart, so let him give; not grudgingly, or of necessity: for God loveth a cheerful giver.*
>
> (2 Corinthians 9:5-7)

You can be assured; God does see and acknowledge your generosity.

> *And God is able to make all grace abound toward you; that ye, always having all sufficiency in all things, may abound to every*

good work: (As it is written, He hath dispersed abroad; he hath given to the poor: his righteousness remaineth for ever. Now he that ministereth seed to the sower both minister bread for your food, and multiply your seed sown, and increase the fruits of your righteousness;) Being enriched in every thing to all bountifulness, which causeth through us thanksgiving to God.

(2 Corinthians 9:8-11)

No, you do not have to do it all alone. I know that there is probably some billionaire out there, who has decided that they will take this challenge on, all by their lonesome, as it is sometimes phrased; but there is no need for that. God, who we serve, truly honors His Son. God, our Father, would not allow the church of His Son to depend on any other human, no matter how well positioned that person is. God knows even better than we do that sometimes people die. Then, if there was only one means of support, the church might be in danger of dying; or, at least, there might have to be some emergency action by God to prevent that. God does not, ever, operate in emergency mode. The LORD is the Master of advance preparedness. For the church's sake, the Father provides a continual supply of resources; not just monetary, but all resources.

And they, continuing daily with one accord in the temple, and breaking bread from house to house, did eat their meat with gladness and singleness of heart, Praising God, and having favour with all the people. And the Lord added to the church daily such as should be saved.

(Acts 2:46-47)

In addition to quantity and quality, the LORD also regulates the limitation of the provisions. For instance, it would be detrimental for a church to receive its total annual—or even monthly—operating provisions (its budget) in one day. If that did happen, the church would have three hundred, sixty and four or five (or twenty seven or nine, or thirty) days in which it had no need for fiscal intervention by the LORD. This could create a great void; a great absence of earnest worship and fervent prayer.

The same limitation of the provisions is applicable for the services in the church.

In the church, God regulates the supply of the message. Regulation is required because the church cannot operate effectively with everybody trying to express themselves at the same time, in their zeal for God. As Moses was taught by his father-in-law, to set up a structure for the management of the nation of Israel; so, too, this method has been passed on to the church. For the church, God has, through His Son, the Christ, established the structure for the management of the church.

> *Now ye are the body of Christ, and members in particular. And God hath set some in the church, first apostles, secondarily prophets, thirdly teachers, after that miracles, then gifts of healings, helps, governments, diversities of tongues.*
> (1 Corinthians 12:27-28)

Oh, and did I forget to mention that we do not have to fly solo, as far as rules are concerned? Oh, yes; I did mention that. To expand upon the mention, let me say that we do not have to invent a new thing for every new situation that comes up. Some may have been wondering why God took so much time with that Old Testament thing. Some may even think that God could have just skipped to the Son part, and left out this son (nation of Israel) thing. For both of these possible groups of folk, let me educate you.

You see, the time of the Old Testament is the time of the writing of the instruction manual for the church. All matters that could ever come before the church were tried out on something else, before we Christians came about. The bulk of the trial and error was done by the nation of Israel.

Let all Christian say, as its younger sibling, in an appreciative and joyful adolescent voice, "Thank you Israel."

Let all lovers of God say, in an even more appreciative, but much more childlike, voice, "Thank you, LORD, for the nation of Israel."

Now, everybody read what the congregation of Israel, and some other names—such as, Pharaoh, Nebuchadnezzar, Belshezzar, Saul, David, and a host of kings and judges—gave us in this instruction manual. Take a look at what we can do with the product of their efforts.

> *All scripture is given by inspiration of God, and is profitable for doctrine, for reproof, for correction, for instruction in righteousness:*

> *That the man of God may be perfect, thoroughly furnished unto all good works.*
>
> (2 Timothy 3:16-17)

Maybe we should also send a, Thank You, to God, for giving us the history of these leaders, and for the present lessons of all leaders today. What do you think?

I think we should.

Well, anyway; that is what we got from the efforts of those who went before us, in the time called, the Old Testament era.

So, knowing this, please understand that you have a function. You are not just filler for gaps in history. Now you know that you do not have to be the chief of operations; for, in God, all functions are important. To man, there are hierarchies; and, too often, only the functions at, or near, the top are considered to be important. But, who should we serve? Should we serve man or should we serve God? The answer to this question is obvious; it is that we must serve God. Thereby, you obtain your rest in the fact that you are not just filler for gaps in history: you are of *the body of Christ, and members in particular.*

> *For the body is not one member, but many. If the foot shall say, Because I am not the hand, I am not of the body; is it therefore not of the body? And if the ear shall say, Because I am not the eye, I am not of the body; is it therefore not of the body? If the whole body were an eye, where were the hearing? If the whole were hearing, where were the smelling? But now hath God set the members every one of them in the body, as it hath pleased him.*
>
> *And if they were all one member, where were the body? But now are they many members, yet but one body. And the eye cannot say unto the hand, I have no need of thee: nor again the head to the feet, I have no need of you. Nay, much more those members of the body, which seem to be more feeble, are necessary: And those members of the body, which we think to be less honourable, upon these we bestow more abundant honour; and our uncomely parts have more abundant comeliness. For our comely parts have no need: but God hath tempered the body together, having given more abundant honour to that part which lacked: That there should be no schism in the body; but that the members should have the*

same care one for another. And whether one member suffer, all the members suffer with it; or one member be honoured, all the members rejoice with it.

Now ye are the body of Christ, and members in particular.
(1 Corinthians 12:14-27)

Therefore, wherever the LORD calls you to serve; do all to the glory of God. This means that you always put your righteous foot forward, as much as you humanly can. God understands that, sometimes the janitor of our temptation to sin leaves the enticement floor wet, and we slip on it and fall from doing the will of God. Oh, the floor was dry, and you still slipped? Well, God understand that too. Just yield your best (trying, not sufficient) to be content in what you are called to do in the service of the Lord, and in his church.

Behold, O God our shield, and look upon the face of thine anointed. For a day in thy courts is better than a thousand. I had rather be a doorkeeper in the house of my God, than to dwell in the tents of wickedness. For the LORD God is a sun and shield: the LORD will give grace and glory: no good thing will he withhold from them that walk uprightly.
O LORD of hosts, blessed is the man that trusteth in thee.
(Psalm 84:9-12)

But do not walk around with your head in the clouds, thinking that everything will be just rosy. Also, be very watchful about those who would demand that you do things in the church because you are just so capable of being . . .

There are specific titles that God has designated for the various offices of the church. When God places you in a church, and it is not as the head; then follow those to whom He has given responsibility for you. He will hold them responsible for the proper performance of their duties; even, their duties toward you.

And for those who are held responsible for the members of the church of Christ, be very careful about the most dangerous part of being in an organization. As I learned when I was a part of a computer security task force, the greatest danger in a company is not from the outside, but from the inside. The greatest danger is from those on the inside who accidentally (or, accidentally on purpose) compromise the systems that are put in place to protect the people and the organization. This is the same danger that floats in the church. Let us look at three dangers, floating in the church.

The danger on the inside, from the inside, arises when there are additions or modifications that are made to the doctrine of Christ. This is the doctrine that is found in the body of Scripture; the body that supersedes all traditions, discoveries, visions, dreams, and revelations of any man. It also supersedes any new statement of any man or woman that they say can be attributed to God. There is a resolution for the pressure to accept any such variance; it was shared by the apostle Paul, through Timothy, to all of us. It carries the full authority of all apostles and prophets, and any other child of God. And this authority is of the Holy Ghost.

> *Hold fast the form of sound words, which thou hast heard of me, in faith and love which is in Christ Jesus. That good thing which was committed unto thee keep by the Holy Ghost which dwelleth in us.*
>
> (2 Timothy 1:13-14)

The next level of danger comes from what I will call the pretenders. These are the folk who look very much like they were called to a position of leadership. They are very adept at talking the talk. However, they fall apart when you really look at how they are walking the walk.

Now, walking the walk is not that difficult, so it will not take, as they say, a rocket scientist, in order for us to see the failing in their walk. Walking the walk is just a matter of adhering to the instruction manual, the Bible; stepping where it says step, and not stepping where it tells you not to step. When you watch these pretenders, you will see them sometimes stepping where the word tells them to step. However, when you really watch them, you will also see them intentionally stepping where the word says not to step: do not follow them there. As a matter of fact, do not, at all, follow them.

> *But there were false prophets also among the people, even as there shall be false teachers among you, who privily shall bring in damnable heresies, even denying the Lord that bought them, and bring upon themselves swift destruction. And many shall follow their pernicious ways; by reason of whom the way of truth shall be evil spoken of. And through covetousness shall they with feigned words make merchandise of you: whose judgment now of a long time lingereth not, and their damnation slumbereth not.*
>
> (2 Peter 2:1-3)

Then, there are probably the easiest ones to ignore, but the hardest ones to deal with: the detractors. It is easy to ignore those who just stand at a distance, and tell you that what you believe is nonsense. It is more difficult to deal with those who tell you this, but have been given, by government, the power to place roadblocks in your path. It is tremendously difficult to deal with those who can, not just put roadblocks in your path, but also take you off the path and destroy it; or, so they think. This, they do, by trying to suppress your witness.

Yes, there may be some things that are able to take you off the path of presenting, in ***their*** world, the verbal path to service to God. However, such detractors cannot destroy the path to God that is illuminated by the example in and of your life. In fact, they do not have any way of getting a focused view of this path to God. Their view is only of pseudo-paths. To move these types of roadblock-builders, you will have to depend totally on God, in the Holy Ghost. There is no other formula or special escape hatch that will cause them to cease-and-desist. Indeed, there is no need to stop them; rather, rejoice in the fact of their existence. For, it is with handling of the detractors that you, in God, get to really work out your soul salvation. And, in this, God will NEVER leave you.

> *And when they bring you unto the synagogues, and unto magistrates, and powers, take ye no thought how or what thing ye shall answer, or what ye shall say: For the Holy Ghost shall teach you in the same hour what ye ought to say.*
>
> (Luke 12:11-12)

Now that we have reviewed all these structural and procedural matters, it is time to get to what is usually covered first. Normally (and I admit to not being very normal) the first thing that organizations like to get out of the way is their mission statement. Well, when this topic came to me, and the outline was presented, I saw that the mission statement was at the end of the list. I thought about moving it to the top, but this is not my work to control, wherefore I must yield to the hand that works within me. So, in closing, here is your mission statement, from Scripture. (Also in closing, I ask that you pray for me, as I pray for all those in the church of Christ—and even for those who are on their way—that, in all things we all will shine only for the Father, and only by the Father.)

> *Ye are the light of the world. A city that is set on an hill cannot be hid. Neither do men light a candle, and put it under a bushel, but on a candlestick; and it giveth light unto all that are in the house. Let your light so shine before men, that they may see your good works, and glorify your Father which is in heaven.*
>
> (Matthew 5:14-16)

THE WORD FROM THE BIBLE

Daniel 7:13-28

I saw in the night visions, and, behold, one like the Son of man came with the clouds of heaven, and came to the Ancient of days, and they brought him near before him. And there was given him dominion, and glory, and a kingdom, that all people, nations, and languages, should serve him: his dominion is an everlasting dominion, which shall not pass away, and his kingdom that which shall not be destroyed.

I Daniel was grieved in my spirit in the midst of my body, and the visions of my head troubled me. I came near unto one of them that stood by, and asked him the truth of all this. So he told me, and made me know the interpretation of the things.

These great beasts, which are four, are four kings, which shall arise out of the earth. But the saints of the most High shall take the kingdom, and possess the kingdom for ever, even for ever and ever.

Then I would know the truth of the fourth beast, which was diverse from all the others, exceeding dreadful, whose teeth were of iron, and his nails of brass; which devoured, brake in pieces, and stamped the residue with his feet; And of the ten horns that were in his head, and of the other which came up, and before whom three fell; even of that horn that had eyes, and a mouth that spake very great things, whose look was more stout than his fellows. I beheld, and the same horn made war with the saints, and prevailed against them; Until the Ancient of days came, and judgment was given to the saints of the most High; and the time came that the saints possessed the kingdom.

Thus he said, The fourth beast shall be the fourth kingdom upon earth, which shall be diverse from all kingdoms, and shall devour the whole earth, and shall tread it down, and break it in pieces. And the ten horns out of this kingdom are ten kings that shall arise: and another shall rise after them; and he shall be diverse from the first, and he shall subdue three kings. And he shall speak great words against the most High, and shall wear out the saints of the most High, and think to change times and laws: and they shall be given into his hand until a time and times and the dividing of time.

But the judgment shall sit, and they shall take away his dominion, to consume and to destroy it unto the end. And the kingdom and dominion, and the greatness of the kingdom under the whole heaven, shall be given to the people of the saints of the most High, whose kingdom is an everlasting kingdom, and all dominions shall serve and obey him. Hitherto is the end of the matter.

As for me Daniel, my cogitations much troubled me, and my countenance changed in me: but I kept the matter in my heart.

Zechariah 9:9-17

Rejoice greatly, O daughter of Zion; shout, O daughter of Jerusalem: behold, thy King cometh unto thee: he is just, and having salvation; lowly, and riding upon an ass, and upon a colt the foal of an ass. And I will cut off the chariot from Ephraim, and the horse from Jerusalem, and the battle bow shall be cut off: and he shall speak peace unto the heathen: and his dominion shall be from sea even to sea, and from the river even to the ends of the earth.

As for thee also, by the blood of thy covenant I have sent forth thy prisoners out of the pit wherein is no water. Turn you to the strong hold, ye prisoners of hope: even to day do I declare that I will render double unto thee; When I have bent Judah for me, filled the bow with Ephraim, and raised up thy sons, O Zion, against thy sons, O Greece, and made thee as the sword of a mighty man. And the LORD shall be seen over them, and his arrow shall go forth as the lightning: and the Lord GOD shall blow the trumpet, and shall go with whirlwinds of the south. The LORD of hosts shall defend them; and they shall devour, and subdue with sling stones; and they shall drink, and make a noise as through wine; and they shall be filled like bowls, and as the corners of the altar.

And the LORD their God shall save them in that day as the flock of his people: for they shall be as the stones of a crown, lifted up as an ensign upon his land. For how great is his goodness, and how great is his beauty! corn shall make the young men cheerful, and new wine the maids.

Revelation 20:1-6

And I saw an angel come down from heaven, having the key of the bottomless pit and a great chain in his hand. And he laid hold on the dragon, that old serpent, which is the Devil, and Satan, and bound him a thousand years, And cast him into the bottomless pit, and shut him up, and set a seal upon him, that he should deceive the nations no more, till the thousand years should be fulfilled: and after that he must be loosed a little season.

And I saw thrones, and they sat upon them, and judgment was given unto them: and I saw the souls of them that were beheaded for the witness of Jesus, and for the word of God, and which had not worshipped the beast, neither his image, neither had received his mark upon their foreheads, or in their hands; and they lived and reigned with Christ a thousand years. But the rest of the dead lived not again until the thousand years were finished. This is the first resurrection. Blessed and holy is he that hath part in the first resurrection: on such the second death hath no power, but they shall be priests of God and of Christ, and shall reign with him a thousand years.

CHAPTER EIGHT

Revelation

Christ Rules

From about 63 AD to about 70 AD was the destruction of Jerusalem. Around 410 AD the Roman Empire started its decline: a range of approximately 340 years (or one hundred plus two hundred plus a part of a hundred). After this time the Roman Empire lost its ability to harass the Christians, as the Scripture foretold. Around 476 AD is the date cited as being the time of its fall.

And he shall speak great words against the most High, and shall wear out the saints of the most High, and think to change times and laws: and they shall be given into his hand until a time and times and the dividing of time.

(Daniel 7:25)

Once this happened, it was time for the rule of Christ in the earth. Now, we must understand this very clearly; Jesus does not have to announce his coming to the earth by way of physical embodiment. In explaining his relationship to the physical realm, Jesus had already told us that his kingdom was not to be formed in this fashion.

Then Pilate entered into the judgment hall again, and called Jesus, and said unto him, Art thou the King of the Jews?

Jesus answered him, Sayest thou this thing of thyself, or did others tell it thee of me?

> *Pilate answered, Am I a Jew? Thine own nation and the chief priests have delivered thee unto me: what hast thou done?*
>
> *Jesus answered, My kingdom is not of this world: if my kingdom were of this world, then would my servants fight, that I should not be delivered to the Jews: but now is my kingdom not from hence.*
> (John 18:33-36)

Furthermore, we know that the servants of God operate on a spiritual level, in their service to Him. This is true even when the result of their spiritual service is manifested in the physical realm, such as in charitable donations.

> *Jesus saith unto her, Woman, believe me, the hour cometh, when ye shall neither in this mountain, nor yet at Jerusalem, worship the Father. Ye worship ye know not what: we know what we worship: for salvation is of the Jews. But the hour cometh, and now is, when the true worshippers shall worship the Father in spirit and in truth: for the Father seeketh such to worship him. God is a Spirit: and they that worship him must worship him in spirit and in truth.*
> (John 4:21-24)

Therefore, when the Bible mentions a thousand year reign, it is not necessary for Jesus Christ to physically announce himself to the earth. "What," you exclaim, "We expect him to come here, announce himself, and then make everything right! We especially expect him to come here and take care of all those degenerate unbelievers."

Well, let us look at that from the records of the revealed events that were done by God, as recorded in the Bible. By a review of history, we see that the hosts of God have been here before, and they also cleaned house then. However, they were only seen by the selected ones of God. Let us look at the record of one of those times, during the building of the nation of Israel.

> *Then the king of Syria warred against Israel, and took counsel with his servants, saying, In such and such a place shall be my camp.*

And the man of God sent unto the king of Israel, saying, Beware that thou pass not such a place; for thither the Syrians are come down.

And the king of Israel sent to the place which the man of God told him and warned him of, and saved himself there, not once nor twice.

Therefore the heart of the king of Syria was sore troubled for this thing; and he called his servants, and said unto them, Will ye not show me which of us is for the king of Israel?

And one of his servants said, None, my lord, O king: but Elisha, the prophet that is in Israel, telleth the king of Israel the words that thou speakest in thy bedchamber.

And he said, Go and spy where he is, that I may send and fetch him.

And it was told him, saying, Behold, he is in Dothan. Therefore sent he thither horses, and chariots, and a great host: and they came by night, and compassed the city about.

And when the servant of the man of God was risen early, and gone forth, behold, an host compassed the city both with horses and chariots.

And his servant said unto him, Alas, my master! how shall we do?

And he answered, Fear not: for they that be with us are more than they that be with them. And Elisha prayed, and said, LORD, I pray thee, open his eyes, that he may see.

And the LORD opened the eyes of the young man; and he saw: and, behold, the mountain was full of horses and chariots of fire round about Elisha.

(2 Kings 6:8-17)

Then, there was that other time; the time when the centurion came to Jesus to petition his intervention in a matter of life and death. Jesus was all set to go, when the centurion, feeling very unworthy, constrained him not to. In giving his reason for his statement, the centurion noted that Jesus, being a man of much authority in God, could perform these sorts of action in one of the most exquisite displays of power that is possible.

The centurion indicated that Jesus could accomplish the healing without being there, but, rather, by sending the ambassador of God that is in the spirit that heals.

> *And when Jesus was entered into Capernaum, there came unto him a centurion, beseeching him, And saying, Lord, my servant lieth at home sick of the palsy, grievously tormented.*
>
> *And Jesus saith unto him, I will come and heal him.*
>
> *The centurion answered and said, Lord, I am not worthy that thou shouldest come under my roof: but speak the word only, and my servant shall be healed. For I am a man under authority, having soldiers under me: and I say to this man, Go, and he goeth; and to another, Come, and he cometh; and to my servant, Do this, and he doeth it.*
>
> *When Jesus heard it, he marvelled, and said to them that followed, Verily I say unto you, I have not found so great faith, no, not in Israel. And I say unto you, That many shall come from the east and west, and shall sit down with Abraham, and Isaac, and Jacob, in the kingdom of heaven. But the children of the kingdom shall be cast out into outer darkness: there shall be weeping and gnashing of teeth.*
>
> *And Jesus said unto the centurion, Go thy way; and as thou hast believed, so be it done unto thee.*
> *And his servant was healed in the selfsame hour.*
> (Matthew 8:5-13)

So, it is perfectly understandable that Jesus can remain back at his place beside God, and still accomplish God's work on earth. If you remember the time he was here, you will recall that he was very anxious to get back to the state that makes him most comfortable. And, I might add, it makes God most comfortable, speaking in the ways of man, for him to be there.

Now is my soul troubled; and what shall I say? Father, save me from this hour: but for this cause came I unto this hour. Father, glorify thy name.

Then came there a voice from heaven, saying, I have both glorified it, and will glorify it again.

The people therefore, that stood by, and heard it, said that it thundered: others said, An angel spake to him.

Jesus answered and said, This voice came not because of me, but for your sakes.

Now is the judgment of this world: now shall the prince of this world be cast out.

And I, if I be lifted up from the earth, will draw all men unto me.

(John 12:27-32)

At the Father's side, in the glory that is his from the foundation of the world, is the state of having Jesus at the center of the power—the Word—of God. Think about it; there are undoubtedly a lot of things for God to do in the universe, and many of these will require the attention of the Lord of the universe. Maybe, just maybe, mankind is preparing some tests of the ability of the Father to control the elements that He placed on this earth; we do have a lot of conversation about man-inspired global warming, for instance. Remember, God did not give man authority over the elements, just over the plants and creatures. Therefore, maybe, just maybe Jesus is also needed on a global scale to control such things as the man's manipulation of subatomic particles. Or, maybe he is sent by God to control the extremely powerful astrological phenomenon that mankind is attempting to manifest within the earth.

So, it seems perfectly reasonable to me that even without coming here to do it, Jesus would activate the cleanup process that he described when he was here. That is, after he had, by the truth of God's Word, taken care of the removal of the major leaders' outsized authority over the peoples and institutions of the earth.

> *Then Jesus sent the multitude away, and went into the house: and his disciples came unto him, saying, Declare unto us the parable of the tares of the field.*
>
> *He answered and said unto them,*
>
> *He that soweth the good seed is the Son of man;*
> *The field is the world;*
> *the good seed are the children of the kingdom;*
>
> *but the tares are the children of the wicked one;*
> *The enemy that sowed them is the devil;*
> *the harvest is the end of the world;*
> *and the reapers are the angels.*
>
> *As therefore the tares are gathered and burned in the fire; so shall it be in the end of this world.*
>
> *The Son of man shall send forth his angels, and they shall gather out of his kingdom all things that offend, and them which do iniquity; And shall cast them into a furnace of fire: there shall be wailing and gnashing of teeth.*
>
> *Then shall the righteous shine forth as the sun in the kingdom of their Father. Who hath ears to hear, let him hear.*
>
> (Matthew 13:36-43)

This is where we are after Babylon has fallen. The center of government over the world, at Rome, has been greatly suppressed, as it moves to the time of its elimination. The whore is gone, but there is still some cleanup to be done. Satan is neutralized in the pit, and the world can now grow into a fuller understanding of the gospel of Jesus Christ. This is the time of the Byzantine Empire. Let me borrow from others some words of history that tell the approximate time of the Byzantine Empire.

Borrowed Thought

> The primary issue historians have looked at when analyzing any theory is the continued existence of the Eastern Empire or Byzantine Empire, which lasted for about a thousand years after the fall of the West.
>
> The eastern half of the Empire, which was even more Christian than the west in geographic extent, fervor, penetration and sheer numbers continued on for a thousand years afterwards. Environmental or weather changes impacted the east as much as the west, yet the east did not "fall."

This is one source's estimation of the period of the Byzantine Empire. Is it coincidence that this matches with the Revelation of Jesus Christ? I don't think so!

> *And he laid hold on the dragon, that old serpent, which is the Devil, and Satan, and bound him a thousand years,*
>
> (Revelation 20:2)

I am not going to give an extensive history lesson, here; however, the Byzantine Empire is generally agreed to be a time of great religious enlightenment and growth of the Christian religion. During this time Christ's spiritual presence was being spread, mightily, throughout the world. Remember, the Bible indicates that the world is not pristine during the thousand year reign; it is still being developed. Christ's Spirit still has to rule with an iron rod, and it has to break some things in pieces.

> *I will declare the decree: the LORD hath said unto me, Thou art my Son; this day have I begotten thee. Ask of me, and I shall give thee the heathen for thine inheritance, and the uttermost parts of the earth for thy possession. Thou shalt break them with a rod of iron; thou shalt dash them in pieces like a potter's vessel.*
>
> (Psalm 2:7-9)

And I saw heaven opened, and behold a white horse; and he that sat upon him was called Faithful and True, and in righteousness he doth judge and make war. His eyes were as a flame of fire, and on his head were many crowns; and he had a name written, that no man knew, but he himself. And he was clothed with a vesture dipped in blood: and his name is called The Word of God.

And the armies which were in heaven followed him upon white horses, clothed in fine linen, white and clean. And out of his mouth goeth a sharp sword, that with it he should smite the nations: and he shall rule them with a rod of iron: and he treadeth the winepress of the fierceness and wrath of Almighty God. And he hath on his vesture and on his thigh a name written, KING OF KINGS, AND LORD OF LORDS.

(Revelation 19:11-16)

Folks, during the Byzantine Empire, it is not over yet. There are many who will die in Christ during this period. These, too, will be accounted for in the continuation of the spiritual kingdom of Christ on the earth. You might say that they are allowed to sleep while Christ takes care of making the world safer for them to observe, once they are brought forth to witness the continuation of existence.

But the rest of the dead lived not again until the thousand years were finished. This is the first resurrection.

(Revelation 20:5)

There is this little matter of the *escape* of Satan. Oh, you say it is not an escape. Well, you are right; it is not an escape; it is a release. And, since Satan is released, there must be some pieces of his dynasty that remain. Like a sponge, he must be released to suck all of them into himself; so that when he is disposed of, all the filth that is accounted to him will go along with him.

And he laid hold on the dragon, that old serpent, which is the Devil, and Satan, and bound him a thousand years, And cast him into the bottomless pit, and shut him up, and set a seal upon him,

that he should deceive the nations no more, till the thousand years should be fulfilled: and after that he must be loosed a little season.
(Revelation 20:2-3)

After an intervening analysis of surrounding events, this will be the next stop, in our journey to identify that which is of the seven, as we look at this part of the Revelation: Satan Released. First, we will go to an exploration of Rightly Dividing: Honoring The Spirit. As preparation, please store this in your soul, if it is not already there. It will help to clarify that God may use indirect means to accomplish His will in our world.

Remember the former things of old: for I am God, and there is none else; I am God, and there is none like me, Declaring the end from the beginning, and from ancient times the things that are not yet done, saying, My counsel shall stand, and I will do all my pleasure: Calling a ravenous bird from the east, the man that executeth my counsel from a far country: yea, I have spoken it, I will also bring it to pass; I have purposed it, I will also do it.

Hearken unto me, ye stouthearted, that are far from righteousness: I bring near my righteousness: it shall not be far off, and my salvation shall not tarry: and I will place salvation in Zion for Israel my glory.
(Isaiah 46:9-13)

They learned, well,
How to roam,
But they wanted
A place to call home.

Their world was often
Dark and cold;
Still, they remained
Strong and bold:

Setting their sights
On things above;
Assuring one another
Of God's great love.

With God's promise being
Their shelter in the storm;
Many days, they only had
This to keep them warm.

They only wanted
To follow God's Way,
So that mankind's soul
Would stop its decay.

They knew their rest
Would come along;
But could they endure,
Could they stay strong?

Their love of the Lord
Set, for them, the pace;
Their greatest hope:
To, one day, see his face.

They were aware that
No man knew the hour
Of the Lord's return
In matchless power.

Then, came the death
Of a powerful threat;
Ennared, by God's word,
In an inescapable net.

This is the dawn
That removed fear;
As the Son's glory,
To all did appear.

Food for Thought

Edward Gibbon's 476 date for the fall of Rome is conventionally acceptable because that's when the Germanic Odoacer deposed the last emperor ruling from Rome. There are, however, other reasonable dates for the Fall of the Roman Empire. Some say Rome fell when it was split in two. Many say the Fall was an ongoing process lasting more than a century.

Additional Food for Thought

Theodosius the Great also starts two other chain reactions. Theodosius split the Roman Empire right down the middle, giving the West and Rome to Honorius and the East and City of Constantine to Arcadia. This is viewed as a possible ending of the Roman Empire. This is especially evident as the Empire weakens when the land gets divided. The other chain reaction started during the Germanic Invasions. The Visigoths traveled south towards Rome to avoid the Huns attack. However while Theodosius the Great was trying to keep Rome together, he experienced a massive invasion of the Visigoths, at which time he gave them permission to settle in the Roman Empire naming them "Federates" so they would fight with him instead of against him.

At this time the Roman Empire did not have a real army and the Federates were used as a "buffer" or protection from the Barbarians. However in 410 CE, the Federates turned on the Roman Empire by attacking and sacking the city of Rome when fellow Goths invaded Rome. This was the first time that Rome had been overrun in over 600 years, and qualifies the event as a cause of the Roman Empire falling

Still More Food for Thought

Egypt is identified in the Bible as the place of refuge that the Holy Family sought in its flight from Judea: "*When he arose, he took the young child and his mother by night, and departed into Egypt: And was there until the death of Herod: that it might be fulfilled which was spoken of the Lord by the prophet, saying, Out of Egypt have I called my son.*" (Matthew 2:14-15). The Egyptian Church, which is now more than nineteen centuries old, was the subject of many prophecies in the Old Testament. "*In that day shall there be an altar to the LORD in the midst of the land of Egypt, and a pillar at the border thereof to the LORD. And it shall be for a sign and for a witness unto the LORD of hosts in the land of Egypt: for they shall cry unto the LORD because of the oppressors, and he shall send them a saviour, and a great one, and he shall deliver them. And the LORD shall be known to Egypt, and the Egyptians shall know the LORD in that day, and shall do sacrifice and oblation; yea, they shall vow a vow unto the LORD, and perform it."* (Isaiah 19:19-21).

The first Christians in Egypt were mainly Alexandrian Jews such as Theophilus, whom Saint Luke the Evangelist addresses in the introductory chapter of his gospel. When the church was founded by Mark during the reign of the Roman emperor Nero, a great multitude of native Egyptians (as opposed to Greeks or Jews) embraced the Christian faith. Christianity spread throughout Egypt within half a century of Saint Mark's arrival in Alexandria as is clear from the New Testament writings found in Bahnasa, in Middle Egypt, which date around the year 200 AD, and a fragment of the Gospel of Saint John, written in Coptic, which was found in Upper Egypt and can be dated to the first half of the second century. In the second century Christianity began to spread to the rural areas, and scriptures were translated into the local language, namely Coptic.

Additional Tidbits

Whereas in an earlier time, man was becoming more Christian, in the 12th century, there were efforts underway to make Christianity more human.

In 1391, intense, pent up anti-Jewish sentiment in Christian Spain erupted, with great violence, against the country's prosperous, well-established Jewish community. Spanish cities were engulfed in ferocious pogroms that destroyed much property and claimed many lives.

This led to the mass expulsion of all Jews from Spain in 1492. (Ten years later, the Muslims were likewise driven out.) In their edict of expulsion, issued on March 31, 1492, King Ferdinand and Queen Isabella announced their "decision to banish all Jews of both sexes forever from the precincts of our realm." Ordered, on pain of death, to leave within four months, the Jews were permitted to take their personal belongings, except for gold, silver, coined money, or jewels. Estimates of the number of Jews banished generally range from about 165,000 to 400,000. An estimated 50,000 Jews chose baptism to avoid expulsion. In his diary Christopher Columbus noted: "In the same month in which Their Majesties issued the edict that all Jews should be driven out of the kingdom and its territories, in the same month they gave me the order to undertake with sufficient men my expedition of discovery to the Indies."

Expulsions of Jews and outbreaks of anti-Jewish violence have been features of both European and non-Western societies over many centuries and under a variety of political and religious regimes. What is noteworthy about these 14th—and 15th-century actions in Spain, however, is that tens of thousands of Jews escaped death or expulsion by converting to Christianity. As a result, by the middle of the 15th century there was a numerically large (perhaps 100,000), and politically and economically significant community of people of Jewish descent in Spain who were, at least outwardly, Christians.

CHAPTER 8A

Honoring the Spirit

Rightly Dividing Scripture

Matthew 12:22-37

Then was brought unto him one possessed with a devil, blind, and dumb: and he healed him, insomuch that the blind and dumb both spake and saw. And all the people were amazed, and said, Is not this the son of David?

But when the Pharisees heard it, they said, This fellow doth not cast out devils, but by Beelzebub the prince of the devils.

And Jesus knew their thoughts, and said unto them, Every kingdom divided against itself is brought to desolation; and every city or house divided against itself shall not stand: And if Satan cast out Satan, he is divided against himself; how shall then his kingdom stand? And if I by Beelzebub cast out devils, by whom do your children cast them out? therefore they shall be your judges. But if I cast out devils by the Spirit of God, then the kingdom of God is come unto you.

Or else how can one enter into a strong man's house, and spoil his goods, except he first bind the strong man? and then he will spoil his house.

He that is not with me is against me; and he that gathereth not with me scattereth abroad. Wherefore I say unto you, All manner of sin and blasphemy shall be forgiven unto men: but the blasphemy against the

Holy Ghost shall not be forgiven unto men. And whosoever speaketh a word against the Son of man, it shall be forgiven him: but whosoever speaketh against the Holy Ghost, it shall not be forgiven him, neither in this world, neither in the world to come.

Either make the tree good, and his fruit good; or else make the tree corrupt, and his fruit corrupt: for the tree is known by his fruit. O generation of vipers, how can ye, being evil, speak good things? for out of the abundance of the heart the mouth speaketh. A good man out of the good treasure of the heart bringeth forth good things: and an evil man out of the evil treasure bringeth forth evil things. But I say unto you, That every idle word that men shall speak, they shall give account thereof in the day of judgment. For by thy words thou shalt be justified, and by thy words thou shalt be condemned.

We have gone through two dimensions of our absorption into the body of Christ. The first one took us deep, by our spirit being overshadowed by the Holy Ghost. This happens when the Spirit of truth moves in you.

Then, we studied the breadth of the body of Christ in the church of Christ. This is where you understand how to move in the Spirit of truth.

There is one more dimension: this is the dimension of being prepared for the heights of service.

> *At that day ye shall know that I am in my Father, and ye in me, and I in you. He that hath my commandments, and keepeth them, he it is that loveth me: and he that loveth me shall be loved of my Father, and I will love him, and will manifest myself to him.*
>
> (John 14:20-21)

As you move forward to independence in Christ, through submission to God, by yielding to the direction of the Holy Ghost; there are several thoughts for you to consider in what we will cover here. These thoughts are good for the teacher, as well as the beginner. The beginner can reference them to know when he or she is receiving sound doctrine. The more advanced, teacher, can reference them to determine when he is giving sound doctrine. As you read the thoughts that follow, please carry the following Scripture in your heart.

> *All things are lawful for me, but all things are not expedient: all things are lawful for me, but all things edify not.*
>
> *Let no man seek his own, but every man another's wealth.*
>
> *Whatsoever is sold in the shambles, that eat, asking no question for conscience sake: For the earth is the Lord's, and the fulness thereof. If any of them that believe not bid you to a feast, and ye be disposed to go; whatsoever is set before you, eat, asking no question for conscience sake.*
>
> *But if any man say unto you, This is offered in sacrifice unto idols, eat not for his sake that showed it, and for conscience sake: for the earth is the Lord's, and the fulness thereof: Conscience, I say, not thine own, but of the other: for why is my liberty judged of another man's conscience? For if I by grace be a partaker, why am I evil spoken of for that for which I give thanks?*
>
> *Whether therefore ye eat, or drink, or whatsoever ye do, do all to the glory of God.*
>
> (1 Corinthians 10:23-31)

When we are first immersed in the Spirit, our eyes are wide with wonder, and our ears are attuned to every sound. We want to know everything that we see or hear. This is why the term babe in Christ became a common expression. By observing the early years of babies, we can understand our fascination with this new *toy*. Fortunately for us, God wants us to enjoy Him, as a child. Unfortunately for us, so do many others.

As a spiritual child, with either a young or a full adult body and mind, we seek out counsel in the Lord. And even if we do not seek it out, it comes to us. The news is full of stories about the poor Christian *Davids,* battling the evil governmental, institutional and lifestyle goliaths. We hear about some of the obvious ones; such as, suppression of human right. We hear about the subtle ones, such as the freedom to partake in what is called, gay marriage. These pull at our little Christian hearts, and move us from east to west and from north to south, attempting to lure us into a fractionated state of mind. If we let them pull us there, our minds can be changed based on the *authority* speaking the message. This is a dangerous position to be in. We must look to God for answers—not, to man.

> *If any of you lack wisdom, let him ask of God, that giveth to all men liberally, and upbraideth not; and it shall be given him. But let him ask in faith, nothing wavering. For he that wavereth is like a wave of the sea driven with the wind and tossed. For let not that man think that he shall receive any thing of the Lord. A double minded man is unstable in all his ways.*
>
> (James 1:5-8)

The church, as a modern institution, has almost stopped being of universal help. Please understand that this is not a slight against the local church; each Christian must petition God for His leading, to deliver them to a local congregation with which the believer can share his and their life. Rather, this is a slam against the organizations of local churches. Unless the organization itself has as its charter the full message of God, as recorded in the Bible; they are of no use. No, I did not say, little use: I said, no use. Let me go one step further. If they are not totally immersed in the truth of the Bible, they are actually doing damage to the emerging Christian.

Whenever there are doctrinal statements that conflict with the words of the Bible, there is a problem. Yes, we know that there is such a thing as the difference between the spirit and the letter. The letter is only a pointer to the Spirit, as it pertains to the Bible: especially, it is this way with prophecy. However, when the interpretation clearly denounces the text of the Bible; it is anathema to the Lord, and to the LORD. Such expressions as, "for that day," "under those circumstances," "considering that group of people," and others of their kind, can become really confusing to the new Christian; and confusing to many older ones, as well. The question arises; who determines what modification must be made to the text in order to live a righteous life?

This discussion could go on and on, but it has only one point: there comes a time when the statements of the institutions of the church have to be passed through the filter. This filter is the Bible as revealed by the Holy Ghost. Christian, you no longer have an excuse. It will not do you any good to say to God, "The minister that thou gavest to me, he gave me this message, and I did absorb it into my soul" (think, Adam, here). You must come to the point at which you try the spirits for yourself.

> *Beloved, believe not every spirit, but try the spirits whether they are of God: because many false prophets are gone out into the world. Hereby know ye the Spirit of God: Every spirit that confesseth that Jesus Christ is come in the flesh is of God: And every spirit that confesseth not that Jesus Christ is come in the flesh is not of God: and this is that spirit of antichrist, whereof ye have heard that it should come; and even now already is it in the world.*
>
> (1 John 4:1-3)

Trying the spirits is the point where you submit yourself to the Spirit. The "take them at their word" way of life, which is sufficient for the child, will be removed from you as you mature.

> *Charity never faileth: but whether there be prophecies, they shall fail; whether there be tongues, they shall cease; whether there be knowledge, it shall vanish away. For we know in part, and we prophesy in part. But when that which is perfect is come, then that which is in part shall be done away. When I was a child, I spake as a child, I understood as a child, I thought as a child: but when I became a man, I put away childish things.*
>
> *For now we see through a glass, darkly; but then face to face: now I know in part; but then shall I know even as also I am known. And now abideth faith, hope, charity, these three; but the greatest of these is charity.*
>
> (1 Corinthians 13:8-13)

Trying the spirits is the point where you walk in the Spirit, and not according to the flesh. Of course, you must first have clear in your heart and mind that you are of the redeemed of Christ. This is the first and easiest step. There is no need to consult with anyone on this earth about this matter. The result of being redeemed is to know that you have eternal life. It is not subject to conjecture, or interpretation by any institution. It is clearly revealed in Scripture, in the Bible.

For Christ is the end of the law for righteousness to every one that believeth.

(Romans 10:4)

But what saith it? The word is nigh thee, even in thy mouth, and in thy heart: that is, the word of faith, which we preach; That if thou shalt confess with thy mouth the Lord Jesus, and shalt believe in thine heart that God hath raised him from the dead, thou shalt be saved. For with the heart man believeth unto righteousness; and with the mouth confession is made unto salvation. For the scripture saith, Whosoever believeth on him shall not be ashamed. For there is no difference between the Jew and the Greek: for the same Lord over all is rich unto all that call upon him.

For whosoever shall call upon the name of the Lord shall be saved.

(Romans 10:8-13)

He that believeth on the Son of God hath the witness in himself: he that believeth not God hath made him a liar; because he believeth not the record that God gave of his Son. And this is the record, that God hath given to us eternal life, and this life is in his Son. He that hath the Son hath life; and he that hath not the Son of God hath not life. These things have I written unto you that believe on the name of the Son of God; that ye may know that ye have eternal life, and that ye may believe on the name of the Son of God.

(1 John 5:10-13)

Let us yield to the Spirit. Let us, daily, pick up our Bible. Let us allow the Spirit to show us what truth is. If you feel bold about it, then challenge the Holy Ghost, the Spirit of truth within you, to do what is its name and what is, too, its joy. Challenge the Holy Ghost to reveal to you the truth—written by the power of God, and not according to the heart of man.

Therefore leaving the principles of the doctrine of Christ, let us go on unto perfection; not laying again the foundation of repentance from dead works, and of faith toward God, Of the doctrine of

> *baptisms, and of laying on of hands, and of resurrection of the dead, and of eternal judgment. And this will we do, if God permit.*
> (Hebrews 6:1-3)

The first step on this route is to truly believe that the Bible is the word of God. This sounds all too simple, but it is really very difficult. When you look, from our modern perspective, at the Old Testament, you see some pretty gory things. In the Old Testament, God seems to have authorized mass killings, extinction of cultures, and even deception of people and peoples that led to their destruction. This can make a servant of the LORD "stand up" for God, and say that He would never do such a thing (without a really good reason). Unfortunately, both the fervor and the defense are not in agreement with modern laws of man, and so they will not convince one who lays the template of man's law over God's revealed works.

Now, I could engage in an attempt to explain all this away, but I will not do that, directly, here. In other places in this book, and other writings of mine, I have shown where this is a matter of action and consequence. Allow the Spirit to enhance your understanding of this concept as you read the text of the Bible. We must believe that all which is accounted to the voice of God actually belongs to that voice. We must believe that *All scripture is given by inspiration of God . . .* (2 Timothy 3:16)

Furthermore, the acts of God, in the Old Testament, as under the Old Covenant, were not directly transcribed into the New Covenant, in the New Testament. Again there is a need for the filter of the Spirit, the Holy Ghost.

> *These things have I spoken unto you, being yet present with you. But the Comforter, which is the Holy Ghost, whom the Father will send in my name, he shall teach you all things, and bring all things to your remembrance, whatsoever I have said unto you. Peace I leave with you, my peace I give unto you: not as the world giveth, give I unto you. Let not your heart be troubled, neither let it be afraid.*
> (John 14:25-27)

And in believing this, we must be willing to wait for God's revelation of the whys of the actions. But above all, we must allow God total sovereignty in our lives. This sovereignty says that God may not let you know the why of a particular action. If it is not relevant to your further service to mankind through Christ, then do not allow the quest for the knowledge to become a stumbling block. You are not required to ***explain*** everything that God did in the Bible. Our search through the Bible is not to find "proofs to present". We study the Bible, in the filling of the Holy Ghost, because we want to know how we should order our lives; we want to know how we ***must*** order our lives.

> *Then said Jesus to those Jews which believed on him, If ye continue in my word, then are ye my disciples indeed; And ye shall know the truth, and the truth shall make you free.*
>
> (John 8:31-32)

Then, having learned that; we want to know the best way to pass it on to others.

> *While I was with them in the world, I kept them in thy name: those that thou gavest me I have kept, and none of them is lost, but the son of perdition; that the scripture might be fulfilled. And now come I to thee; and these things I speak in the world, that they might have my joy fulfilled in themselves. I have given them thy word; and the world hath hated them, because they are not of the world, even as I am not of the world.*
>
> *I pray not that thou shouldest take them out of the world, but that thou shouldest keep them from the evil. They are not of the world, even as I am not of the world. Sanctify them through thy truth: thy word is truth.*
>
> *As thou hast sent me into the world, even so have I also sent them into the world.*
>
> (John 17:12-18)

I have a bias, here: I think the best way to pass anything on to anyone else is by example. If we live the life, and God bestows His peace on our life, then we can go to anyone, and say, "Follow me". This is the mission of the Christian: not, to explain, but instead, to show. We may point to the scriptural reference in the Bible, but the best reference is a life lived in Christ before the eyes of the student seeking wisdom. Yes, we must believe that *All scripture is given by inspiration of God* . . . Furthermore, we must also know that it *is profitable for doctrine, for reproof, for correction, for instruction in righteousness: That the man of God may be perfect, thoroughly furnished unto all good works.* (2 Timothy 3:16-17)

Furthermore, understand this: books about the Bible—**including this one**—do not stand on the same level as the Bible. When the Spirit directs you to them, they may be useful to clarify a portion of the Scripture. However, they are not to be believed just because of the reputation, or the works, of the person who has written them. Above all, they are not to receive acceptance as a part of the truth of God just because "everyone" is reading and reciting them. This goes for songs as well.

The truth of God is certified in the Bible, not in books or songs that represent biblical truth. Too often, these books and songs are based on institutional positions; and there are many institutional positions that are **wrong**. Apply yourself to the kind of wisdom that *the preacher* shared with us.

> *And moreover, because the preacher was wise, he still taught the people knowledge; yea, he gave good heed, and sought out, and set in order many proverbs. The preacher sought to find out acceptable words: and that which was written was upright, even words of truth. The words of the wise are as goads, and as nails fastened by the masters of assemblies, which are given from one shepherd. And further, by these, my son, be admonished: of making many books there is no end; and much study is a weariness of the flesh.*
>
> *Let us hear the conclusion of the whole matter: Fear God, and keep his commandments: for this is the whole duty of man. For God shall bring every work into judgment, with every secret thing, whether it be good, or whether it be evil.*
>
> (Proverbs 12:9-14)

Furthermore, the truth of God was not given to us so that we might transform it to fit the ways of our specific society; or, of any society whatsoever. The prophets of old stood on very firm ground in what they wrote. They wrote it as it was received from God. They did not invent the words and concepts. In each case, they told everyone that the LORD is Who they represented. Thereby, the people knew that the actions carried the Authority of the LORD, whether the actions were words or behaviors. There are many examples in the Bible of the prophetic transfer, in words and calls to action, coming from the LORD God. Some of these are written below.

Now go, write it before them in a table, and note it in a book, that it may be for the time to come for ever and ever:

(Isaiah 30:8)

The word that came to Jeremiah from the LORD, saying, Thus speaketh the LORD God of Israel, saying, Write thee all the words that I have spoken unto thee in a book. For, lo, the days come, saith the LORD, that I will bring again the captivity of my people Israel and Judah, saith the LORD: and I will cause them to return to the land that I gave to their fathers, and they shall possess it.

And these are the words that the LORD spake concerning Israel and concerning Judah.

(Jeremiah 30:1-4)

And it came to pass in the fourth year of Jehoiakim the son of Josiah king of Judah, that this word came unto Jeremiah from the LORD, saying, Take thee a roll of a book, and write therein all the words that I have spoken unto thee against Israel, and against Judah, and against all the nations, from the day I spake unto thee, from the days of Josiah, even unto this day. It may be that the house of Judah will hear all the evil which I purpose to do unto them; that they may return every man from his evil way; that I may forgive their iniquity and their sin.

Then Jeremiah called Baruch the son of Neriah: and Baruch wrote from the mouth of Jeremiah all the words of the LORD, which he had spoken unto him, upon a roll of a book.

(Jeremiah 36:1-4)

I will stand upon my watch, and set me upon the tower, and will watch to see what he will say unto me, and what I shall answer when I am reproved.

And the LORD answered me, and said, Write the vision, and make it plain upon tables, that he may run that readeth it. For the vision is yet for an appointed time, but at the end it shall speak, and not lie: though it tarry, wait for it; because it will surely come, it will not tarry.

(Habakkuk 2:1-3)

Understand clearly that God knows when the requirements of man change, and at that time, He will send an intervention. For instance, at the time of the sending of His Son, God the Father caused such an intervention; because the world had indeed changed, in that it had become almost terminally corrupt. This was the period in history where God reformatted portions of the message of the Bible, as had been provided in the Old Testament. The LORD did not throw the Old Testament out; He just clarified areas that we would need to know about. This clarification is what we refer to as the Gospel of the Kingdom. Once again, in order to deliver this, the LORD God moved in men, by His Spirit . . .

Forasmuch as many have taken in hand to set forth in order a declaration of those things which are most surely believed among us, Even as they delivered them unto us, which from the beginning were eyewitnesses, and ministers of the word; It seemed good to me also, having had perfect understanding of all things from the very first, to write unto thee in order, most excellent Theophilus, That thou mightest know the certainty of those things, wherein thou hast been instructed.

(Luke 1:1-4)

. . . Including, the Spirit of Jesus Christ, which also told others to write.

The Revelation of Jesus Christ, which God gave unto him, to show unto his servants things which must shortly come to pass; and he sent and signified it by his angel unto his servant John: Who bare record of the word of God, and of the testimony of Jesus Christ, and of all things that he saw. Blessed is he that readeth, and they that hear the words of this prophecy, and keep those things which are written therein: for the time is at hand.

(Revelation 1:1-3)

I was in the Spirit on the Lord's day, and heard behind me a great voice, as of a trumpet, Saying, I am Alpha and Omega, the first and the last: and, What thou seest, write in a book, and send it unto the seven churches which are in Asia; unto Ephesus, and unto Smyrna, and unto Pergamos, and unto Thyatira, and unto Sardis, and unto Philadelphia, and unto Laodicea.

(Revelation 1:10-11)

I am he that liveth, and was dead; and, behold, I am alive for evermore, Amen; and have the keys of hell and of death. Write the things which thou hast seen, and the things which are, and the things which shall be hereafter; The mystery of the seven stars which thou sawest in my right hand, and the seven golden candlesticks. The seven stars are the angels of the seven churches: and the seven candlesticks which thou sawest are the seven churches.

(Revelation 1:18-20)

Additionally, there is the matter of the apostles who wrote on behalf of God. Even though they may not have stated that God told them to write, they still had authority for their words. Two of the authorities were observation, and participation. Many of the apostles, whose words we have in the Bible, were eyewitnesses to the events of the life of Jesus. They told what he did, and what he said; and that he said it as a representative—also known as, an angel—of God the Father, as Jesus declared of himself.

> *Philip saith unto him, Lord, show us the Father, and it sufficeth us.*
>
> *Jesus saith unto him, Have I been so long time with you, and yet hast thou not known me, Philip? he that hath seen me hath seen the Father; and how sayest thou then, Show us the Father? Believest thou not that I am in the Father, and the Father in me? the words that I speak unto you I speak not of myself: but the Father that dwelleth in me, he doeth the works. Believe me that I am in the Father, and the Father in me: or else believe me for the very works' sake.*
>
> (John 14:8-11)

In the spirit of authority that was given by the Father, coming through the Son; the apostle presented to the world the Gospel of the Kingdom of God. And a potent statement of the depth and breadth of this type of reporting is seen in the statement of the apostle John.

> *This is the disciple which testifieth of these things, and wrote these things: and we know that his testimony is true. And there are also many other things which Jesus did, the which, if they should be written every one, I suppose that even the world itself could not contain the books that should be written. Amen.*
>
> (John 21:24-25)

Then, there was that maverick, Saul; who became, the apostle Paul. Paul's statements are not purely observation, but are a unique mix of observation and inspiration. In that respect, in all of Scripture, the apostle Paul is one of the most critical examples for our lives. Of course, the best example is the Lord Jesus Christ, in that he was the first one to tell us to believe him based on the works of God that proceeded from his life. This is also the authority for the writings of the apostle Paul.

The presence and protection of God in Paul's life is evident. It is seen throughout the pages of the New Testament of Jesus Christ, which is of

God the Father, as written in the Bible. The apostle Paul's immersion in the Spirit is on the same par with that of those remaining from the original twelve apostles. The other apostles are also Paul's certification, as stated by the apostle Peter in his call for us to persist in Christian service . . .

> *And account that the longsuffering of our Lord is salvation; even as our beloved brother Paul also according to the wisdom given unto him hath written unto you; As also in all his epistles, speaking in them of these things; in which are some things hard to be understood, which they that are unlearned and unstable wrest, as they do also the other scriptures, unto their own destruction.*
> (2 Peter 3:15-16)

This is not watered down certification. This is the certification that Peter was authorized, by the Lord Jesus Christ, to do. It is a part of Peter's portion in the handling of the keys of the Kingdom of Heaven.

> *And I will give unto thee the keys of the kingdom of heaven: and whatsoever thou shalt bind on earth shall be bound in heaven: and whatsoever thou shalt loose on earth shall be loosed in heaven.*
> (Matthew 16:19)

This is the only type of certification—as of an apostle of God, to this level of service—that is recorded in the Bible as having been given by Peter. We say this because there is a group of people that misuse the fervor of Paul, by establishing a hierarchical privilege based collection of certified bishops, with the top level being a bishop of Rome. There is no biblical certification of a unique office of the bishop of Rome, as being superior to any other bishop's office. It would be counterproductive for God to put the center of His authority in a place that was ordained for destruction, in the one part, and that would not exist for almost fifteen centuries in the other part. The written words of the Bible only support a single-level bishopric, as recorded in the following Scripture.

> *This is a true saying, If a man desire the office of a bishop, he desireth a good work. A bishop then must be blameless, the husband of one wife, vigilant, sober, of good behaviour, given to hospitality, apt to teach; Not given to wine, no striker, not greedy of filthy lucre; but*

patient, not a brawler, not covetous; One that ruleth well his own house, having his children in subjection with all gravity; (For if a man know not how to rule his own house, how shall he take care of the church of God?)

Not a novice, lest being lifted up with pride he fall into the condemnation of the devil.

Moreover he must have a good report of them which are without; lest he fall into reproach and the snare of the devil.

(1 Timothy 3:1-7)

Moreover, Peter's certification of anything is a limited certification, as bounds by the keys to the kingdom. The keys are for the dispensation of knowledge that opens the door to the will of God, in Christ Jesus; or closes it off from pretenders at the faith. The keys are not a means to rule. The Bible says that the twelve had authority to bind and loose; not, to control. Furthermore, that which they did bind and loose was delivered to Heaven, and not kept in a state of servitude on the earth. All glory is to God; no control is to man. You have read it for yourself in Matthew 16:19.

Therefore, on this matter of external sources of inspiration, we have a slippery slope situation. First, let me say that the Bible is not a history book. It does not record, blow by blow, the events of the day. There are references in the Bible to other historical texts, but the Bible is not a history book. For instance, in writing about Joshua's service, the scribe of Scripture mentions another reference source . . .

Then spake Joshua to the LORD in the day when the LORD delivered up the Amorites before the children of Israel, and he said in the sight of Israel, Sun, stand thou still upon Gibeon; and thou, Moon, in the valley of Ajalon. And the sun stood still, and the moon stayed, until the people had avenged themselves upon their enemies. Is not this written in the book of Jasher? So the sun stood still in the midst of heaven, and hasted not to go down about a whole day.

(Joshua 10:12-13)

. . . So, too, does the scribe for David.

> *And David lamented with this lamentation over Saul and over Jonathan his son: (Also he bade them teach the children of Judah the use of the bow: behold, it is written in the book of Jasher.)*
> (2 Samuel 1:17-18)

Regardless of any discovery of associated references, we will not be able to validate all the writings in the Bible based on the inclusion of these outside historical texts. We will also not be able to validate all the writings in the Bible based on archaeology. There are some things that God has sealed from our discovery. We will have to accept this as being the will and wisdom of God. Therefore, do not look to the Bible to provide you with all the answer to the historical flow of the lives of the servants in the Bible. Throughout the Bible, we see that God is not showing us the history of mankind. We must remember the purpose for which we were given the Bible: *for doctrine, for reproof, for correction, for instruction in righteousness.* To do this, only those events that give a view of God's working are required.

On an associated matter, there is much debate about the how of the Bible; this is a fruitless endeavor. God is God: this is a simple enough statement, and quite obvious; however, a powerful dose of complexity is embedded in that statement. Let me add that man is man, and not God. To develop an appreciation for the magnitude of that difference; think about a discussion of Plato's total worldview, being engaged between a new born baby and a doctor of philosophy: by absolute design, it is a one-sided communication, which, for most of us, is, at best, a speech, and not a discussion. Moreover, it is a speech without usefulness. The same is the combination of any vision of God explaining His total worldview, and even the entire, end-to-end in time, from everlasting to everlasting, collection of humans.

We sit in the place of that newborn, in our small capacity to absorb the Wisdom that frames our existence. As with the newborn, so, too, are we. Most newborns (I hesitate to say all because I do not want to offend any hopeful parents, out there) do not understand language of this sort. They will not know that they should take these words, and store them. Now, if they are associated with a smile, the newborn can internalize that. Though the trigger for the smile is useful, the newly born does not profit by understanding Plato. This is the state that we are in, most of the time, with God. The way God did what God did falls into this same category of "need to know". Do we really have a need to know how God did what He did? The answer is: some parts, yes; other parts, no. God does allow for a limited amount of human understanding, as He did at this time.

> *Wash you, make you clean; put away the evil of your doings from before mine eyes; cease to do evil; Learn to do well; seek judgment, relieve the oppressed, judge the fatherless, plead for the widow. Come now, and let us reason together, saith the LORD: though your sins be as scarlet, they shall be as white as snow; though they be red like crimson, they shall be as wool.*
>
> *If ye be willing and obedient, ye shall eat the good of the land: But if ye refuse and rebel, ye shall be devoured with the sword: for the mouth of the LORD hath spoken it.*
>
> (Isaiah 1:16-20)

In obtaining the "some parts, yes" knowledge of God's interventions in reality, we still need to be vigilant about how we use the understanding. For, sometimes, when we are given glimpses into the possible workings of God, we get all uppity about it. When He does show us some hint of the power behind the action, we suddenly feel that **we** invented it. We lose sight of the fact that; even when we understand the majesty, it is still the majesty of God that we are observing. It is not the majesty of man because he has received the revelation. Oftentimes, we just do not seem to be able to get this matter through our thick skulls; as my mother would often say about me in reference to my listening skills. The matter at hand is this: what we discover, and when we discover it, are both controlled by God. So do not fall into the trap of trying to prove the science in the Bible—or the philosophy, or the theology, or the other-ology.

> *O Timothy, keep that which is committed to thy trust, avoiding profane and vain babblings, and oppositions of science falsely so*

> *called: Which some professing have erred concerning the faith. Grace be with thee. Amen.*
>
> (1 Timothy 6:20-21)

"Why," you may ask, "doesn't God just clarify this issue? Why doesn't he just indicate what is true science, and what is not? Why does he leave us hanging like this?"

Well, let me highlight a portion of what has been said before. When we discover what we do discover, it is discovered at the time that God knows that we need to discover it: this is a statement for all mankind. For instance, you would not feed a child two thousand pizzas to take care of the food allowance for life. You might provide the means for the child to obtain two thousand pizzas, by training them, over time and at the right time. Indeed, some of us are even able to provide the funds for the two thousand pizzas, right now. But no one would try to feed the child two thousand pizzas, at a single period in time, so that they can be finished with their responsibility for the entire life of the child.

Mankind was made to inhabit the earth. Or should I say that the earth was made for mankind to inhabit, over a long term.

> *For thus saith the LORD that created the heavens; God himself that formed the earth and made it; he hath established it, he created it not in vain, he formed it to be inhabited: I am the LORD; and there is none else.*
>
> (Isaiah 45:18)

Do not be so critical of the progressive nature of the development of our knowledge base. As you look around you, you will see that God has been revealing the working of His universe since the start of the day when we stopped killing folks because they wanted to ask God, *why*. From that time, to now, we have seen advanced discoveries that would have caused the early folks to believe that all mankind were prophets and priests of God. The mysteries that existed then, which are now known by the average school child, are magnificently mind boggling. Assuredly, God has been revealing His majesty to mankind. Mankind has to be patient, and wait until the time when God knows that it will understand, and fully appreciate, the next lesson that He is teaching.

We must learn from the condemnation that was given of those who exalt their search for knowledge, placing it above God THAT gives them knowledge.

> *For the invisible things of him from the creation of the world are clearly seen, being understood by the things that are made, even his eternal power and Godhead; so that they are without excuse: Because that, when they knew God, they glorified him not as God, neither were thankful; but became vain in their imaginations, and their foolish heart was darkened. Professing themselves to be wise, they became fools, And changed the glory of the uncorruptible God into an image made like to corruptible man, and to birds, and fourfooted beasts, and creeping things. Wherefore God also gave them up to uncleanness through the lusts of their own hearts, to dishonour their own bodies between themselves: Who changed the truth of God into a lie, and worshipped and served the creature more than the Creator, who is blessed for ever. Amen.*
>
> (Romans 1:20-25)

Therefore, do not look to the Bible to provide you with all the answer to the scientific manifestation of the workings of God as seen in the Bible, and in the world. In the Bible, God is not showing us how He did what He did. God did not overload the minds of the early recipients of the Bible, and He does not want to overload the minds of modern man, or any possible future man. Therefore, there are things that will just have to wait to be revealed; but, not everything.

God even taught His Son how to protect us from really bad news. This protection was done to keep us from being paralyzed with fear as the times approach. This fear would, then, drive out the love that we needed to exhibit at that time.

> *Verily I say unto you, This generation shall not pass, till all these things be fulfilled. Heaven and earth shall pass away, but my words*

shall not pass away. But of that day and hour knoweth no man, no, not the angels of heaven, but my Father only.

But as the days of Noe were, so shall also the coming of the Son of man be. For as in the days that were before the flood they were eating and drinking, marrying and giving in marriage, until the day that Noe entered into the ark, And knew not until the flood came, and took them all away; so shall also the coming of the Son of man be.

(Matthew 24:34-39)

So, what are our constraints, when it is in our area of service? Don't we have a *right*—oh, pardon me, I meant to say, need—to know what is coming up?

Nope!

Sometimes, even those with whom we must associate will remain something of a mystery to us. On a light note, if God required that we know fully the people with whom we are to bond, there would be no such thing as marriage. And, courtship would definitely be out the window. But back to seriousness (did I ever really leave it) we are in the Spirit. This does not mean that we have a need, or a right, to pull everything around us into the Spirit with us. Actually, we have no right to pull anyone into the Spirit with us; not even our children.

Each person must relate to the Spirit in their own fashion; for, the Spirit will relate to each of us as individuals. This, however, does not release the follower of Christ from setting the example that points the way to receiving the Holy Ghost. The same holds true for the explanations that are given to any child, telling of the hope that is in us. (In this, though, parents must never give up responsibility for steering their children. Sunday school is not a substitute for family worship.) Most often, the example of a life lived in Christ is the answer that any child (or adolescent, or adult) needs. This steering, by example, is done to point the way to residence in the Gospel of Christ. This is the simplicity of the walk.

Ye are the salt of the earth: but if the salt have lost his savour, wherewith shall it be salted? it is thenceforth good for nothing, but to be cast out, and to be trodden under foot of men.

Ye are the light of the world. A city that is set on an hill cannot be hid. Neither do men light a candle, and put it under a bushel, but on a candlestick; and it giveth light unto all that are in the house.

Let your light so shine before men, that they may see your good works, and glorify your Father which is in heaven.

(Matthew 5:13-16)

When we abide in Christ, we will be able to almost effortlessly share, with others, that which we have shared with the Spirit. We will not be speaking supposition, theory, or human potential. We will be displaying the actuality of life in God, as a catalyst for others to open the door to their soul. Let us be content to do that, and not try to control the lives of all in our environment. In this contentment with limited knowledge and reach, we will have episodes with answers; such as this encounter between Peter and Jesus. And, as in the discussion between Jesus and Peter; our sole answer to others, as pertains to the mind of Christ, at the urging of the Spirit of truth, will be this: *follow thou me.*

Then Peter, turning about, seeth the disciple whom Jesus loved following; which also leaned on his breast at supper, and said, Lord, which is he that betrayeth thee? Peter seeing him saith to Jesus, Lord, and what shall this man do?

Jesus saith unto him, If I will that he tarry till I come, what is that to thee? follow thou me.

(John 21:20-22)

These are some of the actions that you will perform as you walk in the Spirit. We will have more to say, on another level, later. Prepare your self with the following:

As many as I love, I rebuke and chasten: be zealous therefore, and repent. Behold, I stand at the door, and knock: if any man hear my voice, and open the door, I will come in to him, and will sup with him, and he with me.

> *To him that overcometh will I grant to sit with me in my throne, even as I also overcame, and am set down with my Father in his throne.*
>
> (Revelation 3:19-21)

THE WORD FROM THE BIBLE

Revelation 20:7-15

And when the thousand years are expired, Satan shall be loosed out of his prison, And shall go out to deceive the nations which are in the four quarters of the earth, Gog and Magog, to gather them together to battle: the number of whom is as the sand of the sea.

And they went up on the breadth of the earth, and compassed the camp of the saints about, and the beloved city: and fire came down from God out of heaven, and devoured them. And the devil that deceived them was cast into the lake of fire and brimstone, where the beast and the false prophet are, and shall be tormented day and night for ever and ever.

And I saw a great white throne, and him that sat on it, from whose face the earth and the heaven fled away; and there was found no place for them. And I saw the dead, small and great, stand before God; and the books were opened: and another book was opened, which is the book of life: and the dead were judged out of those things which were written in the books, according to their works. And the sea gave up the dead which were in it; and death and hell delivered up the dead which were in them: and they were judged every man according to their works. And death and hell were cast into the lake of fire. This is the second death.

And whosoever was not found written in the book of life was cast into the lake of fire.

Chapter Nine

Revelation

Satan Released (for a short time)

Evidence is not evidence until someone sees it. To say that a thing will happen has no proof until it happens. This was the dilemma that faced the early people of God. They needed to know how they would be able to tell who is a true prophet, and who is a false prophet. God gave them the following method.

> *And if thou say in thine heart, How shall we know the word which the LORD hath not spoken?*
>
> *When a prophet speaketh in the name of the LORD, if the thing follow not, nor come to pass, that is the thing which the LORD hath not spoken, but the prophet hath spoken it presumptuously: thou shalt not be afraid of him.*
>
> (Deuteronomy 18:21-22)

God also used as an addendum to this proof to strengthen the nation of Israel. For, during the time of the prophets, sometimes there would be a prophet who could do wonderful works, and still not be of God. The purpose for this additional test is to highlight the need for absolute faith in the word of God, above any words of man.

> *If there arise among you a prophet, or a dreamer of dreams, and giveth thee a sign or a wonder, And the sign or the wonder come to pass, whereof he spake unto thee, saying, Let us go after other gods,*

> *which thou hast not known, and let us serve them; Thou shalt not hearken unto the words of that prophet, or that dreamer of dreams: for the LORD your God proveth you, to know whether ye love the LORD your God with all your heart and with all your soul. Ye shall walk after the LORD your God, and fear him, and keep his commandments, and obey his voice, and ye shall serve him, and cleave unto him.*
>
> (Deuteronomy 13:1-4)

Jesus, by his life and the delivery of the gospel of the Kingdom of God, fulfilled the need of mankind for prophets. When the Messiah was revealed in Jesus Christ, it was no longer necessary for individuals to seek for any other prophet to tell them how they must relate to God.

> *And he saith unto me, Write, Blessed are they which are called unto the marriage supper of the Lamb. And he saith unto me, These are the true sayings of God.*
>
> *And I fell at his feet to worship him.*
>
> *And he said unto me, See thou do it not: I am thy fellowservant, and of thy brethren that have the testimony of Jesus: worship God: for the testimony of Jesus is the spirit of prophecy.*
>
> (Revelation 19:9-10)

For our benefit, some of his works and words were recorded in the Bible; these are the ones that we need to study and accept. To assist us in our studies, Jesus obtained, from God the Father, the release of the Spirit of truth, sent to mankind. This was the fulfillment of the proclamation of God, as given to the prophet Jeremiah.

> *Behold, the days come, saith the LORD, that I will make a new covenant with the house of Israel, and with the house of Judah: Not according to the covenant that I made with their fathers in the day that I took them by the hand to bring them out of the land of Egypt; which my covenant they brake, although I was an husband unto them, saith the LORD: But this shall be the covenant that I will make with the house of Israel; After those days, saith the LORD, I will put my law in their inward parts, and write it in*

> *their hearts; and will be their God, and they shall be my people. And they shall teach no more every man his neighbour, and every man his brother, saying, Know the LORD: for they shall all know me, from the least of them unto the greatest of them, saith the LORD: for I will forgive their iniquity, and I will remember their sin no more.*
>
> (Jeremiah 31:31-34)

Jesus sealed this by his statement about the Gospel and the *kingdom of God.*

> *And he said unto them, Ye are they which justify yourselves before men; but God knoweth your hearts: for that which is highly esteemed among men is abomination in the sight of God. The law and the prophets were until John: since that time the kingdom of God is preached, and every man presseth into it.*
>
> *And it is easier for heaven and earth to pass, than one tittle of the law to fail.*
>
> (Luke 16:15-17)

All this was done to provide us with much needed assistance in recognizing those who carried the truth. To summarize:

- no new revelations are necessary beyond those recorded in the Bible
- the prophets do not have the authority to tell us how we must live, for there is no longer a need for them to do that
- so we have the ability to access the truth of God directly from the Sprit of truth, sent to us from God the Father
- anyone trying to disrupt any of these truths of Scripture is a false prophet

We have already seen that the greatest of the false prophets was cast into the lake of fire and brimstone, along with the beast. This happened before the thousand year reign of Christ. The beast that was thrown into the lake was the authority that pertained to the old Roman Empire. The false prophet, therefore, had to be some institutional center of authority that was persuasive during this time. They were both thrown into the lake at the same time. To fully understand this, we must move away from human limitations.

When Christ revealed the nature of the beast, he was not talking about a human. To see this, notice the anatomy of the participants in the abomination of that day.

> *And the angel said unto me, Wherefore didst thou marvel? I will tell thee the mystery of the woman, and of the beast that carrieth her, which hath the seven heads and ten horns.*
>
> *The beast that thou sawest was, and is not; and shall ascend out of the bottomless pit, and go into perdition: and they that dwell on the earth shall wonder, whose names were not written in the book of life from the foundation of the world, when they behold the beast that was, and is not, and yet is.*
>
> *And here is the mind which hath wisdom. The seven heads are seven mountains, on which the woman sitteth. And there are seven kings: five are fallen, and one is, and the other is not yet come; and when he cometh, he must continue a short space.*
>
> *And the beast that was, and is not, even he is the eighth, and is of the seven, and goeth into perdition.*
>
> (Revelation 17:7-11)

The beast is not one of the seven kings of the Roman Empire; however, the beast is spawned from the seven kings of the Roman Empire. The woman is the hierarchy of the Roman Empire, which controlled all activity in the Empire. It is this hierarchy that was responsible for the atrocities that were performed by the spawn of the Roman Empire. This is not something that I am making up as I go along; this comes from the direct reading of the text of the Bible. In the epistle of Paul the apostle to the Ephesians, we were told that principalities and powers provide the challenges for Christians; not, individual people.

> *Finally, my brethren, be strong in the Lord, and in the power of his might. Put on the whole armour of God, that ye may be able to stand against the wiles of the devil. For we wrestle not against flesh and blood, but against principalities, against powers, against*

> *the rulers of the darkness of this world, against spiritual wickedness in high places.*
>
> (Ephesians 6:10-12)

Please allow me this slight diversion in the flow, as I complete the thought that Paul inspires in Ephesians 6:10-12. For, I do not want to leave you with a challenge to your faith, without giving you the word from God as to how to obtain victory.

> *Wherefore take unto you the whole armour of God, that ye may be able to withstand in the evil day, and having done all, to stand. Stand therefore, having your loins girt about with truth, and having on the breastplate of righteousness; And your feet shod with the preparation of the gospel of peace; Above all, taking the shield of faith, wherewith ye shall be able to quench all the fiery darts of the wicked.*
>
> *And take the helmet of salvation, and the sword of the Spirit, which is the word of God: Praying always with all prayer and supplication in the Spirit, and watching thereunto with all perseverance and supplication for all saints; And for me, that utterance may be given unto me, that I may open my mouth boldly, to make known the mystery of the gospel, For which I am an ambassador in bonds: that therein I may speak boldly, as I ought to speak.*
>
> (Ephesians 6:13-20)

A note of understanding: just because a power is brought low by the LORD does not mean that it is destroyed. Therefore, think about the false prophet not as a person, but as a power. This power was withdrawn from the institution that held it, and thrown as the beast into the lake of fire and brimstone. Thereby, the power of the institution was neutralized, as it pertains to the saints of God. However, even though the institution's power is now suppressed; still, the principal energy signature that empowers such an institution may linger in certain ones of the people of the world. This is the sort of residue of the power of the abomination that Satan used, as seen especially in the time after he was released, as described in the Revelation.

Think clearly about this. The action of Satan when he was released was to gather an army. In doing this, Satan took the residue and consolidated it into an institution, again.

> *And shall go out to deceive the nations which are in the four quarters of the earth, Gog and Magog, to gather them together to battle: . . .*
>
> (Revelation 20:8)

This is not an army of the saints of God in Christ Jesus. This is an army of those who are willing to believe in the destruction of the things of Christ. This is the remnant of the deception of the beast, and of the false prophet. Satan is the master deceiver, and the beast and false prophet had come in the power of Satan. Therefore, they had deceived the nations from the four quarters of the earth. All Satan had to do was to stir up that deception. In order to do that, Satan worked with those who were the followers of the beast and the false prophet—and there were a huge number of them.

> *. . . the number of whom is as the sand of the sea.*
>
> (Revelation 20:8)

Jesus Christ gave us a warning about those who seek, or accept, multitudes of physical signs for spiritual happenings. From the tone of the chastisement by Jesus, as given to those around him, we can know that God is conservative about how many signs He will give us. We only need enough signs to know that what we are seeing in the event is indeed a miracle that comes from God. We do not need a multitude of events of this world to show us that we are receiving a stirring from God. Moreover, we do not need a multitude of events of this world to show us that there is a condemnation of evil men.

> *Then certain of the scribes and of the Pharisees answered, saying, Master, we would see a sign from thee.*
>
> *But he answered and said unto them, An evil and adulterous generation seeketh after a sign; and there shall no sign be given to it, but the sign of the prophet Jonas: For as Jonas was three days*

and three nights in the whale's belly; so shall the Son of man be three days and three nights in the heart of the earth.

(Matthew 12:38-40)

However, even though Satan had deceived many, and through them, he was able to mount a spiritual attack against the saints of God; still, Satan is only allowed to wage this battle for a short time. Oh, did I just put something in here that needs explanation. Yes, I think I did, so here is the explanation. Do not look for only physical manifestations of the battle waged by Satan. The battle is also waged on a spiritual level.

In the physical portion of the battle for control of the institutions of man, there was much loss of life; but the purpose of the battle was to destroy the spirits of those who witnessed the assault against their societal and religious system of order. Among the societies that were under attack is the congregation of Christian—as it still is under attack. But we have the word of God to guide us in this matter.

Satan brings his forces to encamp against the true principles of God's word. They want to destroy the presence of the Holy Ghost in the lives of men and women. Our fear is not properly handled when we raise it because of those who can destroy the body. Our fear—our overwhelming respect—must be reserved for He who can destroy both body and soul, as we persevere in the witness of the Gospel.

The disciple is not above his master, nor the servant above his lord. It is enough for the disciple that he be as his master, and the servant as his lord. If they have called the master of the house Beelzebub, how much more shall they call them of his household? Fear them not therefore: for there is nothing covered, that shall not be revealed; and hid, that shall not be known. What I tell you in darkness, that speak ye in light: and what ye hear in the ear, that preach ye upon the housetops.

And fear not them which kill the body, but are not able to kill the soul: but rather fear him which is able to destroy both soul and body in hell.

(Matthew 10:24-28)

Satan and those who follow his ways seeks to displace God as the one who can also destroy the soul. Satan already knew that he had the power to destroy the body; this was the manner of his work as done by those who perpetrated the atrocities of history. This has been the continued work of those who continue to follow his game plan, even up to now. The satanic plan includes such events as, the holocaust; and the enslavement of large masses of peoples from Africa and other areas of the world, which were labeled, disadvantaged; and the destruction of lives by ethnic cleansing.

Yes, Satan could engineer the destruction of the body; but during this time, he was after the soul. This is the warfare that he incited. This is why his failure was sealed, by ordinance of God.

> *And they went up on the breadth of the earth, and compassed the camp of the saints about, and the beloved city: and fire came down from God out of heaven, and devoured them.*
>
> (Revelation 20:9)

God will allow no one and nothing else to have access to the soul of man. Every soul belongs to him, and is subject to His commandments.

> *The word of the LORD came unto me again, saying, What mean ye, that ye use this proverb concerning the land of Israel, saying, The fathers have eaten sour grapes, and the children's teeth are set on edge? As I live, saith the Lord GOD, ye shall not have occasion any more to use this proverb in Israel.*
>
> *Behold, all souls are mine; as the soul of the father, so also the soul of the son is mine: the soul that sinneth, it shall die.*
>
> *But if a man be just, and do that which is lawful and right, And hath not eaten upon the mountains, neither hath lifted up his eyes to the idols of the house of Israel, neither hath defiled his neighbour's wife, neither hath come near to a menstruous woman, And hath not oppressed any, but hath restored to the debtor his pledge, hath spoiled none by violence, hath given his bread to the hungry, and hath covered the naked with a garment; He that hath not given forth upon usury, neither hath taken any increase, that hath withdrawn his hand from iniquity, hath executed true judgment between man and man, Hath walked in my statutes,*

> *and hath kept my judgments, to deal truly; he is just, he shall surely live, saith the Lord GOD.*
>
> (Ezekiel 18:1-9)

Satan was defeated on the spiritual level, then; and he remains defeated to this day. Whenever anyone or anything tries to come after the soul of one of the saints, it will be stopped. The same Lord that dismissed Satan, by the power of his word, is alive today, and ready to fight. The Lord of the salvation of mankind's soul defeated the demons, then; so, do not think for even a second that he will have any problem chastising any human who dares to try to go head-to-head or toe-to-toe with him in a spiritual confrontation. This is the shield that we receive when we stay in Christ, and yield to the Holy Ghost. Jesus Christ promised us that this shield will not leave us.

> *Let not your heart be troubled: ye believe in God, believe also in me. In my Father's house are many mansions: if it were not so, I would have told you. I go to prepare a place for you. And if I go and prepare a place for you, I will come again, and receive you unto myself; that where I am, there ye may be also.*
>
> (John 14:1-3)

Jesus has kept his promise: he has sealed a remnant unto himself. Among the two or so billion folks who are listed as being Christian—as of this writing—there is a significant number who are truly sealed by God, according to the way of the truth of Christ. Unfortunately, there is, too, a large number that have been deceived into a perception of Christ that is not according to Scripture, but is, instead, according to man.

My prayer is that God protects the innocent among them; and that He releases the full power of Christ to redeem them from error. This is not just a prayer for the follower, but also for the leaders. There are many leaders who have been deceived by the modifications that are of Satan. These modifications still linger in many parts of the Christian world.

Seek God's wisdom on matters of the spirit; this includes the human spirit, the Spirit of truth, the seven Spirits of God, and any other of the spirits that can have a relationship with the heavenly places. Seek God's protection from the spirits that arise according to the things of Satan. It is not necessary for you to understand them, unless God calls you to do so. It is enough that you trust God to protect you from their influence; in your minds, and in your communities. Let me be emphatic about this: unless God calls you to do so, do not study error to know how to avoid it. The Bible tells us what we must study, and how we are to present our petitions for understanding. The apostle Paul sent the word to us, through the Philippians.

> *Be careful for nothing; but in every thing by prayer and supplication with thanksgiving let your requests be made known unto God. And the peace of God, which passeth all understanding, shall keep your hearts and minds through Christ Jesus.*
>
> *Finally, brethren, whatsoever things are true, whatsoever things are honest, whatsoever things are just, whatsoever things are pure, whatsoever things are lovely, whatsoever things are of good report; if there be any virtue, and if there be any praise, think on these things.*
>
> (Philippians 4:6-8)

Additionally, the apostle Paul sent instruction in what we must study, and how we are to present our petitions for understanding, as passing through the Ephesians.

> *Let no man deceive you with vain words: for because of these things cometh the wrath of God upon the children of disobedience. Be not ye therefore partakers with them. For ye were sometimes darkness, but now are ye light in the Lord: walk as children of light: (For the fruit of the Spirit is in all goodness and righteousness and truth;) Proving what is acceptable unto the Lord.*
>
> *And have no fellowship with the unfruitful works of darkness, but rather reprove them. For it is a shame even to speak of those things which are done of them in secret.*
>
> (Ephesians 5:6-12)

As God did with Job, so He will do with us. The life of Job is not just an example of trials that highlight perfection. The life example of Job is also our assurance of God's hedge, which He will build around each one who comes to Him. This is a hedge that endures, even during the roughest of times. Sometimes, it does not seem to be there, but it still is. When you read the story of Job, you will discover that it was the hedge that Satan complained about, first.

> *And the LORD said unto Satan, Whence comest thou?*
>
> *Then Satan answered the LORD, and said, From going to and fro in the earth, and from walking up and down in it.*
>
> *And the LORD said unto Satan, Hast thou considered my servant Job, that there is none like him in the earth, a perfect and an upright man, one that feareth God, and escheweth evil?*
>
> *Then Satan answered the LORD, and said, Doth Job fear God for nought? Hast not thou made an hedge about him, and about his house, and about all that he hath on every side? thou hast blessed the work of his hands, and his substance is increased in the land. But put forth thine hand now, and touch all that he hath, and he will curse thee to thy face.*
>
> *And the LORD said unto Satan, Behold, all that he hath is in thy power; only upon himself put not forth thine hand.*
> *So Satan went forth from the presence of the LORD.*
> (Job 1:7-12)

The devil knew that this hedge was hampering his ability to move Job away from righteousness. However, from the reading of Job, we know that Satan greatly underestimated the power of the hedge of God; for, Satan only saw the physical side. God had implanted, in Job, the spiritual side, which is able to withstand any assault that comes from the natural. And this is the confidence of God that we can also have.

Seek the hedge of God over your life, and thereby hamper the forward progress of the remnant of the evil spiritual seed of Satan. As God provided a hedge for Job, He will also do so for you. The hedge worked quite well in delivering Job from Satan's temptations. It will also work for you. God has not changed. This is our time to shine, by yielding to the Spirit of God, and to the Holy Ghost.

Behold, I will send my messenger, and he shall prepare the way before me: and the Lord, whom ye seek, shall suddenly come to his temple, even the messenger of the covenant, whom ye delight in: behold, he shall come, saith the LORD of hosts. But who may abide the day of his coming? and who shall stand when he appeareth? for he is like a refiner's fire, and like fullers' soap: And he shall sit as a refiner and purifier of silver: and he shall purify the sons of Levi, and purge them as gold and silver, that they may offer unto the LORD an offering in righteousness.

Then shall the offering of Judah and Jerusalem be pleasant unto the LORD, as in the days of old, and as in former years. And I will come near to you to judgment; and I will be a swift witness against the sorcerers, and against the adulterers, and against false swearers, and against those that oppress the hireling in his wages, the widow, and the fatherless, and that turn aside the stranger from his right, and fear not me, saith the LORD of hosts.

For I am the LORD, I change not; therefore ye sons of Jacob are not consumed.

(Malachi 3:1-6)

Surely, God is Holy,
His judgment we face,
In this time of decision
For the human race.

Which way to go;
Either right or left?
No more hiding
In indecision's cleft.

For, one is coming
To gather you in;
It is the spiritual father
Of man's deepest sin.

It has come forth
To help you decide
To stand in tradition;
You can no longer hide.

On the LORD'S side,
Or for the devil's way;
This is the decision
For this day.

Each nation, now,
Must make a choice.
For whom will yours
Raise its voice?

Is yours on the left
Or is it on the right?
Placement is made
Before the fight.

Examples were given,
In times of old:
It may seem hard;
It may seem cold:

Nations on the right
Fulfilled God's desire;
The ones on the left
Are immersed in the fire.

The battle waged
Is swift and complete,
As, willingly, every knee
Now bows at his feet.

Additional Food for Thought

Pope Gregory XI—acting partly on the advice of St. Catherine of Siena and St. Bridget of Sweden—moved the papacy back to Rome. But the church was immediately plunged into the disorder of the Great Schism (1378-1417). There were two or even three rival popes at a time (in later determination of true succession, those claimants ruled out of the succession are called antipopes). The schism ended in the Council of Constance. Since then, apart from the abortive revolt at the Council of Basel there has been no schism in the papacy.

Subsequently, the pope had little real power outside Italy, and no 15th-century pope was prepared to attempt serious reform, which would have required challenging the vested interests of bishops, cardinals, and princes. Indeed, in the 15th century the papal court made Rome a brilliant Renaissance capital, enriched by some of the finest art of the West. The Renaissance popes, however, were little distinguished from other princes in the extravagance and immorality of their courts.

Still More Food for Thought

Papal corruption during the Renaissance provided the background for the Protestant Reformation and alienated many followers of the established church. Martin Luther and his colleagues entered upon a basic theological revolution, reacting in part to the state of the papacy. They denounced the whole accepted view of God's relation to humanity and began a movement that split the Western Church.

Although reformation within the church began in the 1520s, papal involvement did not begin until the election (1534) of Paul III. The Council of Trent (1545-47, 1551-52, 1562-63) undertook to lay out the new definitions and regulations that reconstructed the church, including the papacy. The other major work of the 16th-century popes was the new development of foreign missions, which, as in ancient times, enhanced papal prestige. Of the several orders concerned with reform and missions, the Jesuits were the best known. The 16th century also saw the stabilization of the Papal States as they would remain until the 19th century

CHAPTER 9A

Conquering Doubt

Rightly Dividing Scripture

In a previous chapter we introduced the beauty of our ability to walk in the Holy Ghost; which is, the Spirit of truth. There we presented some of the concepts of the Bible that are written on our hearts. These concepts must be kept at the front of our minds. As we achieve growth by using them, we must never forget to thank God for our newfound knowledge of Him. This is a knowledge that we are trying to allow the Spirit of truth to increase, within us, and, through us, to the world. We are working, in the Spirit, to hold true to the LORD. The power to do this is contained in the type of assistance that the Spirit of truth gives us.

Before we continue in highlighting our interaction with the Spirit of truth, let us look, once again, at the love of Christ. This is the love that he demonstrated by petitioning the Father on our behalf, so that we would receive the Spirit of truth, *the Comforter.*

> *If ye love me, keep my commandments. And I will pray the Father, and he shall give you another Comforter, that he may abide with you for ever; Even the Spirit of truth; whom the world cannot receive, because it seeth him not, neither knoweth him: but ye know him; for he dwelleth with you, and shall be in you.*
>
> *I will not leave you comfortless: I will come to you. Yet a little while, and the world seeth me no more; but ye see me: because I live, ye shall live also.*
>
> *At that day ye shall know that I am in my Father, and ye in me, and I in you. He that hath my commandments, and keepeth*

them, he it is that loveth me: and he that loveth me shall be loved of my Father, and I will love him, and will manifest myself to him.

Judas saith unto him, not Iscariot, Lord, how is it that thou wilt manifest thyself unto us, and not unto the world?

Jesus answered and said unto him, If a man love me, he will keep my words: and my Father will love him, and we will come unto him, and make our abode with him. He that loveth me not keepeth not my sayings: and the word which ye hear is not mine, but the Father's which sent me.

These things have I spoken unto you, being yet present with you. But the Comforter, which is the Holy Ghost, whom the Father will send in my name, he shall teach you all things, and bring all things to your remembrance, whatsoever I have said unto you.

(John 14:15-26)

Please, ask God to keep you away from attempting to obstruct the work of the Holy Ghost in your life, and in the world. In this matter, we are of a dual nature: we have the potential to yield to the Holy Ghost, and we have the ability to resist it. In this relationship, God did not mandate obedience. We must accept the counsel of the Spirit of truth. We must not resist it.

In every thing give thanks: for this is the will of God in Christ Jesus concerning you.

Quench not the Spirit.

Despise not prophesyings.

(1 Thessalonians 5:18-20)

I repeat; if we find that we are resisting the Spirit, let us be instant in asking God for assistance, in Jesus name.

Verily, verily, I say unto you, He that believeth on me, the works that I do shall he do also; and greater works than these shall he do; because I go unto my Father. And whatsoever ye shall ask in my

name, that will I do, that the Father may be glorified in the Son. If ye shall ask any thing in my name, I will do it.
(John 14:12-14)

One of the most difficult parts of being a Christian is overcoming doubt. We neglect to put in the effort that is required to overcome doubt because doubt is one of the easiest seeds to sow, and they grow fast enough to overwhelm us. The world in which we live has a large supply of the seeds of doubt. There are many people sowing them; people that are both in and out of the communities of believers.

One of the first steps to combat doubt is to determine in your spirit that you will accept God's word as being true. This is not done by accepting part of His word. In order for us to accept the truth as being in God's word, we must believe that all of it is true. Therein is an interesting paradox. How does one believe in truth? Isn't truth a thing that must be known? However, isn't it true that; to know something, we must already possess the truth? As I ponder these questions, my mind settles into a recollection of a conversation between Pilate and Jesus Christ. Here, we have included the last part of the conversation.

Pilate therefore said unto him, Art thou a king then?

Jesus answered, Thou sayest that I am a king. To this end was I born, and for this cause came I into the world, that I should bear witness unto the truth. Every one that is of the truth heareth my voice.

Pilate saith unto him, What is truth?

And when he had said this, he went out again unto the Jews, and saith unto them, I find in him no fault at all.
(John 18:37-38)

Pilate asks, *What is truth?* It is of note to me that there is no answer given, at that time. It is my belief that no answer was given because the answer is the property of the Spirit of truth. Jesus did not want to reveal to Pilate, or anyone else, what they would have to later receive from the one that he would ask the Father to send: the Holy Ghost. When we received our introduction to it, then we knew that the name of the Holy Ghost tells us the answer to the question. The Holy Ghost is the Spirit of truth. This is why it is so important that we receive and yield to the Holy Ghost; only in this way will we know what truth is.

Now, if Pilate had asked, "Who is truth", he could have been given a definite answer. (However, he probably would not have received this witness.) This is the answer that he could have been given.

> *Jesus saith unto him, I am the way, the truth, and the life: no man cometh unto the Father, but by me. If ye had known me, ye should have known my Father also: and from henceforth ye know him, and have seen him.*
>
> (John 14:6-7)

The starting point for our yielding to the Spirit of truth is to believe that the words of Jesus are accurate; wherefore let us start there. When we believe that the words that Jesus said are true, then we can see reference in his words to many of the Old Testament actions recorded in the Bible. By extension, this would mean that these are also true. Jesus cannot lie, and he cannot use a false message to prove his point. So, let us read some words of Jesus, as recorded in the New Testament. These words are an assignment given to the twelve disciples.

> *And I will give unto thee the keys of the kingdom of heaven: and whatsoever thou shalt bind on earth shall be bound in heaven: and whatsoever thou shalt loose on earth shall be loosed in heaven.*
>
> (Matthew 16:19)

The keys to the kingdom represent the true message of the Gospel. This was given to the disciples in full force at Pentecost. Therefore, when we read their writings, we know that they too are speaking the truth. This is so because they are speaking by the movement, in them, of the Spirit of truth. In the Spirit, their impact on the world began with their assignment to redeem the lost sheep of the house of Israel.

> *And when he had called unto him his twelve disciples, he gave them power against unclean spirits, to cast them out, and to heal*

> *all manner of sickness and all manner of disease. Now the names of the twelve apostles are these; The first, Simon, who is called Peter, and Andrew his brother; James the son of Zebedee, and John his brother; Philip, and Bartholomew; Thomas, and Matthew the publican; James the son of Alphaeus, and Lebbaeus, whose surname was Thaddaeus; Simon the Canaanite, and Judas Iscariot, who also betrayed him.*
>
> *These twelve Jesus sent forth, and commanded them, saying,*
>
> *Go not into the way of the Gentiles, and into any city of the Samaritans enter ye not: But go rather to the lost sheep of the house of Israel.*
>
> (Matthew 10:1-6)

After that ministry to the lost sheep of the house of Israel was in motion, the salvation of the Gentiles was assigned to the apostle Paul: he was commissioned as the apostle to the Gentiles. This was confirmed by Peter, who was given the ability to bind on earth things that would be confirmed as being bound in Heaven. So, by Peter's action, the words of the apostle Paul are bound in Heaven. This is in addition to the apostle Paul's own possession of the keys, and his consequent ability to bind and loose. In the matter of Paul's keys, Peter and a few others served as a collective second witness.

> *Then fourteen years after I went up again to Jerusalem with Barnabas, and took Titus with me also. And I went up by revelation, and communicated unto them that gospel which I preach among the Gentiles, but privately to them which were of reputation, lest by any means I should run, or had run, in vain. But neither Titus, who was with me, being a Greek, was compelled to be circumcised: And that because of false brethren unawares brought in, who came in privily to spy out our liberty which we have in Christ Jesus, that they might bring us into bondage: To whom we gave place by subjection, no, not for an hour; that the truth of the gospel might continue with you.*

> *But of these who seemed to be somewhat, (whatsoever they were, it maketh no matter to me: God accepteth no man's person:) for they who seemed to be somewhat in conference added nothing to me: But contrariwise, when they saw that the gospel of the uncircumcision was committed unto me, as the gospel of the circumcision was unto Peter; (For he that wrought effectually in Peter to the apostleship of the circumcision, the same was mighty in me toward the Gentiles:) And when James, Cephas, and John, who seemed to be pillars, perceived the grace that was given unto me, they gave to me and Barnabas the right hands of fellowship; that we should go unto the heathen, and they unto the circumcision. Only they would that we should remember the poor; the same which I also was forward to do.*
>
> (Galatians 2:1-10)

Now, let us expand from here. Once we have a substantial portion of a work from the hand of God that is true, then we must look to the Spirit of truth to determine if the whole is true. In this search, the task is actually very easy. When we trust the Spirit of truth to always be what it is, we know that the Bible, by being certified as true in part, is certified as then true in the whole. For, if it were not true in the whole, then the parts would also not be true. This is true because all parts of the Bible complement and support one another. When one part of the support of anything is rotten, the entire structure will collapse. Put simply; for the Bible to stand, it must be indivisible. Therefore, let us accept as emphatically true that the Bible is the indivisible word of God.

We can also come to acceptance by moving in stages. To do that, we begin at the end. Let us read and accept the message given to John the Revelator, as a message that covers this entire book.

> *For I testify unto every man that heareth the words of the prophecy of this book, If any man shall add unto these things, God shall add unto him the plagues that are written in this book: And if any man shall take away from the words of the book of this prophecy, God shall take away his part out of the book of life, and out of the holy city, and from the things which are written in this book.*
>
> (Revelation 22:18-19)

Furthermore, since this warning is true for the book of Revelation we can say that it is also true for the entire Bible. "Why!?"

All the other books of the Bible contain pointers to the events that are written in the Revelation of Jesus Christ. Therefore, if anything is done to add or take away from this book, then the referent pointers are also distorted, and thereby made of non-effect.

Let us go even further in our understanding of the Bible, and the removal of doubt about this work of God. Let us go on to view some of the so called, issues, which are brought up about the perceived problems in some areas of the Bible. No, we cannot just accept them as being transcriber errors. It is not sufficient to say that mistakes might have been made by humans—never forget that we are referring to a work that represents Perfection, in the Being of God. Perfection does not make mistakes, and Perfection does not allow mistakes to appear in His work. Though, Perfection has also told us that we will not always understand Perfection.

> *For my thoughts are not your thoughts, neither are your ways my ways, saith the LORD. For as the heavens are higher than the earth, so are my ways higher than your ways, and my thoughts than your thoughts. For as the rain cometh down, and the snow from heaven, and returneth not thither, but watereth the earth, and maketh it bring forth and bud, that it may give seed to the sower, and bread to the eater: So shall my word be that goeth forth out of my mouth: it shall not return unto me void, but it shall accomplish that which I please, and it shall prosper in the thing whereto I sent it.*
>
> (Isaiah 55:8-11)

Sometimes, people like to consider certain passages, and say that there is a logical disconnect. They read some of the things in the Bible, and then they say that it is illogical for our times. They have even been known to read passages of the Bible that are clearly presented as literal, and to relegate them to the symbolic category. This is most often done to allow the opinions of the day to override the statements of God; statements that

He sent through his messengers, and through the prophets, and through the apostles.

The reading of the Bible is the exercise of faith. When we do not understand, we must still believe God. When there is what is presumed to be a logical disconnect, it is not an error; instead, it is another opportunity to believe God, and to do this in spite of what we see or what we think that we have learned during our time on this earth. God challenged the children of Israel to do that.

> *If there arise among you a prophet, or a dreamer of dreams, and giveth thee a sign or a wonder, And the sign or the wonder come to pass, whereof he spake unto thee, saying, Let us go after other gods, which thou hast not known, and let us serve them; Thou shalt not hearken unto the words of that prophet, or that dreamer of dreams: for the LORD your God proveth you, to know whether ye love the LORD your God with all your heart and with all your soul. Ye shall walk after the LORD your God, and fear him, and keep his commandments, and obey his voice, and ye shall serve him, and cleave unto him.*
>
> (Deuteronomy 13:1-4)

We hinted at this once before, but let us now put it in direct terms: the scholars that were moved by God to produce the King James Version of the Bible did actually read it. This seems like a kind of obvious thing, but it is sometimes the only way that certain challenges can be addressed. Some who have read the Bible have discovered what they believe to be numerical differences in different references to the same episode. These differences have had explanations created for them, but I will not go to that logic at this time. It is sufficient to say that, even if we do not have an explanation, we must not jump to the conclusion that it is a translator error.

Since the scholars read it, they also knew that these, now called, mismatches, were there. But they knew—better than we ever will—that the so-called errors are actually in the texts that they received. I have to believe that the scholars that God allowed to translate His work were intelligent enough to do math, and that they would have known that a certain computation within one passage did not match with another passage. Therefore, it seems reasonable to think that they left them in the translated work because they judged that they belonged in the work.

We choose to think that the translators and transcribers that gave us the King James Version of the Bible must have weighed the perception of the protection of God's reputation. It seems reasonable to think that they must have pondered how His reputation might be affected by the removal of a *perceived disconnection* in the Scripture, as set against the accuracy of God's message by including it. They left it there so that God could explain it, when, or if ever, we have a need to know why it is there. I have to believe that the ones God allowed to translate His work, in the day of King James, felt very confident that God protects His word. This means that they would have believed that what they saw was what God said, and what He did. As far as they were concerned, no change was necessary.

Furthermore, you must understand this: we must not challenge God to prove His work to us. We are also not told to prove His work to other men. Whether they are inside or outside the family, if others choose to challenge the accuracy of a written statement that was received from those who were inspired by God, then stand away from them. Let them take their challenge to God, and ask Him "*why*?" or "*if*?" We have a clear message about what God expects from us, individually, relative to the reading of the Bible. First . . .

> *Study to show thyself approved unto God, a workman that needeth not to be ashamed, rightly dividing the word of truth. But shun profane and vain babblings: for they will increase unto more ungodliness.*
>
> (2 Timothy 2:15-16)

Then, . . .

> *If any of you lack wisdom, let him ask of God, that giveth to all men liberally, and upbraideth not; and it shall be given him. But let him ask in faith, nothing wavering. For he that wavereth is like a wave of the sea driven with the wind and tossed. For let not that man think that he shall receive any thing of the Lord. A double minded man is unstable in all his ways.*
>
> (James 1:5-8)

In studying and asking, our objective is not to prove the accuracy of Scripture; rather, we want to just present the message. And if we only understand a part, we only present a part. Never force the issue of acquiring understanding of the message of God in the Bible. We must remember our place in the ministry of the Gospel. In this matter, we have some insights from the apostle Paul.

> *And I, brethren, could not speak unto you as unto spiritual, but as unto carnal, even as unto babes in Christ. I have fed you with milk, and not with meat: for hitherto ye were not able to bear it, neither yet now are ye able. For ye are yet carnal: for whereas there is among you envying, and strife, and divisions, are ye not carnal, and walk as men? For while one saith, I am of Paul; and another, I am of Apollos; are ye not carnal?*
>
> *Who then is Paul, and who is Apollos, but ministers by whom ye believed, even as the Lord gave to every man? I have planted, Apollos watered; but God gave the increase. So then neither is he that planteth any thing, neither he that watereth; but God that giveth the increase.*
>
> *Now he that planteth and he that watereth are one: and every man shall receive his own reward according to his own labour. For we are labourers together with God: ye are God's husbandry, ye are God's building.*
>
> (1 Corinthians 3:1-9)

Consider this: if the work has mistakes, then it is not a work of Perfection. And if the work is not a work of Perfection, then it is only a thing that is of man. And if it is only a work of man, then it has no bearing or validity on eternity; thus, at some point in time, it will dissolve and become totally ineffective. The Bible is either a work of the Perfect God, or it is worthless as a work of man, which work would not, then, be able to establish us in righteousness. Choose ye this day what ye will believe. As for me and my house, we will choose to believe the Bible—unrefined.

For we have not followed cunningly devised fables, when we made known unto you the power and coming of our Lord Jesus Christ, but were eyewitnesses of his majesty. For he received from God the Father honour and glory, when there came such a voice to him from the excellent glory, This is my beloved Son, in whom I am well pleased. And this voice which came from heaven we heard, when we were with him in the holy mount.

We have also a more sure word of prophecy; whereunto ye do well that ye take heed, as unto a light that shineth in a dark place, until the day dawn, and the day star arise in your hearts: Knowing this first, that no prophecy of the scripture is of any private interpretation. For the prophecy came not in old time by the will of man: but holy men of God spake as they were moved by the Holy Ghost.

(1 Peter 1:16-21)

This extends, too, to the Gospel of the Kingdom of God in Christ.

Now if Christ be preached that he rose from the dead, how say some among you that there is no resurrection of the dead? But if there be no resurrection of the dead, then is Christ not risen: And if Christ be not risen, then is our preaching vain, and your faith is also vain. Yea, and we are found false witnesses of God; because we have testified of God that he raised up Christ: whom he raised not up, if so be that the dead rise not.

For if the dead rise not, then is not Christ raised: And if Christ be not raised, your faith is vain; ye are yet in your sins.

Then they also which are fallen asleep in Christ are perished.

If in this life only we have hope in Christ, we are of all men most miserable.

But now is Christ risen from the dead, and become the firstfruits of them that slept. For since by man came death, by man came also the resurrection of the dead. For as in Adam all die, even so in Christ shall all be made alive. But every man in his own order: Christ the firstfruits; afterward they that are Christ's at his coming.

(1 Corinthians 15:12-23)

Furthermore, please, do not read Old Testament prophecy as you would if you constructed the ideas yourself. Old Testament prophecy is as God says it is, as he spoke of it, both in general and as being a portion of Moses' ministry.

And the LORD came down in the pillar of the cloud, and stood in the door of the tabernacle, and called Aaron and Miriam: and they both came forth. And he said,

Hear now my words: If there be a prophet among you, I the LORD will make myself known unto him in a vision, and will speak unto him in a dream.

My servant Moses is not so, who is faithful in all mine house. With him will I speak mouth to mouth, even apparently, and not in dark speeches; and the similitude of the LORD shall he behold: wherefore then were ye not afraid to speak against my servant Moses?

(Numbers 12:5-8)

Prophecy, in the Old Testament, according to the words from the mouth of God, contains *dark speeches*. And guess what: the same method is used by God in the New Testament's one book of prophecy—Revelation. But we want to take these things one at a time. We want to first look at the Old Testament prophecy. Old Testament prophecy requires the interpretation of it according to the Spirit of God; which, in us, is done by the Spirit of truth, the Holy Ghost, and by God's Angel, Jesus Christ. In the Old Testament times, there were also other angels that delivered interpretations. Let us look at one of those Old Testament times, as recounted in the prophecy of Daniel.

In that book of the Bible, the book of Daniel; Daniel seemed to have a permanent frown as pertained to receiving prophecy. Most often, Daniel is totally mystified by what he is seeing. Daniel makes no pretense of being wise about the messages; they are truly *dark speeches* to him. Sometime this is true even after the angel of the LORD has given him an interpretation. Actually, after the interpretation, he seems to be more concerned about the magnitude of the action of God. This, too, helps us to know that he did not interpret the prophecy himself. Here is an example.

> *I Daniel was grieved in my spirit in the midst of my body, and the visions of my head troubled me. I came near unto one of them that stood by, and asked him the truth of all this. So he told me, and made me know the interpretation of the things.*
>
> (Daniel 7:15-16)

We, too, must depend on God to empower us to receive the interpretation. Moreover, unless God tells us to broadcast the interpretation, we must be comfortable having unique knowledge from Above. Not everyone is ready to receive the interpretation of the prophecy that we have been allowed to understand. This is a matter that requires the intervention of the Holy Ghost; for, because we know a certain thing does not mean that we must tell it to anyone else. This was applied to Daniel's knowledge of the time of the end.

> *And I heard, but I understood not: then said I, O my Lord, what shall be the end of these things?*
>
> *And he said, Go thy way, Daniel: for the words are closed up and sealed till the time of the end.*
>
> (Daniel 12:8-9)

First, however, we must be sure, in God, that we do know. It is very easy to invent an interpretation that fits our wishes for things, such as might happen when we have a desire for solace, vengeance, justice, judgment, or any other such highly charged things.

Prophecy was not designed to be shared in a "God is going to get you" attitude. Look at the most notable of all the prophets, Moses. When he received the word of God about the potential upheaval and reconfiguration of the development of the nation of Israel, he did not revel in the thought of their destruction for their offense toward God. Rather, Moses petitioned

God to stay this judgment. And I am happy to tell you that God listened to what Moses said, and that He gave Moses what he requested.

> *And the LORD said unto Moses, Go, get thee down; for thy people, which thou broughtest out of the land of Egypt, have corrupted themselves: They have turned aside quickly out of the way which I commanded them: they have made them a molten calf, and have worshipped it, and have sacrificed thereunto, and said, These be thy gods, O Israel, which have brought thee up out of the land of Egypt.*
>
> *And the LORD said unto Moses, I have seen this people, and, behold, it is a stiffnecked people: Now therefore let me alone, that my wrath may wax hot against them, and that I may consume them: and I will make of thee a great nation.*
>
> *And Moses besought the LORD his God, and said, LORD, why doth thy wrath wax hot against thy people, which thou hast brought forth out of the land of Egypt with great power, and with a mighty hand? Wherefore should the Egyptians speak, and say, For mischief did he bring them out, to slay them in the mountains, and to consume them from the face of the earth? Turn from thy fierce wrath, and repent of this evil against thy people. Remember Abraham, Isaac, and Israel, thy servants, to whom thou swarest by thine own self, and saidst unto them, I will multiply your seed as the stars of heaven, and all this land that I have spoken of will I give unto your seed, and they shall inherit it for ever.*
>
> *And the LORD repented of the evil which he thought to do unto his people.*
>
> (Exodus 32:7-14)

The following may be one of the most difficult things for many people to believe. In fact, it is one of the major reasons for the delivery of this book. Let it be known that Old Testament prophecy was fulfilled in the time of Christ. Moreover, New Testament prophecy was fulfilled during the thousand years of the Byzantine Empire.

Old Testament prophecy pointed the way to the everlasting kingdom of the Lord Jesus Christ. So, its place as the focal point was filled by the testimony of the life of Jesus Christ.

> *And he saith unto me, Write, Blessed are they which are called unto the marriage supper of the Lamb. And he saith unto me, These are the true sayings of God.*
>
> *And I fell at his feet to worship him.*
>
> *And he said unto me, See thou do it not: I am thy fellowservant, and of thy brethren that have the testimony of Jesus: worship God: for the testimony of Jesus is the spirit of prophecy.*
>
> (Revelation 19:9-10)

The inheritance of God the Father, in the children of Israel, has been joined to the inheritance of the Son of God, consisting of the heathen (also known as the Gentiles). With this joining, the entire world is now under a much more obvious authority of the Kingdom of God. With this joining, the Kingdom of God is with man. Jesus stated that this day would come, and that it would come during the time of certain ones of his followers. Jesus did not give any indication that it would wait for another era. Jesus also did not say that it would tarry until a time that was after that entire generation had already faced death.

> *Immediately after the tribulation of those days shall the sun be darkened, and the moon shall not give her light, and the stars shall fall from heaven, and the powers of the heavens shall be shaken: And then shall appear the sign of the Son of man in heaven: and then shall all the tribes of the earth mourn, and they shall see the Son of man coming in the clouds of heaven with power and great glory. And he shall send his angels with a great sound of a trumpet, and they shall gather together his elect from the four winds, from one end of heaven to the other.*
>
> *Now learn a parable of the fig tree; When his branch is yet tender, and putteth forth leaves, ye know that summer is nigh: So likewise ye, when ye shall see all these things, know that it is near, even at the doors.*

> *Verily I say unto you, This generation shall not pass, till all these things be fulfilled.*
>
> (Matthew 24:29-34)

The first part of Jesus' prophecy was completed when Christ uncovered the mystery of the Old Testament. The mystery of the Old Testament was this: how we might come to righteousness. There is ample evidence in the behavior of the children of Israel that the law of Moses is not the route to righteousness. The lost sheep of the tribes of Israel had the Law, and yet they did not come to righteousness. Jesus Christ, the Son of God, delivered righteousness to mankind.

> *For Christ is the end of the law for righteousness to every one that believeth. For Moses describeth the righteousness which is of the law, That the man which doeth those things shall live by them. But the righteousness which is of faith speaketh on this wise, Say not in thine heart, Who shall ascend into heaven? (that is, to bring Christ down from above:) Or, Who shall descend into the deep? (that is, to bring up Christ again from the dead.)*
>
> *But what saith it? The word is nigh thee, even in thy mouth, and in thy heart: that is, the word of faith, which we preach; That if thou shalt confess with thy mouth the Lord Jesus, and shalt believe in thine heart that God hath raised him from the dead, thou shalt be saved.*
>
> (Romans 10:4-9)

Redemption from the power of sin, as a result of the remission of sin, is done today. It is done in the same fashion as it was done in the day of the apostles. It is done by faith in Jesus Christ.

> *But now the righteousness of God without the law is manifested, being witnessed by the law and the prophets; Even the righteousness of God which is by faith of Jesus Christ unto all and upon all them that believe: for there is no difference: For all have sinned, and come short of the glory of God; Being justified freely by his grace through the redemption that is in Christ Jesus: Whom God hath set forth to be a propitiation through faith in his blood, to declare*

his righteousness for the remission of sins that are past, through the forbearance of God; To declare, I say, at this time his righteousness: that he might be just, and the justifier of him which believeth in Jesus.

(Romans 3:21-26)

Before the day of the Lord, the disciples spent time looking for it. The angels of the LORD told them to stop staring, and, instead, to believe.

When they therefore were come together, they asked of him, saying, Lord, wilt thou at this time restore again the kingdom to Israel?

And he said unto them, It is not for you to know the times or the seasons, which the Father hath put in his own power. But ye shall receive power, after that the Holy Ghost is come upon you: and ye shall be witnesses unto me both in Jerusalem, and in all Judaea, and in Samaria, and unto the uttermost part of the earth.

And when he had spoken these things, while they beheld, he was taken up; and a cloud received him out of their sight.

And while they looked stedfastly toward heaven as he went up, behold, two men stood by them in white apparel; Which also said,

Ye men of Galilee, why stand ye gazing up into heaven? this same Jesus, which is taken up from you into heaven, shall so come in like manner as ye have seen him go into heaven.

(Acts 1:6-11)

Today, while standing in the Kingdom of God, many of us are still standing, gazing up. This is a sign of our doubt about the accuracy of our Lord and Saviour's proclamation of the age of his coming. Jesus clearly identified the era of his return; he identified the events surrounding his return as *things which must shortly come to pass.*

The Revelation of Jesus Christ, which God gave unto him, to show unto his servants things which must shortly come to pass; and he sent and signified it by his angel unto his servant John: Who bare record of the word of God, and of the testimony of Jesus Christ, and of all things that he saw.

(Revelation 1:1-2)

Folks; Jesus of Nazareth was talking to a group of people there, with him. Among those in the group are his apostles. Also among those in the group are ones who believed, but had no idea what prophecy meant. The Lord Jesus would not have made some nebulous statement that applied to several thousand years after the statement was made. The statement he made was for the people to whom he was talking. It is a promise to them.

We receive the blessing of the knowledge of the Gospel of Jesus Christ by the fact that, when we look at history, we can say for sure, to anyone that asks, that Jesus Christ, the Son of God, said what would happen; and, we can say that it did indeed happen. This is a work that comes from God. And, too, it is this work that we must also share with others.

Those who are still busy gazing up—since they have ordered their life as if the Kingdom is not here—are really missing out. They could achieve so much, and receive so much from God, if they would just stop looking up, and believe.

When the disciples stopped looking up, then they went back to living their lives. We have to do the same.

When the disciples received the promise of God, they were energized and changed the world. We have to do the same.

It is time to stop looking for what is already here. As Jesus said of the Kingdom of God, so it is.

And when he was demanded of the Pharisees, when the kingdom of God should come, he answered them and said, The kingdom of God cometh not with observation: Neither shall they say, Lo here! or, lo there! for, behold, the kingdom of God is within you.

(Luke 17:20-21)

Think abut this: the Bible was not just written to provide those of this day with hope in their lives. The Bible was also written to provide salvation for those who lived around Jesus Christ; the saints of Christ, in the day of Christ. And that salvation was not just a way to remove the believer from spiritual death, but also from physical destruction by the spiritually wicked of that day.

And there shall come forth a rod out of the stem of Jesse, and a Branch shall grow out of his roots: And the spirit of the LORD shall rest upon him, the spirit of wisdom and understanding, the spirit of counsel and might, the spirit of knowledge and of the fear of the LORD; And shall make him of quick understanding in the fear of the LORD: and he shall not judge after the sight of his eyes, neither reprove after the hearing of his ears: But with righteousness shall he judge the poor, and reprove with equity for the meek of the earth: and he shall smite the earth with the rod of his mouth, and with the breath of his lips shall he slay the wicked. And righteousness shall be the girdle of his loins, and faithfulness the girdle of his reins.

The wolf also shall dwell with the lamb, and the leopard shall lie down with the kid; and the calf and the young lion and the fatling together; and a little child shall lead them.

And the cow and the bear shall feed; their young ones shall lie down together: and the lion shall eat straw like the ox. And the sucking child shall play on the hole of the asp, and the weaned child shall put his hand on the cockatrice' den.

(Isaiah 11:1-8)

He who hath an ear . . .

Now I would not have you ignorant, brethren, that oftentimes I purposed to come unto you, (but was let hitherto,) that I might have some fruit among you also, even as among other Gentiles. I am debtor both to the Greeks, and to the Barbarians; both to the wise, and to the unwise. So, as much as in me is, I am ready to preach the gospel to you that are at Rome also.

For I am not ashamed of the gospel of Christ: for it is the power of God unto salvation to every one that believeth; to the Jew first, and also to the Greek. For therein is the righteousness of God revealed from faith to faith: as it is written, The just shall live by faith.

(Romans 1:13-17)

The Word from the Bible

Revelation 21:1-8

And I saw a new heaven and a new earth: for the first heaven and the first earth were passed away; and there was no more sea. And I John saw the holy city, new Jerusalem, coming down from God out of heaven, prepared as a bride adorned for her husband.

And I heard a great voice out of heaven saying, Behold, the tabernacle of God is with men, and he will dwell with them, and they shall be his people, and God himself shall be with them, and be their God. And God shall wipe away all tears from their eyes; and there shall be no more death, neither sorrow, nor crying, neither shall there be any more pain: for the former things are passed away.

And he that sat upon the throne said, Behold, I make all things new. And he said unto me, Write: for these words are true and faithful. And he said unto me, It is done. I am Alpha and Omega, the beginning and the end. I will give unto him that is athirst of the fountain of the water of life freely. He that overcometh shall inherit all things; and I will be his God, and he shall be my son. But the fearful, and unbelieving, and the abominable, and murderers, and whoremongers, and sorcerers, and idolaters, and all liars, shall have their part in the lake which burneth with fire and brimstone: which is the second death.

Revelation 21:9-21

And there came unto me one of the seven angels which had the seven vials full of the seven last plagues, and talked with me, saying, Come hither, I will show thee the bride, the Lamb's wife. And he carried me away in the spirit to a great and high mountain, and showed me that great city, the holy Jerusalem, descending out of heaven from God, Having the glory of God: and her light was like unto a stone most precious, even like a jasper stone, clear as crystal; And had a wall great and high, and had twelve gates, and at the gates twelve angels, and names written thereon, which are the names of the twelve tribes of the children of Israel: On the east three gates; on the north three gates; on the south three gates; and on the west three gates.

And the wall of the city had twelve foundations, and in them the names of the twelve apostles of the Lamb.

And he that talked with me had a golden reed to measure the city, and the gates thereof, and the wall thereof. And the city lieth foursquare, and the length is as large as the breadth: and he measured the city with the reed, twelve thousand furlongs. The length and the breadth and the height of it are equal. And he measured the wall thereof, an hundred and forty and four cubits, according to the measure of a man, that is, of the angel. And the building of the wall of it was of jasper: and the city was pure gold, like unto clear glass.

And the foundations of the wall of the city were garnished with all manner of precious stones. The first foundation was jasper; the second, sapphire; the third, a chalcedony; the fourth, an emerald; The fifth, sardonyx; the sixth, sardius; the seventh, chrysolyte; the eighth, beryl; the ninth, a topaz; the tenth, a chrysoprasus; the eleventh, a jacinth; the twelfth, an amethyst.

And the twelve gates were twelve pearls: every several gate was of one pearl: and the street of the city was pure gold, as it were transparent glass.

Revelation 21:22-27

And I saw no temple therein: for the Lord God Almighty and the Lamb are the temple of it. And the city had no need of the sun, neither of the moon, to shine in it: for the glory of God did lighten it, and the Lamb is the light thereof.

And the nations of them which are saved shall walk in the light of it: and the kings of the earth do bring their glory and honour into it. And the gates of it shall not be shut at all by day: for there shall be no night there. And they shall bring the glory and honour of the nations into it. And there shall in no wise enter into it any thing that defileth, neither whatsoever worketh abomination, or maketh a lie: but they which are written in the Lamb's book of life.

Chapter Ten

Revelation

The Historical Completions (World Without End)

We are almost done. What happened to all the fireworks? Why haven't I tried to persuade you to flee the destruction that will come when Jesus returns to stand on this earth, look you in the eye, or snatch you away? Well, I cannot provide that; because that prophecy has already happened. Jesus has already taken control of the religious power of the earth: this is much more than the sort of power that is housed in religious buildings or institutions. The power that Jesus controls is the power that flows, directly and unfiltered, from the Spirit of God. Oh, is the frown of disbelief there because you are looking at this Scripture about every knee bowing, and every tongue confessing?

> *Look unto me, and be ye saved, all the ends of the earth: for I am God, and there is none else. I have sworn by myself, the word is gone out of my mouth in righteousness, and shall not return, That unto me every knee shall bow, every tongue shall swear. Surely, shall one say, in the LORD have I righteousness and strength: even to him shall men come; and all that are incensed against him shall be ashamed.*
>
> *In the LORD shall all the seed of Israel be justified, and shall glory.*
>
> (Isaiah 45:22-25)

The frown intensifies, as you think the following, "Everybody on this earth does not yet profess to be a Christian. So, how can anyone in their right mind say that this Scripture has been fulfilled?"

First, let me assure you that I am not in my right mind; especially, not as I write this. My right mind is anathema to me, in attempting to spread the good news of the glory of God. And yours should also be so to you. There is a better mind to have.

> *Let this mind be in you, which was also in Christ Jesus: Who, being in the form of God, thought it not robbery to be equal with God: But made himself of no reputation, and took upon him the form of a servant, and was made in the likeness of men: And being found in fashion as a man, he humbled himself, and became obedient unto death, even the death of the cross.*
>
> (Philippians 2:5-8)

It is according to the mind of Christ that I write these things. It is my constant prayer that the Holy Ghost continues to override my, all too weak, mind, and fill these messages with the Spirit of truth.

For the sake of our relatively restricted minds, let us review this matter very slowly. First question: Is it Christ's humanity or is it his similitude with God that is the defining essence of who Jesus is in his connection with us?

> *I in them, and thou in me, that they may be made perfect in one; and that the world may know that thou hast sent me, and hast loved them, as thou hast loved me.*
>
> (John 17:23)

Next question: Is Christ's kingdom one that is of this earth?

> *Jesus answered, My kingdom is not of this world: if my kingdom were of this world, then would my servants fight, that I should not be delivered to the Jews: but now is my kingdom not from hence.*
>
> (John 18:36-36)

Next question: Is the Kingdom of God something that can be made with hands?

Thus saith the LORD, The heaven is my throne, and the earth is my footstool: where is the house that ye build unto me? and where is the place of my rest? For all those things hath mine hand made, and all those things have been, saith the LORD: but to this man will I look, even to him that is poor and of a contrite spirit, and trembleth at my word.

(Isaiah 66:1-2)

God that made the world and all things therein, seeing that he is Lord of heaven and earth, dwelleth not in temples made with hands; Neither is worshipped with men's hands, as though he needed any thing, seeing he giveth to all life, and breath, and all things; And hath made of one blood all nations of men for to dwell on all the face of the earth, and hath determined the times before appointed, and the bounds of their habitation; That they should seek the Lord, if haply they might feel after him, and find him, though he be not far from every one of us: For in him we live, and move, and have our being; as certain also of your own poets have said, For we are also his offspring.

(Acts 17:24-28)

Final question: Where is the Kingdom of God housed?

And when he was demanded of the Pharisees, when the kingdom of God should come, he answered them and said, The kingdom of God cometh not with observation: Neither shall they say, Lo here! or, lo there! for, behold, the kingdom of God is within you.

(Luke 17:20-21)

Okay, allow me just one more question: What is the church of Christ?

Having made known unto us the mystery of his will, according to his good pleasure which he hath purposed in himself: That in the dispensation of the fulness of times he might gather together in one all things in Christ, both which are in heaven, and which are on earth; even in him: In whom also we have obtained an inheritance, being predestinated according to the purpose of him

> *who worketh all things after the counsel of his own will: That we should be to the praise of his glory, who first trusted in Christ. In whom ye also trusted, after that ye heard the word of truth, the gospel of your salvation: in whom also after that ye believed, ye were sealed with that holy Spirit of promise, Which is the earnest of our inheritance until the redemption of the purchased possession, unto the praise of his glory.*
>
> *Wherefore I also, after I heard of your faith in the Lord Jesus, and love unto all the saints, Cease not to give thanks for you, making mention of you in my prayers; That the God of our Lord Jesus Christ, the Father of glory, may give unto you the spirit of wisdom and revelation in the knowledge of him: The eyes of your understanding being enlightened; that ye may know what is the hope of his calling, and what the riches of the glory of his inheritance in the saints, And what is the exceeding greatness of his power to us-ward who believe, according to the working of his mighty power, Which he wrought in Christ, when he raised him from the dead, and set him at his own right hand in the heavenly places, Far above all principality, and power, and might, and dominion, and every name that is named, not only in this world, but also in that which is to come: And hath put all things under his feet, and gave him to be the head over all things to the church, Which is his body, the fulness of him that filleth all in all.*
>
> (Ephesians 1:9-23)

Now that we have those answers about the location of the action that is mentioned in the prophecies about the coming Kingdom of God, we can proceed further. Okay, for those who have not caught up yet, here are some key points.

God has established His Kingdom among man, and it is revealed through His Son, Jesus Christ.

- All men are pressing into it.
- Some folks are moving slower than others—Christ is patient.
- The nations who did not honor God have been removed.

- There are some remaining nations that do not honor Christ, but this can be forgiven.
- No, I did not make that last one up.

> *Verily I say unto you, All sins shall be forgiven unto the sons of men, and blasphemies wherewith soever they shall blaspheme:*
> (Mark 3:28)

In the time of the incarnate presence of the Son of God, in Jesus of Nazareth; the leaders in Jerusalem, as well as those in the Roman Empire, before its fall (and maybe, too, up to this day, in its spirit), made the mistake of blaspheming against the Holy Ghost, and, thus, against God. This was not forgiven.

> *But he that shall blaspheme against the Holy Ghost hath never forgiveness, but is in danger of eternal damnation.*
> (Mark 3:29)

Now, it is time for me to step on some seriously sensitive toes: the people of Christ have been given the assignment that was formerly perceived as being exclusively from the nation of Israel. We are sent forth to be the ambassadors and priests of God. God said that He would do this . . .

> *But Jeshurun waxed fat, and kicked: thou art waxen fat, thou art grown thick, thou art covered with fatness; then he forsook God which made him, and lightly esteemed the Rock of his salvation. They provoked him to jealousy with strange gods, with abominations provoked they him to anger. They sacrificed unto devils, not to God; to gods whom they knew not, to new gods that came newly up, whom your fathers feared not. Of the Rock that begat thee thou art unmindful, and hast forgotten God that formed thee. And when the LORD saw it, he abhorred them, because of the provoking of his sons, and of his daughters.*
>
> *And he said, I will hide my face from them, I will see what their end shall be: for they are a very froward generation, children in whom is no faith. They have moved me to jealousy with that which*

is not God; they have provoked me to anger with their vanities: and I will move them to jealousy with those which are not a people; I will provoke them to anger with a foolish nation.

(Deuteronomy 32:15-21)

. . . And Christ confirmed that it was done.

Blessed is he that readeth, and they that hear the words of this prophecy, and keep those things which are written therein: for the time is at hand.

John to the seven churches which are in Asia: Grace be unto you, and peace, from him which is, and which was, and which is to come; and from the seven Spirits which are before his throne; And from Jesus Christ, who is the faithful witness, and the first begotten of the dead, and the prince of the kings of the earth. Unto him that loved us, and washed us from our sins in his own blood, And hath made us kings and priests unto God and his Father; to him be glory and dominion for ever and ever. Amen.

(Revelation 1:3-6)

Please remember this: the first group of people of Christ came from the nation of Israel. At the time of the selection of the twelve disciples, they stood in the place of a former messenger of God. The assignment that was first given to the congregation of Israel, in the day of Moses, was taken from the nation of Israel, and given to the apostles of Christ, as their commission to spread the Gospel.

In time, the ministry of the Gospel was sealed into many more of the servants of the nation of Israel. Thereby, the message was spread to the entire world, as it continued forward in these sealed ones that are of the nation of Israel.

And after these things I saw four angels standing on the four corners of the earth, holding the four winds of the earth, that the wind should not blow on the earth, nor on the sea, nor on any tree. And I saw another angel ascending from the east, having the seal of the living God: and he cried with a loud voice to the four angels, to whom it was given to hurt the earth and the sea, Saying, Hurt not the earth, neither the sea, nor the trees, till we have sealed the servants of our God in their foreheads.

And I heard the number of them which were sealed: and there were sealed an hundred and forty and four thousand of all the tribes of the children of Israel.

Of the tribe of Juda were sealed twelve thousand.
Of the tribe of Reuben were sealed twelve thousand.
Of the tribe of Gad were sealed twelve thousand.
Of the tribe of Aser were sealed twelve thousand.
Of the tribe of Nephthalim were sealed twelve thousand.
Of the tribe of Manasses were sealed twelve thousand.
Of the tribe of Simeon were sealed twelve thousand.
Of the tribe of Levi were sealed twelve thousand.
Of the tribe of Issachar were sealed twelve thousand.
Of the tribe of Zabulon were sealed twelve thousand.
Of the tribe of Joseph were sealed twelve thousand.
Of the tribe of Benjamin were sealed twelve thousand.

(Revelation 7:1-8)

In all these things, the Gospel, as delivered by Jesus of Nazareth—who is, the Son of God—has been placed in our world as an eternal message and method of God.

"But, doesn't the Bible say that everybody will one day be Christians?"

No, it does not.

The Bible says that every knee will bow to God, and proclaim that Jesus Christ is Lord—the world is already doing this. Let us concentrate for a moment on the United States of America. Look at the news. What is the name that is being placed under the greatest scrutiny? Who are some of the top guns of religiosity trying to unseat from his position of power. One does not try to kill a gnat with a shotgun. And there are some serious shotguns being aimed at Christ's spiritual world. Isn't this man's way of admitting that Jesus is Lord? Haven't they bowed the knee, by the attention that they are giving to the Gospel of Jesus Christ?

Come on now, do not think physical, so much; rather, think, spiritual. What do you think is going on in the spirits of those who are fomenting oppression? Well, let me tell you; it is the fear that they will have to face the God of the universe and explain their actions. So, just as it was done in the day of Christ, so it is today: the world outside of the Kingdom of God is trying to remove the spiritual impact of the message of Christ. What we, who believe, have to do is to stop helping them do so.

"Whoa!" you say, "How are we helping them?"

We are helping them by fighting with them on these matters. What was the hallmark of Jesus Christ that caused the officials of the government of that day to say that they saw an innocent man before them? Wasn't it his calm in the face of accusation? Wasn't it that he could look his accusers in the eye, and allow them to vent their hostility, while he kept his peace? And when he did this, didn't God show that the accusers were liars? Christ, the Son, stayed still, as he let God the Father bring his enemies to their knees.

The more we try to bring our enemies to their knees, the more we push God away from the battle. Know this: regardless of our human-only effort, the battle will go on. By standing in humanity alone, we will never seal the victory. For the victory to be sealed, **we must get out of God's way!** God's way is that the Father sent only one ambassador to take control. This ambassador is Jesus Christ. The potency of the ambassador is best seen in the fact that he does not have to take control of the physical world, since this is earth-bound mankind's responsibility.

> *And the LORD God said, Behold, the man is become as one of us, to know good and evil: and now, lest he put forth his hand, and take also of the tree of life, and eat, and live for ever: Therefore the LORD God sent him forth from the garden of Eden, to till the ground from whence he was taken.*
>
> *So he drove out the man; and he placed at the east of the garden of Eden Cherubims, and a flaming sword which turned every way, to keep the way of the tree of life.*
>
> (Genesis 3:22-24)

> *And God blessed Noah and his sons, and said unto them, Be fruitful, and multiply, and replenish the earth. And the fear of you and the dread of you shall be upon every beast of the earth, and upon every fowl of the air, upon all that moveth upon the earth, and upon all the fishes of the sea; into your hand are they delivered.*

Every moving thing that liveth shall be meat for you; even as the green herb have I given you all things.

(Genesis 9:1-3)

And you, be ye fruitful, and multiply; bring forth abundantly in the earth, and multiply therein.

(Genesis 9:7)

The spiritual world is the world of the Father, and of His Son. God the Father gave great authority to His Son, empowering him to supervise the spiritual world of mankind.

Then the eleven disciples went away into Galilee, into a mountain where Jesus had appointed them. And when they saw him, they worshipped him: but some doubted.

And Jesus came and spake unto them, saying, All power is given unto me in heaven and in earth.

(Matthew 28:16-18)

The control that is of the Son is not focused on the physical; it is concentrated in the spiritual.

But the hour cometh, and now is, when the true worshippers shall worship the Father in spirit and in truth: for the Father seeketh such to worship him. God is a Spirit: and they that worship him must worship him in spirit and in truth.

(John 4:23-24)

For, once man's spirit is brought into righteousness, then the proper handling of the physical is just a prayer away.

Ask, and it shall be given you; seek, and ye shall find; knock, and it shall be opened unto you: For every one that asketh receiveth; and he that seeketh findeth; and to him that knocketh it shall be opened.

(Matthew 7:7-8)

Furthermore, understand clearly that whenever God activates His control on the spiritual level, there are some physical results. As we yield to God, we receive the power that we need to have in order to perform the actions that He has ordered for us to do. It seems better to yield and receive God's empowerment; since, whether we yield or not, we are still fulfilling the ordinance of the LORD. The ordinances that spawn actions are in effect both for the church of Christ and for all others who call upon the name of the LORD. In Christ's day, these actions were continued as extensions of the Law and the prophets.

Among the ordinances that continues across the ages are the kind that brings mankind into tangible support of the ministry. This support is of the kind that was emphasized by God's revelation to the prophet Malachi. That revelation tells us that, numbered among our connections with the ministry of the LORD God is our offerings for the spread of the Gospel, throughout the ages.

> *Bring ye all the tithes into the storehouse, that there may be meat in mine house, and prove me now herewith, saith the LORD of hosts, if I will not open you the windows of heaven, and pour you out a blessing, that there shall not be room enough to receive it. And I will rebuke the devourer for your sakes, and he shall not destroy the fruits of your ground; neither shall your vine cast her fruit before the time in the field, saith the LORD of hosts.*
>
> *And all nations shall call you blessed: for ye shall be a delightsome land, saith the LORD of hosts.*
>
> (Malachi 3:10-12)

When we get enough people of God participating in promoting the things of God, major changes will occur. But this is where many people have placed a block between themselves and God; because of their concentration on greedy religious organizations, which sprouts a resistance to supporting any of them. There are too many things that are floating around in the world, claiming to be the thing of God, and requesting funding. There are many Christian this, and Christian that. There are large amounts of funds that are raised so that Christians can send this to that country or that to this country. As a person concentrates on this, they can become weary in giving.

Also adding to the weight of constant church fund-raising, there is the fact that we do not just build church organizations; we now build religious institutions. Is this according to the commandment given by God to bring your tithes into the storehouse? If it is, then why don't we let God open the windows of heaven, and thereby remove the need to raise funds? Are we supposed to ask the world for physical provisions, or are we to wait until God inspires individuals to bring them?

On the other hand, we have created this mess of, for lack of a better term, *voluminosity*. If a person wanted to bring their tithe into the storehouse; which storehouse do they bring it to? Here we have an issue of personal responsibility. God has promised to install the Holy Ghost, as an indwelling component of every believer. The Holy Ghost is the Spirit of truth. When we seek the Spirit's guidance, the Holy Ghost will tell us where to deliver the money. But I do understand your dilemma. Devotion to God persuades us to give: guilt, leveled by man, causes us confusion about where to give. I am really sorry, but I do not have an answer, yet; other than to tell you to pray, as you also do this . . .

> *If any of you lack wisdom, let him ask of God, that giveth to all men liberally, and upbraideth not; and it shall be given him. But let him ask in faith, nothing wavering. For he that wavereth is like a wave of the sea driven with the wind and tossed. For let not that man think that he shall receive any thing of the Lord. A double minded man is unstable in all his ways.*
>
> (James 1:5-8)

Okay, I cannot rest with that answer, alone. God knows that I do not like to leave an issue without receiving some words from Him on the matter. So, I could not leave this one, either. There is another answer. We need to consider returning to the message of Pentecost. We need to go back to concentrating our efforts in our communities; that is, of course, after our own families have been provided for—we have gone so far out into the uttermost parts of the world that Jerusalem is being neglected. Each servant of God must renew their efforts in their personal Jerusalem, before even extending into their personal Judea, and then on from there.

> *When they therefore were come together, they asked of him, saying, Lord, wilt thou at this time restore again the kingdom to Israel?*

> *And he said unto them, It is not for you to know the times or the seasons, which the Father hath put in his own power.*
>
> *But ye shall receive power, after that the Holy Ghost is come upon you: and ye shall be witnesses unto me both in Jerusalem, and in all Judaea, and in Samaria, and unto the uttermost part of the earth.*
>
> (Acts 1:6-8)

However, reestablishing proper family emphasis means that some of the larger institutions will have to focus their ministries at a more local level. As I think about it, Christ could have broadcast his message to the entire world; the apostle Paul did it, and I believe that Christ came to the earth with more power than the very capable and highly effective apostle to the Gentiles. However, Christ's mission is to give us an example of how things are started, and how they are preserved.

Even when the apostle Paul was sent to the Gentiles, he did not form mass groups of peoples covering multiple cities or locations. The ministry of the apostle Paul was concentrated in the locality that he was in. This may be the way back to a clearer spread of the Gospel. We have to always remember that the Gospel is not spread by advertising: the Gospel is spread by living. Those who live the word, entice others to want to imitate them.

It does not matter what we have always done: it does matter what God has told us to do. It is no excuse to say that we have been doing what we are doing for so long, with such a great devotion to it, such that it would be too disruptive to change. A similar situation was faced by others in the Bible times, and the apostle had an answer for them.

> *Forasmuch then as we are the offspring of God, we ought not to think that the Godhead is like unto gold, or silver, or stone, graven by art and man's device. And the times of this ignorance God winked at; but now commandeth all men every where to repent: Because he hath appointed a day, in the which he will judge the world in righteousness by that man whom he hath ordained; whereof he hath given assurance unto all men, in that he hath raised him from the dead.*
>
> (Acts 17:29-31)

The spiritual Kingdom of God is here, and men ought to be pressing into it. It is up to us to show them how to do so; not just, to tell them to do so. The message is substantially the same as it has been since the day of John the Baptist; the only difference is that certain things are no longer *at hand*, as being still in the future tense.

> *In those days came John the Baptist, preaching in the wilderness of Judaea, And saying, Repent ye: for the kingdom of heaven is at hand.*
>
> (Matthew 3:1-2)

Now, the kingdom is, *at hand*, in the sense of being available to us when we stretch out our mind in order to receive it. We can no longer hide behind the word, mystery.

> *Now after that John was put in prison, Jesus came into Galilee, preaching the gospel of the kingdom of God, And saying, The time is fulfilled, and the kingdom of God is at hand: repent ye, and believe the gospel.*
>
> (Mark 1:14-15)

The Kingdom of God was revealed, in tremendous force, with Christ's return, in his glory. We are now faced with a dilemma. We have so many institutions that purport to represent Christ; and I am not saying that they are, all, not sincere; though, I am saying that many of them are unnecessary. However, I do say that some of them are not sincere: the Bible says so.

> *Not every one that saith unto me, Lord, Lord, shall enter into the kingdom of heaven; but he that doeth the will of my Father which is in heaven. Many will say to me in that day, Lord, Lord, have we not prophesied in thy name? and in thy name have cast out devils? and in thy name done many wonderful works? And then will I profess unto them, I never knew you: depart from me, ye that work iniquity.*
>
> (Matthew 7:21-23)

If we do not seek to enter the spiritual kingdom of God, we are now without excuse. This is the message sent to those who are outside. However, another message must be understood by those of us that are inside. We, too, are without excuse if we do not come together with one another, under the Holy Ghost, and determine just who is selected by God to be the leadership among the church of Christ. This is not the physical church only, but also the spiritual church.

Christ said that there would still be kings and priests that would carry the Gospel. The testimony of Jesus Christ did not say that he would do everything personally. We are promised power from God; there must be some responsibility that comes along with this. We need to petition God for a stirring of the Holy Ghost, to give us clear direction about how and where to use the power that has been given to us. At this point in history, of most importance is the where of the matter.

To eliminate the dilemma of choosing between advertised houses of faith, our life has to be conformed to the image of God's Son, Jesus Christ. This must be done, in order for us to be allowed to function in righteousness in the spiritual Kingdom of God. This is why the Bible talks about diligently performing certain daily practices. For we who are alive, maintaining our dwelling in the Kingdom of God is not a one time things. It is a constant thing, where we have to tame the old man, which will be with us all our life.

> *For I say, through the grace given unto me, to every man that is among you, not to think of himself more highly than he ought to think; but to think soberly, according as God hath dealt to every man the measure of faith. For as we have many members in one body, and all members have not the same office: So we, being many, are one body in Christ, and every one members one of another. Having then gifts differing according to the grace that is given to us, whether prophecy, let us prophesy according to the proportion of faith; Or ministry, let us wait on our ministering: or he that teacheth, on teaching; Or he that exhorteth, on exhortation: he that giveth, let him do it with simplicity; he that ruleth, with diligence; he that showeth mercy, with cheerfulness.*
>
> (Romans 12:3-8)

To tame the old man, takes the constant power of the Holy Ghost, speaking Spirit to spirit, to move us to excellence.

Let love be without dissimulation. Abhor that which is evil; cleave to that which is good. Be kindly affectioned one to another with brotherly love; in honour preferring one another; Not slothful in business; fervent in spirit; serving the Lord; Rejoicing in hope; patient in tribulation; continuing instant in prayer; Distributing to the necessity of saints; given to hospitality. Bless them which persecute you: bless, and curse not. Rejoice with them that do rejoice, and weep with them that weep.

Be of the same mind one toward another. Mind not high things, but condescend to men of low estate. Be not wise in your own conceits. Recompense to no man evil for evil. Provide things honest in the sight of all men.

If it be possible, as much as lieth in you, live peaceably with all men. Dearly beloved, avenge not yourselves, but rather give place unto wrath: for it is written, Vengeance is mine; I will repay, saith the Lord. Therefore if thine enemy hunger, feed him; if he thirst, give him drink: for in so doing thou shalt heap coals of fire on his head.

Be not overcome of evil, but overcome evil with good.

(Romans 12:9-21)

This is a change of spirit, not necessarily an immediate change of behavior. The woman at the well probably did not kick her, then latest, man out, immediately upon Jesus' certifying that there was a covered up deficiency in her relationship.

Jesus saith unto her, Go, call thy husband, and come hither.

The woman answered and said, I have no husband.

Jesus said unto her, Thou hast well said, I have no husband: For thou hast had five husbands; and he whom thou now hast is not thy husband: in that saidst thou truly.

The woman saith unto him, Sir, I perceive that thou art a prophet.

(John 4:16-19)

Even so, her mind was renewed by her contact with Christ.

> *Our fathers worshipped in this mountain; and ye say, that in Jerusalem is the place where men ought to worship.*
>
> *Jesus saith unto her, Woman, believe me, the hour cometh, when ye shall neither in this mountain, nor yet at Jerusalem, worship the Father. Ye worship ye know not what: we know what we worship: for salvation is of the Jews. But the hour cometh, and now is, when the true worshippers shall worship the Father in spirit and in truth: for the Father seeketh such to worship him. God is a Spirit: and they that worship him must worship him in spirit and in truth.*
>
> *The woman saith unto him, I know that Messias cometh, which is called Christ: when he is come, he will tell us all things.*
>
> *Jesus saith unto her, I that speak unto thee am he.*
>
> *The woman then left her waterpot, and went her way into the city, and saith to the men, Come, see a man, which told me all things that ever I did: is not this the Christ?*
>
> (John 4:20-26; 4:28-29)

We have evolved into a mess of indecision. There are too many organizations trying to prove their worth. There are too many people striving for the wrong prize, and the wrong crown, and the wrong reward. Not enough understanding of what the prize is, and how it is achieved. It is not a prize of physical substance. It is a prize of excellence in servitude. The prize is the high calling in Christ Jesus. When we are selected by him to do anything for God, we have access to the prize. We must then cherish and nurture it, as we continually press toward the mark.

> *Brethren, I count not myself to have apprehended: but this one thing I do, forgetting those things which are behind, and reaching forth unto those things which are before, I press toward the mark for the prize of the high calling of God in Christ Jesus.*
>
> (Philippians 3:13-14)

As in the days of Noah, so it is now. This, too, is a part of the environment into which God's Kingdom came, as described in the

Revelation: there are still folks around, who have not conformed to the image of the Son of God. This is why there are Scripture passages such as the following.

> *And there shall in no wise enter into it any thing that defileth, neither whatsoever worketh abomination, or maketh a lie: but they which are written in the Lamb's book of life.*
> (Revelation 21:27)

People will experience a change of heart, before they experience a change of circumstances. For this reason, there will be some who are moving toward the Kingdom of God, but who have baggage that they have to unload. Some of us were the same sorts of people that many of us deride as unworthy of eternal life. We changed, and so can they. They will not be forced to change, solely on the basis of our words; rather, they will be persuaded to change by the impact of the image of Christ as it comes through us. This is our challenge.

> *Know ye not that the unrighteous shall not inherit the kingdom of God? Be not deceived: neither fornicators, nor idolaters, nor adulterers, nor effeminate, nor abusers of themselves with mankind, Nor thieves, nor covetous, nor drunkards, nor revilers, nor extortioners, shall inherit the kingdom of God. And such were some of you: but ye are washed, but ye are sanctified, but ye are justified in the name of the Lord Jesus, and by the Spirit of our God.*
> (1 Corinthians 6:9-11)

In the final chapters of the Revelation of Jesus Christ, there are indications that there will be an inner area of the holy city that is reserved for the redeemed in Christ, while there is an outer area that is open to those who are not yet redeemed. This is reminiscent of the Gentiles that trod the outer court of the temple complex. This would seem to be the population that is subjected to the weight of the iron rod of Christ. This is also the population that is under the supervision of the people of Christ. They are not summarily destroyed just because they have a *problem*. They are governed, and eventually broken into conformance with the will of God, in Christ Jesus.

Therefore, for us to announce the total destruction of all who are on the precipice, just about to make a decision for Christ, is not something that we should ever think about accusing God of doing. To say that at some time certain, God will cut off all non-redeemed life from His presence because of a circumstance, occurring at a certain time, is an unnecessary act of dishonoring the power of God. It is, too, an unfortunate rejection of the love of God. For,

> *The Lord is not slack concerning his promise, as some men count slackness; but is longsuffering to us-ward, not willing that any should perish, but that all should come to repentance.*
>
> (2 Peter 3:9)

It is my prayer that conversion goes on for an eternity. Moreover, when I leave this earth, and am absent from the body and present with the Lord; it is my prayer that he continues to assist me to develop into more and more of the image that Christ showed on the earth. I do not ever want to stop my forward development of understanding all that is God; not even because of a little thing like death. Furthermore, I do not want to stop developing because there is no one around to praise me, or give me pep talks, given with the intent of causing me to continue to develop toward full perfection. Yes, I know that then I will receive great enlightenment.

> *For we know in part, and we prophesy in part. But when that which is perfect is come, then that which is in part shall be done away. When I was a child, I spake as a child, I understood as a child, I thought as a child: but when I became a man, I put away childish things.*
>
> *For now we see through a glass, darkly; but then face to face: now I know in part; but then shall I know even as also I am known.*
>
> (1 Corinthians 13:9-12)

Even with—or maybe because of—that enlightenment, it is my prayer that the development of every human will indeed continue for eternity. To be conformed to the image of Christ is, for me, only the first step in moving toward everlasting. God has so much more in Him that no one has ever seen—or could ever see, even in an eternity. Therefore, I never want to stop learning.

And I do not want this earth to end, just because a date, or even an era, along the path to everlasting has been reached.

Yes, I want everyone to be a Christian. I want them to be that not because they must fear placement in negative situations—hell, or the lake of fire. I want them to become Christians because this is the route to the fullest life that is possible on this side of Heaven. There is no occupation, lifestyle or state of mind that comes close to the glory that is presented by God to those who follow His Son: *world without end.*

> *Therefore, brethren, we are debtors, not to the flesh, to live after the flesh. For if ye live after the flesh, ye shall die: but if ye through the Spirit do mortify the deeds of the body, ye shall live. For as many as are led by the Spirit of God, they are the sons of God.*
>
> *For ye have not received the spirit of bondage again to fear; but ye have received the Spirit of adoption, whereby we cry, Abba, Father.*
>
> *The Spirit itself beareth witness with our spirit, that we are the children of God: And if children, then heirs; heirs of God, and joint-heirs with Christ; if so be that we suffer with him, that we may be also glorified together.*
>
> *For I reckon that the sufferings of this present time are not worthy to be compared with the glory which shall be revealed in us.*
>
> (Romans 8:12-18)

I pray that the ending portion of the following Scripture is an actual statement of the heart of God. I want the earth to go on—well—forever. I want each generation of humans to have the joy of coming closer and closer to God.

> *Now unto him that is able to do exceeding abundantly above all that we ask or think, according to the power that worketh in us, Unto him be glory in the church by Christ Jesus throughout all ages, world without end.*
>
> *Amen.*
>
> (Ephesians 3:20-21)

Spending much time
Looking to the skies,
A childlike wonder
Fills our eyes.

Our thoughts moving
To things above,
In a final expectation
Of God's great love

Coming to the earth,
To the kingdom of man;
It is what they say
Is in His Plan.

The Lord of Heaven,
Coming with the cloud;
The trumpets blaring
Long and loud:

Riding above
The land and sea,
Providing deliverance
For you and me:

Well, maybe not
For everyone;
Just for those
Who follow the Son.

Is this a way of saying,
God's reach cannot span
Beyond the faithful,
To tame defiance in man?

If that is true,
Then tell me how
Will God cause
Every knee to bow?

Rest, believing that
There is surely a day
When, in each life,
*He **will** have His say.*

God need not destroy
What He can mend,
And place them in His
World without end.

CHAPTER 10A

Empowering Mankind

Rightly Dividing Scripture

Acts 1:1-9

The former treatise have I made, O Theophilus, of all that Jesus began both to do and teach, Until the day in which he was taken up, after that he through the Holy Ghost had given commandments unto the apostles whom he had chosen: To whom also he showed himself alive after his passion by many infallible proofs, being seen of them forty days, and speaking of the things pertaining to the kingdom of God: And, being assembled together with them, commanded them that they should not depart from Jerusalem, but wait for the promise of the Father, which, saith he, ye have heard of me. For John truly baptized with water; but ye shall be baptized with the Holy Ghost not many days hence.

When they therefore were come together, they asked of him, saying, Lord, wilt thou at this time restore again the kingdom to Israel?

And he said unto them, It is not for you to know the times or the seasons, which the Father hath put in his own power. But ye shall receive power, after that the Holy Ghost is come upon you: and ye shall be witnesses unto me both in Jerusalem, and in all Judaea, and in Samaria, and unto the uttermost part of the earth.

And when he had spoken these things, while they beheld, he was taken up; and a cloud received him out of their sight.

The greatest power to witness to the world is in a full acceptance of the message of God as being infallible. This is closely joined with believing the Bible to be accurate and complete. This is so because when we go to the world to present the Gospel of Jesus Christ, the source that we have that was written to chronicle this unfolding of the Gospel, as certified by the Father God, is the Bible. Any book written by man (including this one) is an interpretation of the words of God that are in the Bible. If it does not state that it is an interpretation, we should not present any of its contents to a searching world. And when it does say that it is interpretive, we must include this designation whenever we pass its words on to others.

Therefore, we have to obtain power-of-presence for the Bible, within our being. When we do this, the Bible is a living testament to the introduction of the Son of man, to all humanity. To do this, we have to fix in ourselves some beliefs that carry for us the closest weight to fact that we as humans can achieve. This closeness to fact must be a part of our spirit. In this way, the Spirit of truth will have access to these beliefs, which we hold so dearly. And once the Spirit of truth gets a hold on a belief, which is its fact in reality, it will magnify it in our lives, and in the lives of those we touch. This is the transcendence of belief beyond the limits of mankind; by the added ingredient of God's Spirit. In the following words from the Bible, Jesus calls for the expansion of belief to encompass reality.

> *Jesus saith unto him, Thomas, because thou hast seen me, thou hast believed: blessed are they that have not seen, and yet have believed.*
>
> (John 20:29)

Therefore, let us grab hold of some of the principles of the Bible, and apply them to our self, in order to incorporate the Bible into our being as the true and living word of God.

God does not have a gray area. There is no place for a lukewarm issue with God. In the Revelation of Jesus Christ, Jesus tells us God's view of our lukewarm behavior toward Him.

And unto the angel of the church of the Laodiceans write; These things saith the Amen, the faithful and true witness, the beginning of the creation of God; I know thy works, that thou art neither cold nor hot: I would thou wert cold or hot. So then because thou art lukewarm, and neither cold nor hot, I will spue thee out of my mouth.

(Revelation 3:14-16)

To avoid the pitfall of being lukewarm, we must be able to clearly separate the absolutes in the Bible from the relatives. When God makes a pronouncement, we can be sure that it is an absolute. However, not all the words in the Bible are by pronouncements from God to man. Moses is known to have received pronouncements from God, as well as direct products of the work of God, in the tablets of the Ten Commandments. In an even more direct fashion, Jesus received the message of God, as the Son of man; as a hearer, as a witness, and as a participant in the events that are the foundation of the pronouncements. In this aspect, Jesus was there when God did things. The Son of man saw what God did, and he heard what God said, across time. And, too, the soul of the Son of man absorbed all this; sitting it in its place, for the time of his appearing.

John answered and said, A man can receive nothing, except it be given him from heaven. Ye yourselves bear me witness, that I said, I am not the Christ, but that I am sent before him. He that hath the bride is the bridegroom: but the friend of the bridegroom, which standeth and heareth him, rejoiceth greatly because of the bridegroom's voice: this my joy therefore is fulfilled. He must increase, but I must decrease. He that cometh from above is above all: he that is of the earth is earthly, and speaketh of the earth: he that cometh from heaven is above all. And what he hath seen and heard, that he testifieth; and no man receiveth his testimony.

(John 3:27-32)

Jesus answered them, Verily, verily, I say unto you, Whosoever committeth sin is the servant of sin. And the servant abideth not in the house for ever: but the Son abideth ever. If the Son therefore shall make you free, ye shall be free indeed.

I know that ye are Abraham's seed; but ye seek to kill me, because my word hath no place in you. I speak that which I have seen with my Father: and ye do that which ye have seen with your father.

(John 8:34-38)

This is the soul that was placed in the man we call, Jesus of Nazareth. What he said was of a direct pronouncement of God, but not by a direct pronouncement of God to him; instead, they are pronouncements of God <u>for</u> him. Because of this; those things that Jesus, the Son of man, said are direct pronouncements of the Son of God, which carries the full weight of the authority of the LORD God the Father. Thus, Jesus Christ is more than just a prophet; he is also a teacher; among many other things. Therefore, to highlight the nature of absolutes and relatives, we will start with some of Jesus' pronouncements.

Jesus absolutely said that he is the Son of man, and the Son of God. There are many references to this absolute: listed below are two.

And, behold, they brought to him a man sick of the palsy, lying on a bed: and Jesus seeing their faith said unto the sick of the palsy; Son, be of good cheer; thy sins be forgiven thee.

And, behold, certain of the scribes said within themselves, This man blasphemeth.

And Jesus knowing their thoughts said, Wherefore think ye evil in your hearts? For whether is easier, to say, Thy sins be forgiven thee; or to say, Arise, and walk? But that ye may know that the Son of man hath power on earth to forgive sins,

(then saith he to the sick of the palsy,) Arise, take up thy bed, and go unto thine house.

(Matthew 9:2-6)

And when he was come to the other side into the country of the Gergesenes, there met him two possessed with devils, coming out of the tombs, exceeding fierce, so that no man might pass by that way. And, behold, they cried out, saying, What have we to do with

> *thee, Jesus, thou Son of God? art thou come hither to torment us before the time?*
>
> (Matthew 8:28-29)

There are some relative, or fluid, concepts in the compendium of Jesus' statements. These relative statements, we will call recommendations. Recommendations are clearly stated in the Bible. Before we list any of the recommendations; please understand that if you can do what is stated in these pronouncements, you will achieve the optimum in God. However, if you cannot do what is stated herein, you do not have to feel like a second-class citizen of the Kingdom of God. God knows our limitations, and this is why he allows us to forego adhering to certain things. However, the allowance only lasts until we have strengthened our connection with God, in the Spirit of truth. In order to help you understand this better, here is an example.

> *He saith unto them, Moses because of the hardness of your hearts suffered you to put away your wives: but from the beginning it was not so. And I say unto you, Whosoever shall put away his wife, except it be for fornication, and shall marry another, committeth adultery: and whoso marrieth her which is put away doth commit adultery.*
>
> *His disciples say unto him, If the case of the man be so with his wife, it is not good to marry.*
>
> *But he said unto them, All men cannot receive this saying, save they to whom it is given. For there are some eunuchs, which were so born from their mother's womb: and there are some eunuchs, which were made eunuchs of men: and there be eunuchs, which have made themselves eunuchs for the kingdom of heaven's sake. He that is able to receive it, let him receive it.*
>
> (Matthew 19:8-12)

Let me differentiate here between recommendations, and the permissive will of God. Recommendations are a much narrower category than the permissive will of God. Recommendations are those things that we do in righteousness, for which if we can achieve them, we do well. The permissive will of God can cover everything from those things done in righteousness to those things done in willful self-service. The nation of

Israel was constantly receiving the permissive will of God. An example of this is seen in their request for a king.

> *And it came to pass, when Samuel was old, that he made his sons judges over Israel. Now the name of his firstborn was Joel; and the name of his second, Abiah: they were judges in Beersheba. And his sons walked not in his ways, but turned aside after lucre, and took bribes, and perverted judgment.*
>
> *Then all the elders of Israel gathered themselves together, and came to Samuel unto Ramah, And said unto him, Behold, thou art old, and thy sons walk not in thy ways: now make us a king to judge us like all the nations.*
>
> *But the thing displeased Samuel, when they said, Give us a king to judge us. And Samuel prayed unto the LORD.*
>
> *And the LORD said unto Samuel, Hearken unto the voice of the people in all that they say unto thee: for they have not rejected thee, but they have rejected me, that I should not reign over them. According to all the works which they have done since the day that I brought them up out of Egypt even unto this day, wherewith they have forsaken me, and served other gods, so do they also unto thee.*
>
> (1 Samuel 8:1-8)

Considering the text and the tone of what the LORD said unto Samuel, it is clear that their request for a king was not done in righteousness. Even so, the request was allowed according to the permissive will of God. It was not a recommendation of God that they not have a king; it was a requirement of righteousness that they not have a king. This requirement was both for the nation's sake, as well as for the sake of whoever would become king. As contained in the following Scripture, God clearly showed how the nation would suffer under a king.

> *Now therefore hearken unto their voice: howbeit yet protest solemnly unto them, and show them the manner of the king that shall reign over them.*

> *And Samuel told all the words of the LORD unto the people that asked of him a king. And he said, This will be the manner of the king that shall reign over you: He will take your sons, and appoint them for himself, for his chariots, and to be his horsemen; and some shall run before his chariots. And he will appoint him captains over thousands, and captains over fifties; and will set them to ear his ground, and to reap his harvest, and to make his instruments of war, and instruments of his chariots. And he will take your daughters to be confectionaries, and to be cooks, and to be bakers. And he will take your fields, and your vineyards, and your oliveyards, even the best of them, and give them to his servants. And he will take the tenth of your seed, and of your vineyards, and give to his officers, and to his servants. And he will take your menservants, and your maidservants, and your goodliest young men, and your asses, and put them to his work. He will take the tenth of your sheep: and ye shall be his servants.*
>
> *And ye shall cry out in that day because of your king which ye shall have chosen you; and the LORD will not hear you in that day.*
>
> (1 Samuel 8:9-18)

In many other places in the Bible, God also let us know how any person taking on the mantle of king would be subject to falling away from God. Thus, the person who became king was placing himself in the way of becoming unrighteous. Among them is this one . . .

> *When thou art come unto the land which the LORD thy God giveth thee, and shalt possess it, and shalt dwell therein, and shalt say, I will set a king over me, like as all the nations that are about me; Thou shalt in any wise set him king over thee, whom the LORD thy God shall choose: one from among thy brethren shalt thou set king over thee: thou mayest not set a stranger over thee, which is not thy brother.*
>
> *But he shall not multiply horses to himself, nor cause the people to return to Egypt, to the end that he should multiply horses: forasmuch as the LORD hath said unto you, Ye shall henceforth return no more that way. Neither shall he multiply wives to himself,*

> *that his heart turn not away: neither shall he greatly multiply to himself silver and gold.*
>
> *And it shall be, when he sitteth upon the throne of his kingdom, that he shall write him a copy of this law in a book out of that which is before the priests the Levites: And it shall be with him, and he shall read therein all the days of his life: that he may learn to fear the LORD his God, to keep all the words of this law and these statutes, to do them: That his heart be not lifted up above his brethren, and that he turn not aside from the commandment, to the right hand, or to the left: to the end that he may prolong his days in his kingdom, he, and his children, in the midst of Israel.*
>
> (Deuteronomy 17:14-20)

This has been brought to light for you so that you will understand that we need to avoid situations that trigger the LORD'S permissive will. Moreover, we must be careful about labeling any one of God's messages for man, as being a recommendation that is not a thing that must be done. The more prudent stance to take is to say that each one of the calls to action that is in Scripture is a declaration; not, a recommendation.

Old Testament declaratives are collected together as, the Law and the prophets, and both have the full authority of God as their strength. New Testament declarations are expressed as doctrine, not as suggestions. In order for us to remain in the righteousness of God, we must pattern our life in accordance with both, the Law and the prophets of the Old Testament, and, the doctrine of the New Testament. As you look at the New Testament doctrine that Jesus Christ presents, here; please notice the declarative tone that is in the answer that he gives.

> *There was a man of the Pharisees, named Nicodemus, a ruler of the Jews: The same came to Jesus by night, and said unto him, Rabbi, we know that thou art a teacher come from God: for no man can do these miracles that thou doest, except God be with him.*
>
> *Jesus answered and said unto him, Verily, verily, I say unto thee, Except a man be born again, he cannot see the kingdom of God.*

Nicodemus saith unto him, How can a man be born when he is old? can he enter the second time into his mother's womb, and be born?

Jesus answered, Verily, verily, I say unto thee, Except a man be born of water and of the Spirit, he cannot enter into the kingdom of God. That which is born of the flesh is flesh; and that which is born of the Spirit is spirit. Marvel not that I said unto thee, Ye must be born again.

(John 3:1-7)

The declarative tone is also in the ministry of the Gospel that is a part of the mission of the apostles. Here are three examples, from the ministry of the apostle Paul.

Let your women keep silence in the churches: for it is not permitted unto them to speak; but they are commanded to be under obedience, as also saith the law. And if they will learn any thing, let them ask their husbands at home: for it is a shame for women to speak in the church. What? came the word of God out from you? or came it unto you only?

If any man think himself to be a prophet, or spiritual, let him acknowledge that the things that I write unto you are the commandments of the Lord. But if any man be ignorant, let him be ignorant.

(1 Corinthians 14:34-38)

Husbands, love your wives, even as Christ also loved the church, and gave himself for it; That he might sanctify and cleanse it with the washing of water by the word, That he might present it to himself a glorious church, not having spot, or wrinkle, or any such thing; but that it should be holy and without blemish. So ought men to love their wives as their own bodies. He that loveth his wife loveth himself.

> *For no man ever yet hated his own flesh; but nourisheth and cherisheth it, even as the Lord the church: For we are members of his body, of his flesh, and of his bones.*
>
> *For this cause shall a man leave his father and mother, and shall be joined unto his wife, and they two shall be one flesh.*
>
> (Ephesians 5:25-31)

> *Submitting yourselves one to another in the fear of God. Wives, submit yourselves unto your own husbands, as unto the Lord. For the husband is the head of the wife, even as Christ is the head of the church: and he is the saviour of the body. Therefore as the church is subject unto Christ, so let the wives be to their own husbands in every thing.*
>
> (Ephesians 5:21-24)

Of course, the declarative tone is, too, an attribute of the requirements for obedience that the LORD sent through the Old Testament prophets. Moreover, the power of the tone had a forceful impact in the time of the New Testament. At that time, portions of the declarations were embedded in the tone of negotiation, which was expressed by Jesus Christ. The tone of negotiation carried us up to the time at which Christ fulfilled portions of the Old Testament declaratives, for righteousness sake. Among the still active statements are the following necessary practices for righteous living.

> *Train up a child in the way he should go: and when he is old, he will not depart from it.*
>
> (Proverbs 22:6)

> *Now therefore hearken, O Israel, unto the statutes and unto the judgments, which I teach you, for to do them, that ye may live, and go in and possess the land which the LORD God of your fathers giveth you. Ye shall not add unto the word which I command you, neither shall ye diminish ought from it, that ye may keep the commandments of the LORD your God which I command you.*
>
> (Deuteronomy 4:1-2)

As we move to a consideration of negotiation, keep its difference from recommendation and declaration clearly in mind: negotiations are their own sort of interaction. In the Spirit, negotiations are much like recommendations, in that if we do not follow them, we only hurt our self. To give you a better sense of negotiations, here is a Scripture in which this tone was used.

> *Wash you, make you clean; put away the evil of your doings from before mine eyes; cease to do evil; Learn to do well; seek judgment, relieve the oppressed, judge the fatherless, plead for the widow.*
>
> *Come now, and let us reason together, saith the LORD: though your sins be as scarlet, they shall be as white as snow; though they be red like crimson, they shall be as wool.*
>
> *If ye be willing and obedient, ye shall eat the good of the land: But if ye refuse and rebel, ye shall be devoured with the sword: for the mouth of the LORD hath spoken it.*
>
> (Isaiah 1:16-20)

Also, know this: regardless of the tone of Scripture, there are no missing pieces in the Bible; there is nothing to be filled in, not even as based on changed human conditions. This pertains to the family, as well as the church. The church was set up with a particular structure; the family, too, was established in a particular fashion by God. God's ordinance for the family dates back to Creation, and it has not been changed by God since that time.

> *And the LORD God caused a deep sleep to fall upon Adam, and he slept: and he took one of his ribs, and closed up the flesh instead thereof; And the rib, which the LORD God had taken from man, made he a woman, and brought her unto the man.*

And Adam said, This is now bone of my bones, and flesh of my flesh: she shall be called Woman, because she was taken out of Man. Therefore shall a man leave his father and his mother, and shall cleave unto his wife: and they shall be one flesh.

And they were both naked, the man and his wife, and were not ashamed.

(Genesis 2:21-25)

In a time that is between Creation, and now; Jesus Christ, speaking as the Son of God, once again stressed the ancient architecting of the family. By these, his words, he declared the ancient architecture as being binding still in that day.

The Pharisees also came unto him, tempting him, and saying unto him, Is it lawful for a man to put away his wife for every cause?

And he answered and said unto them, Have ye not read, that he which made them at the beginning made them male and female, And said, For this cause shall a man leave father and mother, and shall cleave to his wife: and they twain shall be one flesh? Wherefore they are no more twain, but one flesh. What therefore God hath joined together, let not man put asunder.

(Matthew 19:3-6)

Moreover, because of the unchanging nature of Jesus Christ, the declaration of the continued authority of the Creation architecting of marriage continues to this day. Because of this unchanging nature of Jesus Christ, the forward motion of his authority goes across all time.

Jesus Christ the same yesterday, and to day, and for ever.

(Hebrews 13:8)

The true church, built on the rock of the Son of God, is an unchanging declaration that is of Jesus Christ. The church that rests on the rock was announced by Jesus Christ, and it is built on the truth that he is *the Christ, the Son of the living God.* There is no other truth that can form the basis for the church. No man, other than Jesus, has a place as being the foundation, or as the chief architect, of the church of God, in Christ. Yes, there may be some *assistant* architects, and there are definitely master builders that, both, have assigned tasks; but there is only one chief architect. Furthermore, even the assistant architects, along with the master builders, are crafted by God according to clear specifications. These are some of the specifications that are listed in the Bible . . .

> *This is a true saying, If a man desire the office of a bishop, he desireth a good work. A bishop then must be blameless, the husband of one wife, vigilant, sober, of good behaviour, given to hospitality, apt to teach; Not given to wine, no striker, not greedy of filthy lucre; but patient, not a brawler, not covetous; One that ruleth well his own house, having his children in subjection with all gravity; (For if a man know not how to rule his own house, how shall he take care of the church of God?)*
>
> *Not a novice, lest being lifted up with pride he fall into the condemnation of the devil. Moreover he must have a good report of them which are without; lest he fall into reproach and the snare of the devil.*
>
> (1 Timothy 3:1-7)

> *Likewise must the deacons be grave, not doubletongued, not given to much wine, not greedy of filthy lucre; Holding the mystery of the faith in a pure conscience. And let these also first be proved; then let them use the office of a deacon, being found blameless.*
>
> *Even so must their wives be grave, not slanderers, sober, faithful in all things. Let the deacons be the husbands of one wife, ruling their children and their own houses well.*
>
> *For they that have used the office of a deacon well purchase to themselves a good degree, and great boldness in the faith which is in Christ Jesus.*
>
> (1 Timothy 3:8-13)

Any other person, or anything else, from anywhere else, which enters into, or incites, conflict with these requisites is promoting unrighteousness. This is true for anything that conflicts with the Bible. There are no missing pieces in the Bible.

There is a clear reason why there can be no missing pieces in the Bible. If God had left things up to man, then He would have opened up a possibility for *righteous* conflict between God and man. That is, if man had a say in the matter of his own righteousness before God; and, if man decided to say something different from God; then, we would be left with a question of who has precedence over whom, and under what circumstances the one or the other precedent is activated? This is not the way of God. God does not have a kingdom that can be divided against its self. Jesus told us why this is so, as he described the devastating result for such a conflict.

> *And Jesus knew their thoughts, and said unto them, Every kingdom divided against itself is brought to desolation; and every city or house divided against itself shall not stand: And if Satan cast out Satan, he is divided against himself; how shall then his kingdom stand? And if I by Beelzebub cast out devils, by whom do your children cast them out? therefore they shall be your judges. But if I cast out devils by the Spirit of God, then the kingdom of God is come unto you.*
>
> (Matthew 12:25-28)

God, in His righteousness, makes no allowance for confusing situations. We see this in operation in the churches of the saints.

> *If any man speak in an unknown tongue, let it be by two, or at the most by three, and that by course; and let one interpret. But if there be no interpreter, let him keep silence in the church; and let him speak to himself, and to God.*
>
> *Let the prophets speak two or three, and let the other judge. If any thing be revealed to another that sitteth by, let the first hold his peace. For ye may all prophesy one by one, that all may learn, and all may be comforted. And the spirits of the prophets are subject to the prophets.*
>
> *For God is not the author of confusion, but of peace, as in all churches of the saints.*
>
> (1 Corinthians 14:27-33)

God does not cause man to have to select between one truth and the other. God makes no allowances for creating double minded servants. To prevent us from being double minded, God has given us access to wisdom.

> *If any of you lack wisdom, let him ask of God, that giveth to all men liberally, and upbraideth not; and it shall be given him. But let him ask in faith, nothing wavering. For he that wavereth is like a wave of the sea driven with the wind and tossed. For let not that man think that he shall receive any thing of the Lord. A double minded man is unstable in all his ways.*
>
> (James 1:5-8)

This brings us to a very easy point of understanding, which is this: when something is said by Jesus Christ, it is to be believed as written. Jesus clearly identifies when there is a mystery contained in anything he says; but, Jesus himself has no mystery. Moreover, Jesus is the final answer to all the mysteries that were laid out by the prophets in the Old Testament. In this, Jesus did not walk alone. In the revelation of the answers to the mystery of the prophets of the Old Testament, the first seed of this understanding was planted by John the Baptist.

> *And he said unto them, Ye are they which justify yourselves before men; but God knoweth your hearts: for that which is highly esteemed among men is abomination in the sight of God. The law and the prophets were until John: since that time the kingdom of God is preached, and every man presseth into it. And it is easier for heaven and earth to pass, than one tittle of the law to fail.*
>
> (Luke 16:15-17)

Jesus brought to us the way, the truth and the life: not a way, a truth, or a life. He who hath an ear; let him hear

> *Let not your heart be troubled: ye believe in God, believe also in me. In my Father's house are many mansions: if it were not so, I would have told you. I go to prepare a place for you. And if I go and prepare a place for you, I will come again, and receive you*

> *unto myself; that where I am, there ye may be also. And whither I go ye know, and the way ye know.*
>
> *Thomas saith unto him, Lord, we know not whither thou goest; and how can we know the way?*
>
> *Jesus saith unto him, I am the way, the truth, and the life: no man cometh unto the Father, but by me. If ye had known me, ye should have known my Father also: and from henceforth ye know him, and have seen him.*
>
> (John 14:1-7)

As we evaluate the clarity of Jesus' collection of proclamations, let us look at a specific statement of Jesus that many have assumed was somehow veiled in mystery.

> *Then said Jesus unto his disciples, If any man will come after me, let him deny himself, and take up his cross, and follow me. For whosoever will save his life shall lose it: and whosoever will lose his life for my sake shall find it. For what is a man profited, if he shall gain the whole world, and lose his own soul? or what shall a man give in exchange for his soul? For the Son of man shall come in the glory of his Father with his angels; and then he shall reward every man according to his works.*
>
> *Verily I say unto you, There be some standing here, which shall not taste of death, till they see the Son of man coming in his kingdom.*
>
> (Matthew 16:24-28)

The verse that is written immediately above is absolute. The thing Jesus said unto his disciples did happen. During the generation to which he was speaking, the destruction of Jerusalem happened, and the kingdom of Christ settled into its place. Furthermore, even if we extended the generation out to the size of an age—which it is not—the statement was still fulfilled.

The first part, which was to happen while some of those listening were alive, is the destruction of Jerusalem. This happened in about 70 AD. The age itself ended in about 476 AD when the Roman Empire fell. After that empire fell, we entered the time of prominence of the Byzantine Empire. Then, at the time that we moved beyond the time of prominence of that empire, the Revelation of Jesus Christ had been accomplished. After that day (and we are there), there is no need to wait anymore for what has already happened. We have already witnessed *the Son of man coming in his kingdom*, and so much more—this we will share with you, soon.

By the way, there has been some talk about someone hiding meaning in their statements. It is said that they did this to prevent the leaders of that day from taking offense at them, and killing somebody. This somebody is usually seen to be the apostle or disciple who made the statement. Well, I think you will agree with me that this statement could never have been applied to Jesus. You need never believe that Jesus Christ would have been too afraid of anyone, such that he would not speak clearly and directly. Jesus Christ did not have to hide the meaning of his words, so as not to offend anyone, or not to get himself killed—the world had already done that; then, they were overruled by his resurrection.

> *I am the good shepherd, and know my sheep, and am known of mine. As the Father knoweth me, even so know I the Father: and I lay down my life for the sheep.*
>
> *And other sheep I have, which are not of this fold: them also I must bring, and they shall hear my voice; and there shall be one fold, and one shepherd. Therefore doth my Father love me, because I lay down my life, that I might take it again. No man taketh it from me, but I lay it down of myself. I have power to lay it down, and I have power to take it again. This commandment have I received of my Father.*
>
> (John 10:14-18)

To say it bluntly: this is why the Son of God came to this earth. The Son of God, in Jesus of Nazareth, came here to show us that life is only important when it is lived for God, in spite of threats and actions of man.

> *Think not that I am come to send peace on earth: I came not to send peace, but a sword. For I am come to set a man at variance against his father, and the daughter against her mother, and the daughter in law against her mother in law. And a man's foes shall be they of his own household. He that loveth father or mother more*

than me is not worthy of me: and he that loveth son or daughter more than me is not worthy of me.

And he that taketh not his cross, and followeth after me, is not worthy of me. He that findeth his life shall lose it: and he that loseth his life for my sake shall find it.

He that receiveth you receiveth me, and he that receiveth me receiveth him that sent me.

(Matthew 10:34-40)

And, I am fairly certain that the scribes and Pharisees were not confused about any hidden meanings in these words of Jesus of Nazareth. Moreover, I am sure that these are words that would have emboldened them to kill Jesus, if they could have done so. First, Jesus discussed general issues with their pattern of worship.

But woe unto you, scribes and Pharisees, hypocrites! for ye shut up the kingdom of heaven against men: for ye neither go in yourselves, neither suffer ye them that are entering to go in.

Woe unto you, scribes and Pharisees, hypocrites! for ye devour widows' houses, and for a pretence make long prayer: therefore ye shall receive the greater damnation.

Woe unto you, scribes and Pharisees, hypocrites! for ye compass sea and land to make one proselyte, and when he is made, ye make him twofold more the child of hell than yourselves.

Woe unto you, ye blind guides, which say, Whosoever shall swear by the temple, it is nothing; but whosoever shall swear by the gold of the temple, he is a debtor! Ye fools and blind: for whether is greater, the gold, or the temple that sanctifieth the gold? And, Whosoever shall swear by the altar, it is nothing; but whosoever sweareth by the gift that is upon it, he is guilty. Ye fools and blind: for whether is greater, the gift, or the altar that sanctifieth the gift? Whoso therefore shall swear by the altar, sweareth by it, and by all things thereon. And whoso shall swear by the temple, sweareth by it, and by him that dwelleth therein. And he that shall swear by heaven, sweareth by the throne of God, and by him that sitteth thereon.

(Matthew 23:13-22)

Then, to add salt to their wounds; Jesus spread their deficient worship out before the people who were around them. This is where he was tampering with the generosity that might have been a good source of offerings for their coffers. Still to this day, this is a good way of inciting violence from greedy people, including some of the more well known spiritual figureheads.

> *Woe unto you, scribes and Pharisees, hypocrites! for ye pay tithe of mint and anise and cummin, and have omitted the weightier matters of the law, judgment, mercy, and faith: these ought ye to have done, and not to leave the other undone. Ye blind guides, which strain at a gnat, and swallow a camel.*
>
> *Woe unto you, scribes and Pharisees, hypocrites! for ye make clean the outside of the cup and of the platter, but within they are full of extortion and excess. Thou blind Pharisee, cleanse first that which is within the cup and platter, that the outside of them may be clean also.*
>
> *Woe unto you, scribes and Pharisees, hypocrites! for ye are like unto whited sepulchres, which indeed appear beautiful outward, but are within full of dead men's bones, and of all uncleanness. Even so ye also outwardly appear righteous unto men, but within ye are full of hypocrisy and iniquity.*
>
> *Woe unto you, scribes and Pharisees, hypocrites! because ye build the tombs of the prophets, and garnish the sepulchres of the righteous, And say, If we had been in the days of our fathers, we would not have been partakers with them in the blood of the prophets. Wherefore ye be witnesses unto yourselves, that ye are the children of them which killed the prophets. Fill ye up then the measure of your fathers.*
>
> *Ye serpents, ye generation of vipers, how can ye escape the damnation of hell?*
>
> (Matthew 23:23-33)

The things stated above about the boldness of Jesus, are the same for the apostles, on all counts. Their words are from the Holy Ghost, and their words are truth; and, they, too, would have had no fear of dying. In fact, the apostles expected to be placed in positions where they would be killed; this is the nature of their calling. The apostles are the selected ones of Jesus, for their day. Moreover, the apostles were equipped, by Jesus, for service. Jesus did this by giving them a generous portion of the Son's Spirit.

> *And when he had called unto him his twelve disciples, he gave them power against unclean spirits, to cast them out, and to heal all manner of sickness and all manner of disease. Now the names of the twelve apostles are these; The first, Simon, who is called Peter, and Andrew his brother; James the son of Zebedee, and John his brother; Philip, and Bartholomew; Thomas, and Matthew the publican; James the son of Alphaeus, and Lebbaeus, whose surname was Thaddaeus; Simon the Canaanite, and Judas Iscariot, who also betrayed him.*
>
> *These twelve Jesus sent forth, and commanded them, saying, Go not into the way of the Gentiles, and into any city of the Samaritans enter ye not: But go rather to the lost sheep of the house of Israel. And as ye go, preach, saying, The kingdom of heaven is at hand. Heal the sick, cleanse the lepers, raise the dead, cast out devils: freely ye have received, freely give.*
>
> (Matthew 10:1-8)

In sharing his particular generous portion of the Spirit, and regardless of the consequence to him, the apostle Peter set the religious leaders straight about his commitment to the Lord Jesus Christ.

> *And it came to pass on the morrow, that their rulers, and elders, and scribes, And Annas the high priest, and Caiaphas, and John, and Alexander, and as many as were of the kindred of the high priest, were gathered together at Jerusalem. And when they had set them in the midst, they asked, By what power, or by what name, have ye done this?*
>
> *Then Peter, filled with the Holy Ghost, said unto them, Ye rulers of the people, and elders of Israel, If we this day be examined of the good deed done to the impotent man, by what means he is made whole; Be it known unto you all, and to all the people of Israel, that by the name of Jesus Christ of Nazareth, whom ye crucified, whom God raised from the dead, even by him doth this man stand*

> *here before you whole. This is the stone which was set at nought of you builders, which is become the head of the corner. Neither is there salvation in any other: for there is none other name under heaven given among men, whereby we must be saved.*
>
> (Acts 4:5-12)

In fact, as a result of the Spirit of truth being in Peter's world, the religious leaders were, as they say, thrown off their game. Wherefore the religious leaders had to take a time-out, to regroup.

> *Now when they saw the boldness of Peter and John, and perceived that they were unlearned and ignorant men, they marvelled; and they took knowledge of them, that they had been with Jesus. And beholding the man which was healed standing with them, they could say nothing against it. But when they had commanded them to go aside out of the council, they conferred among themselves, Saying, What shall we do to these men? for that indeed a notable miracle hath been done by them is manifest to all them that dwell in Jerusalem; and we cannot deny it. But that it spread no further among the people, let us straitly threaten them, that they speak henceforth to no man in this name.*
>
> *And they called them, and commanded them not to speak at all nor teach in the name of Jesus.*
>
> *But Peter and John answered and said unto them, Whether it be right in the sight of God to hearken unto you more than unto God, judge ye. For we cannot but speak the things which we have seen and heard.*
>
> (Acts 4:13-22)

On the Damascus road, the apostle Paul (formerly named, Saul) was given his marching orders by the Lord Jesus Christ.

> *And Saul, yet breathing out threatenings and slaughter against the disciples of the Lord, went unto the high priest, And desired of him letters to Damascus to the synagogues, that if he found any of this way, whether they were men or women, he might bring them bound unto Jerusalem. And as he journeyed, he came near*

Damascus: and suddenly there shined round about him a light from heaven: And he fell to the earth, and heard a voice saying unto him,

Saul, Saul, why persecutest thou me?
And he said, Who art thou, Lord?

And the Lord said, I am Jesus whom thou persecutest: it is hard for thee to kick against the pricks.
And he trembling and astonished said, Lord, what wilt thou have me to do?
And the Lord said unto him, Arise, and go into the city, and it shall be told thee what thou must do.

And the men which journeyed with him stood speechless, hearing a voice, but seeing no man.
(Acts 9:1-7)

Moreover, if he had any misunderstanding about the risk that he faced, a certain disciple of the Lord was directed to tell Paul just how much he would have to suffer for Jesus' name's sake.

And Saul arose from the earth; and when his eyes were opened, he saw no man: but they led him by the hand, and brought him into Damascus. And he was three days without sight, and neither did eat nor drink.

And there was a certain disciple at Damascus, named Ananias; and to him said the Lord in a vision,

Ananias.
And he said, Behold, I am here, Lord.

And the Lord said unto him, Arise, and go into the street which is called Straight, and inquire in the house of Judas for one called Saul, of Tarsus: for, behold, he prayeth, And hath seen in a vision a man named Ananias coming in, and putting his hand on him, that he might receive his sight.

Then Ananias answered, Lord, I have heard by many of this man, how much evil he hath done to thy saints at Jerusalem: And here he hath authority from the chief priests to bind all that call on thy name.

But the Lord said unto him, Go thy way: for he is a chosen vessel unto me, to bear my name before the Gentiles, and kings, and the children of Israel: For I will show him how great things he must suffer for my name's sake.

(Acts 9:8-16)

Apostles are the first ones in the line of fire.

Now ye are the body of Christ, and members in particular. And God hath set some in the church, first apostles, secondarily prophets, thirdly teachers, after that miracles, then gifts of healings, helps, governments, diversities of tongues.

(1 Corinthians 12:27-28)

The apostle cannot let a paralyzing fear of harm against his person overtake him, in anticipation of the behavior of evil, sinful, or even misguided, men. In actuality, they have to expect it to come; or at least, expect it to be tried by someone, in some form. Whether it is physical or spiritual, or even emotional, they have to expect that it will be tried. Wherefore they had to walk in the authority of Christ until the end of their individual life. Then, their authorization moved on.

For we know that if our earthly house of this tabernacle were dissolved, we have a building of God, an house not made with hands, eternal in the heavens. For in this we groan, earnestly desiring to be clothed upon with our house which is from heaven: If so be that being clothed we shall not be found naked. For we that are in this tabernacle do groan, being burdened: not for that we would be unclothed, but clothed upon, that mortality might be swallowed up of life.

(2 Corinthians 5:1-4)

Now, once the apostles of Christ died, their authority returned, with them, to Jesus; it did not pass on, in some stale fashion, to anyone else.

God sends a fresh batch of servants to replenish the church; filling them with a renewed and refreshed cup of power. This thought is in accordance with a declaration of Jesus.

> *And Jesus went about all the cities and villages, teaching in their synagogues, and preaching the gospel of the kingdom, and healing every sickness and every disease among the people. But when he saw the multitudes, he was moved with compassion on them, because they fainted, and were scattered abroad, as sheep having no shepherd. Then saith he unto his disciples, The harvest truly is plenteous, but the labourers are few; Pray ye therefore the Lord of the harvest, that he will send forth labourers into his harvest.*
> (Matthew 9:35-38)

Moreover, when the Father sends laborers, He gives to each man the authority that is required for the position to which they are elected.

> *And we know that all things work together for good to them that love God, to them who are the called according to his purpose. For whom he did foreknow, he also did predestinate to be conformed to the image of his Son, that he might be the firstborn among many brethren. Moreover whom he did predestinate, them he also called: and whom he called, them he also justified: and whom he justified, them he also glorified. What shall we then say to these things? If God be for us, who can be against us?*
> (Romans 8:28-31)

Therefore, there is no cloaking of the Scripture because of fear. What the Bible says, the Bible means. If we cannot live by a piece of Scripture, let us be honest with God, first; with ourselves, second; and with the church, third. Do not try to water down, or, in any other way, change the Scripture to fit the weaknesses of a man, an organized religious group, a community, a state, a nation, or a planet; or even, a world.

> *I charge thee therefore before God, and the Lord Jesus Christ, who shall judge the quick and the dead at his appearing and his kingdom; Preach the word; be instant in season, out of season;*

> *reprove, rebuke, exhort with all longsuffering and doctrine. For the time will come when they will not endure sound doctrine; but after their own lusts shall they heap to themselves teachers, having itching ears; And they shall turn away their ears from the truth, and shall be turned unto fables. But watch thou in all things, endure afflictions, do the work of an evangelist, make full proof of thy ministry.*
>
> (2 Timothy 4:1-5)

God, first; ourselves, second; and the church, third: why are they written in that order?

We are true to God first because there will be times when we cannot even believe that we are where we are. However, during those times, God still lets us know that we need something more; and that this can only come from Him. Then, we will answer as this father did: *Lord, I believe; help thou mine unbelief.*

> *And they brought him unto him: and when he saw him, straightway the spirit tare him; and he fell on the ground, and wallowed foaming.*
>
> *And he asked his father, How long is it ago since this came unto him? And he said, Of a child. And ofttimes it hath cast him into the fire, and into the waters, to destroy him: but if thou canst do any thing, have compassion on us, and help us.*
>
> *Jesus said unto him, If thou canst believe, all things are possible to him that believeth.*
>
> *And straightway the father of the child cried out, and said with tears, Lord, I believe; help thou mine unbelief.*
>
> (Mark 9:20-24)

Next, when God shows us his answer to our prayer, we must be honest with our self: people have this tendency to say that it is "the other guy". When we have been convicted of God that there is a problem, let us look to ourselves to see if we are a part of the problem, or if we are the whole problem. Until you know that it is not you, do not look out into the world to see who is causing the problem.

> *Judge not, that ye be not judged. For with what judgment ye judge, ye shall be judged: and with what measure ye mete, it shall be measured to you again.*
>
> *And why beholdest thou the mote that is in thy brother's eye, but considerest not the beam that is in thine own eye? Or how wilt thou say to thy brother, Let me pull out the mote out of thine eye; and, behold, a beam is in thine own eye?*
>
> *Thou hypocrite, first cast out the beam out of thine own eye; and then shalt thou see clearly to cast out the mote out of thy brother's eye.*
>
> (Matthew 7:1-5)

Then, once we either know that it is not us, or we have yielded to God and He has empowered us to remove the beam from our eye, then we may proceed. If we still see the problem in society at large, we must understand that we are now an empowered individual. As an empowered individual, it is our responsibility to make ourselves available to God to empower others. This is how mankind is empowered. It is done by the one-on-one empowerment of individuals by God, who are then sent forth to empower others, according to the Spirit of God. We, in the Holy Ghost, are the empowerment of mankind.

> *Also I heard the voice of the Lord, saying, Whom shall I send, and who will go for us?*
>
> *Then said I, Here am I; send me.*
>
> (Isaiah 6:8)

The Word from the Bible

Isaiah 45:11-17

Thus saith the LORD, the Holy One of Israel, and his Maker, Ask me of things to come concerning my sons, and concerning the work of my hands command ye me. I have made the earth, and created man upon it: I, even my hands, have stretched out the heavens, and all their host have I commanded. I have raised him up in righteousness, and I will direct all his ways: he shall build my city, and he shall let go my captives, not for price nor reward, saith the LORD of hosts.

Thus saith the LORD, The labour of Egypt, and merchandise of Ethiopia and of the Sabeans, men of stature, shall come over unto thee, and they shall be thine: they shall come after thee; in chains they shall come over, and they shall fall down unto thee, they shall make supplication unto thee, saying, Surely God is in thee; and there is none else, there is no God.

Verily thou art a God that hidest thyself, O God of Israel, the Saviour. They shall be ashamed, and also confounded, all of them: they shall go to confusion together that are makers of idols. But Israel shall be saved in the LORD with an everlasting salvation: ye shall not be ashamed nor confounded world without end.

Ephesians 3:14-21

For this cause I bow my knees unto the Father of our Lord Jesus Christ, Of whom the whole family in heaven and earth is named, That he would grant you, according to the riches of his glory, to be strengthened with might by his Spirit in the inner man; That Christ may dwell in your hearts by faith; that ye, being rooted and grounded in love, May be able to comprehend with all saints what is the breadth, and length, and depth, and height; And to know the love of Christ, which passeth knowledge, that ye might be filled with all the fulness of God.

Now unto him that is able to do exceeding abundantly above all that we ask or think, according to the power that worketh in us, Unto him be glory in the church by Christ Jesus throughout all ages, world without end. Amen.

Genesis 8:20-22

And Noah builded an altar unto the LORD; and took of every clean beast, and of every clean fowl, and offered burnt offerings on the altar.

And the LORD smelled a sweet savour; and the LORD said in his heart, I will not again curse the ground any more for man's sake; for the imagination of man's heart is evil from his youth; neither will I again smite any more every thing living, as I have done. While the earth remaineth, seedtime and harvest, and cold and heat, and summer and winter, and day and night shall not cease.

CHAPTER ELEVEN

Revelation

What to Expect Now

God said that he would not again destroy all mankind. This is another statement from God to which I strongly cling; not for my sake alone, but for the sake of all mankind. Fellow humans; please keep moving forward. Trust in God. He will show you the way, and give you ample time to clearly understand it. This is my prayer; in Jesus name, and for his sake.

> *And God spake unto Noah, and to his sons with him, saying, And I, behold, I establish my covenant with you, and with your seed after you; And with every living creature that is with you, of the fowl, of the cattle, and of every beast of the earth with you; from all that go out of the ark, to every beast of the earth. And I will establish my covenant with you; neither shall all flesh be cut off any more by the waters of a flood; neither shall there any more be a flood to destroy the earth.*

> *And God said, This is the token of the covenant which I make between me and you and every living creature that is with you, for perpetual generations: I do set my bow in the cloud, and it shall be for a token of a covenant between me and the earth. And it shall come to pass, when I bring a cloud over the earth, that the bow shall be seen in the cloud: And I will remember my covenant, which is between me and you and every living creature of all flesh; and the waters shall no more become a flood to destroy all flesh. And the bow shall be in the cloud; and I will look upon it, that*

> *I may remember the everlasting covenant between God and every living creature of all flesh that is upon the earth.*
>
> *And God said unto Noah, This is the token of the covenant, which I have established between me and all flesh that is upon the earth.*
> (Genesis 9:8-17)

God will not *again smite any more every thing living*. As recorded in the Bible, God also says that *While the earth remaineth, seedtime and harvest, and cold and heat, and summer and winter, and day and night shall not cease.* (Genesis 8:22) God always performs his promises. Mankind is not so consistent in performing its obligations. Even so, we are required by God to be caretakers of the earth. The ball is in our court.

Mankind has, within its power, the means to destroy its tenure on earth; directly, by destructive bombing, or indirectly, by making the earth uninhabitable for humans. This would not be an act of God; it would be one that is of man. If we truly honor God, we must live every day, every minute, even every second with the knowledge that we owe Him the best we can do. Maybe, just maybe, if we ask Him nicely; He will not let us destroy what He has built for us. Maybe, just maybe; He will compensate for our ignorance. Maybe, just maybe, He will do that; if we ask Him nicely.

Now, if you follow God with the intention of escaping destruction, you are missing the message. Furthermore, to cling to God because you may be left behind is not to follow God, at all. In that fear, you are not following anything: you are running from something. The only way to follow God is as we follow our good fathers on this earth. We must follow God because He made the Way. This is the same Way that He gave us through the Lord Jesus Christ. This is the Way that we must demonstrate to others.

It is not sufficient for us to just tell others to follow the way of the Gospel; they must see it, in us. They do not see it by hearing us tell them to run from the destruction that some think is written in the book of Revelation and other prophetic texts. This prophetic destruction is complete, and ended with the first century devastation in Jerusalem and, later, the unrepentant Roman Empire. Moreover, any additional destruction that may come is in the Hand of God, and it is superseded by the peace that we have in the Lord Jesus Christ. This is the way it must be; especially, in the church of Christ.

Now, in this time, too, the Kingdom of God, in the Lord Jesus Christ, is with us; and it is the eternal Kingdom. Let us all, as individuals and as ambassadors, say, to ourselves and to others, the words Simon Peter used to give an answer to the Lord.

> *From that time many of his disciples went back, and walked no more with him.*
>
> *Then said Jesus unto the twelve, Will ye also go away?*
>
> *Then Simon Peter answered him,*
>
> *Lord, to whom shall we go? thou hast the words of eternal life. And we believe and are sure that thou art that Christ, the Son of the living God.*
>
> (John 6:66-69)

We turn to Jesus, and the Gospel, to deliver us to God. The message is not to turn to Christ because he has the way to escape destruction. Rather, our advice to the world is that each member of it must come to Christ because he has the way to life. This is life eternal with the Spirit of truth, which is of the Spirits of God. This is our life eternal: to be caught up in the Holy Ghost. And this life eternal is in full effect, now.

> *Jesus said unto her, I am the resurrection, and the life: he that believeth in me, though he were dead, yet shall he live: And whosoever liveth and believeth in me shall never die.*
>
> *Believest thou this?*
>
> (John 11:25-26)

What if this is all that there is? What if this world, as we see it now, with all its problems and issues, is all we have to work with for the "to everlasting" of mankind? I believe that it is. Coming to this point is the most difficult thing that has ever been done to me. Some part of me feels cheated at this thought.

I am of the order of those who listened to the powerful stories about Christ coming with things like the Rapture, the human false prophet, some man who would be ***the Anti-christ***, and other such earth shaking things. Then, into the middle of all this chaos, I was told; Jesus would fly through the air, and establish a new world order on the earth. No man told me that all this has already happened.

Then, when I was educated by the Truth, I said to the Spirit, "What do I do now, since this is it? What do I do, knowing that this earth, as it is now, is what the diversity of mankind, which resides on this earth, will have to work with for an eternity? Can this earth, as it is, hold the substance of the eternal Kingdom?" I needed an answer. I requested one from God the Father. Walk with me, please, as I summarize the answer that was given to me through the Holy Ghost.

Speaking through the prophet and king, David, God stated that He would take care of Christ's enemies. After that, an eternal Kingdom would be established.

> *I will declare the decree: the LORD hath said unto me, Thou art my Son; this day have I begotten thee. Ask of me, and I shall give thee the heathen for thine inheritance, and the uttermost parts of the earth for thy possession.*
>
> (Psalm 2:7-8)

> *A Psalm of David.*
>
> *The LORD said unto my Lord, Sit thou at my right hand, until I make thine enemies thy footstool.*
>
> *The LORD shall send the rod of thy strength out of Zion: rule thou in the midst of thine enemies. Thy people shall be willing in the day of thy power, in the beauties of holiness from the womb of the morning: thou hast the dew of thy youth. The LORD hath sworn, and will not repent, Thou art a priest for ever after the order of Melchizedek.*

The Lord at thy right hand shall strike through kings in the day of his wrath. He shall judge among the heathen, he shall fill the places with the dead bodies; he shall wound the heads over many countries. He shall drink of the brook in the way: therefore shall he lift up the head.

(Psalm 110:1-7)

Well, if the Bible is to be believed as written, then we have a totally different future than the one that has been highly publicized under the catch phrase, *left behind.* The flow of this study of the Bible indicates that a totally different future is exactly what we have. With this in mind, let us look at where we are, keeping this in mind, as you go forward: *rule thou in the midst of thine enemies.*

We are definitely told that God will establish an eternal kingdom, and that His people will have dominion in that kingdom.

Thus he said, The fourth beast shall be the fourth kingdom upon earth, which shall be diverse from all kingdoms, and shall devour the whole earth, and shall tread it down, and break it in pieces. And the ten horns out of this kingdom are ten kings that shall arise: and another shall rise after them; and he shall be diverse from the first, and he shall subdue three kings. And he shall speak great words against the most High, and shall wear out the saints of the most High, and think to change times and laws: and they shall be given into his hand until a time and times and the dividing of time. But the judgment shall sit, and they shall take away his dominion, to consume and to destroy it unto the end.

And the kingdom and dominion, and the greatness of the kingdom under the whole heaven, shall be given to the people of the saints of the most High, whose kingdom is an everlasting kingdom, and all dominions shall serve and obey him. Hitherto is the end of the matter.

As for me Daniel, my cogitations much troubled me, and my countenance changed in me: but I kept the matter in my heart.
(Daniel 7:23-28)

If the world around us is in the eternal Kingdom, how is it possible that Christ is ruling now? Also, as we look at things from the perspective of the nation of Israel, we have other questions. It might be that, by a study of the words of the Gospel, as they pertain to the nation of Israel, we may be able to discover the next level of the interaction of God with man. This seems to be a good place to start, because Israel housed a kingdom formed by God under an Old Covenant, in an Old Testament. We want to expand from there, into the New Covenant.

According to a New Testament, in which there is a New Covenant, the Gospel tells of a Kingdom that is built on the being that was formed of the Holy Ghost of God. The, being that is of Divine birth, is Jesus of Nazareth, called the Christ, the Son of man, and the Son of God. Though, before we proceed further, let us review two portions of the New Covenant. First is provision for the people of God.

Behold, the days come, saith the LORD, that I will make a new covenant with the house of Israel, and with the house of Judah: Not according to the covenant that I made with their fathers in the day that I took them by the hand to bring them out of the land of Egypt; which my covenant they brake, although I was an husband unto them, saith the LORD: But this shall be the covenant that I will make with the house of Israel; After those days, saith the LORD, I will put my law in their inward parts, and write it in their hearts; and will be their God, and they shall be my people.

And they shall teach no more every man his neighbour, and every man his brother, saying, Know the LORD: for they shall all know me, from the least of them unto the greatest of them, saith the LORD: for I will forgive their iniquity, and I will remember their sin no more.
(Jeremiah 31:31-34)

Next, there is a promise of a Heavenly example for the behavior, ministries and missions of the people of God.

Nevertheless the dimness shall not be such as was in her vexation, when at the first he lightly afflicted the land of Zebulun and the land of Naphtali, and afterward did more grievously afflict her by the way of the sea, beyond Jordan, in Galilee of the nations. The people that walked in darkness have seen a great light: they that dwell in the land of the shadow of death, upon them hath the light shined.

Thou hast multiplied the nation, and not increased the joy: they joy before thee according to the joy in harvest, and as men rejoice when they divide the spoil. For thou hast broken the yoke of his burden, and the staff of his shoulder, the rod of his oppressor, as in the day of Midian.

For every battle of the warrior is with confused noise, and garments rolled in blood; but this shall be with burning and fuel of fire. For unto us a child is born, unto us a son is given: and the government shall be upon his shoulder: and his name shall be called Wonderful, Counsellor, The mighty God, The everlasting Father, The Prince of Peace. Of the increase of his government and peace there shall be no end, upon the throne of David, and upon his kingdom, to order it, and to establish it with judgment and with justice from henceforth even for ever. The zeal of the LORD of hosts will perform this.

(Isaiah 9:1-7)

Let us start down this path of greater understanding of the New Covenant, with a question from Scripture. It came from the disciples, and was asked in order for them to obtain understanding of when the kingdom would be restored to Israel.

When they therefore were come together, they asked of him, saying, Lord, wilt thou at this time restore again the kingdom to Israel?

And he said unto them, It is not for you to know the times or the seasons, which the Father hath put in his own power.

(Acts 1:6-7)

With Israel as the center of it, this is an important question for us, too; because Christ's mission was mainly to the lost sheep of Israel. Though, occasionally Jesus did undertake a brief extension, here.

> *Then Jesus went thence, and departed into the coasts of Tyre and Sidon. And, behold, a woman of Canaan came out of the same coasts, and cried unto him, saying, Have mercy on me, O Lord, thou son of David; my daughter is grievously vexed with a devil.*
>
> *But he answered her not a word.*
> *And his disciples came and besought him, saying, Send her away; for she crieth after us.*
> *But he answered and said, I am not sent but unto the lost sheep of the house of Israel.*
>
> *Then came she and worshipped him, saying, Lord, help me.*
> *But he answered and said, It is not meet to take the children's bread, and to cast it to dogs.*
> *And she said, Truth, Lord: yet the dogs eat of the crumbs which fall from their masters' table.*
> *Then Jesus answered and said unto her, O woman, great is thy faith: be it unto thee even as thou wilt.*
> *And her daughter was made whole from that very hour.*
> (Matthew 15:21-28)

Thus, in that fashion, Jesus did allow for the entry into his grace of others who were not an obvious part of his kingdom because she was not a lost sheep of the tribes of Israel. Other folks that were like the woman of Canaan who we have just read about, include a Samaritan and a Centurion. By Jesus' ministry to them, we know that the total mission was more than just to provide for the lost sheep of Israel; however, it is significant that Jesus' ministry did start there. This is obvious, in that eleven (possibly twelve) of the twelve disciples were of *the lost sheep of the house of Israel.* These were the first of the lost sheep for which the Son of God extended his presence to be widely seen in the earth.

> *Jesus answered them, Have not I chosen you twelve, and one of you is a devil? He spake of Judas Iscariot the son of Simon: for he it was that should betray him, being one of the twelve.*
>
> (John 6:70-71)

As we know, once Jesus had made provision for the children of Israel, in the persons of the twelve disciples, a group of seventy, as well as many others among the Hebrew nation. Then, Jesus sent an apostle to take care of the rest of the world. Yes, Jesus came to retrieve the lost sheep of Israel, but the total mission, which was given to him by God, included many more than that.

> *I am the good shepherd, and know my sheep, and am known of mine. As the Father knoweth me, even so know I the Father: and I lay down my life for the sheep.*
>
> *And other sheep I have, which are not of this fold: them also I must bring, and they shall hear my voice; and there shall be one fold, and one shepherd.*
>
> *Therefore doth my Father love me, because I lay down my life, that I might take it again. No man taketh it from me, but I lay it down of myself. I have power to lay it down, and I have power to take it again. This commandment have I received of my Father.*
>
> (John 10:14-18)

Thus, through the other sheep, which are not of this fold, Jesus' service to God continues beyond Israel, and even beyond his physical manifestation on earth. From this extension of the mission of Jesus to Israel, we will find the answer to the question of Christ's kingdom. But, before we go to logic derived from the Bible, let us hear the words of the Christ of the Bible.

> *Then Pilate entered into the judgment hall again, and called Jesus, and said unto him, Art thou the King of the Jews?*
>
> *Jesus answered him, Sayest thou this thing of thyself, or did others tell it thee of me?*

Pilate answered, Am I a Jew? Thine own nation and the chief priests have delivered thee unto me: what hast thou done?

Jesus answered, My kingdom is not of this world: if my kingdom were of this world, then would my servants fight, that I should not be delivered to the Jews: but now is my kingdom not from hence.

Pilate therefore said unto him, Art thou a king then?

Jesus answered, Thou sayest that I am a king.

To this end was I born, and for this cause came I into the world, that I should bear witness unto the truth. Every one that is of the truth heareth my voice.

(John 18:33-37)

My kingdom is not of this world: how can humans be a part of a kingdom that is not of this world? Is there any precedent in Scripture that we can use as an example?

Yes, there is an example. In the ancient time, shortly before it became a nation, the congregation of Israel was ruled by God; and they were as humans as we are. When the nation of Israel made a move away from God by selecting a king, it was made clear that God had been directly ruling over infant Israel. This is the message contained in the words that God gave to Samuel. God told Samuel that they were not rejecting him, but they were rejecting their true ruler, God.

Then all the elders of Israel gathered themselves together, and came to Samuel unto Ramah, And said unto him, Behold, thou art old, and thy sons walk not in thy ways: now make us a king to judge us like all the nations.

But the thing displeased Samuel, when they said, Give us a king to judge us. And Samuel prayed unto the LORD.

And the LORD said unto Samuel, Hearken unto the voice of the people in all that they say unto thee: for they have not rejected thee, but they have rejected me, that I should not reign over them.

(1 Samuel 8:4-7)

In God's reign over Israel, He did not physically sit on a throne in the presence of the people, and issue orders to them. God raised up representatives to take His rule, and His righteousness, to the people. He was the original absentee Landlord, as speaking from a human perspective. Though the LORD God owns all that is counted as belonging to the people of Israel, He never appeared in person, in the sight of the people.

Yes, the LORD'S power was obvious everywhere in Israel, but His "body" was shrouded from their eyes. Now, do not become angry with Him for this. If He had not done it in this fashion, everybody there would have been dead. Moses, the one man who saw the similitude of God, received the word about this limitation, and he relayed the information to all mankind.

> *And the LORD spake unto Moses face to face, as a man speaketh unto his friend. And he turned again into the camp: but his servant Joshua, the son of Nun, a young man, departed not out of the tabernacle. And Moses said unto the LORD, See, thou sayest unto me, Bring up this people: and thou hast not let me know whom thou wilt send with me. Yet thou hast said, I know thee by name, and thou hast also found grace in my sight. Now therefore, I pray thee, if I have found grace in thy sight, shew me now thy way, that I may know thee, that I may find grace in thy sight: and consider that this nation is thy people.*
>
> *And he said, My presence shall go with thee, and I will give thee rest.*
>
> *And he said unto him, If thy presence go not with me, carry us not up hence. For wherein shall it be known here that I and thy people have found grace in thy sight? is it not in that thou goest with us? so shall we be separated, I and thy people, from all the people that are upon the face of the earth.*
>
> *And the LORD said unto Moses, I will do this thing also that thou hast spoken: for thou hast found grace in my sight, and I know thee by name.*
>
> *And he said, I beseech thee, shew me thy glory.*

And he said, I will make all my goodness pass before thee, and I will proclaim the name of the LORD before thee; and will be gracious to whom I will be gracious, and will shew mercy on whom I will shew mercy. And he said, Thou canst not see my face: for there shall no man see me, and live.

And the LORD said, Behold, there is a place by me, and thou shalt stand upon a rock: And it shall come to pass, while my glory passeth by, that I will put thee in a clift of the rock, and will cover thee with my hand while I pass by: And I will take away mine hand, and thou shalt see my back parts: but my face shall not be seen.

(Exodus 33:11-23)

This lesson in effective performance of control from afar and without visible presence, is one that Jesus Christ received while he was with the Father; from before the foundation of the world. Furthermore, Jesus learned that, in heading toward perfection, we must collect and use the things and methods of God, to give us a richer relationship with Him. And Jesus was all about a rich relationship with God. He had always had such a relationship, and he was not about to do anything, or to let anyone else do anything, to disrupt this.

Satan tried to interrupt the relationship of the Son with the Father (remember the promises of grandeur that Satan presented to Jesus, which he did indeed have the authority to deliver). For Jesus Christ, the relationship with his Father greatly overshadowed Satan's temptations.

Remember also, Satan tried to take over one of the disciples; but, Jesus prayed for him, and repelled Satan.

And the Lord said, Simon, Simon, behold, Satan hath desired to have you, that he may sift you as wheat: But I have prayed for thee, that thy faith fail not: and when thou art converted, strengthen thy brethren.

(Luke 22:31-32)

This is the power of the man who was sent from God, as the Messiah. This power is reflected in his ability to use the methods of the Father, in order to perform the Father's work. As the Father ruled Israel from the Heavens, so also can the Son rule the heathen (also known as the Gentile) from his place by the Father in Heaven. As Moses gave the children of Israel the Law; in like fashion, Jesus Christ delivered the message of the Father to his followers. In this way, the message—also known as the Gospel of the Kingdom—provides the words of the rule of the Son of God. This is the rule of the Spirit, and not of the flesh.

The Gospel of the Kingdom is the sword of Jesus' mouth that is written in our hearts, wherefore we no longer need to depend on scrolls, tablets or paper. The Gospel is refreshed and renewed by the indwelling presence of the Holy Ghost; which was sent by God the Father, at the request of the Son. The Holy Ghost was not just sent here to make us feel good. The Holy Ghost was sent to empower us to transform the world to Christ Jesus. For, to transform the world, is the commandment of Jesus Christ. Call it the condition of employment, if you will.

We have been called to service by Jesus Christ. The Father has equipped us with the power of the Holy Ghost. It is now time for us to use it, and to use it in its fullness.

> *But ye shall receive power, after that the Holy Ghost is come upon you: and ye shall be witnesses unto me both in Jerusalem, and in all Judaea, and in Samaria, and unto the uttermost part of the earth.*
>
> (Acts 1:8)

Even though the world seems to be, collectively, trying to resurrect hell; God is still in control. Hell is in the lake of fire, along with all those other things. The Son of God now rules in the Kingdom of God, in which the kingdom of man resides and to which it is subservient. The Son of God, Jesus Christ, rules through the power and presence of the Holy Ghost in regenerate man. In case I did not say it before, let me do so now: ***This is active now.***

> *Jesus answered and said unto him, If a man love me, he will keep my words: and my Father will love him, and we will come unto him, and make our abode with him. He that loveth me not keepeth not my sayings: and the word which ye hear is not mine, but the Father's which sent me.*

> *These things have I spoken unto you, being yet present with you. But the Comforter, which is the Holy Ghost, whom the Father will send in my name, he shall teach you all things, and bring all things to your remembrance, whatsoever I have said unto you.*
>
> *Peace I leave with you, my peace I give unto you: not as the world giveth, give I unto you. Let not your heart be troubled, neither let it be afraid.*
>
> (John 14:23-27)

On this journey, we have tracked mankind through various stages of growth. For all mankind, this is visible in the example of the nation of Israel. This nation moved from the womb of Egypt, on to adulthood, and then it tried to establish its own way, without regard for God. In like fashion, mankind has entered the adulthood of its expectations from God. We can no longer sit back and whine; saying that we do not know what we must do. For those who are true believers in Christ Jesus; if you say that (and I hope you never do), you are insulting the Holy Ghost, and through that process you are insulting God.

The power that God released to us in the Holy Ghost is not the power that would be given to a child. The power that God released to us in the Holy Ghost is the power that is manifested in the life of an adult, in reality. No, this does not mean that we will do everything right; but it does mean that we have no excuse for doing nothing. We must walk in God, in the fashion described in the statement made by the apostle Paul—we must put away childish things.

> *Charity never faileth: but whether there be prophecies, they shall fail; whether there be tongues, they shall cease; whether there be knowledge, it shall vanish away. For we know in part, and we prophesy in part. But when that which is perfect is come, then that which is in part shall be done away.*
>
> *When I was a child, I spake as a child, I understood as a child, I thought as a child: but when I became a man, I put away childish things.*
>
> (1 Corinthians 13:8-11)

Many of us seem to be looking to Jesus to solve a problem for which he has already provided the answer. Mankind does not need to be destroyed as a part of reality, in order to fix the problems of mankind. The real need is for the Holy Ghost to dwell in all mankind. This is the beginning, if not the complete substance, of the glorified body.

Imagine the early Christians, when they started to see the message of Christ fulfilled. Flee with those who left Jerusalem before the destruction. Praise God with them, in their knowledge that Jesus had given them clear signs to watch for. Understand with them, as they come to fully trust in God, knowing that the power they hold is indeed the power of God. Move forward with them as they go out to sway the world to the way of the Lord, for its own good. If you can do this, you will know that they were indeed changed: and this, done in an instant.

> *Behold, I show you a mystery; We shall not all sleep, but we shall all be changed, In a moment, in the twinkling of an eye, at the last trump: for the trumpet shall sound, and the dead shall be raised incorruptible, and we shall be changed. For this corruptible must put on incorruption, and this mortal must put on immortality.*
>
> *So when this corruptible shall have put on incorruption, and this mortal shall have put on immortality, then shall be brought to pass the saying that is written, Death is swallowed up in victory. O death, where is thy sting? O grave, where is thy victory?*
>
> *The sting of death is sin; and the strength of sin is the law. But thanks be to God, which giveth us the victory through our Lord Jesus Christ. Therefore, my beloved brethren, be ye stedfast, unmoveable, always abounding in the work of the Lord, forasmuch as ye know that your labour is not in vain in the Lord.*
>
> (1 Corinthians 15:51-58)

When we fully deliver our offering of service to God, according to the Great Commission, on the microscopic level as well as the macroscopic level, then there will be no need for Rapture, or for any other major upheaval in the system of mankind. This offering of service must be done in the flow that Jesus mentioned. Let us go through it, once again.

> *Afterward he appeared unto the eleven as they sat at meat, and upbraided them with their unbelief and hardness of heart, because they believed not them which had seen him after he was risen. And he said unto them,*
>
> *Go ye into all the world, and preach the gospel to every creature. He that believeth and is baptized shall be saved; but he that believeth not shall be damned.*
>
> *And these signs shall follow them that believe; In my name shall they cast out devils; they shall speak with new tongues; They shall take up serpents; and if they drink any deadly thing, it shall not hurt them; they shall lay hands on the sick, and they shall recover.*
>
> *So then after the Lord had spoken unto them, he was received up into heaven, and sat on the right hand of God.*
>
> *And they went forth, and preached every where, the Lord working with them, and confirming the word with signs following. Amen.*
>
> (Mark 16:14-20)

The words for that time, then, are, too, the words for us now.

> *Go ye therefore, and teach all nations, baptizing them in the name of the Father, and of the Son, and of the Holy Ghost: Teaching them to observe all things whatsoever I have commanded you: and, lo, I am with you alway, even unto the end of the world. Amen.*
>
> (Matthew 28:19-20)

Jesus told us that *ye shall witnesses unto me both in Jerusalem* . . . (at home, with the family, and others who are near us) . . .

> *While he yet talked to the people, behold, his mother and his brethren stood without, desiring to speak with him. Then one said unto him, Behold, thy mother and thy brethren stand without, desiring to speak with thee.*

But he answered and said unto him that told him, Who is my mother? and who are my brethren?

And he stretched forth his hand toward his disciples, and said,

Behold my mother and my brethren! For whosoever shall do the will of my Father which is in heaven, the same is my brother, and sister, and mother.

(Matthew 12:46-50)

. . . *and in all Judaea* . . . (in the broader community) . . .

And, behold, a certain lawyer stood up, and tempted him, saying, Master, what shall I do to inherit eternal life?

He said unto him, What is written in the law? how readest thou?

And he answering said, Thou shalt love the Lord thy God with all thy heart, and with all thy soul, and with all thy strength, and with all thy mind; and thy neighbour as thyself.

And he said unto him, Thou hast answered right: this do, and thou shalt live.

But he, willing to justify himself, said unto Jesus, And who is my neighbour?

And Jesus answering said, A certain man went down from Jerusalem to Jericho, and fell among thieves, which stripped him of his raiment, and wounded him, and departed, leaving him half dead. And by chance there came down a certain priest that way: and when he saw him, he passed by on the other side. And likewise a Levite, when he was at the place, came and looked on him, and passed by on the other side. But a certain Samaritan, as he journeyed, came where he was: and when he saw him, he had compassion on him, And went to him, and bound up his wounds, pouring in oil and wine, and set him on his own beast, and brought him to an inn, and took care of him. And on the morrow when he departed, he took out two pence, and gave them to the host, and said unto him, Take care of him; and whatsoever thou spendest more, when I come again, I will repay thee.

Which now of these three, thinkest thou, was neighbour unto him that fell among the thieves?
And he said, He that shewed mercy on him.
Then said Jesus unto him, Go, and do thou likewise.
(Luke 10:25-37)

. . . *and in Samaria* . . . (to our unbelieving neighbor) . . .

And if any man will sue thee at the law, and take away thy coat, let him have thy cloak also. And whosoever shall compel thee to go a mile, go with him twain. Give to him that asketh thee, and from him that would borrow of thee turn not thou away.
(Matthew 5:40-42)

. . . *and unto the uttermost part of the earth* . . . (among those who have forgotten what is the solved mystery of God, in Jesus Christ).

Ye are the light of the world. A city that is set on an hill cannot be hid. Neither do men light a candle, and put it under a bushel, but on a candlestick; and it giveth light unto all that are in the house. Let your light so shine before men, that they may see your good works, and glorify your Father which is in heaven.
(Matthew 5:14-16)

However, let us not get this thing backwards. There are so many organizations and institutions that are sending folks to other countries, especially many that are in the United States of America. They say that they want the other people to know the Lord. Too often, this is a veiled attempt to rush God on that non-existent matter of the Rapture. They feel that if they can somehow preach what they consider to be the gospel, to every nook and cranny of the earth; then, Christ will be obligated to physically return, in accordance with their interpretation of the Bible. It is only fair, they think; after all, he did promise it.

Let me be a little generous here. Even if—which I will state for the record, Christ did not do—he had indicated that there would be some rapid removal of all Christians from the earth, prior to some cataclysmic disruption of the remainder of humanity; this still does not give you license to ignore the commandment, known as the Great Commission. This is a known commandment of the Lord Jesus Christ, and one which is easily understood from the text of the Bible. Let me be blunt here. ***We have not taken care of our house yet.*** Our Jerusalem is waiting.

Speaking of things that I see in the United States of America; we have not spread the Gospel to every part of our own house. What gives us the right to ignore our own families, in an attempt to impress someone else's family? How can we say that it is righteous to ignore the needs of our families, by sending our substance abroad to feed other families?

One simple example—oh, instead, let me ask some questions. Are there any hungry children in this country? Are there any sick children who have no hope of receiving care, in this country? Are there churches or other religious organizations around these children?

If the answer to those questions is, yes; then there is no excuse for sending even one dime to another country, not even to another area of this country, until the organizations and institutions of God have taken care of the problem that is staring them in the face. The nation is at real risk of suffocating itself in this type of behavior, and joining a certain flock of goats of the following Scripture. After you have read that Scripture; please take some time to research what happened to the goats of that time, on the left side of the Son of man.

> *When the Son of man shall come in his glory, and all the holy angels with him, then shall he sit upon the throne of his glory: And before him shall be gathered all nations: and he shall separate them one from another, as a shepherd divideth his sheep from the goats: And he shall set the sheep on his right hand, but the goats on the left.*
>
> (Matthew 25:31-33)

No, this is not saying that you will lose your salvation by your inaction, or by your incorrect action. However, this is telling you that God will not honor your work as being for him, since it has been laid on a carnal foundation. We need to stay with the faithful and true foundation.

> *For other foundation can no man lay than that is laid, which is Jesus Christ. Now if any man build upon this foundation gold,*

> *silver, precious stones, wood, hay, stubble; Every man's work shall be made manifest: for the day shall declare it, because it shall be revealed by fire; and the fire shall try every man's work of what sort it is.*
>
> *If any man's work abide which he hath built thereupon, he shall receive a reward.*
>
> *If any man's work shall be burned, he shall suffer loss: but he himself shall be saved; yet so as by fire.*
>
> (1 Corinthians 3:11-15)

Equally as urgent is the fact that there is a danger on a personal level for those who never really took care of that little matter of yielding to the way of Christ.

> *Not every one that saith unto me, Lord, Lord, shall enter into the kingdom of heaven; but he that doeth the will of my Father which is in heaven.*
>
> *Many will say to me in that day, Lord, Lord, have we not prophesied in thy name? and in thy name have cast out devils? and in thy name done many wonderful works? And then will I profess unto them, I never knew you: depart from me, ye that work iniquity.*
>
> *Therefore whosoever heareth these sayings of mine, and doeth them, I will liken him unto a wise man, which built his house upon a rock: And the rain descended, and the floods came, and the winds blew, and beat upon that house; and it fell not: for it was founded upon a rock. And every one that heareth these sayings of mine, and doeth them not, shall be likened unto a foolish man, which built his house upon the sand: And the rain descended, and the floods came, and the winds blew, and beat upon that house; and it fell: and great was the fall of it.*
>
> (Matthew 7:21-27)

Study the Bible. Your objective is to clearly understand your obligation to those who are of the family of God, first; and then, to understand your obligation to the remainder of humanity. Is this an exclusionist type statement? YES! Any member of any family has an obligation to be exclusionist as pertains to the welfare of other members of his or her family. This is not a negative; it is an aspect of being human; moreover, it is according to divinity. Until we can look God in the Spirit, and say that all is well with our house; we need to stop looking for problems in the rest of the world. God is not impressed with your ability to spread what belongs to your family, laying it over the rest of the world.

> *And he spake a parable unto them, Can the blind lead the blind? shall they not both fall into the ditch? The disciple is not above his master: but every one that is perfect shall be as his master. And why beholdest thou the mote that is in thy brother's eye, but perceivest not the beam that is in thine own eye? Either how canst thou say to thy brother, Brother, let me pull out the mote that is in thine eye, when thou thyself beholdest not the beam that is in thine own eye? Thou hypocrite, cast out first the beam out of thine own eye, and then shalt thou see clearly to pull out the mote that is in thy brother's eye.*
>
> (Luke 6:39-42)

However, when you have prayed to God for workers in your neighborhood, and when He has provided them; and when God does cleanse your house, and your neighborhood; then, go with boldness into the world. It is no accident that once active believers enter an area, there are major revivals. The spirits of the humans in the area are receiving a reminder of what they already knew. The history of God in their lives, and in the lives of their community, had been misfiled. We are just bringing it from the back of the file cabinet, to the desk, for review; as Paul did, here.

> *Then Paul stood in the midst of Mars' hill, and said, Ye men of Athens, I perceive that in all things ye are too superstitious. For as I passed by, and beheld your devotions, I found an altar with this inscription, TO THE UNKNOWN GOD. Whom therefore ye ignorantly worship, him declare I unto you.*
>
> *God that made the world and all things therein, seeing that he is Lord of heaven and earth, dwelleth not in temples made with hands; Neither is worshipped with men's hands, as though he needed any thing, seeing he giveth to all life, and breath, and all*

things; And hath made of one blood all nations of men for to dwell on all the face of the earth, and hath determined the times before appointed, and the bounds of their habitation; That they should seek the Lord, if haply they might feel after him, and find him, though he be not far from every one of us: For in him we live, and move, and have our being; as certain also of your own poets have said, For we are also his offspring.

(Acts 17:22-28)

What do we do now?
We pray, and live.

And Jesus went about all the cities and villages, teaching in their synagogues, and preaching the gospel of the kingdom, and healing every sickness and every disease among the people. But when he saw the multitudes, he was moved with compassion on them, because they fainted, and were scattered abroad, as sheep having no shepherd. Then saith he unto his disciples, The harvest truly is plenteous, but the labourers are few; Pray ye therefore the Lord of the harvest, that he will send forth labourers into his harvest.

(Matthew 9:35-38)

How do we do it?

And it came to pass, that, as he was praying in a certain place, when he ceased, one of his disciples said unto him, Lord, teach us to pray, as John also taught his disciples.

And he said unto them, When ye pray, say,

Our Father which art in heaven, Hallowed be thy name. Thy kingdom come. Thy will be done, as in heaven, so in earth. Give us day by day our daily bread. And forgive us our sins; for we also forgive every one that is indebted to us. And lead us not into temptation; but deliver us from evil.

(Luke 11:1-4)

We need to evaluate the full scope of the Lord's Prayer. This is what we must do; now that God has established His eternal Kingdom with man. The early Christians fulfilled the first part, for us. We have to continue with the latter part. Then, complete paradise will be re-opened to mankind on this earth. It will be a paradise of the mind, and of the spirit; and, of the Spirit.

> *And one of the malefactors which were hanged railed on him, saying, If thou be Christ, save thyself and us.*
>
> *But the other answering rebuked him, saying, Dost not thou fear God, seeing thou art in the same condemnation? And we indeed justly; for we receive the due reward of our deeds: but this man hath done nothing amiss. And he said unto Jesus, Lord, remember me when thou comest into thy kingdom.*
>
> *And Jesus said unto him, Verily I say unto thee, To day shalt thou be with me in paradise.*
>
> (Luke 23:39-43)

When we truly enter the service of God according to the commandments of Jesus Christ, we will have more than enough work to do in his service. We will be so busy that we will not want any Rapture; since, for our spirit, it would only be a thing that would disrupt the flow of God's goodness to the world. Even if Christ were to come, and announce to us that the Rapture is starting (which he WILL NOT); our response would be to ask him for more time. We will be so in love with God's power and majesty, as it fulfills the needs of all mankind; so much so that we will want to continue to share this power, in the love of God, as long as we can. The apostle Paul stated it much better than I can. Think about this, and live in Christ.

> *According to my earnest expectation and my hope, that in nothing I shall be ashamed, but that with all boldness, as always, so now also Christ shall be magnified in my body, whether it be by life, or by death. For to me to live is Christ, and to die is gain.*

But if I live in the flesh, this is the fruit of my labour: yet what I shall choose I wot not. For I am in a strait betwixt two, having a desire to depart, and to be with Christ; which is far better: Nevertheless to abide in the flesh is more needful for you. And having this confidence, I know that I shall abide and continue with you all for your furtherance and joy of faith; That your rejoicing may be more abundant in Jesus Christ for me by my coming to you again.
(Philippians 1:20-26)

The weapon of choice,
A threatening word,
To show other
Just how absurd

Are their efforts
To resist the plea
To order their life
As we say it must be.

They must live
According to the plan
That we say existed
Before there was man:

The plan that we say
Was established on earth,
To serve as the measure
For mankind's worth.

If they do not submit,
The result is dire:
They will spend eternity
In the lake of fire.

Then, in a flash of logic,
Things are rearranged;
As mankind's whims,
Over time, have changed.

But, if it is from God,
Who is unchanging,
Then why is its doctrine
Constantly rearranging?

We need a return
To the absolute source:
The ancient and holy one,
Which God did endorse:

As written in the blood
Of the righteous band
That spread Christ's love
Throughout the land.

Let us preach Jesus, only,
On whom we all depend;
As we move, on this earth,
In the world without end.

CHAPTER 11A

Heralding the Kingdom

Rightly Dividing Scripture

Luke 9:57-62

And it came to pass, that, as they went in the way, a certain man said unto him, Lord, I will follow thee whithersoever thou goest.

And Jesus said unto him, Foxes have holes, and birds of the air have nests; but the Son of man hath not where to lay his head. And he said unto another, Follow me.

But he said, Lord, suffer me first to go and bury my father.

Jesus said unto him, Let the dead bury their dead: but go thou and preach the kingdom of God.

And another also said, Lord, I will follow thee; but let me first go bid them farewell, which are at home at my house.

And Jesus said unto him, No man, having put his hand to the plough, and looking back, is fit for the kingdom of God.

Well what do we do, now that we do not have to keep looking to the skies for a host of beings descending upon us? Do we spend our time in a renewed state of depression because we will not receive the bonus of escape? Speaking of that word, *bonus*; might there be a lesson in that? I think so!

Let us say that all your friends told you that there was this really great job. They told you about the big bonuses they got; not to mention, the very decent salary. They convinced you to join them. You worked really hard, but at the end of the year, guess what? Of course, you guessed it: no bonus. "This can't be!" You had planned your life around that bonus. This is similar to what Jesus said about the Kingdom of Heaven.

> *For the kingdom of heaven is like unto a man that is an householder, which went out early in the morning to hire labourers into his vineyard. And when he had agreed with the labourers for a penny a day, he sent them into his vineyard.*
>
> *And he went out about the third hour, and saw others standing idle in the marketplace, And said unto them; Go ye also into the vineyard, and whatsoever is right I will give you. And they went their way.*
>
> *Again he went out about the sixth and ninth hour, and did likewise.*
>
> *And about the eleventh hour he went out, and found others standing idle, and saith unto them, Why stand ye here all the day idle?*
>
> *They say unto him, Because no man hath hired us.*
>
> *He saith unto them, Go ye also into the vineyard; and whatsoever is right, that shall ye receive.*
>
> *So when even was come, the lord of the vineyard saith unto his steward, Call the labourers, and give them their hire, beginning from the last unto the first. And when they came that were hired about the eleventh hour, they received every man a penny.*
>
> *But when the first came, they supposed that they should have received more; and they likewise received every man a penny. And when they had received it, they murmured against the goodman of the house, Saying, These last have wrought but one hour, and thou hast made them equal unto us, which have borne the burden and heat of the day.*
>
> *But he answered one of them, and said, Friend, I do thee no wrong: didst not thou agree with me for a penny? Take that thine*

is, and go thy way: I will give unto this last, even as unto thee. Is it not lawful for me to do what I will with mine own? Is thine eye evil, because I am good?

So the last shall be first, and the first last: for many be called, but few chosen.

(Matthew 20:1-16)

But, let us make it even worse. Let us say that you have charged many things on your credit cards because you just ***knew*** that there would be a bonus. Of course, you will quit that stupid job; won't you?

I THINK, NOT! However, this is what many people do with the Lord.

Why didn't you quit that stupid job; with no bonus?

Probably because of the salary it does give.

But, surely you will go to the management and ask them where that bonus is; won't you? You know something; that is just like what the disciples did.

Then answered Peter and said unto him, Behold, we have forsaken all, and followed thee; what shall we have therefore?

(Matthew 19:27)

However, in the world of being an employee; usually, this is not what we do. Why don't we do that?

We do not do that because we know that the bonus is not a part of either the explicit or implied contract of employment. We also understand that, in this world, there are rare occasions when we get a bonus for anything. Usually, we understand that if there is a company that gives any kind of bonus, it is also one that has many other benefits. At least this is what the disciples learned.

And Jesus said unto them, Verily I say unto you, That ye which have followed me, in the regeneration when the Son of man shall sit in the throne of his glory, ye also shall sit upon twelve thrones, judging the twelve tribes of Israel.

And every one that hath forsaken houses, or brethren, or sisters, or father, or mother, or wife, or children, or lands, for my name's sake, shall receive an hundredfold, and shall inherit everlasting life.

But many that are first shall be last; and the last shall be first.

(Matthew 19:28-30)

So, you don't "cut off your nose, to spite your face", as the saying goes. You continue to work in the company, and draw your salary. Besides, we all know that anyone who does not want to work because they cannot get what they want is not worth retaining as an employee; especially not, when there are so many other qualified candidates. Besides, we do not want to be an ungrateful lout, do we?

Now, let us tilt the focus even more away from the natural, toward the supernatural. We do this so that you will understand what it means to work in the company known as, the Kingdom of God. We will begin in the day of Jesus of Nazareth. Though, before we do, you need to know that in the day of Jesus of Nazareth, the landscape of the supernatural was slightly different than it is now. In his day, we were waiting for the "world to come". This started with John the Baptist.

In those days came John the Baptist, preaching in the wilderness of Judaea, And saying, Repent ye: for the kingdom of heaven is at hand. For this is he that was spoken of by the prophet Esaias, saying, The voice of one crying in the wilderness, Prepare ye the way of the Lord, make his paths straight.

(Matthew 3:1-3)

As John's ministry spread, our yearning for the new world was intensified. Then, in Jesus Christ, the meaning of our yearning was clarified, and given real immediacy.

And as they departed, Jesus began to say unto the multitudes concerning John, What went ye out into the wilderness to see? A reed shaken with the wind? But what went ye out for to see? A man clothed in soft raiment? behold, they that wear soft clothing are in kings' houses. But what went ye out for to see? A prophet? yea, I say unto you, and more than a prophet. For this is he, of whom it is written, Behold, I send my messenger before thy face, which shall prepare thy way before thee. Verily I say unto you, Among them that are born of women there hath not risen a greater than John the Baptist: notwithstanding he that is least in the kingdom of heaven is greater than he.

And from the days of John the Baptist until now the kingdom of heaven suffereth violence, and the violent take it by force. For all the prophets and the law prophesied until John.

And if ye will receive it, this is Elias, which was for to come. He that hath ears to hear, let him hear.

(Matthew 11:7-15)

Then, Jesus came to a significant fork in the road: he made a *choice* between the revelation of the Kingdom of God, and the continuation of the sovereignty of man—and of Satan over man. Blessedly, and most predictably, Jesus made the decision to endure in God's mission

And he came out, and went, as he was wont, to the mount of Olives; and his disciples also followed him. And when he was at the place, he said unto them, Pray that ye enter not into temptation. And he was withdrawn from them about a stone's cast, and kneeled down, and prayed, Saying, Father, if thou be willing, remove this cup from me: nevertheless not my will, but thine, be done.

And there appeared an angel unto him from heaven, strengthening him. And being in an agony he prayed more earnestly: and his sweat was as it were great drops of blood falling down to the ground.

(Luke 22:39-44)

As a result of Jesus' decision to persist in the Kingdom of God, he went to the cross. In the meantime, all Heaven was breaking loose: Satan was being dismissed, lessons were being prepared, and God was readying the fulfillment of His promises to His Son.

I will declare the decree: the LORD hath said unto me, Thou art my Son; this day have I begotten thee. Ask of me, and I shall give thee the heathen for thine inheritance, and the uttermost parts of the earth for thy possession.

(Psalm 2:7-8)

> *A Psalm of David.*
> *The LORD said unto my Lord, Sit thou at my right hand, until I make thine enemies thy footstool. The LORD shall send the rod of thy strength out of Zion: rule thou in the midst of thine enemies.*
> *Thy people shall be willing in the day of thy power, in the beauties of holiness from the womb of the morning: thou hast the dew of thy youth.*
> (Psalm 110:1-3)

Then it happened: Glory hit the fan of reality, and it was dispersed throughout the natural world. In that day, the Kingdom was sealed by a very simple statement from Jesus; the last one that he made from the cross.

> *When Jesus therefore had received the vinegar, he said, It is finished: and he bowed his head, and gave up the ghost.*
> (John 19:30)

It is finished: with the spiritual structure created, and the twelve gates—named after the twelve tribes of Israel—put in place; there were two other matters remaining. The first was to strengthen the foundation. This was done by sending forth the disciples; one in absentia, almost. These twelve went out into the world to deliver foundational truth—even, Judas Iscariot.

"What", you rhetorically declare, "that traitor Judas? He was dead at the time, and good riddance to him!"

On the contrary my friends and sibling in the Lord, Judas was very much alive. Just as the blood of Abel cried out to God, so, too, the blood of Judas also cried out. The blood of Judas has two lessons for us. The first is what can happen when we think we have a right to provide our own interpretation for God's mission. This happens when we think that we can modify God's purpose, by adding the flavoring of man to it. These attempts are just as pre-ordained to die as Judas was for his part in second-guessing the Lord of the universe. This is a foundational truth of Christianity. *He that hath ears to hear, let him hear.*

And then if any man shall say to you, Lo, here is Christ; or, lo, he is there; believe him not: For false Christs and false prophets shall rise, and shall shew signs and wonders, to seduce, if it were possible, even the elect. But take ye heed: behold, I have foretold you all things.

(Mark 13:21-23)

The second foundational truth of Judas tells of the absolute authority of Christ to forgive all sins done against him. Hear Jesus on this matter!

Wherefore I say unto you, All manner of sin and blasphemy shall be forgiven unto men: but the blasphemy against the Holy Ghost shall not be forgiven unto men. And whosoever speaketh a word against the Son of man, it shall be forgiven him: but whosoever speaketh against the Holy Ghost, it shall not be forgiven him, neither in this world, neither in the world to come.

(Matthew 12:31-32)

So, the foundation was laid, and the walls have gates in them. What, then, is left to do? Well, let us drop back to earth for a moment, and consider this: when we are about to deliver a mansion to a blighted area, we do not just drop the building down. Before delivering the mansion, we will do some urban renewal; we will revitalize the area. And that is what God did.

God cleaned out the old spiritual center: the temple in Jerusalem. Jesus, the prophet, had declared the coming of this event.

And Jesus went out, and departed from the temple: and his disciples came to him for to shew him the buildings of the temple. And Jesus said unto them, See ye not all these things? verily I say unto you, There shall not be left here one stone upon another, that shall not be thrown down.

(Matthew 24:1-2)

In that era, God totally displaced the main gang that was oppressing the followers of His Son—the gang that was the Roman Empire and that which is of the seven. This is the same gang that was attempting to suppress the spread of the Gospel of the Kingdom of God, in that day.

> *And the angel said unto me, Wherefore didst thou marvel? I will tell thee the mystery of the woman, and of the beast that carrieth her, which hath the seven heads and ten horns. The beast that thou sawest was, and is not; and shall ascend out of the bottomless pit, and go into perdition: and they that dwell on the earth shall wonder, whose names were not written in the book of life from the foundation of the world, when they behold the beast that was, and is not, and yet is. And here is the mind which hath wisdom.*
>
> *The seven heads are seven mountains, on which the woman sitteth. And there are seven kings: five are fallen, and one is, and the other is not yet come; and when he cometh, he must continue a short space. And the beast that was, and is not, even he is the eighth, and is of the seven, and goeth into perdition.*
>
> *And the ten horns which thou sawest are ten kings, which have received no kingdom as yet; but receive power as kings one hour with the beast. These have one mind, and shall give their power and strength unto the beast. These shall make war with the Lamb, and the Lamb shall overcome them: for he is Lord of lords, and King of kings: and they that are with him are called, and chosen, and faithful.*
>
> *And he saith unto me, The waters which thou sawest, where the whore sitteth, are peoples, and multitudes, and nations, and tongues.*
>
> *And the ten horns which thou sawest upon the beast, these shall hate the whore, and shall make her desolate and naked, and shall eat her flesh, and burn her with fire. For God hath put in their hearts to fulfil his will, and to agree, and give their kingdom unto the beast, until the words of God shall be fulfilled.*
>
> *And the woman which thou sawest is that great city, which reigneth over the kings of the earth.*
>
> (Revelation 17:7-18)

Then, God delivered the model home; the new spiritual center of religious worship: the new spiritual Jerusalem.

> *And I saw a new heaven and a new earth: for the first heaven and the first earth were passed away; and there was no more sea. And I*

John saw the holy city, new Jerusalem, coming down from God out of heaven, prepared as a bride adorned for her husband.
(Revelation 21:1-2)

Then, God started the process, as declared by His Son. The spiritual area upon which God has placed His name went through a massive construction process. This is a builder's dream; at least it is for those who can build on a spiritual level.

And I heard a great voice out of heaven saying, Behold, the tabernacle of God is with men, and he will dwell with them, and they shall be his people, and God himself shall be with them, and be their God. And God shall wipe away all tears from their eyes; and there shall be no more death, neither sorrow, nor crying, neither shall there be any more pain: for the former things are passed away.

And he that sat upon the throne said, Behold, I make all things new.

And he said unto me, Write: for these words are true and faithful.

And he said unto me, It is done. I am Alpha and Omega, the beginning and the end. I will give unto him that is athirst of the fountain of the water of life freely. He that overcometh shall inherit all things; and I will be his God, and he shall be my son.
(Revelation 21:3-7)

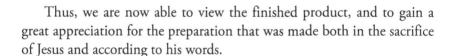

Thus, we are now able to view the finished product, and to gain a great appreciation for the preparation that was made both in the sacrifice of Jesus and according to his words.

Let not your heart be troubled: ye believe in God, believe also in me. In my Father's house are many mansions: if it were not so, I would have told you. I go to prepare a place for you. And if I go and prepare a place for you, I will come again, and receive you

> *unto myself; that where I am, there ye may be also. And whither I go ye know, and the way ye know.*
>
> (John 14:1-4)

And now, YOU ARE HERE (as is often written on directories in shopping malls). The eternal, spiritual kingdom of the Lord Jesus Christ is active now. This is our *salary* (*ask any thing in my name*), and our *bonus* (*another Comforter*).

> *Verily, verily, I say unto you, He that believeth on me, the works that I do shall he do also; and greater works than these shall he do; because I go unto my Father. And whatsoever ye shall ask in my name, that will I do, that the Father may be glorified in the Son. If ye shall ask any thing in my name, I will do it.*
>
> *If ye love me, keep my commandments. And I will pray the Father, and he shall give you another Comforter, that he may abide with you for ever; Even the Spirit of truth; whom the world cannot receive, because it seeth him not, neither knoweth him: but ye know him; for he dwelleth with you, and shall be in you.*
>
> (John 14:12-17)

We do not have to wait for some non-defined event, of a major disruptive nature. We have the clearly defined power to make all the descriptions of reality that we want to—in righteousness. For, we can do it as the force of one-in-one that is by ordinance of God, as proclaimed by His Son, Jesus Christ.

> *But ye shall receive power, after that the Holy Ghost is come upon you: and ye shall be witnesses unto me both in Jerusalem, and in all Judaea, and in Samaria, and unto the uttermost part of the earth.*
>
> (Acts 1:8)

As for earning this *salary* and *bonus*; all we have to do is to announce the Kingdom, in a fashion that is like the introduction of one of our most praiseworthy celebrities of this day. Then, the Kingdom will lay out its credentials in its own Voice, and in its own great power; for, it is fully live.

> *And he said unto them, Go ye into all the world, and preach the gospel to every creature. He that believeth and is baptized shall be saved; but he that believeth not shall be damned. And these signs shall follow them that believe; In my name shall they cast out devils; they shall speak with new tongues; They shall take up serpents; and if they drink any deadly thing, it shall not hurt them; they shall lay hands on the sick, and they shall recover.*
>
> *So then after the Lord had spoken unto them, he was received up into heaven, and sat on the right hand of God. And they went forth, and preached every where, the Lord working with them, and confirming the word with signs following.*
>
> *Amen.*
>
> (Mark 16:15-20)

Just be sure to wait for instruction from *the Spirit of your Father*, please, before you try to do this; because:

> *Behold, I send you forth as sheep in the midst of wolves: be ye therefore wise as serpents, and harmless as doves. But beware of men: for they will deliver you up to the councils, and they will scourge you in their synagogues; And ye shall be brought before governors and kings for my sake, for a testimony against them and the Gentiles.*
>
> *But when they deliver you up, take no thought how or what ye shall speak: for it shall be given you in that same hour what ye shall speak. For it is not ye that speak, but the Spirit of your Father which speaketh in you.*
>
> (Matthew 10:16-20)

This is the Dream Job!

> *And we know that all things work together for good to them that love God, to them who are the called according to his purpose. For whom he did foreknow, he also did predestinate to be conformed to*

the image of his Son, that he might be the firstborn among many brethren. Moreover whom he did predestinate, them he also called: and whom he called, them he also justified: and whom he justified, them he also glorified.

What shall we then say to these things? If God be for us, who can be against us?

(Romans 8:28-31)

In My Conclusion (Almost)

Daniel 7:15-28

I Daniel was grieved in my spirit in the midst of my body, and the visions of my head troubled me. I came near unto one of them that stood by, and asked him the truth of all this. So he told me, and made me know the interpretation of the things.

These great beasts, which are four, are four kings, which shall arise out of the earth. But the saints of the most High shall take the kingdom, and possess the kingdom for ever, even for ever and ever.

Then I would know the truth of the fourth beast, which was diverse from all the others, exceeding dreadful, whose teeth were of iron, and his nails of brass; which devoured, brake in pieces, and stamped the residue with his feet; And of the ten horns that were in his head, and of the other which came up, and before whom three fell; even of that horn that had eyes, and a mouth that spake very great things, whose look was more stout than his fellows. I beheld, and the same horn made war with the saints, and prevailed against them; Until the Ancient of days came, and judgment was given to the saints of the most High; and the time came that the saints possessed the kingdom.

Thus he said, The fourth beast shall be the fourth kingdom upon earth, which shall be diverse from all kingdoms, and shall devour the whole earth, and shall tread it down, and break it in pieces. And the ten horns out of this kingdom are ten kings that shall arise: and another shall rise after them; and he shall be diverse from the first, and he shall subdue three kings. And he shall speak great words against the most High, and shall wear out the saints of the most High, and think to change times and laws: and they shall be given into his hand until a time and times and the dividing of time. But the judgment shall sit, and they shall take away his dominion, to consume and to destroy it unto the end. And the kingdom and dominion, and the greatness of the kingdom under the whole heaven, shall be given to the people of the saints of the most High, whose kingdom is an everlasting kingdom, and all dominions shall serve and obey him. Hitherto is the end of the matter.

As for me Daniel, my cogitations much troubled me, and my countenance changed in me: but I kept the matter in my heart.

Revelation 17:7-18

And the angel said unto me, Wherefore didst thou marvel? I will tell thee the mystery of the woman, and of the beast that carrieth her, which hath the seven heads and ten horns. The beast that thou sawest was, and is not; and shall ascend out of the bottomless pit, and go into perdition: and they that dwell on the earth shall wonder, whose names were not written in the book of life from the foundation of the world, when they behold the beast that was, and is not, and yet is.

And here is the mind which hath wisdom. The seven heads are seven mountains, on which the woman sitteth. And there are seven kings: five are fallen, and one is, and the other is not yet come; and when he cometh, he must continue a short space. And the beast that was, and is not, even he is the eighth, and is of the seven, and goeth into perdition.

And the ten horns which thou sawest are ten kings, which have received no kingdom as yet; but receive power as kings one hour with the beast. These have one mind, and shall give their power and strength unto the beast. These shall make war with the Lamb, and the Lamb shall overcome them: for he is Lord of lords, and King of kings: and they that are with him are called, and chosen, and faithful.

And he saith unto me, The waters which thou sawest, where the whore sitteth, are peoples, and multitudes, and nations, and tongues. And the ten horns which thou sawest upon the beast, these shall hate the whore, and shall make her desolate and naked, and shall eat her flesh, and burn her with fire. For God hath put in their hearts to fulfil his will, and to agree, and give their kingdom unto the beast, until the words of God shall be fulfilled.

And the woman which thou sawest is that great city, which reigneth over the kings of the earth.

As I looked at this topic, I became more and more afraid. My fear was that God had allowed me to see an idea with no solution. I do not call it a problem because the answer was always known to God. Also, I had full confidence that the LORD will reveal it to one of His saints. So, I analyzed the idea that presented itself, and I determined that the answer is, Competition. When we study the children of Israel, we see many episodes of *falling away*; which are primarily a matter of competition. God said it.

> *But Jeshurun waxed fat, and kicked: thou art waxen fat, thou art grown thick, thou art covered with fatness; then he forsook God which made him, and lightly esteemed the Rock of his salvation. They provoked him to jealousy with strange gods, with abominations provoked they him to anger. They sacrificed unto devils, not to God; to gods whom they knew not, to new gods that came newly up, whom your fathers feared not. Of the Rock that begat thee thou art unmindful, and hast forgotten God that formed thee.*
> (Deuteronomy 32:15-18)

> *And when the LORD saw it, he abhorred them, because of the provoking of his sons, and of his daughters. And he said, I will hide my face from them, I will see what their end shall be: for they are a very froward generation, children in whom is no faith. They have moved me to jealousy with that which is not God; they have provoked me to anger with their vanities: and I will move them to jealousy with those which are not a people; I will provoke them to*

anger with a foolish nation. For a fire is kindled in mine anger, and shall burn unto the lowest hell, and shall consume the earth with her increase, and set on fire the foundations of the mountains.

I will heap mischiefs upon them; I will spend mine arrows upon them. They shall be burnt with hunger, and devoured with burning heat, and with bitter destruction: I will also send the teeth of beasts upon them, with the poison of serpents of the dust. The sword without, and terror within, shall destroy both the young man and the virgin, the suckling also with the man of gray hairs.

I said, I would scatter them into corners, I would make the remembrance of them to cease from among men: Were it not that I feared the wrath of the enemy, lest their adversaries should behave themselves strangely, and lest they should say, Our hand is high, and the LORD hath not done all this.

(Deuteronomy 32:19-27)

Competition creates an environment of alternatives. Competition is the order of our day. In this environment, there are all sorts of entities; including, people, groups, and organizations. It seems that everything competes with everything else. We, humans, have even taught the animals how to compete with one another. There are dog fights, bird soccer, hamster races, and all other manner of competition that we have manufactured in the animal kingdom. It was not enough for us that competition is destroying the fabric of humanity; we wanted more than just this . . .

From whence come wars and fightings among you? come they not hence, even of your lusts that war in your members? Ye lust, and have not: ye kill, and desire to have, and cannot obtain: ye fight and war, yet ye have not, because ye ask not. Ye ask, and receive not, because ye ask amiss, that ye may consume it upon your lusts. Ye adulterers and adulteresses, know ye not that the friendship of the world is enmity with God? whosoever therefore will be a friend of the world is the enemy of God.

(James 4:1-4)

. . . And we rejected the only sure solution to the negativity of unrestrained competition, as that solution is stated in Scripture.

> *Do ye think that the scripture saith in vain, The spirit that dwelleth in us lusteth to envy? But he giveth more grace. Wherefore he saith, God resisteth the proud, but giveth grace unto the humble.*
>
> *Submit yourselves therefore to God. Resist the devil, and he will flee from you. Draw nigh to God, and he will draw nigh to you. Cleanse your hands, ye sinners; and purify your hearts, ye double minded.*
>
> (James 4:5-8)

Then, it happened. Before we talk about the "then, it happened" of today, let us review the "then, it happened" in the early nation of Israel. As you carefully read God's word in Deuteronomy 32:18, please note that the LORD did not indicate that the Israelites' congregational competition with Him ***might*** happen; instead, the tone is absolute. The LORD absolutely said, *thou art unmindful, and hast forgotten God.* The LORD forewarned Jeshurun that they will succumb to competition. And, they did. It started somewhat innocently . . .

> *Nevertheless the people refused to obey the voice of Samuel; and they said, Nay; but we will have a king over us; That we also may be like all the nations; and that our king may judge us, and go out before us, and fight our battles.*
>
> (1 Samuel 8:19-20)

. . . From there it kept building. The office of the king was where the major carnal construction was done. In support of these building projects, a significant number of the kings of Israel *did that which was evil in the sight of the LORD*; many of the kings of Judah did the same. Finally, there was one king of Judah who was so competitive that he performed a blood bath among the people of his own nation.

> *And the LORD spake by his servants the prophets, saying, Because Manasseh king of Judah hath done these abominations, and hath done wickedly above all that the Amorites did, which were before him, and hath made Judah also to sin with his idols: Therefore*

> *thus saith the LORD God of Israel, Behold, I am bringing such evil upon Jerusalem and Judah, that whosoever heareth of it, both his ears shall tingle.*
>
> *And I will stretch over Jerusalem the line of Samaria, and the plummet of the house of Ahab: and I will wipe Jerusalem as a man wipeth a dish, wiping it, and turning it upside down. And I will forsake the remnant of mine inheritance, and deliver them into the hand of their enemies; and they shall become a prey and a spoil to all their enemies; Because they have done that which was evil in my sight, and have provoked me to anger, since the day their fathers came forth out of Egypt, even unto this day.*
>
> *Moreover Manasseh shed innocent blood very much, till he had filled Jerusalem from one end to another; beside his sin wherewith he made Judah to sin, in doing that which was evil in the sight of the LORD.*
>
> (2 Kings 21:10-16)

Very ferociously, the competition continued, and the associated wickedness was continually pressed toward God. Finally, all of Israel had reached the point where it had become a hopeless cause, as far as reformation was concerned. They were in the state that the apostle Paul would tell them about, some time later.

> *For it is impossible for those who were once enlightened, and have tasted of the heavenly gift, and were made partakers of the Holy Ghost, And have tasted the good word of God, and the powers of the world to come, If they shall fall away, to renew them again unto repentance; seeing they crucify to themselves the Son of God afresh, and put him to an open shame.*
>
> (Hebrews 6:4-6)

So, God pulled His name from the nation which was born of the seed of Jacob. The LORD, then, gave custody of the nation's presence in the world to the remnant of the seed, and He scattered the much larger portion of the people to the four winds. In order to reduce their ability to participate in competition, the LORD took away their opportunity to compete, at all.

> *For, behold, the Lord, the LORD of hosts, doth take away from Jerusalem and from Judah the stay and the staff, the whole stay of bread, and the whole stay of water. The mighty man, and the man of war, the judge, and the prophet, and the prudent, and the ancient, The captain of fifty, and the honourable man, and the counsellor, and the cunning artificer, and the eloquent orator. And I will give children to be their princes, and babes shall rule over them. And the people shall be oppressed, every one by another, and every one by his neighbour: the child shall behave himself proudly against the ancient, and the base against the honourable.*
>
> *When a man shall take hold of his brother of the house of his father, saying, Thou hast clothing, be thou our ruler, and let this ruin be under thy hand: In that day shall he swear, saying, I will not be an healer; for in my house is neither bread nor clothing: make me not a ruler of the people. For Jerusalem is ruined, and Judah is fallen: because their tongue and their doings are against the LORD, to provoke the eyes of his glory. The show of their countenance doth witness against them; and they declare their sin as Sodom, they hide it not. Woe unto their soul! for they have rewarded evil unto themselves.*
>
> (Isaiah 3:1-9)

Without the ability to rule, they were once again in the Egyptian mode of Moses' time; under new types of Pharaohs. And just as they did then; again, for their deliverance, they called upon the name of the LORD. And when those who are sealed by God called upon Him, He answered.

> *And after these things I saw four angels standing on the four corners of the earth, holding the four winds of the earth, that the wind should not blow on the earth, nor on the sea, nor on any tree. And I saw another angel ascending from the east, having the seal of the living God: and he cried with a loud voice to the four angels, to whom it was given to hurt the earth and the sea, Saying, Hurt*

not the earth, neither the sea, nor the trees, till we have sealed the servants of our God in their foreheads.

And I heard the number of them which were sealed: and there were sealed an hundred and forty and four thousand of all the tribes of the children of Israel.

Of the tribe of Juda were sealed twelve thousand.
Of the tribe of Reuben were sealed twelve thousand.
Of the tribe of Gad were sealed twelve thousand.
Of the tribe of Aser were sealed twelve thousand.
Of the tribe of Nephthalim were sealed twelve thousand.
Of the tribe of Manasses were sealed twelve thousand.
Of the tribe of Simeon were sealed twelve thousand.
Of the tribe of Levi were sealed twelve thousand.
Of the tribe of Issachar were sealed twelve thousand.
Of the tribe of Zabulon were sealed twelve thousand.
Of the tribe of Joseph were sealed twelve thousand.
Of the tribe of Benjamin were sealed twelve thousand.

(Revelation 7:1-8)

This is where we can shift to the time of transition—from the era of then, on toward the era of now. This is where we have our global introduction to what may be referred to as, *the nation of Christianity. The nation of Christianity*, as born of the Gospel of Jesus of Nazareth, is the grafted in portion of God's son, Israel, as collected together in the Son of God. We are born again into the family of the Father God, in full relationship with the Son, and the son.

There was a man of the Pharisees, named Nicodemus, a ruler of the Jews: The same came to Jesus by night, and said unto him, Rabbi, we know that thou art a teacher come from God: for no man can do these miracles that thou doest, except God be with him.

Jesus answered and said unto him, Verily, verily, I say unto thee, Except a man be born again, he cannot see the kingdom of God.

(John 3:1-3)

Thus, we have the same "opportunities" that beset the nation of Israel, and we, too, must do battle with the competitiveness of our world. But we cannot do so on the world's terms. We must not try to go toe-to-toe with the world, by operating according to the methods of the world. We must learn and utilize the methods of the Lord Jesus Christ. They are not the same as the methods of the world that is around us.

> *Ye have not chosen me, but I have chosen you, and ordained you, that ye should go and bring forth fruit, and that your fruit should remain: that whatsoever ye shall ask of the Father in my name, he may give it you.*
>
> *These things I command you, that ye love one another. If the world hate you, ye know that it hated me before it hated you. If ye were of the world, the world would love his own: but because ye are not of the world, but I have chosen you out of the world, therefore the world hateth you.*
>
> (John 15:16-19)

If we are to have success in Christ, we cannot say to God that we want a king. Christ Jesus, the Son of God, is our King. No longer is he just King of the Jews. He is now, and has been since his resurrection, King of kings and Lord of lords. We are the extended fold.

> *I am the good shepherd, and know my sheep, and am known of mine. As the Father knoweth me, even so know I the Father: and I lay down my life for the sheep. And other sheep I have, which are not of this fold: them also I must bring, and they shall hear my voice; and there shall be one fold, and one shepherd. Therefore doth my Father love me, because I lay down my life, that I might take it again.*
>
> (John 10:14-17)

Let me repeat that. We ***must not ask God for a king.***

"And, what," you ask, "is this king thing that you're talking about?"

The king is of the same order as the one asked for by the children of Israel. It is the one that makes us similar to the rest of the world. It is this thing of equal rights under the laws of the land. This message is only for those who are in leadership positions as the elect of God; remember that it was the leaders who came to Samuel to demand equality under the psychological laws of their land. We must not do that.

Too often, I hear or read about some attack on a Christian organization, and how they have gone to court to settle the matter. I will leave this question (with my prayer that if it is the LORD'S will, God guides you to an answer): "Does this not advertise to the world that, for this organization, their God is impotent?" We have our answers in the Scripture.

Yes, I know that the world is rapidly decaying, from the perspective of some. Yes, I know that the decadence of society is being painted over the brilliance of God. Yes, I know that "we've had enough, and we won't take it anymore." But, hold on! Do ***we*** really matter? Are we going forth into the world to take something? Or, are we going forth to give?

The answers to the questions above are very important. For, if we do not "take it" to begin with, then we will never have to "take it anymore".

"Solutions!" you scream. "Give me solutions!"

The solution is for all those who call themselves by God's name to follow the Scripture.

First, all who love the LORD must *humble themselves.*

> *And the LORD appeared to Solomon by night, and said unto him, I have heard thy prayer, and have chosen this place to myself for an house of sacrifice. If I shut up heaven that there be no rain, or if I command the locusts to devour the land, or if I send pestilence among my people; If my people, which are called by my name, shall humble themselves, and pray, and seek my face, and turn from their wicked ways; then will I hear from heaven, and will forgive their sin, and will heal their land.*
>
> (2 Chronicles 7:12-14)

Second, pray! But, do not pray just any prayer. Pray as Jesus taught us to. And if you do not want to be creative about it, just recite the words, sincerely, to God.

> *After this manner therefore pray ye:*
>
> *Our Father which art in heaven, Hallowed be thy name. Thy kingdom come, Thy will be done in earth, as it is in heaven. Give*

us this day our daily bread. And forgive us our debts, as we forgive our debtors. And lead us not into temptation, but deliver us from evil: For thine is the kingdom, and the power, and the glory, for ever. Amen.

(Matthew 6:9-13)

Third, pray the way that we were told to pray.

And when thou prayest, thou shalt not be as the hypocrites are: for they love to pray standing in the synagogues and in the corners of the streets, that they may be seen of men. Verily I say unto you, They have their reward. But thou, when thou prayest, enter into thy closet, and when thou hast shut thy door, pray to thy Father which is in secret; and thy Father which seeth in secret shall reward thee openly. But when ye pray, use not vain repetitions, as the heathen do: for they think that they shall be heard for their much speaking. Be not ye therefore like unto them: for your Father knoweth what things ye have need of, before ye ask him.

(Matthew 6:5-8)

Fourth, add a footnote, if you will, to your prayer; a footnote that raises the leadership up to God.

Let every soul be subject unto the higher powers. For there is no power but of God: the powers that be are ordained of God. Whosoever therefore resisteth the power, resisteth the ordinance of God: and they that resist shall receive to themselves damnation. For rulers are not a terror to good works, but to the evil.

Wilt thou then not be afraid of the power? do that which is good, and thou shalt have praise of the same: For he is the minister of God to thee for good. But if thou do that which is evil, be afraid; for he beareth not the sword in vain: for he is the minister of God, a revenger to execute wrath upon him that doeth evil. Wherefore ye must needs be subject, not only for wrath, but also for conscience sake.

For for this cause pay ye tribute also: for they are God's ministers, attending continually upon this very thing. Render therefore to all their dues: tribute to whom tribute is due; custom to whom custom; fear to whom fear; honour to whom honour. Owe no man any thing, but to love one another: for he that loveth another hath fulfilled the law.

(Romans 13:1-8)

Fifth, be an example.

Ye are the light of the world. A city that is set on an hill cannot be hid. Neither do men light a candle, and put it under a bushel, but on a candlestick; and it giveth light unto all that are in the house. Let your light so shine before men, that they may see your good works, and glorify your Father which is in heaven.

(Matthew 5:14-16)

Sixth, wait on God's opportunity

But sanctify the Lord God in your hearts: and be ready always to give an answer to every man that asketh you a reason of the hope that is in you with meekness and fear: Having a good conscience; that, whereas they speak evil of you, as of evildoers, they may be ashamed that falsely accuse your good conversation in Christ. For it is better, if the will of God be so, that ye suffer for well doing, than for evil doing.

(1 Peter 3:15-17)

And, seventh, reject the urge to create your own message.

For other foundation can no man lay than that is laid, which is Jesus Christ. Now if any man build upon this foundation gold, silver, precious stones, wood, hay, stubble; Every man's work shall be made manifest: for the day shall declare it, because it shall be revealed by fire; and the fire shall try every man's work of what sort it is. If any man's work abide which he hath built thereupon, he shall receive a reward. If any man's work shall be burned, he shall suffer loss: but he himself shall be saved; yet so as by fire.

(1 Corinthians 3:11-15)

Furthermore, if you are an elect of God, you must make yourself available to God. This does not mean that you force the issue. It means that you live the life and you share what you live, to empower others to do the same.

> *And Jesus came and spake unto them, saying, All power is given unto me in heaven and in earth. Go ye therefore, and teach all nations, baptizing them in the name of the Father, and of the Son, and of the Holy Ghost: Teaching them to observe all things whatsoever I have commanded you: and, lo, I am with you alway, even unto the end of the world. Amen.*
>
> (Matthew 28:18-20)

In this way we will never find ourselves being a kind of residual fallout Of the Seven.

> *Nicodemus saith unto him, How can a man be born when he is old? can he enter the second time into his mother's womb, and be born?*
>
> *Jesus answered, Verily, verily, I say unto thee, Except a man be born of water and of the Spirit, he cannot enter into the kingdom of God. That which is born of the flesh is flesh; and that which is born of the Spirit is spirit.*
>
> *Marvel not that I said unto thee, Ye must be born again.*
>
> (John 3:4-7)

If truly all is
As you have read,
My prayer is that
You stay ahead

Of today's trend that
Presses you to swerve
Away from God,
Others to serve.

For, kings of empires
Have a limited day
In which to press all
To follow their way.

In the day of the Son,
The place called Rome,
Ruled over the kingdom,
Making it her home.

Watching, from Heaven,
Standing by God;
The Son readied a
Great and terrible rod.

The first act was done
By the Father above,
Who removed the place
That shunned His love.

With Christ's enemies
Now his footstool,
The Son was set
To establish his rule.

Then, Rome felt
God's Almighty Hand,
With judgment delivered
Throughout its land.

Then from this chaos,
Of a religious kind,
Sprung a thing most evil,
To enslave man's mind.

But God stopped it,
And snatched its power,
As the Beast reached
Its preset hour.

Then, peace reigned
On earth and in Heaven:
In the Lake is the Beast
That is Of the Seven.

Concern for Democracy

Then if any man shall say unto you, Lo, here is Christ, or there; believe it not. For there shall arise false Christs, and false prophets, and shall shew great signs and wonders; insomuch that, if it were possible, they shall deceive the very elect. Behold, I have told you before.

Wherefore if they shall say unto you, Behold, he is in the desert; go not forth: behold, he is in the secret chambers; believe it not. For as the lightning cometh out of the east, and shineth even unto the west; so shall also the coming of the Son of man be.

(Matthew 24:23-27)

Throughout history, and particularly in Old Testament times, God has shown that He prospers the earth by strong rulers. These rulers are not just of the devout flavor. God uses a variety of types of rulers to manifest His purpose. All of these rulers are made to have this authorization: for the time of their rule, they are given the power to bend their designated portion of the world to their way of life. This is done to give their portion a focal point from which to continue its march toward God.

In the ancient world, we had the witness of king Nebuchadnezzar, in testifying to the overriding authority of God as a key factor in the king's exercise of dominion over his world.

Then Nebuchadnezzar spake, and said, Blessed be the God of Shadrach, Meshach, and Abednego, who hath sent his angel, and delivered his servants that trusted in him, and have changed the king's word, and yielded their bodies, that they might not serve nor worship any god, except their own God. Therefore I make a decree, That every people, nation, and language, which speak any thing amiss against the God of Shadrach, Meshach, and Abednego, shall be cut in pieces, and their houses shall be made a dunghill: because there is no other God that can deliver after this sort.

(Daniel 3:28-29)

Also from the ancient world, we have the witness of king Darius.

Then king Darius wrote unto all people, nations, and languages, that dwell in all the earth; Peace be multiplied unto you. I make a decree, That in every dominion of my kingdom men tremble and fear before the God of Daniel: for he is the living God, and stedfast for ever, and his kingdom that which shall not be destroyed, and his dominion shall be even unto the end. He delivereth and rescueth, and he worketh signs and wonders in heaven and in earth, who hath delivered Daniel from the power of the lions.

(Daniel 6:25-27)

And do not forget such rulers as Cyrus and Artaxerxes. These are two of the other kings that were selected by God to be His representative, to show forth His glory to the nations. Also, alongside these rulers, there were chosen spokesmen of God, who we call prophets, to present the will of God to the rulers. Daniel and three other captives, Shadrach, Meshach and Abednego, are among those who were placed in that position in the ancient times.

To continue in the pattern of Daniel and the kings of his time; in the times of the start of the Gospel of Jesus Christ, the purpose that God had set for the world was accomplished through the ascendance of the Roman Empire. Then, as the LORD'S connection to those rulers; for a great part, the purpose that God had set for the world was presented to them by the apostle Paul; through whom God presented the Gospel, to the world that was outside of the nation of Israel, in the Gentile nations. Thus, once again a powerful spokesman of God—an apostle of God, and, too, an apostle of Christ—was selected to present the truth of God to the focal king of the world, in that day. Then, from the focal kings of the Roman Empire, the message reached out into the remainder of the world.

Now, in the present day, the democratic system of the United States of America is sitting in a place as one of the kings of the world, and it is vying for the position of being the central kingdom of the world. In the United States of America, the Presidents bear the burden of presenting to the world the message of God that He has embedded in this form of government. Moreover, the President has an additional responsibility to continually refresh his nation's citizens' recollection of the value and values that God has placed in the United States of America. However, there are significant constraints.

The strength of any system is the support structure that makes up its foundation. When this foundation is a sound principle of God, it can give the assurance that the structure will both stand and withstand; because the foundation is secure.

> *Therefore whosoever heareth these sayings of mine, and doeth them, I will liken him unto a wise man, which built his house upon a rock: And the rain descended, and the floods came, and the winds blew, and beat upon that house; and it fell not: for it was founded upon a rock.*
>
> (Matthew 7:24-25)

But if the foundation is flawed, then, in time, the entire complex will collapse; no matter how strong the overlying structure may be.

> *And every one that heareth these sayings of mine, and doeth them not, shall be likened unto a foolish man, which built his house upon the sand: And the rain descended, and the floods came, and the winds blew, and beat upon that house; and it fell: and great was the fall of it.*
>
> (Matthew 7:26-27)

The foundation of democracy was once sound. It was based on the theocratic maxim, "one nation **under** God". Not, one nation above God; or, one nation standing beside God; but, wisely in focus, one nation under God. The courts—by the allowance of the elected officials—have started a great falling away of democracy from that principle. The foundation is beginning to shift on the sand of appropriateness. The people of the nation are in the structure above the rapidly shifting foundation of the revising principles of democracy, and they, too, are starting to show signs of double mindedness, and, even, duplicity. The present signs are such that, if it were possible, they shall deceive the very elect.

The people of the United States of America are the energy behind the legislation. It is they, who, in a democracy, can set the pace. This has been viewed as the strength of democracy; that is, "that government of the people, by the people and for the people shall not perish from the earth". This is fine when the people are in tune with God, and, might I add, are yielding to the Holy Ghost. But that is not sufficient in a democracy. At a level that is above the citizens, yielding is especially necessary in the judges and the princes (Senators and Representatives) and the king (President).

We have not included the Judges because they are not originators of the rules. In the modern day, the judges of the land are constrained by the collective actions of the Senators, Representatives and Presidents. Thus, judges are more like the centurion that is described here:

> *And when Jesus was entered into Capernaum, there came unto him a centurion, beseeching him, And saying, Lord, my servant lieth at home sick of the palsy, grievously tormented.*
>
> *And Jesus saith unto him, I will come and heal him.*
>
> *The centurion answered and said, Lord, I am not worthy that thou shouldest come under my roof: but speak the word only, and my servant shall be healed. For I am a man under authority, having soldiers under me: and I say to this man, Go, and he goeth; and to another, Come, and he cometh; and to my servant, Do this, and he doeth it.*
>
> (Matthew 8:5-9)

In that respect, the judges of today occupy a place that is similar to the prophets of old, as pertains to governance. This is, in no way, a trivial position to occupy. In their place, they are a critical part of the type of governance that was established, by God, through Moses, in the time of Israel's initial development as a nation. Let us look at the separation of responsibility and the allocation of authority of that time.

Here are the duties that were allocated then, and that are now performed by the full complement of local and national senators, representatives, governors, mayors, along with the President of a democratic system of governance.

> *And it came to pass on the morrow, that Moses sat to judge the people: and the people stood by Moses from the morning unto the*

evening. And when Moses' father in law saw all that he did to the people, he said, What is this thing that thou doest to the people? why sittest thou thyself alone, and all the people stand by thee from morning unto even?

And Moses said unto his father in law, Because the people come unto me to enquire of God: When they have a matter, they come unto me; and I judge between one and another, and I do make them know the statutes of God, and his laws.

And Moses' father in law said unto him, The thing that thou doest is not good. Thou wilt surely wear away, both thou, and this people that is with thee: for this thing is too heavy for thee; thou art not able to perform it thyself alone.

Hearken now unto my voice, I will give thee counsel, and God shall be with thee: Be thou for the people to God-ward, that thou mayest bring the causes unto God: And thou shalt teach them ordinances and laws, and shalt shew them the way wherein they must walk, and the work that they must do.

Moreover thou shalt provide out of all the people able men, such as fear God, men of truth, hating covetousness; and place such over them, to be rulers of thousands, and rulers of hundreds, rulers of fifties, and rulers of tens: And let them judge the people at all seasons: and it shall be, that every great matter they shall bring unto thee, but every small matter they shall judge: so shall it be easier for thyself, and they shall bear the burden with thee.

If thou shalt do this thing, and God command thee so, then thou shalt be able to endure, and all this people shall also go to their place in peace.

So Moses hearkened to the voice of his father in law, and did all that he had said. And Moses chose able men out of all Israel, and made them heads over the people, rulers of thousands, rulers of hundreds, rulers of fifties, and rulers of tens. And they judged the people at all seasons: the hard causes they brought unto Moses, but every small matter they judged themselves.

(Exodus 18:13-26)

Here is the work that is now done, in substance, by the judges of the land.

> *And Moses said, The people, among whom I am, are six hundred thousand footmen; and thou hast said, I will give them flesh, that they may eat a whole month. Shall the flocks and the herds be slain for them, to suffice them? or shall all the fish of the sea be gathered together for them, to suffice them?*
>
> *And the LORD said unto Moses, Is the LORD'S hand waxed short? thou shalt see now whether my word shall come to pass unto thee or not.*
> *And Moses went out, and told the people the words of the LORD, and gathered the seventy men of the elders of the people, and set them round about the tabernacle.*
>
> *And the LORD came down in a cloud, and spake unto him, and took of the spirit that was upon him, and gave it unto the seventy elders: and it came to pass, that, when the spirit rested upon them, they prophesied, and did not cease.*
>
> (Numbers 11:21-25)

But, what happens when the men that have these responsibilities reveal themselves, in large part, to be governed by their sinful nature; as they have started to do more vigorously now? Then, the "man of sin is revealed the son of perdition". The result will be the same as it was in a similar time of the early Christian era; in that, the reign of Christ will be forcefully applied to the world. For, Christ still rules today, and shall forever rule; wherefore as was done then with the Roman Empire, international cleansing may be in order now. The signs are beginning to point in that direction.

> *Now we beseech you, brethren, by the coming of our Lord Jesus Christ, and by our gathering together unto him, That ye be not soon shaken in mind, or be troubled, neither by spirit, nor by word, nor by letter as from us, as that the day of Christ is at hand. Let no man deceive you by any means: for that day shall not come, except there come a falling away first, and that man of sin be revealed, the*

> *son of perdition; Who opposeth and exalteth himself above all that is called God, or that is worshipped; so that he as God sitteth in the temple of God, showing himself that he is God. Remember ye not, that, when I was yet with you, I told you these things?*
> (2 Thessalonians 2:1-5)

Two things have been set forth as the sign that we need a change. The first is this shift in the emphasis of the government. As you read further, please remember this: what is being said by the government is perfectly consistent with the concept of a democracy; however, it is not consistent with the rule of God in the world. A democracy is run by people, in a measure of allowed isolation from God. This is becoming evident in the various actions that are being taken against those who wish to express their beliefs in public; especially, against beliefs of a Christian nature. It is no accident that the Christian principles are seeing the most attack. This is because the Christian principles are the most absolute of all religious expressions.

To establish the liberalism of democracy, anything that is absolute must be watered down; or, just plain suppressed. This poses a problem for any man or nation standing under God in a democracy of this sort; for, God is not a relative being. By the nature, and the definition, of God, He cannot be relative. God cannot have a plethora of ways to arrive at unity with Him. Optional approaches may be available for a non-personal god, but that is not possible with the Living God. The non-personal god can allow men to stumble in the dark, and reach for things that will damage them. This would be like a parent placing a bottle of warm milk somewhere in the house, and allowing their four month old baby to crawl around until it had found the bottle. And, if it didn't; I guess, it would just die.

We are infant—or even younger—to God. The Living God places the bottle clearly within the reach of his children. Yes, when the child of God finds it, he has to reach out, grab it, and tip it to his mouth. No, once they do, they are not disappointed because it is actually empty. For the child of God that is reaching out for the things of the Living God, the milk is always at just the right level for proper nourishment: never too much, never too little.

> *Then Paul stood in the midst of Mars' hill, and said, Ye men of Athens, I perceive that in all things ye are too superstitious. For as*

> *I passed by, and beheld your devotions, I found an altar with this inscription, TO THE UNKNOWN GOD. Whom therefore ye ignorantly worship, him declare I unto you.*
>
> *God that made the world and all things therein, seeing that he is Lord of heaven and earth, dwelleth not in temples made with hands; Neither is worshipped with men's hands, as though he needed any thing, seeing he giveth to all life, and breath, and all things; And hath made of one blood all nations of men for to dwell on all the face of the earth, and hath determined the times before appointed, and the bounds of their habitation; That they should seek the Lord, if haply they might feel after him, and find him, though he be not far from every one of us: For in him we live, and move, and have our being; as certain also of your own poets have said, For we are also his offspring.*
>
> (Acts 17:22-28)

Whereas, in our practice of worship, we are accepted as children to God; democracy confers upon all inhabitants of the nation, individually and collectively, the status of adult. To anyone who chooses to use it; logic would inform them that One as powerful as God can have no peer. No nation is the peer of the Living God, and certainly no man on this earth is either; or, even, any one or thing that has ever been on this earth. Only God can dispense the power that is necessary for any man, or any nation, to do the things that He requires of them; however, democracy says that a collection of humans can control the destiny of that collection. This is the first foundational weakness of this structure known as democracy.

The second foundational weakness, as a second sign that we need to change, is that the only text that can govern the actions of the members of the nation is composed of the laws of the nation. This is really an easy one to discard. One of the more famous foundational structures that were built upon the Law of God is the one called, the law of Moses. The nation of Israel was given the Perfect Law, from the Perfect God; however, He gave it to the imperfect structure known as, the mixed multitude of Israel. This is not to say that this congregation is any different from any other. All congregations on this earth, including nations, are rife with imperfections. This is the reason that before the foundation of the world, God brought forth His Son, the Christ. The prophet Isaiah described our need for this intercession.

> *For since the beginning of the world men have not heard, nor perceived by the ear, neither hath the eye seen, O God, beside thee, what he hath prepared for him that waiteth for him. Thou meetest him that rejoiceth and worketh righteousness, those that remember thee in thy ways: behold, thou art wroth; for we have sinned: in those is continuance, and we shall be saved. But we are all as an unclean thing, and all our righteousnesses are as filthy rags; and we all do fade as a leaf; and our iniquities, like the wind, have taken us away. And there is none that calleth upon thy name, that stirreth up himself to take hold of thee: for thou hast hid thy face from us, and hast consumed us, because of our iniquities.*
>
> *But now, O LORD, thou art our father; we are the clay, and thou our potter; and we all are the work of thy hand. Be not wroth very sore, O LORD, neither remember iniquity for ever: behold, see, we beseech thee, we are all thy people.*
>
> (Isaiah 64:4-9)

As members of the family of God, we sit in a sensitive position in a democracy; because, in a democracy, the laws, as established by the minds of men, are set up to control the actions of the citizens. This leaves us in double jeopardy, as follows: we have imperfect laws, with imperfect application of these laws. If it could ever happen, this would be a very good time for two wrongs to make a right. But, alas, this does not happen, here.

To more fully understand the weight of democracy's double jeopardy as being contained in its laws; let us look in history at a single jeopardy environment: imperfect application of perfect laws. This is the start of the jeopardy . . .

> *And the LORD said unto Moses, Hew thee two tables of stone like unto the first: and I will write upon these tables the words that were in the first tables, which thou brakest. And be ready in the*

morning, and come up in the morning unto mount Sinai, and present thyself there to me in the top of the mount. And no man shall come up with thee, neither let any man be seen throughout all the mount; neither let the flocks nor herds feed before that mount.

And he hewed two tables of stone like unto the first; and Moses rose up early in the morning, and went up unto mount Sinai, as the LORD had commanded him, and took in his hand the two tables of stone.

And the LORD descended in the cloud, and stood with him there, and proclaimed the name of the LORD. And the LORD passed by before him, and proclaimed, The LORD, The LORD God, merciful and gracious, longsuffering, and abundant in goodness and truth, Keeping mercy for thousands, forgiving iniquity and transgression and sin, and that will by no means clear the guilty; visiting the iniquity of the fathers upon the children, and upon the children's children, unto the third and to the fourth generation.

And Moses made haste, and bowed his head toward the earth, and worshipped. And he said, If now I have found grace in thy sight, O LORD, let my LORD, I pray thee, go among us; for it is a stiffnecked people; and pardon our iniquity and our sin, and take us for thine inheritance.

And he said, Behold, I make a covenant: before all thy people I will do marvels, such as have not been done in all the earth, nor in any nation: and all the people among which thou art shall see the work of the LORD: for it is a terrible thing that I will do with thee.

(Exodus 34:1-10)

Here is an explanation of the single jeopardy environment of human application of perfect laws.

What shall we say then? is the law sin? God forbid. Nay, I had not known sin, but by the law: for I had not known lust, except the law had said, Thou shalt not covet. But sin, taking occasion by the commandment, wrought in me all manner of concupiscence. For without the law sin was dead. For I was alive without the law once: but when the commandment came, sin revived, and I died.

And the commandment, which was ordained to life, I found to be unto death.

For sin, taking occasion by the commandment, deceived me, and by it slew me.

(Romans 7:7-11)

As history has shown, it was not the law of Moses that failed, but the nation's continuation in it. This was God's biggest lesson to the nations of laws (I think that is every one of them). Any piece of law, even the noblest portions of the Law, will see failure among mankind, unless mankind is willing to honor the author of the law. Furthermore, unless the author of the laws is steeped in the mind of God, then these laws have already failed, from the start. This also applies to any revision of a once perfect law.

These two must be in any law that is meant to last: honor for the authority of the law, and one or more of God's principles at the core of the law. Jesus said it best, about himself, when he established, for all mankind, the law of love, from within himself.

And as Moses lifted up the serpent in the wilderness, even so must the Son of man be lifted up: That whosoever believeth in him should not perish, but have eternal life. For God so loved the world, that he gave his only begotten Son, that whosoever believeth in him should not perish, but have everlasting life. For God sent not his Son into the world to condemn the world; but that the world through him might be saved.

He that believeth on him is not condemned: but he that believeth not is condemned already, because he hath not believed in the name of the only begotten Son of God.

And this is the condemnation, that light is come into the world, and men loved darkness rather than light, because their deeds were evil. For every one that doeth evil hateth the light, neither cometh to the light, lest his deeds should be reproved.

But he that doeth truth cometh to the light, that his deeds may be made manifest, that they are wrought in God.

(John 3:14-21)

It is not my intent to negotiate with anyone about the error of their choices; or, even, the wisdom thereof. I am in this respect, an old-school, adopted Israel, follower of Christ; so, the message that Jesus gave when he sent out the twelve disciples is a deep part of my heart. This is what controls my outreach to anyone, in the name of Jesus.

> *Then he called his twelve disciples together, and gave them power and authority over all devils, and to cure diseases. And he sent them to preach the kingdom of God, and to heal the sick. And he said unto them, Take nothing for your journey, neither staves, nor scrip, neither bread, neither money; neither have two coats apiece.*
>
> *And whatsoever house ye enter into, there abide, and thence depart. And whosoever will not receive you, when ye go out of that city, shake off the very dust from your feet for a testimony against them.*
>
> (Luke 9:1-5)

To give us greater understanding of his doctrine and its intention, Jesus also sent out seventy others.

> *After these things the Lord appointed other seventy also, and sent them two and two before his face into every city and place, whither he himself would come. Therefore said he unto them, The harvest truly is great, but the labourers are few: pray ye therefore the Lord of the harvest, that he would send forth labourers into his harvest.*
>
> *Go your ways: behold, I send you forth as lambs among wolves. Carry neither purse, nor scrip, nor shoes: and salute no man by the way. And into whatsoever house ye enter, first say, Peace be to this house. And if the son of peace be there, your peace shall rest upon it: if not, it shall turn to you again. And in the same house remain, eating and drinking such things as they give: for the labourer is worthy of his hire. Go not from house to house.*
>
> *And into whatsoever city ye enter, and they receive you, eat such things as are set before you: And heal the sick that are therein, and say unto them, The kingdom of God is come nigh unto you.*

> *But into whatsoever city ye enter, and they receive you not, go your ways out into the streets of the same, and say, Even the very dust of your city, which cleaveth on us, we do wipe off against you: notwithstanding be ye sure of this, that the kingdom of God is come nigh unto you.*
>
> *But I say unto you, that it shall be more tolerable in that day for Sodom, than for that city.*
>
> *Woe unto thee, Chorazin! woe unto thee, Bethsaida! for if the mighty works had been done in Tyre and Sidon, which have been done in you, they had a great while ago repented, sitting in sackcloth and ashes. But it shall be more tolerable for Tyre and Sidon at the judgment, than for you. And thou, Capernaum, which art exalted to heaven, shalt be thrust down to hell.*
>
> *He that heareth you heareth me; and he that despiseth you despiseth me; and he that despiseth me despiseth him that sent me.*
>
> (Luke 10:1-16)

As they say, "you know the deal". The increase of immoral behavior—disguised as freedom of choice—is evidence enough of the drift of democracy from the message of God. We can strain all we want to at a gnat of propriety, so that we can swallow the camel of these immoralities; the truth of their nature will not change. Let me just mention a few.

Same sex unions, of any sort, should not be an issue, at all. The Bible has a direct statement about such people who are involved in actions of this sort.

> *There shall be no whore of the daughters of Israel, nor a sodomite of the sons of Israel. Thou shalt not bring the hire of a whore, or the price of a dog, into the house of the LORD thy God for any vow: for even both these are abomination unto the LORD thy God.*
>
> (Deuteronomy 23:17-18)

A decision for abortion, as being a very dangerous one, is nestled in words of the Lord Jesus Christ. However, to understand this, we have to first believe that God is ever-present in the process of birth; starting in the womb. We have to believe that human life is more than an incident of mutual agreement between humans. We have to understand that bringing a human life into the world is establishing a contract with God. And that this contract is written when the *deed is done*, and the result is acknowledged by the womb, as being active; In other words, when the man and women have sex and the embryo is implanted. This is when God's presence in us, for our sake, recognizes that there is a contract to carry a child; whether we do so, or not. Note the already-accomplished, though scheduled for a future time, tense of the words of the angel that came to the Virgin Mary.

> *And in the sixth month the angel Gabriel was sent from God unto a city of Galilee, named Nazareth, To a virgin espoused to a man whose name was Joseph, of the house of David; and the virgin's name was Mary. And the angel came in unto her, and said, Hail, thou that art highly favoured, the Lord is with thee: blessed art thou among women.*
>
> *And when she saw him, she was troubled at his saying, and cast in her mind what manner of salutation this should be.*
>
> *And the angel said unto her, Fear not, Mary: for thou hast found favour with God. And, behold, thou shalt conceive in thy womb, and bring forth a son, and shalt call his name JESUS. He shall be great, and shall be called the Son of the Highest: and the Lord God shall give unto him the throne of his father David: And he shall reign over the house of Jacob for ever; and of his kingdom there shall be no end.*
>
> *Then said Mary unto the angel, How shall this be, seeing I know not a man?*
>
> *And the angel answered and said unto her, The Holy Ghost shall come upon thee, and the power of the Highest shall overshadow thee: therefore also that holy thing which shall be born of thee shall be called the Son of God.*
>
> (Luke 1:26-35)

And, note the tense of the words that were spoken to the mother and father of John the Baptist.

> *But the angel said unto him, Fear not, Zacharias: for thy prayer is heard; and thy wife Elisabeth shall bear thee a son, and thou shalt call his name John. And thou shalt have joy and gladness; and many shall rejoice at his birth. For he shall be great in the sight of the Lord, and shall drink neither wine nor strong drink; and he shall be filled with the Holy Ghost, even from his mother's womb. And many of the children of Israel shall he turn to the Lord their God.*
>
> (Luke 1:13-16)

And, note the actions of the child in the womb (especially, you blessed mothers that now feel them in their own, developing treasure).

> *And Mary arose in those days, and went into the hill country with haste, into a city of Juda; And entered into the house of Zacharias, and saluted Elisabeth. And it came to pass, that, when Elisabeth heard the salutation of Mary, the babe leaped in her womb; and Elisabeth was filled with the Holy Ghost: And she spake out with a loud voice, and said, Blessed art thou among women, and blessed is the fruit of thy womb.*
>
> (Luke 1:39-42)

God's view on this matter is constant, and specific. The challenge to anyone who would defy it is contained in the words of the Lord Jesus Christ. This describes the factors that are in play, once God has sealed the contract, and designated the fruit of the womb as being *one of these little ones.* (Though, we caution you; no man can mandate when the contract is sealed, or not.)

> *At the same time came the disciples unto Jesus, saying, Who is the greatest in the kingdom of heaven?*
>
> *And Jesus called a little child unto him, and set him in the midst of them, And said, Verily I say unto you, Except ye be converted, and become as little children, ye shall not enter into the kingdom*

> *of heaven. Whosoever therefore shall humble himself as this little child, the same is greatest in the kingdom of heaven. And whoso shall receive one such little child in my name receiveth me. But whoso shall offend one of these little ones which believe in me, it were better for him that a millstone were hanged about his neck, and that he were drowned in the depth of the sea.*
>
> (Matthew 18:1-6)

> *Take heed that ye despise not one of these little ones; for I say unto you, That in heaven their angels do always behold the face of my Father which is in heaven.*
>
> (Matthew 18:10)

Do I believe that implanted John the Baptist, and implanted Jesus of Nazareth had angels that *always behold the face of my Father which is in heaven*? Well, actually, I believe they had Something better than that. The implanted John the Baptist, and implanted Jesus of Nazareth had the Holy Ghost, which was in residence, abiding beside them, as each cell split and as the cells specialized to form each organ, and as the child finally erupted into the world, and on thereafter.

Those are only two of the modern atrocities that have taken root in the world. They are only at the visible tip of the iceberg; there are so many others that are subtlety hidden, not subjected to public announcement. These include matters such as the argument about evolution and intelligent design. Each one of them is a quiet evil that should not be going on. We only need to allow God to settle the matter, in His time. We do not even need to have the discussion. For, as we turn our minds to Him, in the brilliance of our relationship with God; the discussion will lose its savor—but not for everyone.

For those who are straddling the fence, still; evolution and intelligent design are the sort of waste-of-time issues that come into the minds of those who have become enamored with this thing known as democracy. Yes, many of us that believe in God have also been bitten by the democracy bug. We have forgotten that God does not have a democracy. We have forgotten that Christ rules; and that his rule is the same today, as it was when it was first revealed to us in the Bible.

> *Thou shalt break them with a rod of iron; thou shalt dash them in pieces like a potter's vessel. Be wise now therefore, O ye kings: be instructed, ye judges of the earth. Serve the LORD with fear, and rejoice with trembling. Kiss the Son, lest he be angry, and ye perish from the way, when his wrath is kindled but a little. Blessed are all they that put their trust in him.*
>
> (Psalm 2:9-12)

As pertains to such hypotheses as evolution and intelligent design, I do not have to get into scientific arguments with you about how God did what. All I have to do is ask you what you believe about God. And if what you believe about God does not conform to the message of Christ, then it is time for me to pray for you, and for me. My prayer will be that God open a window of opportunity for you to either hear from me, or to see in me, the message of Jesus Christ. Preaching is done not just by words, but also by living the life, as an example.

> *And I, brethren, when I came to you, came not with excellency of speech or of wisdom, declaring unto you the testimony of God. For I determined not to know any thing among you, save Jesus Christ, and him crucified. And I was with you in weakness, and in fear, and in much trembling. And my speech and my preaching was not with enticing words of man's wisdom, but in demonstration of the Spirit and of power: That your faith should not stand in the wisdom of men, but in the power of God.*
>
> (1 Corinthians 2:1-5)

We might find it helpful, in this democracy, to review the lesson of Jonah, and to do as the people of Nineveh did.

> *And Jonah began to enter into the city a day's journey, and he cried, and said, Yet forty days, and Nineveh shall be overthrown.*
>
> *So the people of Nineveh believed God, and proclaimed a fast, and put on sackcloth, from the greatest of them even to the least of them. For word came unto the king of Nineveh, and he arose*

> *from his throne, and he laid his robe from him, and covered him with sackcloth, and sat in ashes. And he caused it to be proclaimed and published through Nineveh by the decree of the king and his nobles, saying, Let neither man nor beast, herd nor flock, taste any thing: let them not feed, nor drink water: But let man and beast be covered with sackcloth, and cry mightily unto God: yea, let them turn every one from his evil way, and from the violence that is in their hands. Who can tell if God will turn and repent, and turn away from his fierce anger, that we perish not?*
>
> *And God saw their works, that they turned from their evil way; and God repented of the evil, that he had said that he would do unto them; and he did it not.*
>
> (Jonah 3:4-10)

However, in a democracy, it will require not just the one king; for, in a democracy the king is in four parts: executive, legislative, judicial, and a collection that is made up of all the other citizens of the nation. We must put on the sackcloth of simpler times, in reverence to God and His principles; while sprinkling on ourselves the ashes of commitment to His way, which we have burned by our sinfulness. We must do this in order to push our soul to renew our commitment to the Living God, and to His way.

Might all this fail?

If we continue to depend on democratic systems, based on human initiative; yes!

Might we be past the limit?

If our leaders, like those of the biblical nation of Israel—as from Egypt, on to the Roman Empire—become so engrossed in what is called "personal freedom" that they do not adhere to the sound and healthy commandments of God; yes!

If so, then it is time for God to direct the wrap-up; in a day that only He knows, and in a way that only He knows; and, even this is good because it renews God in the world. But its *fallout* will be the chaining of democracy, and of its collective king. The four parts then become like unto the angels of Satan, and are eligible for the place that was prepared for the devil and his angels. As Jesus did before to the nations; so, too, he can do now.

When the Son of man shall come in his glory, and all the holy angels with him, then shall he sit upon the throne of his glory: And before him shall be gathered all nations: and he shall separate them one from another, as a shepherd divideth his sheep from the goats: And he shall set the sheep on his right hand, but the goats on the left.

Then shall the King say unto them on his right hand, Come, ye blessed of my Father, inherit the kingdom prepared for you from the foundation of the world: For I was an hungred, and ye gave me meat: I was thirsty, and ye gave me drink: I was a stranger, and ye took me in: Naked, and ye clothed me: I was sick, and ye visited me: I was in prison, and ye came unto me.

Then shall the righteous answer him, saying, Lord, when saw we thee an hungred, and fed thee? or thirsty, and gave thee drink? When saw we thee a stranger, and took thee in? or naked, and clothed thee? Or when saw we thee sick, or in prison, and came unto thee?

And the King shall answer and say unto them, Verily I say unto you, Inasmuch as ye have done it unto one of the least of these my brethren, ye have done it unto me.

Then shall he say also unto them on the left hand, Depart from me, ye cursed, into everlasting fire, prepared for the devil and his angels: For I was an hungred, and ye gave me no meat: I was thirsty, and ye gave me no drink: I was a stranger, and ye took me not in: naked, and ye clothed me not: sick, and in prison, and ye visited me not.

Then shall they also answer him, saying, Lord, when saw we thee an hungred, or athirst, or a stranger, or naked, or sick, or in prison, and did not minister unto thee?

Then shall he answer them, saying, Verily I say unto you, Inasmuch as ye did it not to one of the least of these, ye did it not to me.

And these shall go away into everlasting punishment: but the righteous into life eternal.

(Matthew 25:31-46)

Oh, you thought this referred to human beings? Sorry to disappoint you. There have been a few historic and powerful empires that were relegated to the lake of fire and brimstone because of their leaders' disavowal of God's vision. One of the best known is the Roman Empire.

So, why might I, personally, feel justified in retaining my fear for democracy? I fear for it because I love it; and because it has lost its first love! We started out as a nation under God; now, there are now many forces that are pressing for us to become a nation without God. They may say that they want to open up the nation to all gods; however, if this were true, then there should indeed be a place for the Living God. No, the current trend is not to open up the nation to all gods, but just to eliminate the Living God. The real eventual purpose is so that the nation will have no god, other than man.

We are right back to the serpent in the garden, and we, as a nation, can be cast out of the sight of God, as surely as Adam was cast out of the Garden of Eden. It is time for all democracies on this earth to review basic Christianity, 001, and stop listening to our modern serpent of unrestrained freedom; pointing at the fruit of licentious behavior. The insight about our jeopardy is of very old wisdom.

> *Now the serpent was more subtle than any beast of the field which the LORD God had made. And he said unto the woman, Yea, hath God said, Ye shall not eat of every tree of the garden?*
>
> *And the woman said unto the serpent, We may eat of the fruit of the trees of the garden: But of the fruit of the tree which is in the midst of the garden, God hath said, Ye shall not eat of it, neither shall ye touch it, lest ye die.*
>
> *And the serpent said unto the woman, Ye shall not surely die: For God doth know that in the day ye eat thereof, then your eyes shall be opened, and ye shall be as gods, knowing good and evil.*
>
> *And when the woman saw that the tree was good for food, and that it was pleasant to the eyes, and a tree to be desired to make one wise, she took of the fruit thereof, and did eat, and gave also unto*

> *her husband with her; and he did eat. And the eyes of them both were opened, and they knew that they were naked; and they sewed fig leaves together, and made themselves aprons.*
>
> (Genesis 3:1-7)

Therefore, be careful about the fruits of, privilege and freedom of expression, which are being presented to you. As individuals, and as the nation, be careful. For, once you consume them, as you ignore God's command to heed His word; then, you will be naked before Him. And, just as in the Garden, there will be no place for you—the person or the nation—to hide from His recompense of consequence. Pursue instead, the repentance of Nineveh; as citizens of a true nation under God. Do not continue on the course that will place you in the group of the ones that *fall away.*

> *Therefore leaving the principles of the doctrine of Christ, let us go on unto perfection; not laying again the foundation of repentance from dead works, and of faith toward God, Of the doctrine of baptisms, and of laying on of hands, and of resurrection of the dead, and of eternal judgment. And this will we do, if God permit.*
>
> *For it is impossible for those who were once enlightened, and have tasted of the heavenly gift, and were made partakers of the Holy Ghost, And have tasted the good word of God, and the powers of the world to come, If they shall fall away, to renew them again unto repentance; seeing they crucify to themselves the Son of God afresh, and put him to an open shame.*
>
> (Hebrews 6:1-6)

In the glory of God, pursue the path of grace; and, in that path, channel your concern for democracy, as well as any other form of government, through the Spirit of God, in the power of the Spirit of truth. These are words that will inspire and energize us to do so.

> *But, beloved, we are persuaded better things of you, and things that accompany salvation, though we thus speak. For God is not unrighteous to forget your work and labour of love, which ye have showed toward his name, in that ye have ministered to the saints, and do minister. And we desire that every one of you do show the*

same diligence to the full assurance of hope unto the end: That ye be not slothful, but followers of them who through faith and patience inherit the promises.

(Hebrews 6:9-12)

Even Atheists Receive

Isaiah 45:1-7

> Thus saith the LORD to his anointed, to Cyrus, whose right hand I have holden, to subdue nations before him; and I will loose the loins of kings, to open before him the two leaved gates; and the gates shall not be shut; I will go before thee, and make the crooked places straight: I will break in pieces the gates of brass, and cut in sunder the bars of iron: And I will give thee the treasures of darkness, and hidden riches of secret places, that thou mayest know that I, the LORD, which call thee by thy name, am the God of Israel. For Jacob my servant's sake, and Israel mine elect, I have even called thee by thy name: I have surnamed thee, though thou hast not known me.
>
> I am the LORD, and there is none else, there is no God beside me: I girded thee, though thou hast not known me: That they may know from the rising of the sun, and from the west, that there is none beside me. I am the LORD, and there is none else. I form the light, and create darkness: I make peace, and create evil: I the LORD do all these things.

There is no learning or understanding that comes of the Scripture, or of the things of God outside of God. Even many of those who are in institutions of higher learning, and in religious school, do not know what to make of this God thing. This is because the knowledge of God is achieved from God, and from God alone. This may be extremely uncomfortable for those who think that they, by being religious, are the sole recipients of God's wisdom. However, think about this: at the time

Peter received the revelation of the nature of Jesus Christ, he was, at best, an agnostic, relative to the mission of Christ.

Whoa!!!

Well, yes, this is what is written here. As illustrated in later actions by Peter during his early walk with Jesus, he did not fully understand the mission. Peter did believe that there was a mission, but he had no understanding of what that mission fully entailed. And even after receiving a significant revelation from God's ambassador in Jesus Christ, it is obvious that he did not fully accept this revelation; he still fell back on his humanity, while protecting himself during his denial. God has no respect of persons; He sends His rain on the just and the unjust. Wherefore, O religious one, prepare to share in an aggravating rain of facts of Scripture.

It is time to aggravate some groups of peoples, on both sides of the aisle. To do that, we begin with a description of two very prominent religious entities: Atheist and Agnostic. By way of warning, we say that in this observation of tangential worship, the breadth of these two religious groups will be greatly expanded beyond their currently acknowledged bounds. They will not, however, be changed; but, only, shown in their true light. First, the definitions:

Atheist: One who disbelieves or denies the existence of God or gods.

Agnostic: One who believes that it is impossible to know whether there is a God.

One who is skeptical about the existence of God but does not profess true atheism.

So, let us start the angst. The first groups who will be offended are those who believe that we must tolerate all forms of belief. This view is basic cowardice. It does not want to take a stand for a being that is uniform in its aspects. It is much like a man who would say that we must tolerate all forms of behaviors. Those who say this are also among those who decry the criminal element. Well, if we must tolerate all forms of behavior, then we have to even tolerate the criminally violent and exploitive factions of mankind. If such were done, this would invalidate laws and legislatures; and almost all elected officials. There are very few people that would endorse this level of tolerance—if it can be called that, at all. Almost unanimously, mankind believes that there must be bounds to what can be tolerated.

Almost unanimously, we also all believe that there is a superior being that rules over our lives; or, at least, one that has the authority and the power to do so. Some of us may call this being, "Baby," "Darling," "Momma", "Sweetie," "Boss," "Richman," "THE Man," "BIG Brother," or any of a whole series of human titles. These are the forces that we know have a sway, of an absolute sort, over our lives. They have a life and death grip on our existence. They can destroy us mentally, and in some cases physically. We know this, and we accept it. These are our gods, in the same way that the idols of the, so-called, primitive peoples, were their gods. And we esteem them in the same way, and for the same reasons.

Therefore, working from the premise that we all have gods in our lives, the only task at hand is to define the God that rules over all the gods of our lives, and, thus, over all aspects and affiliations of our lives. We are in our Athenian phase, here.

> *Then Paul stood in the midst of Mars' hill, and said, Ye men of Athens, I perceive that in all things ye are too superstitious. For as I passed by, and beheld your devotions, I found an altar with this inscription, TO THE UNKNOWN GOD. Whom therefore ye ignorantly worship, him declare I unto you.*
>
> *God that made the world and all things therein, seeing that he is Lord of heaven and earth, dwelleth not in temples made with hands; Neither is worshipped with men's hands, as though he needed any thing, seeing he giveth to all life, and breath, and all things; And hath made of one blood all nations of men for to dwell on all the face of the earth, and hath determined the times before appointed, and the bounds of their habitation; That they should seek the Lord, if haply they might feel after him, and find him, though he be not far from every one of us: For in him we live, and move, and have our being; as certain also of your own poets have said, For we are also his offspring.*
>
> (Acts 17:22-28)

Okay, I will now aggravate the other side of the aisle. There are those who say that we can inherently know this, or we can inherently know that about God. Well, those who have talked with God, as recorded in the Bible, can say that they know this or that about God; however, for the rest of us, we have to say that we believe this, or we believe that about God. This is really the most basic of requirements in the formation of any kind of awareness of God.

> *Now faith is the substance of things hoped for, the evidence of things not seen. For by it the elders obtained a good report. Through faith we understand that the worlds were framed by the word of God, so that things which are seen were not made of things which do appear.*
>
> *By faith Abel offered unto God a more excellent sacrifice than Cain, by which he obtained witness that he was righteous, God testifying of his gifts: and by it he being dead yet speaketh. By faith Enoch was translated that he should not see death; and was not found, because God had translated him: for before his translation he had this testimony, that he pleased God.*
>
> *But without faith it is impossible to please him: for he that cometh to God must believe that he is, and that he is a rewarder of them that diligently seek him.*
>
> (Hebrews 11:1-6)

I am impressed by the dictionary's use of the word *God* in defining an agnostic. This does not mean the same as the use of the word *god*. There can be many gods, but there is only one God: for this reason the dictionary states it as being a certain belief in the God. To say that we cannot have certainty about the God is the dilemma that mankind has faced throughout its history.

The agnostic takes the position that there are forces that rise to the level of god in the universe, but it is unclear whether these forces have a leader who rises to the level of being the God. This is actually the position of all who seek God, before they have come into a personal connection with Him. We all start as agnostics. The atheist is just an agnostic reacting against organized religion; not against a god, in the absolute sense of the word.

Let us look at an example of a time in the Bible when a large section of the nation of Israel went the agnostic route.

> *Then all the men which knew that their wives had burned incense unto other gods, and all the women that stood by, a great multitude, even all the people that dwelt in the land of Egypt, in Pathros, answered Jeremiah, saying, As for the word that thou hast spoken unto us in the name of the LORD, we will not hearken unto thee. But we will certainly do whatsoever thing goeth forth out of our own mouth, to burn incense unto the queen of heaven, and to pour out drink offerings unto her, as we have done, we, and our fathers, our kings, and our princes, in the cities of Judah, and in the streets of Jerusalem: for then had we plenty of victuals, and were well, and saw no evil. But since we left off to burn incense to the queen of heaven, and to pour out drink offerings unto her, we have wanted all things, and have been consumed by the sword and by the famine. And when we burned incense to the queen of heaven, and poured out drink offerings unto her, did we make her cakes to worship her, and pour out drink offerings unto her, without our men?*
>
> *Then Jeremiah said unto all the people, to the men, and to the women, and to all the people which had given him that answer, saying, The incense that ye burned in the cities of Judah, and in the streets of Jerusalem, ye, and your fathers, your kings, and your princes, and the people of the land, did not the LORD remember them, and came it not into his mind? So that the LORD could no longer bear, because of the evil of your doings, and because of the abominations which ye have committed; therefore is your land a desolation, and an astonishment, and a curse, without an inhabitant, as at this day. Because ye have burned incense, and because ye have sinned against the LORD, and have not obeyed the voice of the LORD, nor walked in his law, nor in his statutes, nor in his testimonies; therefore this evil is happened unto you, as at this day.*
>
> (Jeremiah 44:15-23)

Let us indulge ourselves in an interlude of meditation on this passage.

This is a complex matter of circular reasoning. When they were sacrificing to other gods, the LORD absorbed this, and, in His forbearance, allowed them a space of time to repent. However, because they had this space of time, they counted it to the benefit of the worship of the other gods. Thus, when the LORD issued a stern reminder of Who they should worship, by removing their benefits; they thought that they had been punished by the other gods for leaving them. I wonder if they actually thought through the matter, and questioned the truth of their thoughts.

Did the problems really come at the same time that they stopped worshipping the other gods, or did they come even while they were worshipping the other gods? Did they ever stop worshipping the other gods; even during the reminders that the LORD was giving them, or are they just looking for an excuse to do what they want to do? To analyze this, remember that worship is in the mind, and in the heart; not, in the mouth and the hands.

Sometimes, we can see "calamity" as a reason to stop worshipping God. We say within ourselves that, when we worship God, bad things happen; but when we follow the crowd, we have joy and peace. But the question we should pose to ourselves is the same one listed above. Have we really stopped serving our other gods of personal pleasure, and thus received trials; or did the trials start during the time of worshipping the other gods? And, even if we believe that the trials came after we stopped worshipping the other gods; do we not understand that in the same way that our parents learned from the LORD God to do with their children, so does the LORD God do with his mankind-child?

Our parents know that when we are "bad", we need to get a spanking. It is not sufficient for us to say that we will not be bad anymore. The consequences of having been bad must be demonstrated to us, by the spanking. This is done so that we have a memory of the reason we should never be disobedient, or do bad things. For, once we have this memory (as best humans can retain such a memory), and have accepted the justice in our father giving us the spanking, and have returned to him for further counsel on how to resist the urge to do bad things; then, our father will receive our acknowledgment of his wisdom in chastening us, and he will be able to repent of any further deprivation that he had in store for us. For our ensample, this is also what our Heavenly Father has always done. For, our earthly fathers—those who are truly fathers—learned this from the Father God, in the first place.

Therefore, in this case, the "proof of the pudding", as is said, would come when the God produced an effect against all the gods that they were worshipping; such that He would show that they were not gods of any real consequence.

> *Therefore, behold, the days come, saith the LORD, that it shall no more be said, The LORD liveth, that brought up the children of Israel out of the land of Egypt; But, The LORD liveth, that brought up the children of Israel from the land of the north, and from all the lands whither he had driven them: and I will bring them again into their land that I gave unto their fathers. Behold, I will send for many fishers, saith the LORD, and they shall fish them; and after will I send for many hunters, and they shall hunt them from every mountain, and from every hill, and out of the holes of the rocks. For mine eyes are upon all their ways: they are not hid from my face, neither is their iniquity hid from mine eyes.*
>
> *And first I will recompense their iniquity and their sin double; because they have defiled my land, they have filled mine inheritance with the carcases of their detestable and abominable things.*
>
> *O LORD, my strength, and my fortress, and my refuge in the day of affliction, the Gentiles shall come unto thee from the ends of the earth, and shall say, Surely our fathers have inherited lies, vanity, and things wherein there is no profit. Shall a man make gods unto himself, and they are no gods?*
>
> *Therefore, behold, I will this once cause them to know, I will cause them to know mine hand and my might; and they shall know that my name is The LORD.*
>
> (Jeremiah 16:14-21)

Okay, let us get back to work.

We, who study the Bible and are charged by God to present meaning from His living word, to the world, must show the world the first level of evidence of the one, Faithful and True, God. To do this, we must first firmly plant our own faith; for, we sometimes get caught up in the discovery of whether we have two versions of God contained in the Bible. Too often, we separate the God of Abraham, Isaac and Jacob from the God of Jesus of Nazareth. Then, we do not see the line that runs from Creation, to now. So, in our mind there is a great separation between Malachi and Matthew. This is not recognized as the transformative event that solidifies our Age. It is not generally understood that during this time mankind was being remodeled in preparation for a newly emerging image. We do not seem to understand that we were being moved from adolescences in our dealings with God, to a more adult-like stance in reality.

> *For we know in part, and we prophesy in part. But when that which is perfect is come, then that which is in part shall be done away. When I was a child, I spake as a child, I understood as a child, I thought as a child: but when I became a man, I put away childish things. For now we see through a glass, darkly; but then face to face: now I know in part; but then shall I know even as also I am known.*
>
> (1 Corinthians 13:11-12)

Too often, we forget our own roots in agnosticism, and we want everybody to transform themselves; ***now***! Let me state clearly that what is written next applies only to the conversion of a seeker. In other places, we have presented words for those who feel that they have everything all sewed up about this matter of their god. For now, let us think about those who are sitting in a position where they hear our message, and are intrigued by it. Understand clearly that not everyone who knows God will react just like us. This is seen in the continuation of the Athenian matter.

> *And when they heard of the resurrection of the dead, some mocked: and others said, We will hear thee again of this matter.*
>
> *So Paul departed from among them. Howbeit certain men clave unto him, and believed: among the which was Dionysius the Areopagite, and a woman named Damaris, and others with them.*
>
> (Acts 17:32-34)

Again, a lesson from Jeremiah is appropriate, here. By the Old Testament, we are made aware of the position of the nation of Israel, as being a peculiar treasure of the LORD God; however, the nation of Israel sometimes thought that they were the only ones holding that position. Surely, in their early years, they were told that they must not adopt the ways of any other nations around them, and this could have placed them in an increasingly separatist frame of mind; but, the congregation of Israel was also told that there would be others who would see the glory that God had demonstrated in their nation. These others would become jealous to have what they had, and would come to God for it. There is such a man in Jeremiah's life.

> *Now when Ebedmelech the Ethiopian, one of the eunuchs which was in the king's house, heard that they had put Jeremiah in the dungeon; the king then sitting in the gate of Benjamin; Ebedmelech went forth out of the king's house, and spake to the king, saying, My lord the king, these men have done evil in all that they have done to Jeremiah the prophet, whom they have cast into the dungeon; and he is like to die for hunger in the place where he is: for there is no more bread in the city.*
>
> *Then the king commanded Ebedmelech the Ethiopian, saying, Take from hence thirty men with thee, and take up Jeremiah the prophet out of the dungeon, before he die.*
>
> *So Ebedmelech took the men with him, and went into the house of the king under the treasury, and took thence old cast clouts and old rotten rags, and let them down by cords into the dungeon to Jeremiah. And Ebedmelech the Ethiopian said unto Jeremiah, Put now these old cast clouts and rotten rags under thine armholes under the cords. And Jeremiah did so.*
>
> *So they drew up Jeremiah with cords, and took him up out of the dungeon: and Jeremiah remained in the court of the prison.*
>
> (Jeremiah 38:7-13)

And lest you think that *Ebedmelech the Ethiopian* was treated as just one more good man who had pity on the downtrodden, let us take a look at God's view of his actions. For, in this view, of God, we see a place of recognition of non-Israelis into the service of God, through faith.

> *Now the word of the LORD came unto Jeremiah, while he was shut up in the court of the prison, saying, Go and speak to Ebedmelech the Ethiopian, saying,*
>
> *Thus saith the LORD of hosts, the God of Israel;*
>
> *Behold, I will bring my words upon this city for evil, and not for good; and they shall be accomplished in that day before thee. But I will deliver thee in that day, saith the LORD: and thou shalt not be given into the hand of the men of whom thou art afraid. For I will surely deliver thee, and thou shalt not fall by the sword, but thy life shall be for a prey unto thee: because thou hast put thy trust in me, saith the LORD.*
>
> (Jeremiah 39:15-18)

There were also those who would be perceived as being on the outside, who still held reverence for God, and for the man of God. One of the most notable of these is Nebuchadrezzar king of Babylon. Some of the things that he did that show his position relative to God are recorded in the book of Daniel. Nebuchadrezzar king of Babylon was, by no means, a firm believer in the God of Abraham, Isaac and Jacob. Really, he might be described as the "test-the-waters" type of agnostic. He did not disbelieve in God, but he did believe that there were other gods that just might be superior to God. Even with this belief, he had respect for the messenger of God.

> *Now Nebuchadrezzar king of Babylon gave charge concerning Jeremiah to Nebuzaradan the captain of the guard, saying, Take him, and look well to him, and do him no harm; but do unto him even as he shall say unto thee.*
>
> (Jeremiah 39:11-12)

"So, what is the point," you ask, with a measure of antagonism in your projected voice.

It really does not matter if a person wishes to hide behind the labels of atheist, to keep from having to face the reality of limited control; or the label of agnostic, to escape from being accountable to a definite sphere of order; they must, each one, be brought before God just as they are. We who know God, must constantly petition God that he bring forth His kingdom on the earth. In the Lord's Prayer, the, kingdom coming, precedes the, will being done. This is not, the kingdom being built, or, the kingdom being torn down; this is, the kingdom coming.

Guess who is the only Being THAT can deliver His kingdom to this world?

Now, that was an easy question; wasn't it? We have to allow that God does send blessings to those who have not yet directly faced Him in their lives. To say that terrible things will happen to anyone, because they do not immediately conform to this or the other, is to deny the progressive nature of God. God did not destroy Nebuchadnezzar whenever he veered from His path. This is because, like all the rest of us, Nebuchadnezzar was a tool in God's Total Design. This is the Design that unfolds for the benefit of all mankind, and not just for building the membership of any religious group or organization.

> *Then said Jesus unto them again, Verily, verily, I say unto you, I am the door of the sheep. All that ever came before me are thieves and robbers: but the sheep did not hear them. I am the door: by me if any man enter in, he shall be saved, and shall go in and out, and find pasture. The thief cometh not, but for to steal, and to kill, and to destroy: I am come that they might have life, and that they might have it more abundantly. I am the good shepherd: the good shepherd giveth his life for the sheep.*
>
> (John 10:7-11)

When we truly understand the global nature of God's provisions for mankind, it becomes easier to continue the walk with the God of Abraham, Isaac and Jacob, as traveling along the path to the righteousness set by Jesus of Nazareth. Once we know that it is life that God is seeking—even in the mass of destruction that was visited on His chosen people, as well as those who defied Him in the Old Testament era—we can begin, at least, to believe that there must be some kind of ordered reason to His construction of the world.

The stance of the agnostic is somewhat easy to have when you try to understand God in light of a single event, or a personal collection of events of the world. This is the most limited of views. God cannot be understood in this way. He can only be understood in light of the events of all beings, not even as they are considered across all time, in both Heaven and earth. Therefore, we must not present God as owned property of our intellect. Indeed, except for by our good works, we must not, at all, present God. This is how we must express God to those who are, by their definition of themselves, saying something different from what we want to hear.

> *Ye are the light of the world. A city that is set on an hill cannot be hid. Neither do men light a candle, and put it under a bushel, but on a candlestick; and it giveth light unto all that are in the house.*
>
> *Let your light so shine before men, that they may see your good works, and glorify your Father which is in heaven.*
>
> (Matthew 5:14-16)

The agnostic is telling us that what we are presenting is so confusing as to be basically worthless, as a thing around which one can order ones life. Additionally, the person who would label himself an atheist is telling us that our presentations of God are to them not presentations of a god, but of something else.

No, it is not sufficient to quote Scripture to others, with the expectation that suddenly we will sway them by the massive weight of our arguments; they, too, feel that they have a brain and an intellect. This type of behavior is one among those things that we were told not to do.

> *Of these things put them in remembrance, charging them before the Lord that they strive not about words to no profit, but to the subverting of the hearers.*
>
> (2 Timothy 2:14-14)

In our conversations on Scripture, as informed by our preparation; this is what we must do, in faith and truth.

> *Study to show thyself approved unto God, a workman that needeth not to be ashamed, rightly dividing the word of truth. But shun*

profane and vain babblings: for they will increase unto more ungodliness.

(2 Timothy 2:15-16)

Maybe it is time for some, if not all, of our noise to cease.

Be still, and know that I am God: I will be exalted among the heathen, I will be exalted in the earth. The LORD of hosts is with us; the God of Jacob is our refuge. Selah.

(Psalm 4610-11)

It is time for us to reassess the directions in which we have been leading the ministries that purport to represent God: the ministry of the word is not as powerful as the ministry of the life. Yes, the disciples were sent into the world to teach . . .

And Jesus came and spake unto them, saying, All power is given unto me in heaven and in earth. Go ye therefore, and teach all nations, baptizing them in the name of the Father, and of the Son, and of the Holy Ghost: Teaching them to observe all things whatsoever I have commanded you: and, lo, I am with you alway, even unto the end of the world. Amen.

(Matthew 28:18-20)

. . . But, it would have been a wasted task if they did not live the life that they were teaching. The song of the life lived will always overwhelm the sound of any voice of admonition. It wasn't the words that Jesus said that he put forward as the proof of his divinity. It wasn't because he told good stories about his relationship with God that men were moved. It wasn't that he could quote the Old Testament, and move even the religious leaders to be impressed with his knowledge and grasp of Scripture. It was the works that he did for the Father, and the life that he lived.

Philip saith unto him, Lord, show us the Father, and it sufficeth us.

Jesus saith unto him, Have I been so long time with you, and yet hast thou not known me, Philip? he that hath seen me hath seen

> *the Father; and how sayest thou then, Show us the Father? Believest thou not that I am in the Father, and the Father in me? the words that I speak unto you I speak not of myself: but the Father that dwelleth in me, he doeth the works. Believe me that I am in the Father, and the Father in me: or else believe me for the very works' sake.*
>
> (John 14:8-11)

God has no respect of persons: He will deliver his word to all mankind; whether they listen, or not. Even the atheist will receive the message of God. However, we might find that the strongest message of God, sent to all mankind, is done in that same format that He did it in times of old. This is the message of the life that is lived for Him. It is no wonder that the Bible tells us to become as a little child, in our approach to serving God. It is given to the little child to know how to live a true life. When they are angry, they do not try to pretend that they are happy. When they are happy, they do not mask it in order to keep you from stealing their joy. When they are sick, they let you know.

We have worn the world out, with words with no substance. We need to release that inner child, whose Father is God. Let the world see you running to Daddy, to tell Him that those, who call themselves atheists and agnostics, are "hurting" you. And let those who you feel have "hurt" you, know that you have told Dad about what they are doing. Then step back; and let Dad "get them".

I invite all those who know God, to, in prayer, deliver to Him anyone that they meet who sits under one of these titles. Then watch Dad work in their lives. By this writing, I raise all, especially those who go by these names, up to You, Dad. And I do so in the name of my Elder Brother, Jesus Christ, and for his name's sake. Amen.

It is time for we who know Him, to get back to living the life in Him; and, to do so in the sight of each one we meet, person-to-person. In this way, even the atheist will not only receive, but truly they will accept.

And the angel of the Lord spake unto Philip, saying, Arise, and go toward the south unto the way that goeth down from Jerusalem unto Gaza, which is desert.

And he arose and went: and, behold, a man of Ethiopia, an eunuch of great authority under Candace queen of the Ethiopians, who had the charge of all her treasure, and had come to Jerusalem for to worship, Was returning, and sitting in his chariot read Esaias the prophet.

Then the Spirit said unto Philip, Go near, and join thyself to this chariot.

And Philip ran thither to him, and heard him read the prophet Esaias, and said, Understandest thou what thou readest?

And he said, How can I, except some man should guide me? And he desired Philip that he would come up and sit with him.

The place of the scripture which he read was this, He was led as a sheep to the slaughter; and like a lamb dumb before his shearer, so opened he not his mouth: In his humiliation his judgment was taken away: and who shall declare his generation? for his life is taken from the earth.

And the eunuch answered Philip, and said, I pray thee, of whom speaketh the prophet this? of himself, or of some other man?

Then Philip opened his mouth, and began at the same scripture, and preached unto him Jesus.

And as they went on their way, they came unto a certain water: and the eunuch said, See, here is water; what doth hinder me to be baptized?

And Philip said, If thou believest with all thine heart, thou mayest.

And he answered and said, I believe that Jesus Christ is the Son of God. And he commanded the chariot to stand still: and they went down both into the water, both Philip and the eunuch; and he baptized him.

And when they were come up out of the water, the Spirit of the Lord caught away Philip, that the eunuch saw him no more: and he went on his way rejoicing.

(Acts 8:26-39)

Not by the Hand of Man

There are times when things seem to be going in a direction that requires a Christian to stand up and make a difference. The issue of democracy is not one of these times. Democracy is not the means for the conversion of mankind: Jesus Christ, and him crucified, is. There are many Christians hanging their hopes on this form of government to bring peace to the world. This is not what government was created by God to do. Let me begin by saying that, as Christians, we are told that we must pray for the leaders of our governments; also, we are told why we must do so.

> *I exhort therefore, that, first of all, supplications, prayers, intercessions, and giving of thanks, be made for all men; For kings, and for all that are in authority; that we may lead a quiet and peaceable life in all godliness and honesty. For this is good and acceptable in the sight of God our Saviour; Who will have all men to be saved, and to come unto the knowledge of the truth.*
>
> (1 Timothy 2:1-4)

Prayer for leaders is required, but I must point out that there is no mention of providing God's peace to the world through any government, even when we diligently pray for our leaders. In fact, Jesus made a clear distinction between the peace of the world, and the peace of God.

> *These things have I spoken unto you, being yet present with you. But the Comforter, which is the Holy Ghost, whom the Father will send in my name, he shall teach you all things, and bring all things to your remembrance, whatsoever I have said unto you. Peace I leave with you, my peace I give unto you: not as the world*

giveth, give I unto you. Let not your heart be troubled, neither let it be afraid.

(John 14:25-27)

There are many organizations that have been formed, carrying the title of Christian, but that are actually performing the work of the world. This is not a criticism of their work; only a clarification of for whom the work is being done. These types of works are present in many of the head-to-head clashes between Christian organizations, and governmental entities.

It is, of course, our right, according to the laws of democracy, to disagree with the government; however, we have no right to say that this is being done on behalf of God and His Kingdom, in the world. This is a very delicate subject, for there are many organizations that strive against the government on the basis of actions that could cause suppression of rights of Christians. Even so, this does not provide a justification for placing this work that is being done at a level that is equal with the message of Christ. This is especially a delicate issue for those Christian churches involved in such outreaches.

Let me state again, and, this time, emphatically: there is nothing wrong with challenging the government; however, such challenges must be pursued as a normal part of the democratic process. Such pursuits must not be portrayed as being a message from God. Of equal importance; the actions of the government must not be raised to the level of violations of God's law, unless it is obviously among those things that God requires of governments. Jesus Christ told us the things that cause nations to be in violation of God's law.

Then shall he say also unto them on the left hand, Depart from me, ye cursed, into everlasting fire, prepared for the devil and his angels: For I was an hungred, and ye gave me no meat: I was thirsty, and ye gave me no drink: I was a stranger, and ye took me not in: naked, and ye clothed me not: sick, and in prison, and ye visited me not.

Then shall they also answer him, saying, Lord, when saw we thee an hungred, or athirst, or a stranger, or naked, or sick, or in prison, and did not minister unto thee?

Then shall he answer them, saying, Verily I say unto you, Inasmuch as ye did it not to one of the least of these, ye did it not to me.
(Matthew 25:41-45)

Yes, when we see a nation misbehaving in the fashion described above, we have every reason to warn the nation of the judgment from God that it may be facing. It is, however, up to God to perform the change. And yes, God does use the political process, sometimes, to accomplish change in the world. This was done during the time of Nebuchadrezzar king of Babylon, when God told the land of Judah that He had established a new political center for the world. The LORD told them that they must submit to this new political center; and He told them the consequences of not doing so.

The word which came unto Jeremiah from the LORD, when king Zedekiah sent unto him Pashur the son of Melchiah, and Zephaniah the son of Maaseiah the priest, saying, Inquire, I pray thee, of the LORD for us; for Nebuchadrezzar king of Babylon maketh war against us; if so be that the LORD will deal with us according to all his wondrous works, that he may go up from us.

Then said Jeremiah unto them, Thus shall ye say to Zedekiah: Thus saith the LORD God of Israel; Behold, I will turn back the weapons of war that are in your hands, wherewith ye fight against the king of Babylon, and against the Chaldeans, which besiege you without the walls, and I will assemble them into the midst of this city. And I myself will fight against you with an outstretched hand and with a strong arm, even in anger, and in fury, and in great wrath. And I will smite the inhabitants of this city, both man and beast: they shall die of a great pestilence. And afterward, saith the LORD, I will deliver Zedekiah king of Judah, and his servants, and the people, and such as are left in this city from the pestilence, from the sword, and from the famine, into the hand of Nebuchadrezzar king of Babylon, and into the hand of their enemies, and into the hand of those that seek their life: and he shall smite them with the edge of the sword; he shall not spare them, neither have pity, nor have mercy.

And unto this people thou shalt say, Thus saith the LORD; Behold, I set before you the way of life, and the way of death. He that abideth in this city shall die by the sword, and by the famine, and by the pestilence: but he that goeth out, and falleth to the Chaldeans that besiege you, he shall live, and his life shall be unto him for a prey.

(Jeremiah 21:1-9)

Then, once God had established the dominant political force in the world; the LORD took over full responsibility for making the political center perform according to His will. Let us share some episodes of God's intervention to correct the kings in Babylon and Persia.

EPISODE ONE—king Nebuchadnezzar (Babylon)

Blessed be the God of Shadrach, Meshach, and Abednego

. . . there is no other God that can deliver after this sort

The king performed a foolish political move, in not honoring a sensible separation of church and state.

Nebuchadnezzar spake and said unto them, Is it true, O Shadrach, Meshach, and Abednego, do not ye serve my gods, nor worship the golden image which I have set up? Now if ye be ready that at what time ye hear the sound of the cornet, flute, harp, sackbut, psaltery, and dulcimer, and all kinds of music, ye fall down and worship the image which I have made; well: but if ye worship not, ye shall be cast the same hour into the midst of a burning fiery furnace; and who is that God that shall deliver you out of my hands?

Shadrach, Meshach, and Abednego, answered and said to the king, O Nebuchadnezzar, we are not careful to answer thee in this matter. If it be so, our God whom we serve is able to deliver us from the burning fiery furnace, and he will deliver us out of thine hand, O king. But if not, be it known unto thee, O king, that we will not serve thy gods, nor worship the golden image which thou hast set up.

(Daniel 3:14-18)

Even though king Nebuchadnezzar received a none too subtle reminder of the political reach of a king, as he stretches his authority into the domain of the Spirit; still, the king pressed his political advantage, over the, perceived to be weaker, religious folks. Even so, you can be sure that life and death is a part of the authorization for the exercise of a king's authority.

Then was Nebuchadnezzar full of fury, and the form of his visage was changed against Shadrach, Meshach, and Abednego: therefore he spake, and commanded that they should heat the furnace one seven times more than it was wont to be heated. And he commanded the most mighty men that were in his army to bind Shadrach, Meshach, and Abednego, and to cast them into the burning fiery furnace.

Then these men were bound in their coats, their hosen, and their hats, and their other garments, and were cast into the midst of the burning fiery furnace. Therefore because the king's commandment was urgent, and the furnace exceeding hot, the flame of the fire slew those men that took up Shadrach, Meshach, and Abednego. And these three men, Shadrach, Meshach, and Abednego, fell down bound into the midst of the burning fiery furnace.

Then Nebuchadnezzar the king was astonied, and rose up in haste, and spake, and said unto his counsellors, Did not we cast three men bound into the midst of the fire?

They answered and said unto the king, True, O king.

He answered and said, Lo, I see four men loose, walking in the midst of the fire, and they have no hurt; and the form of the fourth is like the Son of God.

(Daniel 3:19-25)

Even though a king does have authority for life and death; God reserves, to Himself, the final transition from one, to the other. In other words, God can override the order of a king, without touching the order itself, or even announcing that it has been overruled.

> *Then Nebuchadnezzar came near to the mouth of the burning fiery furnace, and spake, and said, Shadrach, Meshach, and Abednego, ye servants of the most high God, come forth, and come hither.*
>
> *Then Shadrach, Meshach, and Abednego, came forth of the midst of the fire. And the princes, governors, and captains, and the king's counsellors, being gathered together, saw these men, upon whose bodies the fire had no power, nor was an hair of their head singed, neither were their coats changed, nor the smell of fire had passed on them.*
>
> *Then Nebuchadnezzar spake, and said, Blessed be the God of Shadrach, Meshach, and Abednego, who hath sent his angel, and delivered his servants that trusted in him, and have changed the king's word, and yielded their bodies, that they might not serve nor worship any god, except their own God.*
>
> *Therefore I make a decree, That every people, nation, and language, which speak any thing amiss against the God of Shadrach, Meshach, and Abednego, shall be cut in pieces, and their houses shall be made a dunghill: because there is no other God that can deliver after this sort.*
>
> (Daniel 3:26-29)

EPISODE TWO—king Nebuchadnezzar (Babylon)

mine understanding returned unto me, and I blessed the most High, and I praised and honoured him that liveth for ever

This is an episode where God issued correction, by debasing a politician . . .

> *All this came upon the king Nebuchadnezzar.*

At the end of twelve months he walked in the palace of the kingdom of Babylon. The king spake, and said, Is not this great Babylon, that I have built for the house of the kingdom by the might of my power, and for the honour of my majesty?

While the word was in the king's mouth, there fell a voice from heaven, saying, O king Nebuchadnezzar, to thee it is spoken; The kingdom is departed from thee. And they shall drive thee from men, and thy dwelling shall be with the beasts of the field: they shall make thee to eat grass as oxen, and seven times shall pass over thee, until thou know that the most High ruleth in the kingdom of men, and giveth it to whomsoever he will.

The same hour was the thing fulfilled upon Nebuchadnezzar: and he was driven from men, and did eat grass as oxen, and his body was wet with the dew of heaven, till his hairs were grown like eagles' feathers, and his nails like birds' claws.

(Daniel 4:28-34)

. . . Then, enlightening him, in order to restore him to his throne, and so that he can educate others as to the indisputable Authority of God, the Most High.

And at the end of the days I Nebuchadnezzar lifted up mine eyes unto heaven, and mine understanding returned unto me, and I blessed the most High, and I praised and honoured him that liveth for ever, whose dominion is an everlasting dominion, and his kingdom is from generation to generation: . . .

(Daniel 4:34)

EPISODE THREE—king Belshazzar (Babylon)

This episode, with king Belshazzar, is particularly striking in its obvious movement of the Hand of God, in issuing judgment. God had chastised king Nebuchadnezzar, and the king had placed his testimony on record for all future generations; however, king Belshazzar did not honor the message. Therefore, God issued a clear message of judgment against him. There may be some who believe that this is the position that the modern Christian organization must take against the *evil* of governmental entities. Yes, this has a similar tone as the modern warnings that are being given by some Christian organizations, but theirs seem to carry neither the imprint of God, nor the power of His Word.

I refer to king Belshazzar in order to highlight the obvious visible intervention of the Hand of God. The others actions from God, mentioned in the prior episodes, brought about internal change in the kings. This, too, is from the Hand of God, but it is not as publicly obvious as king Belshazzar's episode. Changes that are a matter of the mind can be mistaken for a human move toward maturity, or toward greater understanding of God. These are often not attributed to the Hand of God, even though they are just as real a part of His work as what we will discuss now. Also, messages from God that are given to individuals sometimes bring out the skeptics among those people or group that did not ***see*** what God has done.

Mankind likes signs. So, sometimes, God makes them crystal clear, and highly visible to the public. This is the witness of Belshazzar, where, to provide visible evidence, God did not choose a man to convert the king; God chose one of His angels to deliver judgment against the king. The event started like this: there was writing on the wall by a hand from God.

> *Belshazzar the king made a great feast to a thousand of his lords, and drank wine before the thousand. Belshazzar, whiles he tasted the wine, commanded to bring the golden and silver vessels which his father Nebuchadnezzar had taken out of the temple which was in Jerusalem; that the king, and his princes, his wives, and his concubines, might drink therein. Then they brought the golden vessels that were taken out of the temple of the house of God which was at Jerusalem; and the king, and his princes, his wives, and his concubines, drank in them. They drank wine, and praised the gods of gold, and of silver, of brass, of iron, of wood, and of stone.*
>
> *In the same hour came forth fingers of a man's hand, and wrote over against the candlestick upon the plaster of the wall of the king's palace: and the king saw the part of the hand that wrote.*
>
> (Daniel 5:1-5)

To correct this nation, God sent a clear, superhuman message. This is an example for every nation; though, we may be somewhat immune to it now. Obviously, God can use the same method to correct nations now; however, because of our advanced state, we would presume that the message was an *accident* or *natural phenomenon*, or some form of clandestine operation, maybe, even, a magic trick. Therefore, a thing that is perceived as being either a natural phenomenon or a contrived feat of man may not immediately be recognized as supernatural. But, sometimes, if we look carefully, we will recognize it as being beyond the current abilities of man to produce.

Digressing for just a moment; on a positive note, this was the same type of message that God gave to the world when Jesus was conceived. Jesus was not conceived in the, then possible, way; he was born of a virgin. This was not an artificial insemination from the hand of man, but an overshadowing of the Holy Ghost. By this event, God sent a clear message to the world, so that we cannot forget that the LORD is working in our midst, nor ignore the uniqueness of this manifestation of God's overriding Authority over the things of this world; in this case, biological science. Having said that, let us return to Belshazzar.

The impact of the message was not lost on king Belshazzar. When he saw it, fear and trembling overwhelmed the king.

> *Then the king's countenance was changed, and his thoughts troubled him, so that the joints of his loins were loosed, and his knees smote one against another.*
>
> (Daniel 5:6)

There was no doubt in the king's mind that this was something out of the realm of human capabilities. No matter how strong a person may be; when the power of God enters the room or the event, it can be the cause of overwhelming impotence on the part of man.

Now, even though He did in this case, God does not always use fear. He can also use respect and obedience to manifest His presence to the person within the event. But, king Belshazzar needed the fear factor to give him, and all mankind after him, the knowledge that God is a sure part of this lesson.

The impotence of mankind is highlighted in that, as the episode continued, the king had to take things up a notch, beyond simple human reasoning skills. Wherefore king Belshazzar tried to use the resources of his kingdom; calling on the best he had available.

> *The king cried aloud to bring in the astrologers, the Chaldeans, and the soothsayers. And the king spake, and said to the wise men of Babylon, Whosoever shall read this writing, and show me the interpretation thereof, shall be clothed with scarlet, and have a chain of gold about his neck, and shall be the third ruler in the kingdom.*
>
> (Daniel 5:7)

But even with the availability of such a great reward, the human resources of the kingdom failed to provide the remedy.

> *Then came in all the king's wise men: but they could not read the writing, nor make known to the king the interpretation thereof.*
>
> (Daniel 5:8)

So, next, it was time to rely upon God, through his representative, Daniel. It is not always necessary for the man of God to announce himself to the king, or the President, or the governor, or anyone else; oftentimes, God will cause the man of God to be brought to the event. This reminds me of something a pastor taught us youngsters in the faith; way back in my emerging adult years. Our youth pastor told us that sometimes the most lasting message is a result of someone coming and asking; not, someone going to tell. Someone coming and asking seems to be the approach that God used in this episode, to get His message across. Now, this does not mean that God does not also direct his prophets to go and tell: He does. However, in this case, it was a "come and ask" type situation, and the king was more than ready for the answer.

> *Then was Daniel brought in before the king. And the king spake and said unto Daniel, Art thou that Daniel, which art of the children of the captivity of Judah, whom the king my father brought out of Jewry?*
>
> (Daniel 5:13)

Then Daniel answered and said before the king, Let thy gifts be to thyself, and give thy rewards to another; yet I will read the writing unto the king, and make known to him the interpretation.
(Daniel 5:17)

So, once the message was revealed to the king, he knew that there was no way to escape the consequence of his actions. Relatively quickly, the correction came from God as indicated; in that, God sent His ambassador to perform the correction that had been declared.

In that night was Belshazzar the king of the Chaldeans slain.
(Daniel 5:30)

"But, why", you may ask, "didn't God just correct the king? Why didn't God **make** Him do it His way?"

Well, God definitely has the power to do that; and as we have seen, in some cases He does use that technique. As far as why He did not apply that methodology to Belshazzar; this is a matter for revelation from the Holy Ghost. However, as we look at the statements that Daniel made to the king, we might get a somewhat clearer image of why.

O thou king, the most high God gave Nebuchadnezzar thy father a kingdom, and majesty, and glory, and honour: And for the majesty that he gave him, all people, nations, and languages, trembled and feared before him: whom he would he slew; and whom he would he kept alive; and whom he would he set up; and whom he would he put down. But when his heart was lifted up, and his mind hardened in pride, he was deposed from his kingly throne, and they took his glory from him: And he was driven from the sons of men; and his heart was made like the beasts, and his dwelling was with the wild asses: they fed him with grass like oxen, and his body was wet with the dew of heaven; till he knew that the most high God ruled in the kingdom of men, and that he appointeth over it whomsoever he will.

And thou his son, O Belshazzar, hast not humbled thine heart, though thou knewest all this; But hast lifted up thyself against the Lord of heaven; and they have brought the vessels of his house before thee, and thou, and thy lords, thy wives, and thy concubines, have drunk wine in them; and thou hast praised the gods of silver, and gold, of brass, iron, wood, and stone, which see not, nor hear, nor know: and the God in whose hand thy breath is, and whose are all thy ways, hast thou not glorified: Then was the part of the hand sent from him; and this writing was written.

(Daniel 5:18-24)

The implication from this message is that Belshazzar had no excuse for his actions. The king had an example that had been given to him through Nebuchadnezzar's correction, and, that was known by the entire royal family. They all knew what had happened to Nebuchadnezzar, and they all knew who the Architect of that action is. However, even while knowing this, the king snubbed his nose at God. Belshazzar thought that he was bigger than God. Moreover, the king displayed this arrogance to the world. Therefore, God issued His judgment in the sight of the world.

Not only was the king chastised, but his entire family was also chastised. The throne was not just taken from Belshazzar and given to another Babylonian, to continue the Babylonian empire; rather, the throne was taken totally out of Chaldean control. Another political center was selected to carry forward the message of the existence of the Most High God.

And Darius the Median took the kingdom, being about threescore and two years old.

(Daniel 5:31)

EPISODE FOUR—king Darius (Persia)

I make a decree, That in every dominion of my kingdom men tremble and fear before the God of Daniel: for he is the living God, and stedfast for ever

Again, a king was persuaded to extend politics, over religion.

All the presidents of the kingdom, the governors, and the princes, the counsellors, and the captains, have consulted together to establish a royal statute, and to make a firm decree, that whosoever shall ask a petition of any God or man for thirty days, save of thee, O king, he shall be cast into the den of lions. Now, O king, establish the decree, and sign the writing, that it be not changed, according to the law of the Medes and Persians, which altereth not.

Wherefore king Darius signed the writing and the decree.

(Daniel 6:7-9)

As you read; the persuasion was somewhat weak. In fact, it seems that the king needed no persuasion; it seems that he was anxious to recast his political pride as a religious ornament. This sort of thing is a loud call for automatic disavowal, as could be done by a servant of God. The automatic part of it is that, instead of standing in open defiance, the servant of God just continues in uninterrupted service. This, by itself, is defiance of any such political recasting. Thereby, the battle lines are drawn.

Now when Daniel knew that the writing was signed, he went into his house; and his windows being open in his chamber toward Jerusalem, he kneeled upon his knees three times a day, and prayed, and gave thanks before his God, as he did aforetime.

Then these men assembled, and found Daniel praying and making supplication before his God. Then they came near, and spake before the king concerning the king's decree; Hast thou not signed a decree, that every man that shall ask a petition of any God or man within thirty days, save of thee, O king, shall be cast into the den of lions?

The king answered and said, The thing is true, according to the law of the Medes and Persians, which altereth not.

Then answered they and said before the king, That Daniel, which is of the children of the captivity of Judah, regardeth not thee, O king, nor the decree that thou hast signed, but maketh his petition three times a day.

(Daniel 6:10-13)

Sometimes, when the battle lines are drawn by political advisors (or, even, any other worldly advisor), and the king lazily certifies them, then the one who stands in foolishness is the king.

> *Then the king, when he heard these words, was sore displeased with himself, and set his heart on Daniel to deliver him: and he laboured till the going down of the sun to deliver him.*
>
> *Then these men assembled unto the king, and said unto the king, Know, O king, that the law of the Medes and Persians is, That no decree nor statute which the king establisheth may be changed.*
>
> *Then the king commanded, and they brought Daniel, and cast him into the den of lions. Now the king spake and said unto Daniel, Thy God whom thou servest continually, he will deliver thee.*
>
> *And a stone was brought, and laid upon the mouth of the den; and the king sealed it with his own signet, and with the signet of his lords; that the purpose might not be changed concerning Daniel. Then the king went to his palace, and passed the night fasting: neither were instruments of music brought before him: and his sleep went from him.*
>
> (Daniel 6:14-18)

There is a somewhat crude statement, of the modern day: "Providence protects children and idiots. I know because I have tested it;" and sometimes, the word, fools, is inserted, or substituted for the word, idiots. In either of the latter categories is where king Darius found himself. In his rush to glory, the king had discarded a very strong advisor, Daniel, in exchange for a host of maliciously manipulative ones. Still, it seems that the modern saying was in effect; for, God did protect the king and his kingdom.

> *Then the king arose very early in the morning, and went in haste unto the den of lions. And when he came to the den, he cried with a lamentable voice unto Daniel: and the king spake and said to Daniel, O Daniel, servant of the living God, is thy God, whom thou servest continually, able to deliver thee from the lions?*

Then said Daniel unto the king, O king, live for ever. My God hath sent his angel, and hath shut the lions' mouths, that they have not hurt me: forasmuch as before him innocency was found in me; and also before thee, O king, have I done no hurt.

Then was the king exceeding glad for him, and commanded that they should take Daniel up out of the den.

So Daniel was taken up out of the den, and no manner of hurt was found upon him, because he believed in his God.
(Daniel 6:19-23)

Then, there is this lesson for political advisors: though God suspends the authority of the king to decide life and death, sometimes; at other times, the LORD will allow the king to exercise that authority, without imposing any restriction or restraint. Then, once the king's hand is released, he might use it to slap you, O manipulative advisor--and it might be done with an irreparable outcome. (In respect to that, remember this too: sometimes, the death of a reputation can make a physical death seem like a welcome alternative.)

And the king commanded, and they brought those men which had accused Daniel, and they cast them into the den of lions, them, their children, and their wives; and the lions had the mastery of them, and brake all their bones in pieces or ever they came at the bottom of the den.

Then king Darius wrote unto all people, nations, and languages, that dwell in all the earth; Peace be multiplied unto you. I make a decree, That in every dominion of my kingdom men tremble and fear before the God of Daniel: for he is the living God, and stedfast for ever, and his kingdom that which shall not be destroyed, and his dominion shall be even unto the end. He delivereth and rescueth, and he worketh signs and wonders in heaven and in earth, who hath delivered Daniel from the power of the lions.
(Daniel 6:24-27)

Some of you may have thought that God had no firm purpose in causing the children of Israel to serve their penance among the 'heathen'. It seems—no, it is—that, thereby, the children of Israel became an international messengers of salvation to those who had conquered them. It is my prayer that we all can be so blessed, and so fruitful, in our efforts for the Lord.

There are useful lessons here, for us. Let us extract some of them.

Any man, or nation, trying to correct the problem in the world of democracy may well be getting in the way of God's correction. Daniel was only a messenger; he was not given power, by God, to alter the situation; nor was it necessary for him to do so. The hand from God delivered the message. God effected the correction. When this happens, any change that will come about is from God, and through God, Above. Here is an example of that kind of dispensation.

> *A Psalm of David.*
>
> *The LORD said unto my Lord, Sit thou at my right hand, until I make thine enemies thy footstool. The LORD shall send the rod of thy strength out of Zion: rule thou in the midst of thine enemies. Thy people shall be willing in the day of thy power, in the beauties of holiness from the womb of the morning: thou hast the dew of thy youth.*
>
> (Psalm 110:1-3)

The Lord is the one known as, the Son of God. The Son of God has come, and now sits at the right hand of God the Father, the LORD. It is the Father that has interceded to deliver the world to Christ. For any other to attempt to usurp this work of the Spirit of God is to go against the gift of God to the Son. It is the Son who has the power to work God's will on the earth.

> *And Jesus came and spake unto them, saying, All power is given unto me in heaven and in earth.*
>
> (Matthew 28:18)

It is by the power of Christ that democracy will be healed, if healing is called for; or chained, if it is not. For, this power now works in the world, by the gift of the Holy Ghost; and not, by the hand of man.

> *When they therefore were come together, they asked of him, saying, Lord, wilt thou at this time restore again the kingdom to Israel?*
>
> *And he said unto them, It is not for you to know the times or the seasons, which the Father hath put in his own power. But ye shall receive power, after that the Holy Ghost is come upon you: and ye shall be witnesses unto me both in Jerusalem, and in all Judaea, and in Samaria, and unto the uttermost part of the earth.*
>
> *And when he had spoken these things, while they beheld, he was taken up; and a cloud received him out of their sight.*
>
> (Acts 1:6-9)

We, who are Christians—including any organization that says it was created to do the will of God in Christ Jesus—need to take a good look at this. We need to evaluate our operations in the light of the working of God in the kingdom of democracy. We need to place the template of Belshazzar on the governmental system that is known as, democracy; to see if it either totally fits, or is starting to fit. When we find that it does fit; then, we must understand that this is a matter that will receive the direct intervention of God. Actually, in this new era, it is more correct to say that it will receive the direct intervention of His Son, Jesus Christ. We, who were once called the heathen, are his inheritance.

> *I will declare the decree: the LORD hath said unto me, Thou art my Son; this day have I begotten thee. Ask of me, and I shall give thee the heathen for thine inheritance, and the uttermost parts of the earth for thy possession.*
>
> (Psalm 2:7-8)

Any nation, person or establishment that chooses to correct the "problem" of democracy will find themselves in direct confrontation with God, and subject to His full wrath. This is not a matter for the hand of man. Yes, we are to work in the vineyard of souls. Yes, this also includes the *souls* of the nations that proclaim democracy. Moreover, this also includes the *soul* of democracy itself. Jesus told us what our part is in bringing greater participation in the fulfillment of the great need in the world.

> *After these things the Lord appointed other seventy also, and sent them two and two before his face into every city and place, whither he himself would come. Therefore said he unto them, The harvest truly is great, but the labourers are few: pray ye therefore the Lord of the harvest, that he would send forth labourers into his harvest.*
> (Luke 10:1-2)

This is our *weapon*: prayer. Our strength is in the *Lord of the harvest*; we are just the workers he calls. As the workers, we have a clear description of what we are to do.

> *Afterward he appeared unto the eleven as they sat at meat, and upbraided them with their unbelief and hardness of heart, because they believed not them which had seen him after he was risen. And he said unto them, Go ye into all the world, and preach the gospel to every creature. He that believeth and is baptized shall be saved; but he that believeth not shall be damned.*
> (Mark 16:14-16)

We are not told to demand that anyone or anything adjust itself to fit the message. We are not told to make anything perform the actions that we teach. We are commanded to present the message. The process of transforming the minds of man belongs to two entities. The first is, of course, God. The second is the political system that God has given the power to perform this work, on His behalf.

Democracy made the choice to invest the power for change in the hands of humans. This was the failing of the nation of Israel that brought about the selection of king Saul. They were told what the stakes were.

> *And Samuel told all the words of the LORD unto the people that asked of him a king.*
>
> *And he said, This will be the manner of the king that shall reign over you: He will take your sons, and appoint them for himself, for his chariots, and to be his horsemen; and some shall run before his chariots. And he will appoint him captains over thousands, and captains over fifties; and will set them to ear his ground, and to reap his harvest, and to make his instruments of war, and instruments of his chariots. And he will take your daughters to be confectionaries, and to be cooks, and to be bakers. And he will take your fields, and your vineyards, and your oliveyards, even the best of them, and give them to his servants. And he will take the tenth of your seed, and of your vineyards, and give to his officers, and to his servants. And he will take your menservants, and your maidservants, and your goodliest young men, and your asses, and put them to his work. He will take the tenth of your sheep: and ye shall be his servants.*
>
> *And ye shall cry out in that day because of your king which ye shall have chosen you; and the LORD will not hear you in that day.*
>
> (1 Samuel 8:10-18)

With full knowledge of the stakes, the congregation of Israel made their choice of governance—as we have done, too.

> *Nevertheless the people refused to obey the voice of Samuel; and they said, Nay; but we will have a king over us; That we also may be like all the nations; and that our king may judge us, and go out before us, and fight our battles.*
>
> (1 Samuel 8:19-20)

If we want to promote the power of democracy, over the power of God; then, we will be subject to the same treatment that was given to the nation of Israel by the kings. However, if we turn our eyes back to God, and lay at His feet the full responsibility for our governments—and this means all governments of the earth—then, we will see miraculous results. There is not a single man, or a single nation, or a single natural anything that will prevail to transform a government back to God. It is only done by the supernatural Spirit of God, in the name of the Son of God. In prayer, let us be like the widow who came to the wicked judge. In a similar fashion, let us raise our cries for vengeance; pressing the matter to the Highest Level.

> *And he spake a parable unto them to this end, that men ought always to pray, and not to faint; Saying,*
>
> *There was in a city a judge, which feared not God, neither regarded man: And there was a widow in that city; and she came unto him, saying, Avenge me of mine adversary. And he would not for a while: but afterward he said within himself, Though I fear not God, nor regard man; Yet because this widow troubleth me, I will avenge her, lest by her continual coming she weary me.*
>
> *And the Lord said, Hear what the unjust judge saith.*
>
> *And shall not God avenge his own elect, which cry day and night unto him, though he bear long with them? I tell you that he will avenge them speedily. Nevertheless when the Son of man cometh, shall he find faith on the earth?*
>
> (Luke 18:1-8)

Let us go back to the time when we realized that such matters of reformation are not by the hand of man; this, we accepted by faith, then. Let us, now, strengthen our belief that reformation will happen only by the Hand of God. There was an evangelist who said something like "the world has not seen what God can do through the life of one committed man." This is a nice expression, but it is too late. The world has seen this with Jesus of Nazareth, the Messiah. And the world was given further glimpses of it in the apostle Paul, and in his labors on behalf of the Kingdom of God, in Christ Jesus.

Instead of looking to democracy's strength; let us, as a people of God, stand together and share in Christ's victory. The blessings we need, and even those that we desire, are there.

> *For since the beginning of the world men have not heard, nor perceived by the ear, neither hath the eye seen, O God, beside thee, what he hath prepared for him that waiteth for him. Thou meetest him that rejoiceth and worketh righteousness, those that remember thee in thy ways: behold, thou art wroth; for we have sinned: in those is continuance, and we shall be saved.*
>
> (Isaiah 64:4-5)

Let us, therefore, not attempt to overrule God's authority on this earth, including that portion which is embodied in the way that is Jesus Christ. Present it to others, yes: overrule it, no.

> *And at that time Hanani the seer came to Asa king of Judah, and said unto him, Because thou hast relied on the king of Syria, and not relied on the LORD thy God, therefore is the host of the king of Syria escaped out of thine hand. Were not the Ethiopians and the Lubims a huge host, with very many chariots and horsemen? yet, because thou didst rely on the LORD, he delivered them into thine hand.*
>
> *For the eyes of the LORD run to and fro throughout the whole earth, to show himself strong in the behalf of them whose heart is perfect toward him.*
>
> (2 Chronicles 16:7-9a)

No Man Cometh unto the Father

John 14:1-12

Let not your heart be troubled: ye believe in God, believe also in me.

In my Father's house are many mansions: if it were not so, I would have told you. I go to prepare a place for you. And if I go and prepare a place for you, I will come again, and receive you unto myself; that where I am, there ye may be also. And whither I go ye know, and the way ye know.

Thomas saith unto him, Lord, we know not whither thou goest; and how can we know the way?

Jesus saith unto him, I am the way, the truth, and the life: no man cometh unto the Father, but by me. If ye had known me, ye should have known my Father also: and from henceforth ye know him, and have seen him.

Philip saith unto him, Lord, show us the Father, and it sufficeth us.

Jesus saith unto him, Have I been so long time with you, and yet hast thou not known me, Philip? he that hath seen me hath seen the Father; and how sayest thou then, Show us the Father? Believest thou not that I am in the Father, and the Father in me? the words that I speak unto you I speak not of myself: but the Father that dwelleth in me, he doeth the works.

Believe me that I am in the Father, and the Father in me: or else believe me for the very works' sake.

Verily, verily, I say unto you, He that believeth on me, the works that I do shall he do also; and greater works than these shall he do; because I go unto my Father.

I am the way, the truth, and the life: no man cometh unto the Father, but by me.

This short statement from Jesus contains so much: I pray that I can do it justice in this discussion. That short statement is the essence of what we believe, and the summation of all for which mankind has been striving. It seems, to many, to be a rather exclusive statement by Jesus; and so it is. Truth, by its nature, is exclusive. Most folks, who are able to read this book, would agree that 2+2=4. They would not believe that 2+2=5 or that 2+2=20,000; they would believe that 2+2 always equals 4. This is the nature of truth. The sum of the parts of a truthful statement always arrives at the same result. This is especially true where God is concerned.

Do not err, my beloved brethren. Every good gift and every perfect gift is from above, and cometh down from the Father of lights, with whom is no variableness, neither shadow of turning.

(James 1:16-17)

For a long time, God had sent his prophets to deliver His word. This was done uniquely for each historical episode. Sometimes, more than one prophet tried to deliver the same message of the LORD; it can be difficult to convince those affected by the prophecy that the words of the prophet are indeed from God. Because of the skepticism, sometimes, and arrogance, at other times; the prophet could have experiences such as this one.

Since the day that your fathers came forth out of the land of Egypt unto this day I have even sent unto you all my servants the prophets, daily rising up early and sending them: Yet they hearkened not unto me, nor inclined their ear, but hardened their neck: they did worse than their fathers.

(Jeremiah 7:25-26)

The prophets came with the word from God, to the world. Some may think of the prophets, and their prophecies, as being centered solely on the nation of Israel: this is too narrow a focus. When you read the messages that were delivered by the prophet Jeremiah, you get a much bigger picture of God's communion with man, as done by way of prophecy. Here are some visits to other nations.

The word of the LORD which came to Jeremiah the prophet against the Gentiles; Against Egypt, against the army of Pharaohnecho king of Egypt, which was by the river Euphrates in Carchemish, which Nebuchadrezzar king of Babylon smote in the fourth year of Jehoiakim the son of Josiah king of Judah.

(Jeremiah 46:1-2)

The word of the LORD that came to Jeremiah the prophet against the Philistines, before that Pharaoh smote Gaza.

(Jeremiah 47:1)

The word that the LORD spake against Babylon and against the land of the Chaldeans by Jeremiah the prophet. Declare ye among the nations, and publish, and set up a standard; publish, and conceal not: say, Babylon is taken, Bel is confounded, Merodach is broken in pieces; her idols are confounded, her images are broken in pieces.

(Jeremiah 50:1-2)

The prophets of old were God's message in flesh, to the world. The LORD constantly told the world to come to Him: to help you achieve a greater understanding of this, we begin with a review of the development of the nation of Israel, as God revealed it in the Bible. God tells us how He started the process of preparing the nation.

And Moses went up unto God, and the LORD called unto him out of the mountain, saying, Thus shalt thou say to the house of

Jacob, and tell the children of Israel; Ye have seen what I did unto the Egyptians, and how I bare you on eagles' wings, and brought you unto myself.

(Exodus 19:3-4)

Though this specifically refers to Israel, it also gives us the hint that there is a greater requirement for the world than it had yet perceived. The requirement was embedded in the preparation of Israel. Consider this: God created the eagle, and commanded it to be fruitful. In obedience, by being fruitful, the eagle bears young; this is obvious. Equally obvious is the fact that the young are brought forth to grow up. And, although they may be carried for a while; the child will not always ride on the wings of the parent. The child is being prepared for a time when it will recognize the example that has been given by the parent. At that time, they child will soar on its own. This is like the training that is given to a human child during the process of teaching it how to walk. Israel is the son that was taught how to soar among the other nations of the world. One of the evidences of its flight is prophecy itself.

God's message that was sent through the prophets is consistent; and, it is this: come to Me, little ones. In the early days of the nation of Israel, they crawled to Him. This was primarily because whenever He picked them up to their feet, they looked at the other nations crawling; and deciding to limit themselves in the same fashion, they fell back down to their knees for the world: it seems that they really did not want to be a peculiar treasure of the LORD. In that day, shifting peer pressure overruled solid family values, as it still does, now.

But Jeshurun waxed fat, and kicked: thou art waxen fat, thou art grown thick, thou art covered with fatness; then he forsook God which made him, and lightly esteemed the Rock of his salvation. They provoked him to jealousy with strange gods, with abominations provoked they him to anger. They sacrificed unto devils, not to God; to gods whom they knew not, to new gods that came newly up, whom your fathers feared not. Of the Rock that begat thee thou art unmindful, and hast forgotten God that formed thee.

(Deuteronomy 32:15-18)

Still, God constantly delivered His message to the nation of Israel. The message teaches that, surely God gave birth to the nation, and that the LORD did so for the nation to walk among the other nations of the world. Moreover, the LORD'S message was specific about how the people of Israel must walk among the nations. The way they must walk is as priests of God; ministering unto Him, and thereby benefiting the entire world.

> *Now therefore, if ye will obey my voice indeed, and keep my covenant, then ye shall be a peculiar treasure unto me above all people: for all the earth is mine: And ye shall be unto me a kingdom of priests, and an holy nation. These are the words which thou shalt speak unto the children of Israel.*
>
> (Exodus 19:5-6)

The nation of Israel is called to set the example for the entire world, and to deliver the message of the LORD. They are called peculiar because there was no other nation with a single focus on God. The other nations had gods, and they had a *lead* god; but no other nation had only one God. To be fair to history, I must add that some nations tried to have one god, but their efforts were rejected by the people. Also, some nations, for a limited time, endured in service to one god; but when new leaders arose, this trend was quickly reversed. Their lack of consistency of worship is because none of the other gods displayed a personal interest in the people. Personal interest in the people that serve was done, and is still being done, by the God of Abraham, Isaac and Jacob, and of Jesus of Nazareth—which is, the Father God.

> *Let all the nations be gathered together, and let the people be assembled: who among them can declare this, and show us former things? let them bring forth their witnesses, that they may be justified: or let them hear, and say, It is truth. Ye are my witnesses, saith the LORD, and my servant whom I have chosen: that ye may know and believe me, and understand that I am he: before me there was no God formed, neither shall there be after me. I, even I, am the LORD; and beside me there is no saviour. I have declared, and have saved, and I have showed, when there was no strange god among you: therefore ye are my witnesses, saith the LORD, that I*

am God. Yea, before the day was I am he; and there is none that can deliver out of my hand: I will work, and who shall let it?

Thus saith the LORD, your redeemer, the Holy One of Israel; For your sake I have sent to Babylon, and have brought down all their nobles, and the Chaldeans, whose cry is in the ships. I am the LORD, your Holy One, the creator of Israel, your King.
(Isaiah 43:9-15)

The nation of Israel was the example that the LORD prepared, to show the way. The priests and prophets carried the words to declare God's way, working according to God's ordinance, for the benefit of the nations. But the nations are made up of people who are subject to rulers. Wherefore the message of the prophets was directed at principally one type of people in the nation. These messages were specifically directed at the leaders of the nations. This is still God's way.

Surely, God holds the leaders of nations responsible for the behavior of the nations. But in the ancient time of the patriarchs, as nations grew and de-centralized their national authority (in more regional chunks, among many leaders); it became necessary to start a re-direction. For, several of these new, regional leaders were not trustworthy in delivering the message to their charges; they were only concerned about themselves. The seed of, the concentration of power in a self-centered expression of authority, was planted early in mankind's life on the earth.

And it came to pass, when men began to multiply on the face of the earth, and daughters were born unto them, That the sons of God saw the daughters of men that they were fair; and they took them wives of all which they chose.
(Genesis 6:1-2)

And God saw that the wickedness of man was great in the earth, and that every imagination of the thoughts of his heart was only evil continually.
(Genesis 6:5)

The period of the birth of Israel was not the first time that those in power had misused their position—and it would not be the last. Those early behaviors still flourished in mankind in the time of Jesus Christ's sojourn on earth in the flesh.

> *And as it was in the days of Noe, so shall it be also in the days of the Son of man. They did eat, they drank, they married wives, they were given in marriage, until the day that Noe entered into the ark, and the flood came, and destroyed them all. Likewise also as it was in the days of Lot; they did eat, they drank, they bought, they sold, they planted, they builded; But the same day that Lot went out of Sodom it rained fire and brimstone from heaven, and destroyed them all. Even thus shall it be in the day when the Son of man is revealed.*
>
> (Luke 17:26-30)

As in the days of Noah, the leaders were practicing consumption—almost exclusively for their own individual pleasure, and not for the nation's prosperity. Later, this is what God also endured for the sake of the nation of Israel. It seems that we, as humans, are all too willing to give up God's spiritual blessing, in order to gain natural benefits—chief among these is physical protection. In their selection of a king, the congregation of Israel did this.

> *Then all the elders of Israel gathered themselves together, and came to Samuel unto Ramah, And said unto him, Behold, thou art old, and thy sons walk not in thy ways: now make us a king to judge us like all the nations.*
>
> (1 Samuel 8:4-5)

> *And the LORD said unto Samuel, Hearken unto the voice of the people in all that they say unto thee: for they have not rejected thee, but they have rejected me, that I should not reign over them. According to all the works which they have done since the day that I brought them up out of Egypt even unto this day, wherewith they have forsaken me, and served other gods, so do they also unto thee. Now therefore hearken unto their voice: howbeit yet protest solemnly unto them, and show them the manner of the king that shall reign over them.*
>
> (1 Samuel 8:7-9)

> *Nevertheless the people refused to obey the voice of Samuel; and they said, Nay; but we will have a king over us; That we also may be like all the nations; and that our king may judge us, and go out before us, and fight our battles.*
>
> (1 Samuel 8:19-20)

A very important concept that was not generally accepted by the people is the principle of the power of example. Once they had established the practice of choosing man over God, within their generation; it was most likely to continue from generation to generation. And, so it did.

The LORD sent His prophets with the constant message that you can have both protection and prosperity in God, but that, in order for them to fall under His protection, the possessions must be centered on God and His mission. The message is timeless; it appeared still in the prophecies of the latter day, as it shined brightly in a message of the New Age, as given during an answer to an apostle's concern about recompense for service. No, we do not have to ask such questions now; because, now we know that faith is sufficient. Even so, we must not retroactively criticize the apostle, because the inspiration to ask the question is from the LORD. The inspiration was placed in the apostle so that we would have a definite statement, of a very high level of authority, saying that faith is indeed both sufficient and prosperous.

> *Then Peter began to say unto him, Lo, we have left all, and have followed thee.*
>
> *And Jesus answered and said, Verily I say unto you, There is no man that hath left house, or brethren, or sisters, or father, or mother, or wife, or children, or lands, for my sake, and the gospel's, But he shall receive an hundredfold now in this time, houses, and brethren, and sisters, and mothers, and children, and lands, with persecutions; and in the world to come eternal life.*
>
> (Mark 10:28-30)

I am sure that you know that God has no reason to take anything from you; that God does not need your possessions. Surely, you know that the LORD has his own possessions; that they are—well—everything.

Since you do know that, then you must also know that the LORD can be very generous in distributing from this vast storehouse.

> *Hear, O my people, and I will speak; O Israel, and I will testify against thee: I am God, even thy God. I will not reprove thee for thy sacrifices or thy burnt offerings, to have been continually before me. I will take no bullock out of thy house, nor he goats out of thy folds. For every beast of the forest is mine, and the cattle upon a thousand hills. I know all the fowls of the mountains: and the wild beasts of the field are mine. If I were hungry, I would not tell thee: for the world is mine, and the fulness thereof. Will I eat the flesh of bulls, or drink the blood of goats? Offer unto God thanksgiving; and pay thy vows unto the most High: And call upon me in the day of trouble: I will deliver thee, and thou shalt glorify me.*
>
> (Psalm 50:7-15)

Surely, all our possessions are lessons from God, to prepare us for the next stage. The next stage is greater service to God; going to the final stage, which is death. We need to understand that our assets are only held in trust, until God releases them to somewhere else. A scribe of Scripture told us about the way this occurs at the final redistribution.

> *Yea, I hated all my labour which I had taken under the sun: because I should leave it unto the man that shall be after me. And who knoweth whether he shall be a wise man or a fool? yet shall he have rule over all my labour wherein I have laboured, and wherein I have showed myself wise under the sun. This is also vanity.*
>
> (Ecclesiastes 2:18-19)

At all times, we need to manage all assets as if we are approaching the final redistribution; for, this is the state of mind in which the ability to use what we have received from God takes blessed flight. At that time, the power that is in the example of lives that are lived for God is revealed to us.

Most definitely, the words of the prophets are informative; and we needed examples, to serve as our preparation to receive a special example. The sacrifices to God that are ordained by the Law prodded us to give our life to Him, but these are only tangible things: animals, plants, gold and silver, and, sometimes, the service of a person. These things are eventually consumed, and they pass away, both physically and mentally. We need an example that we can never forget, and never ignore. The words that we hear need life, and that life has to be human. And so, God provided such a life.

> *And the Word was made flesh, and dwelt among us, (and we beheld his glory, the glory as of the only begotten of the Father,) full of grace and truth. John bare witness of him, and cried, saying, This was he of whom I spake, He that cometh after me is preferred before me: for he was before me. And of his fulness have all we received, and grace for grace. For the law was given by Moses, but grace and truth came by Jesus Christ.*
>
> (John 1:14-17)

Jesus is the message that was evidenced way back with the creation of Israel.

> *Our fathers had the tabernacle of witness in the wilderness, as he had appointed, speaking unto Moses, that he should make it according to the fashion that he had seen. Which also our fathers that came after brought in with Jesus into the possession of the Gentiles, whom God drave out before the face of our fathers, unto the days of David; Who found favour before God, and desired to find a tabernacle for the God of Jacob.*
>
> (Acts 7:44-46)

Jesus Christ, the Son of God, is the message that was on the lips of all the prophets

> *And he saith unto me, Write, Blessed are they which are called unto the marriage supper of the Lamb. And he saith unto me, These are the true sayings of God.*
>
> *And I fell at his feet to worship him.*
>
> *And he said unto me, See thou do it not: I am thy fellowservant, and of thy brethren that have the testimony of Jesus: worship God: for the testimony of Jesus is the spirit of prophecy.*
>
> (Revelation 19:9-10)

The example of Jesus' life is *the way* to God. This example sets the stage for those who are seeking God, as they move toward an understanding of the life and soul saving nature of Jesus Christ. The true search for God is the first and most important step, and it is the one that originates in the will of man, though it is only partially by the will of man: all else is up to God to do.

> *Therefore take no thought, saying, What shall we eat? or, What shall we drink? or, Wherewithal shall we be clothed? (For after all these things do the Gentiles seek:) for your heavenly Father knoweth that ye have need of all these things. But seek ye first the kingdom of God, and his righteousness; and all these things shall be added unto you. Take therefore no thought for the morrow: for the morrow shall take thought for the things of itself. Sufficient unto the day is the evil thereof.*
>
> (Matthew 6:31-34)

The example of Jesus' death is *the truth* of God.

> *He was oppressed, and he was afflicted, yet he opened not his mouth: he is brought as a lamb to the slaughter, and as a sheep before her shearers is dumb, so he openeth not his mouth. He was taken from prison and from judgment: and who shall declare his generation? for he was cut off out of the land of the living: for the transgression of my people was he stricken. And he made his grave with the wicked, and with the rich in his death; because he had done no violence, neither was any deceit in his mouth.*
>
> *Yet it pleased the LORD to bruise him; he hath put him to grief: when thou shalt make his soul an offering for sin, he shall see his seed, he shall prolong his days, and the pleasure of the LORD shall prosper in his hand. He shall see of the travail of his soul, and shall be satisfied: by his knowledge shall my righteous servant justify many; for he shall bear their iniquities. Therefore will I divide him a portion with the great, and he shall divide the spoil*

with the strong; because he hath poured out his soul unto death: and he was numbered with the transgressors; and he bare the sin of many, and made intercession for the transgressors.

(Isaiah 53:7-12)

Then said Jesus unto his disciples, If any man will come after me, let him deny himself, and take up his cross, and follow me. For whosoever will save his life shall lose it: and whosoever will lose his life for my sake shall find it. For what is a man profited, if he shall gain the whole world, and lose his own soul? or what shall a man give in exchange for his soul?

(Matthew 16:24-26)

The example of Jesus' resurrection is *the life* that must be applied to every one of us, as lived in God.

I am the good shepherd, and know my sheep, and am known of mine. As the Father knoweth me, even so know I the Father: and I lay down my life for the sheep. And other sheep I have, which are not of this fold: them also I must bring, and they shall hear my voice; and there shall be one fold, and one shepherd. Therefore doth my Father love me, because I lay down my life, that I might take it again. No man taketh it from me, but I lay it down of myself. I have power to lay it down, and I have power to take it again. This commandment have I received of my Father.

(John 10:14-18)

Jesus saith unto him,
I am the way, the truth, and the life:
no man cometh unto the Father, but by me.

To clearly see the message of Jesus is to view God, as we see the Father.

> *If ye had known me, ye should have known my Father also: and from henceforth ye know him, and have seen him.*
>
> (John 14:7)

In the following short exchange, two disciples asked for two pieces of knowledge that direct us to God. The first one asked, on our behalf, how we can direct our steps toward God.

> *Thomas saith unto him, Lord, we know not whither thou goest; and how can we know the way?*
>
> (John 14:5)

The other disciple asked, on our behalf, how we can have assurance that we are heading in the right direction; a direction that is focused on God.

> *Philip saith unto him, Lord, show us the Father, and it sufficeth us.*
>
> (John 14:8)

We need Jesus as the filter between mankind and God. A discovery that is of the time of Moses, teaches us that we need something to span the gap. In that time, Moses wanted to see God, directly. This request was denied, and the LORD told Moses, and us too, why this is not possible . . .

> *And the LORD said unto Moses, I will do this thing also that thou hast spoken: for thou hast found grace in my sight, and I know thee by name.*
>
> *And he said, I beseech thee, shew me thy glory.*
>
> *And he said, I will make all my goodness pass before thee, and I will proclaim the name of the LORD before thee; and will be gracious to whom I will be gracious, and will shew mercy on whom I will shew mercy. And he said, Thou canst not see my face: for there shall no man see me, and live.*
>
> (Exodus 33:17-20)

But we did receive an incentive to pursue our understanding of the LORD, and a method by which we are able to do so. The LORD said that we would be able to see Him in an indirect fashion.

> *And the LORD said, Behold, there is a place by me, and thou shalt stand upon a rock: And it shall come to pass, while my glory passeth by, that I will put thee in a clift of the rock, and will cover thee with my hand while I pass by: And I will take away mine hand, and thou shalt see my back parts: but my face shall not be seen.*
> (Exodus 33:21-23)

In this answer from God, we can see our great need for a mediator, to add further clarity to the indirect view. The Mediator, Jesus Christ, is the one who, in a personal way, shows us the glory of God. Moses delivered the word from God that heralded the coming of the Mediator that would be, to us, the Messiah. Moses showed mankind the written glory of God. As an extension of the written glory of God, the Bible tells of one who was to come to show mankind the personal glory of God; starting with the nation of Israel.

> *The LORD thy God will raise up unto thee a Prophet from the midst of thee, of thy brethren, like unto me; unto him ye shall hearken; According to all that thou desiredst of the LORD thy God in Horeb in the day of the assembly, saying, Let me not hear again the voice of the LORD my God, neither let me see this great fire any more, that I die not.*
>
> *And the LORD said unto me, They have well spoken that which they have spoken. I will raise them up a Prophet from among their brethren, like unto thee, and will put my words in his mouth; and he shall speak unto them all that I shall command him. And it shall come to pass, that whosoever will not hearken unto my words which he shall speak in my name, I will require it of him.*
> (Deuteronomy 18:15-19)

The Prophet is the man, Jesus of Nazareth; his words carried, and still carry, the full power of God.

A personal note, here: for a time, it almost angered me that these two arrogant "sinners", Thomas and Philip, would dare question the Son of the Living God. Then, God, through the Holy Ghost in me, calmed me down, with a simple revelation: it said, "Hear the questions. Are they not your questions as well?" To which I said, "Yes, my Comforter, they are." Then, my follow-up question to the Spirit of Truth was, "How can I see Jesus, since he now sits at the right hand of the Father?" That is a question that others have asked, as well.

Yes, I have read the Scripture in John 20:29, where *Jesus saith unto him, Thomas, because thou hast seen me, thou hast believed: blessed are they that have not seen, and yet have believed.* But, how do I believe without seeing?"

And then, the power of this apostolic admonition came to bear.

> *Of these things put them in remembrance, charging them before the Lord that they strive not about words to no profit, but to the subverting of the hearers. Study to show thyself approved unto God, a workman that needeth not to be ashamed, rightly dividing the word of truth. But shun profane and vain babblings: for they will increase unto more ungodliness.*
>
> (2 Timothy 2:14-16)

Then, the mystery of belief was unveiled.

> *Believe me that I am in the Father, and the Father in me: or else believe me for the very works' sake.*
>
> (John 14:11)

Once those insights were stored in my soul, things became almost crystal clear (I am still human, and I still see through a glass darkly). Progressing slowly, I recounted how I was started on the path to belief in God.

> *Now faith is the substance of things hoped for, the evidence of things not seen. For by it the elders obtained a good report. Through faith we understand that the worlds were framed by the word of God, so that things which are seen were not made of things which do appear.*

By faith Abel offered unto God a more excellent sacrifice than Cain, by which he obtained witness that he was righteous, God testifying of his gifts: and by it he being dead yet speaketh. By faith Enoch was translated that he should not see death; and was not found, because God had translated him: for before his translation he had this testimony, that he pleased God.

But without faith it is impossible to please him: for he that cometh to God must believe that he is, and that he is a rewarder of them that diligently seek him.

(Hebrews 11:1-6)

Let us say, for the sake of discussion, that there are other ways to God, besides being called a Christian. Even if there are, these other methods will still end up facing the same Mediator, Jesus Christ. These other methods will still receive their power on the basis of the sacrifice of the Mediator, who is the Messiah. This was the case even of the law of Moses. The law of Moses was a preview of the coming of the Messiah, in Jesus Christ. Its power is fully contained in the Mediator, and without the Mediator it has no power.

For there is one God, and one mediator between God and men, the man Christ Jesus; Who gave himself a ransom for all, to be testified in due time.

(1 Timothy 2:5-6)

The belief in God that is in me came from the Spirit striving with me. It was then enhanced by my Bible study. Also contained in the Bible—and in the Koran, and in every religious text of any sort (I made an extremely bold statement here)—are the works of Jesus Christ. The names may be different, in some; but the works are there. Thus, by moving in the Spirit of God, in the desire to understand God, is how I am able to understand and accept Jesus Christ.

Expanding a thought, as inspired by Scripture, I say that to please God through Jesus Christ, you must first believe that he is, and that he performed the works that the Bible records that he did. The works of Jesus is the way of God. When you believe them, you have seen the Father.

Moreover, Jesus did not leave us without a means of proving his works. The proof of his works is in ours.

> *Verily, verily, I say unto you, He that believeth on me, the works that I do shall he do also; and greater works than these shall he do; because I go unto my Father.*
>
> (John 14:12)

This method of proof was forcefully pressed at the hearts of the Pharisees, by Jesus of Nazareth, the Christ

> *Then was brought unto him one possessed with a devil, blind, and dumb: and he healed him, insomuch that the blind and dumb both spake and saw. And all the people were amazed, and said, Is not this the son of David?*
>
> *But when the Pharisees heard it, they said, This fellow doth not cast out devils, but by Beelzebub the prince of the devils.*
>
> *And Jesus knew their thoughts, and said unto them, Every kingdom divided against itself is brought to desolation; and every city or house divided against itself shall not stand: And if Satan cast out Satan, he is divided against himself; how shall then his kingdom stand?*
>
> *And if I by Beelzebub cast out devils, by whom do your children cast them out? therefore they shall be your judges.*
>
> *But if I cast out devils by the Spirit of God, then the kingdom of God is come unto you.*
>
> (Matthew 12:22-28)

In conclusion, the following is a question and response that is for all those who seek to serve in the way of Jesus.

Question: How do we show the world Jesus?

Answer: By doing the works that he did, and letting the world see Jesus in us; so that they will see God in Jesus. And once they see God in Jesus, they will know that they have, too, the protection of the Father, for all time. This is eternal life.

Whosoever believeth that Jesus is the Christ is born of God: and every one that loveth him that begat loveth him also that is begotten of him. By this we know that we love the children of God, when we love God, and keep his commandments. For this is the love of God, that we keep his commandments: and his commandments are not grievous.

For whatsoever is born of God overcometh the world: and this is the victory that overcometh the world, even our faith. Who is he that overcometh the world, but he that believeth that Jesus is the Son of God? This is he that came by water and blood, even Jesus Christ; not by water only, but by water and blood. And it is the Spirit that beareth witness, because the Spirit is truth. For there are three that bear record in heaven, the Father, the Word, and the Holy Ghost: and these three are one. And there are three that bear witness in earth, the Spirit, and the water, and the blood: and these three agree in one.

If we receive the witness of men, the witness of God is greater: for this is the witness of God which he hath testified of his Son. He that believeth on the Son of God hath the witness in himself: he that believeth not God hath made him a liar; because he believeth not the record that God gave of his Son.

And this is the record, that God hath given to us eternal life, and this life is in his Son. He that hath the Son hath life; and he that hath not the Son of God hath not life.

These things have I written unto you that believe on the name of the Son of God; that ye may know that ye have eternal life, and that ye may believe on the name of the Son of God.

(1 John 5:1-13)

THE PARALLEL OF ISRAEL

The people of Israel received the law, crafted by the Hand of God, and delivered to the man Moses; and they became one nation under God. The people on the North American continent, in the section known as the United States of America, pieced together their laws, modeled after the commandments of God, and declared themselves "one nation under God".

The people of Israel were administered by judges, during their early existence. The judges of Israel interpreted and managed the law. The people of the United States of America did the same. And in both cases the judges manipulated the administration of the law, sometimes in unrighteous ways.

The people of Israel cried for a king; so, God allowed them what they did not need, but what they insisted on having. The people of the United States of America cried for a representative to replace the king, and God allowed them to have their form of a king. The people of the United States called their king, *Constitution.* In both cases, the warning of God has been fulfilled.

> *And he will take the tenth of your seed, and of your vineyards, and give to his officers, and to his servants. And he will take your menservants, and your maidservants, and your goodliest young men, and your asses, and put them to his work. He will take the tenth of your sheep: and ye shall be his servants. And ye shall cry out in that day because of your king which ye shall have chosen you; and the LORD will not hear you in that day.*
>
> (1 Samuel 8:15-18)

In the nation of Israel, the people of God strayed away from God, and were subjected to captivity. Then, they started their search for the rule of a Messiah, on earth.

In the United States of America, the people of God are now in captivity to those who use the methods of the king Constitution to inflict unrighteous ways and grievous burdens on them. They are crying for the rule, on earth, of the Messiah. Some believe that this will be Jesus. Others just want an extremely good man to step into this position: maybe, even, a President.

The world seems to have gone in a circle; especially, for the portion that is in the United States of America. We move from the desire for a king, to a press for individual responsibility, back to a yearning for a king. I suspect that the same thing has happened in every other nation in the world. In every new generation, the world has been looking for a sign that fits with what the, then, modern man perceives as being relevant to its time. Most often, this sign is sought from God. This is the way it was in the time of Jesus of Nazareth; however, Jesus told the nation of Israel that they would have no signs, except one.

> *Then certain of the scribes and of the Pharisees answered, saying, Master, we would see a sign from thee.*
>
> *But he answered and said unto them, An evil and adulterous generation seeketh after a sign; and there shall no sign be given to it, but the sign of the prophet Jonas: For as Jonas was three days and three nights in the whale's belly; so shall the Son of man be three days and three nights in the heart of the earth.*
>
> (Matthew 12:38-40)

In order to fully understand this thing about signs, you must think beyond societal conditioning. Jesus was not saying that the world would have no evidences of God's movement among man: Jesus had already given the world plenty of evidence that he is, in fact, the full representative of God, with us.

> *Jesus saith unto him, Have I been so long time with you, and yet hast thou not known me, Philip? he that hath seen me hath seen the Father; and how sayest thou then, Show us the Father? Believest thou not that I am in the Father, and the Father in me? the words that I speak unto you I speak not of myself: but the Father that dwelleth in me, he doeth the works.*
>
> (John 14:9-10)

However, the world did not want to just see the power of God, as expressed through a man. The world wanted to see the power of God as it had been expressed in the times of old. This is the power that comes when God says, and there is; as He did, here.

> *In the beginning God created the heaven and the earth. And the earth was without form, and void; and darkness was upon the face of the deep. And the Spirit of God moved upon the face of the waters.*
>
> *And God said, Let there be light: and there was light.*
> (Genesis 1:1-3)

In a time of disempowerment, when the nation could not resist being dominated by others, the Israelites yearned for this time; Israel wanted to see the Father, in action. Eventually, the world wanted to see the Father. This yearning is heard in a request that of one of the disciples of Jesus made.

> *Jesus saith unto him, I am the way, the truth, and the life: no man cometh unto the Father, but by me. If ye had known me, ye should have known my Father also: and from henceforth ye know him, and have seen him.*
>
> *Philip saith unto him, Lord, show us the Father, and it sufficeth us.*
> (John 14:6-8)

The same mentality is present in this day, especially among Christians. We are the new Israel, as pertains to challenges to God. The things that I now say about the Christian world have direct parallels in the development of the nation of Israel. Let us walk, awhile, down that parallel path.

One of the first things that the Christian world did was to try to harness the power of God, and re-package it in a form that fit their requirements. This was done by some of the early Christians, who were not content with the power of God resting in Christ Jesus. They tried to usurp the authority and position of Jesus, by transferring the power of God from him into a man. This is the man, Simon Peter. Oh, by the way; they had neither Peter's permission, nor his concurrence in this matter. If they had asked him, Peter would have vigorously opposed this type of assignment of the power of God in Christ Jesus.

Later, they continued this practice of attempting to transfer the power of God from one person to another. They called these succeeding persons, the heirs of Peter. But it seems that no one consulted God no this matter. Had they done so, they would have been reminded by Him that He gave the heathen as an inheritance to His only begotten Son, Jesus Christ; and to no one else. Furthermore, the Son, who has all power in Heaven and earth, really does not need any help controlling his inheritance. Yes, the Son does commission *tour guides*, to show others the way; but still, control belongs only to Jesus.

A parallel to the attempted transfer of God's Authorization is seen in this event of the nation of Israel. In that situation, it involved the authority that God place in certain of the kings of Israel.

> *Yet Jeroboam the son of Nebat, the servant of Solomon the son of David, is risen up, and hath rebelled against his lord. And there are gathered unto him vain men, the children of Belial, and have strengthened themselves against Rehoboam the son of Solomon, when Rehoboam was young and tenderhearted, and could not withstand them.*
>
> *And now ye think to withstand the kingdom of the LORD in the hand of the sons of David; and ye be a great multitude, and there are with you golden calves, which Jeroboam made you for gods. Have ye not cast out the priests of the LORD, the sons of Aaron, and the Levites, and have made you priests after the manner of the nations of other lands? so that whosoever cometh to consecrate himself with a young bullock and seven rams, the same may be a priest of them that are no gods.*
>
> (2 Chronicles 13:6-9)

Once they had established these other gods, in, for instance, Peter and his so-called heirs; some of the early Christians then set out to transform the written text of the Bible to fit into the mold of their new gods. This continued with other gods; several of which were used to form the various denominations that exist among the Christian churches. Let me clarify for you, so that there is no misunderstanding: the new gods are humans.

Rules were established to replace the law of love; as established, paid for, and delivered by Jesus Christ, the Messiah. These rules are said to have come about to make it possible for the people to more clearly understand God. However, God and His Son know better than that. They know that the new rules have been delivered to further enslave the people of God.

> *But woe unto you, scribes and Pharisees, hypocrites! for ye shut up the kingdom of heaven against men: for ye neither go in yourselves, neither suffer ye them that are entering to go in.*
> (Matthew 23:13)

The Father and the Son know that the new rules have come about to place new burdens on mankind. These new burdens are designed to allow those in power to wield authority over those who do not have earthly power. It is not sufficient that Jesus said that the meek shall inherit the earth; to those who modify the law of love, the meek are not qualified to inherit the earth. By their reasoning, the earth must be inherited by those who are able to wield the words of God as modified to fit the aims of those who seek power.

> *Then answered one of the lawyers, and said unto him, Master, thus saying thou reproachest us also.*
>
> *And he said, Woe unto you also, ye lawyers! for ye lade men with burdens grievous to be borne, and ye yourselves touch not the burdens with one of your fingers.*
> (Luke 11:45-46)

The ultimate end of the modifications—which are being done to the written word of God contained in the Bible—is to make new converts to hell. Please forgive me for being so direct, but these are not my thoughts; it is in line with a condemnation that is from Jesus, for those who, in his day, were modifying the delivered word of God. This is the condemnation:

> *Woe unto you, scribes and Pharisees, hypocrites! for ye compass sea and land to make one proselyte, and when he is made, ye make him twofold more the child of hell than yourselves.*
> (Matthew 23:15)

The modern flurry of modification that is being done by those who claim to worship Christ is remarkably like those that were done in the ancient nation of Israel, as recorded in the Bible. The modifiers and their modifications are starting to remove the old landmarks, as made up of sound Biblical doctrine; and they are replacing them with their own. This is, by the way, one of the things that God said must not be done.

> *Thou shalt not remove thy neighbour's landmark, which they of old time have set in thine inheritance, which thou shalt inherit in the land that the LORD thy God giveth thee to possess it.*
> (Deuteronomy 19:14)

You need to understand that we must make a separation between true Christians, and those who are only followers of Christ in name. In case you feel uneasy about this treatment, let us look into the Bible. Jesus had many disciples, but not all disciples were his followers. How was this revealed? There came a time when Jesus made a most startling statement—at least it was startling for those folk who did not understand God. Once Jesus had made this statement, some of the disciples separated themselves from him. They, thus, clearly showed that there is a distinction between followers and disciples.

The distinction between followers and disciples is that a disciple is an intellectual entity that requires a certain formula in order for him or her to stay the course. On the other hand, a follower recognizes a leader, and will follow that leader based on the integrity of the leader. Thus, anyone who is truly a follower of Jesus will never leave him, because Jesus' great integrity cannot change.

> *When Jesus knew in himself that his disciples murmured at it, he said unto them, Doth this offend you? What and if ye shall see the Son of man ascend up where he was before? It is the spirit that quickeneth; the flesh profiteth nothing: the words that I speak unto you, they are spirit, and they are life. But there are some of you that believe not.*
>
> *For Jesus knew from the beginning who they were that believed not, and who should betray him.*
>
> *And he said, Therefore said I unto you, that no man can come unto me, except it were given unto him of my Father.*

> *From that time many of his disciples went back, and walked no more with him.*
>
> (John 6:61-66)

When the nation of Israel heard the requirements of God, they, too, separated themselves into two factions. The nation of Israel split into the people of the gods, and the people of God. The people of the gods were the ones who, hearing the commandments of God, decided to walk away. The following Scripture is about a group of Israelites that were people of the gods.

> *Then all the men which knew that their wives had burned incense unto other gods, and all the women that stood by, a great multitude, even all the people that dwelt in the land of Egypt, in Pathros, answered Jeremiah, saying,*
>
> *As for the word that thou hast spoken unto us in the name of the LORD, we will not hearken unto thee. But we will certainly do whatsoever thing goeth forth out of our own mouth, to burn incense unto the queen of heaven, and to pour out drink offerings unto her, as we have done, we, and our fathers, our kings, and our princes, in the cities of Judah, and in the streets of Jerusalem: for then had we plenty of victuals, and were well, and saw no evil. But since we left off to burn incense to the queen of heaven, and to pour out drink offerings unto her, we have wanted all things, and have been consumed by the sword and by the famine. And when we burned incense to the queen of heaven, and poured out drink offerings unto her, did we make her cakes to worship her, and pour out drink offerings unto her, without our men?*
>
> (Jeremiah 44:15-19)

The other part of the nation of Israel consisted of those who retained their place in God's heart, as His people: God referred to them as the remnant. The LORD declared that He would forever take care of the remnant. This is the group that God promised to re-collect from the nations of the world, to which they had been scattered. This is the group that included people with devotion to God that was similar to that of

Daniel, Shadrach, Meshach and Abednego, as well as all the prophets that carried the word of God to the peoples of the world.

> *And I will bring Israel again to his habitation, and he shall feed on Carmel and Bashan, and his soul shall be satisfied upon mount Ephraim and Gilead. In those days, and in that time, saith the LORD, the iniquity of Israel shall be sought for, and there shall be none; and the sins of Judah, and they shall not be found: for I will pardon them whom I reserve.*
>
> (Jeremiah 50:19-20)

It is to this remnant that Jesus came. These are *the lost sheep of the house of Israel*, as he described them in a certain conversation.

> *Then Jesus went thence, and departed into the coasts of Tyre and Sidon. And, behold, a woman of Canaan came out of the same coasts, and cried unto him, saying, Have mercy on me, O Lord, thou son of David; my daughter is grievously vexed with a devil.*
>
> *But he answered her not a word.*
>
> *And his disciples came and besought him, saying, Send her away; for she crieth after us.*
>
> *But he answered and said, I am not sent but unto the lost sheep of the house of Israel.*
>
> (Matthew 15:21-24)

But even though he was sent but unto the lost sheep of the house of Israel; still, Jesus of Nazareth was also a keen judge of character. Therefore, sometimes, Jesus perceived that there were others, who, though they did not fit into the natural genealogy of Israel, will be added to the nation of God, because they are of the nature of God's Israel. These are the *adopted* seed of Abraham. Therefore, when he met someone who believed in him, he did not turn them away. Yes, he had his primary mission, but he also was here to serve the entire world: he did this by making preparation for, and showing the world, the way to salvation.

> *Then came she and worshipped him, saying, Lord, help me.*

But he answered and said, It is not meet to take the children's bread, and to cast it to dogs.

And she said, Truth, Lord: yet the dogs eat of the crumbs which fall from their masters' table.

Then Jesus answered and said unto her, O woman, great is thy faith: be it unto thee even as thou wilt.
And her daughter was made whole from that very hour.
(Matthew 15:25-28)

Jesus' primary mission was to re-energize Israel's walk in the commandments that it had received from God. Moreover, Jesus' task is to take us beyond just the written text, into the fullness of God's message in the words. This, he did, by the life that he led, the death that he endured, and the resurrection that he accomplished. Christ's service to God was successful in that day, and the remnant was sealed into service to God.

And after these things I saw four angels standing on the four corners of the earth, holding the four winds of the earth, that the wind should not blow on the earth, nor on the sea, nor on any tree. And I saw another angel ascending from the east, having the seal of the living God: and he cried with a loud voice to the four angels, to whom it was given to hurt the earth and the sea, Saying, Hurt not the earth, neither the sea, nor the trees, till we have sealed the servants of our God in their foreheads.

And I heard the number of them which were sealed: and there were sealed an hundred and forty and four thousand of all the tribes of the children of Israel.
Of the tribe of Juda were sealed twelve thousand.
Of the tribe of Reuben were sealed twelve thousand.
Of the tribe of Gad were sealed twelve thousand.
Of the tribe of Aser were sealed twelve thousand.
Of the tribe of Nephthalim were sealed twelve thousand.
Of the tribe of Manasses were sealed twelve thousand.
Of the tribe of Simeon were sealed twelve thousand.
Of the tribe of Levi were sealed twelve thousand.

Of the tribe of Issachar were sealed twelve thousand.
Of the tribe of Zabulon were sealed twelve thousand.
Of the tribe of Joseph were sealed twelve thousand.
Of the tribe of Benjamin were sealed twelve thousand.
(Revelation 7:1-8)

Once the nation was re-energized, it became the force that proceeded, from there, to the world. Jesus Christ did not plan on leaving anyone out, but things must start somewhere. Jesus knew that when the remnant of the nation of Israel was restored, according to its original purpose; then, the nation would be able to take care of the rest of the world. You see, this nation was created to be priests and prophets of God. God created the nation so that they would be a holy people of God, to the world.

This day the LORD thy God hath commanded thee to do these statutes and judgments: thou shalt therefore keep and do them with all thine heart, and with all thy soul. Thou hast avouched the LORD this day to be thy God, and to walk in his ways, and to keep his statutes, and his commandments, and his judgments, and to hearken unto his voice: And the LORD hath avouched thee this day to be his peculiar people, as he hath promised thee, and that thou shouldest keep all his commandments; And to make thee high above all nations which he hath made, in praise, and in name, and in honour; and that thou mayest be an holy people unto the LORD thy God, as he hath spoken.
(Deuteronomy 26:16-19)

The mission of the nation of Israel, as a holy people unto the LORD for the sake of the world, is perfected; first, in Jesus, then, in those sent by him from Israel, into the world, in that day and this one. Now, in this day, those who he sends into the world are being called from all nations of the earth. Jesus is the example and the pattern. Jesus performs both these functions, in order to deliver the everlasting Kingdom of God, to mankind. This is why Jesus Christ is referred to as both, a high priest, and, the Prophet.

Priest:

But we see Jesus, who was made a little lower than the angels for the suffering of death, crowned with glory and honour; that he by the grace of God should taste death for every man. For it became him, for whom are all things, and by whom are all things, in bringing many sons unto glory, to make the captain of their salvation perfect through sufferings. For both he that sanctifieth and they who are sanctified are all of one: for which cause he is not ashamed to call them brethren, Saying, I will declare thy name unto my brethren, in the midst of the church will I sing praise unto thee. And again, I will put my trust in him. And again, Behold I and the children which God hath given me.

Forasmuch then as the children are partakers of flesh and blood, he also himself likewise took part of the same; that through death he might destroy him that had the power of death, that is, the devil; And deliver them who through fear of death were all their lifetime subject to bondage.

For verily he took not on him the nature of angels; but he took on him the seed of Abraham. Wherefore in all things it behoved him to be made like unto his brethren, that he might be a merciful and faithful high priest in things pertaining to God, to make reconciliation for the sins of the people. For in that he himself hath suffered being tempted, he is able to succour them that are tempted.

(Hebrews 2:9-18)

Prophet:

And he saith unto me, Write, Blessed are they which are called unto the marriage supper of the Lamb. And he saith unto me, These are the true sayings of God.

And I fell at his feet to worship him.

And he said unto me, See thou do it not: I am thy fellowservant, and of thy brethren that have the testimony of Jesus: worship God: for the testimony of Jesus is the spirit of prophecy.

(Revelation 19:9-10)

But just as the nation of Israel wanted a king, in order to replace God; so, too, do many of those who call themselves disciples (or even Christians). And, just as the nation of Israel wanted someone to speak to the world on their behalf, in the world's language; so, too, do these incomplete disciples (remember, these are not Christians, yet). This attempt at transformation of the message of God is proceeding, in earnest. The refitting of the things of Christ, to fit the world, is proceeding with an escalating fervor. Those of this persuasion are determined to outdo the world, at the world's own game. They have forgotten, or conveniently modified, these words of Jesus Christ . . .

Ye have not chosen me, but I have chosen you, and ordained you, that ye should go and bring forth fruit, and that your fruit should remain: that whatsoever ye shall ask of the Father in my name, he may give it you. These things I command you, that ye love one another. If the world hate you, ye know that it hated me before it hated you. If ye were of the world, the world would love his own: but because ye are not of the world, but I have chosen you out of the world, therefore the world hateth you.

(John 15:16-19)

More correctly, I should say that these words of Jesus Christ provide further enlightenment for ones that his Father gave us. Jesus, the Son of man, learned these things while observing his Father's work with the nation of Israel (and with the world, through them). Even from the beginning of the command to serve only the LORD, we have been pressed to avoid imitating the world.

These are the statutes and judgments, which ye shall observe to do in the land, which the LORD God of thy fathers giveth thee to possess it, all the days that ye live upon the earth. Ye shall utterly destroy all the places, wherein the nations which ye shall possess served their gods, upon the high mountains, and upon the hills, and under every green tree: And ye shall overthrow their altars, and break their pillars, and burn their groves with fire; and ye shall hew down the graven images of their gods, and destroy the names of them out of that place.

(Deuteronomy 12:1-3)

The old landmarks have been replaced: or maybe I should say they have been displaced. Yes, let us say, displaced; for, there are still Christians who are intent on serving God, and they are working to locate and re-map them. These are the ones who do not seek publicity for what they do. They are the ones who do not want any man bowing to them because of their works. They are the ones who do not work for any earthly crown. They are the ones who do not look to mankind to provide the sign of their deliverance. The only sign that they need is the sign that Jesus promised, as recorded in Matthew 12:38-40.

These Christians do not spend time fretting about the *second coming of Christ.* They do not spend time telling others to fear this event. They do not ever intend to try to scare anyone toward the Kingdom of God. They are content to do just what Jesus told them to do: no more, no less.

Go ye therefore, and teach all nations, baptizing them in the name of the Father, and of the Son, and of the Holy Ghost: Teaching them to observe all things whatsoever I have commanded you: and, lo, I am with you alway, even unto the end of the world. Amen.

(Matthew 28:19-20)

Oh, you think that we should always try to do more for God. Well, don't be too sure about that. The Bible tells us that we must not add to, or take away from, the word of God. It tells us that there is real danger in doing so. Let me share both the words of the LORD God, and the words of Jesus, on this matter.

Now therefore hearken, O Israel, unto the statutes and unto the judgments, which I teach you, for to do them, that ye may live, and go in and possess the land which the LORD God of your fathers giveth you. Ye shall not add unto the word which I command

> *you, neither shall ye diminish ought from it, that ye may keep the commandments of the LORD your God which I command you.*
> (Deuteronomy 4:1-2)

> *For I testify unto every man that heareth the words of the prophecy of this book, If any man shall add unto these things, God shall add unto him the plagues that are written in this book: And if any man shall take away from the words of the book of this prophecy, God shall take away his part out of the book of life, and out of the holy city, and from the things which are written in this book.*
> (Revelation 22:18-19)

The Christians that truly follow Christ are content to work with the word of God *to the letter*, in the Spirit of truth. In fact, they have a difficult time when they try to do otherwise. For you see, they truly believe that each jot and each tittle of the word of God is according to the will of God; and, even beyond that, it is according to the perfect ordinance of God. Mankind, in general, has a saying, that you cannot improve on perfection. These Christians understand this fully. They see the word of God as perfection. Therefore, they have no thoughts about changing the words, or the message. Indeed, they would not know how to do so, since they ***cannot*** improve on perfection.

To those who are among the disciples that are leaving the true message behind, totally—let us call them, disciples-without-attitude—let me remind you of the outcome of the last great earthly prince. No, this is not Jesus. Jesus was not limited to being an earthly prince; his titles come from a realm that is far beyond this earth. We heard this in Jesus' very limited testimony as he stood in Pilate's presence.

> *Then Pilate entered into the judgment hall again, and called Jesus, and said unto him, Art thou the King of the Jews?*

> *Jesus answered him, Sayest thou this thing of thyself, or did others tell it thee of me?*
>
> *Pilate answered, Am I a Jew? Thine own nation and the chief priests have delivered thee unto me: what hast thou done?*

Jesus answered, My kingdom is not of this world: if my kingdom were of this world, then would my servants fight, that I should not be delivered to the Jews: but now is my kingdom not from hence.
Pilate therefore said unto him, Art thou a king then?

Jesus answered, Thou sayest that I am a king.
To this end was I born, and for this cause came I into the world, that I should bear witness unto the truth. Every one that is of the truth heareth my voice.

(John 18:33-37)

Jesus Christ, the Son of God, is royalty of the Highest level. As for our much lower level of existence, the last great prince of the entire earth was Satan. Written below is the final disposition of his kingdom. First, Satan's ambassadors were dismissed from power, and more.

And I saw the beast, and the kings of the earth, and their armies, gathered together to make war against him that sat on the horse, and against his army. And the beast was taken, and with him the false prophet that wrought miracles before him, with which he deceived them that had received the mark of the beast, and them that worshipped his image. These both were cast alive into a lake of fire burning with brimstone. And the remnant were slain with the sword of him that sat upon the horse, which sword proceeded out of his mouth: and all the fowls were filled with their flesh.

(Revelation 19:19-21)

Then, Satan itself was removed from dominion in the earth, or anywhere else.

And when the thousand years are expired, Satan shall be loosed out of his prison, And shall go out to deceive the nations which are in the four quarters of the earth, Gog and Magog, to gather them together to battle: the number of whom is as the sand of the sea. And they went up on the breadth of the earth, and compassed the camp of the saints about, and the beloved city: and fire came down from God out of heaven, and devoured them. And the devil that deceived them was cast into the lake of fire and brimstone, where

> *the beast and the false prophet are, and shall be tormented day and night for ever and ever.*
>
> (Revelation 20:7-10)

To the disciples-without-attitude, I say; God is not impressed by your efforts to transform His message to fit the modern times. The Father God is not impressed by your perceived need for a representative from mankind, to create a new way for you, O modern man. As you strain at a gnat and swallow a camel, you may find that you are placing yourself in an elite group. You may find that you have also become an almost perfect reflection of the beast that is of the seven.

> *The beast that thou sawest was, and is not; and shall ascend out of the bottomless pit, and go into perdition: and they that dwell on the earth shall wonder, whose names were not written in the book of life from the foundation of the world, when they behold the beast that was, and is not, and yet is.*
>
> *And here is the mind which hath wisdom. The seven heads are seven mountains, on which the woman sitteth.*
>
> *And there are seven kings: five are fallen, and one is, and the other is not yet come; and when he cometh, he must continue a short space. And the beast that was, and is not, even he is the eighth, and is of the seven, and goeth into perdition.*
>
> (Revelation 17:8-11)

To the yielded and committed Christians, who I am striving mightily in the Spirit to be one of, I say; hold on to the truths of the Bible. Let no man persuade you that God needs any modification to fit a new time. Let no man tell you that the Bible is fluid, and can be manipulated to conform to the signs of the time. Listen only to God through the Holy Ghost. Know that the same God that dwells in us now, is the same God that authored the Bible. The LORD knew, then, who mankind is; and He knows that just as well now. The words that He crafted have the exact same usefulness now as they did then—without modification: let them be forever, for you and yours, unchanging.

> *All scripture is given by inspiration of God, and is profitable for doctrine, for reproof, for correction, for instruction in righteousness: That the man of God may be perfect, thoroughly furnished unto all good works.*
>
> (2 Timothy 3:16-17)

My prayer is that each of those who *went back, and walked no more with him*, will be moved to release their grip on their human spirit, and yield it to the Holy Ghost. My prayer for the Christians is that they be empowered by the Holy Ghost to continue in steadfastness in the Kingdom. It is my most fervent prayer that God totally transform, according to His righteousness, anything that continues to operate as if it is *of the seven.*

In Jesus name, and for his sake, I raise this plea to God the Father.

Amen